Complete Aramaic

Teach® Yourself

Complete Aramaic

Eric D. Reymond

First published in Great Britain by Teach Yourself in 2021
An imprint of John Murray Press
A division of Hodder & Stoughton Ltd,
An Hachette UK company

2

A CIP catalogue record for this title is available from the British Library

ISBN 978 1 473 62776 5

Typeset by KnowledgeWorks Global Ltd.

Printed and bound by CPI Group (UK) Ltd, Croydon CR0 4YY

John Murray Press policy is to use papers that are natural, renewable and recyclable products and made from wood grown in sustainable forests. The logging and manufacturing processes are expected to conform to the environmental regulations of the country of origin.

John Murray Press
Carmelite House
50 Victoria Embankment
London EC4Y 0DZ

www.teachyourself.com

Contents

Acknowledgements

The present work began as a series of handouts to my students at the University of Michigan, where I taught Aramaic for several years. The handouts then became a rudimentary website. Now, they have become a book. I wish to thank, first, my teachers who were generous is their time and energy in helping me learn Aramaic at the University of Chicago; my colleagues at the University of Michigan and here at Yale Divinity School who have always encouraged my research and teaching; but most of all my students who inspired this work and who, with their enthusiasm for ancient Semitic languages and texts, continue to inspire my study of Aramaic. I wish also to thank the team of editors and copy editors who have helped bring this project to its conclusion, in particular Jen Campbell, Emma Green and Victoria Roddam at John Murray Learning. They have shown great patience in accommodating my many corrections and then the inevitable corrections of the corrections. Finally, I thank my family, my parents Patricia and Ralph, my wife, Robin, and my children, Oliver and Lucy, who someday may turn to these pages to learn Aramaic themselves.

About the author

Eric D. Reymond is Senior Lector in Biblical Hebrew at Yale Divinity School in New Haven Connecticut (USA). He has also taught at the University of Michigan, Ann Arbor and at universities in New York City. At the University of Michigan, he focused primarily on the teaching of Aramaic and the history of the civilizations whose peoples spoke and wrote Aramaic. His research interests include post-biblical Hebrew and Aramaic poetry. He is currently working on a commentary and edition of the Wisdom of Ben Sira, a book of the apocrypha that is preserved primarily in Hebrew, Greek, and Syriac (a dialect of Aramaic).

Introduction

Introduction to Aramaic, its history, and its people

Aramaic is perhaps the earliest attested continuously spoken language still in use today. Its first attestations are in the early part of the first millennium BCE in the region of upper Mesopotamia. The earliest use of the label 'Aramean' is still earlier, dating to around the year 1100 BCE. It appears in Akkadian cuneiform, in reference to a group of people from northern Mesopotamia, from the region known at the time as 'Aram'. It is from the name of the people and place, of course, that we get the name of the language (in Akkadian **armaya** is the adjective Aramaic). Originally, the Aramaic language would have been spoken by just this group of people, though in its history its users would eventually include most peoples of the Middle East and some groups in Africa and Central Asia!

The early Aramaic-speakers were like all their neighbours in living a largely agrarian lifestyle. Their cities were relatively small. Archaeologists have unearthed many small palaces and temples from these towns. In some, the imagery on statues and orthostats is reminiscent of the imagery found in grander form in eastern Mesopotamia, in places like Nineveh.

Aramaic's expansion is tied to the rise of empires and religions. In the middle of the first millennium BCE, the Assyrians (a population whose homeland included the ancient cities of Assur and Nineveh, along the Tigris river in contemporary Kurdistan, Iraq, and who spoke a distinct Semitic language, called Akkadian) began extending their political and military control over cities and regions in the northern stretch of Mesopotamia. The result was increasing contact with the local, Aramaic-speaking population. No doubt for practical purposes, the Assyrians chose to incorporate speakers of this Semitic language into their administrative apparatus. In wall reliefs that depict the Assyrian army attacking, looting, and capturing various cities of this region, there are scribes tallying the booty and/or the casualties. There are often two scribes depicted. One writes cuneiform with a stylus on a clay tablet, making a record in Akkadian; another scribe writes with a pen on either leather or papyrus, making a record in Aramaic. During the seventh century BCE, although the two languages, Akkadian and Aramaic, continued to be used together in the Assyrian empire, it is clear (through various references to the language and the increasing number of documents in Aramaic) that Aramaic was becoming more and more important. During the subsequent centuries it continued its ascendancy.

During the Persian empire (from Cyrus the Great in the 500s BCE through to the rise of Alexander the Great in the 300s), although the rulers and high officials spoke a form of Persian (an Indo-European language distantly related to English and Latin), the administrators and scribes of the empire used Aramaic to communicate, even in the heartland of the empire, in Persepolis (Iran). Many documents have survived from this era. Letters, legal documents, and inscriptions have been found throughout the regions of

Persian hegemony, from Egypt in the west to Afghanistan in the east. Even rulers outside the Persian empire used Aramaic, like the Indian ruler Ashoka who promulgated Buddhist ideas in the western edge of his empire in Aramaic inscriptions.

As Latin had in Roman times, Aramaic by the time of the Persian empire had become standardized in order to ease communication between different administrators and scribes. This form of Aramaic, called Official or Imperial Aramaic, was the literary dialect of the second half of the first millennium BCE. 'Biblical Aramaic', that is, the Aramaic found in portions of the books of Ezra and Daniel, is extremely close to this standardized form of administrative Aramaic. For this reason, a knowledge of Biblical Aramaic is often the foundation for further study into this broader dialect. Knowing Biblical Aramaic will make it possible to read other ancient literary works like *The Words of Aḥiqar* (known from a manuscript found in Egypt, dating to the 400s BCE) as well as letters and legal documents preserved from the same time period in Egypt.

With the fragmentation of the Persian empire into separate Greek and Parthian kingdoms, the standardized form of Aramaic slowly decreased in significance. But, new varieties of Aramaic began to appear in written form. Eventually, one of these dialects, Syriac, would emerge as the common language of Middle Eastern Christianity. Like Official Aramaic before it, Syriac would become standardized. Many important works of philosophy, theology, poetry, and history are preserved in this dialect.

Many other regional dialects of Aramaic emerged after the Persian empire dissolved and are preserved in various texts and inscriptions. Particularly important are the numerous Jewish works, including the Targums, which are Aramaic translations of the Hebrew Bible or Old Testament. These Jewish works are written in different dialects of Aramaic. Other varieties of Aramaic were preserved for centuries in small communities in the Middle East, often never being written down. In recent years, scholars like Geoffrey Khan of Cambridge University have made great efforts in seeking out the last speakers of some of these dialects and recording their grammar and vocabulary. Although many dialects of Aramaic are dying, still there are vibrant communities of Aramaic speakers, some in places that you might not expect to find them, as in Detroit, Michigan and Chicago, Illinois.

In this course, we will begin our study with Biblical Aramaic, a variety of the language preserved in what is called the Tanakh, or Old Testament, or (paradoxically) the Hebrew Bible. The texts are the following: a portion of Genesis 31:47; Jeremiah 10:11; Daniel 2:4–7:28; Ezra 4:8–6:18, 7:12–26. This dialect is useful for two reasons. First, texts which preserve this dialect are familiar to many people and are often the inspiration for learning the language in the first place. Second, this dialect was supplied with vowels in the Middle Ages, by scribes who wanted to preserve the oral version of their scripture. Most Aramaic texts from antiquity had no way of indicating all the vowels of words. The vowels allow us a clearer picture of the language and its inflection. This will help ground our reading of other ancient texts that lack vowels. It is easier to read an unvocalized text like *The Words of Aḥiqar*, which employs only a very limited system for indicating vowels, once the full system of vowel representation found in medieval biblical manuscripts is fully understood.

How the course works

The aim of this course is to present the basics of Biblical Aramaic clearly enough that in due course you will be able to read passages of the Bible in Aramaic. It can take time to achieve fluency in Biblical Aramaic, and you should not expect to be fluent by the end of this course. However, the course should give you a fundamental knowledge of the language, and the skills to develop your Aramaic beyond the limits of an introductory course. By the time you reach the end of this course, you should have acquired a knowledge of some fundamental vocabulary and grammar and should have acquired the skills to read and translate simple passages from the biblical text.

The course contains 24 units. Units 1–21 each address some facet of Biblical Aramaic grammar. Units 22–24 offer glimpses into other varieties of Aramaic and Aramaic texts.

Note that all verse numbers are according to the Hebrew/Aramaic Bible. Some of these numbers differ from the verse numbers in English Bibles. Correspondences are listed at the back of the book. It is best to work through the course in order, since later units build on material presented in earlier units. After Unit 24, additional reading practice is offered through the inclusion of the text of Daniel 4-5 as it appears in the Leningrad Codex B19a, the earliest complete manuscript of the Hebrew (and Aramaic) Bible.

In the initial units, the spelling of the words has been simplified in order to introduce distinct aspects of the writing system separately (i.e., the consonantal alphabet, the vowel symbols, etc.). The benefit of this is that you do not need to know all the details of the orthography in order to begin reading Aramaic texts. By Unit 3, however, the words are spelled mostly as they appear in the Bible. This means that it is a good idea not to start memorizing words and phrases from the exercises in Unit 2.

The first part of the course (Units 1–3) introduces the alphabet, the manner in which vowels were written, and other matters pertaining to pronunciation. In these units, we will practise transferring Aramaic words into the Roman alphabet, a process called transliteration. The second part (Units 4–10) introduces the basic elements of the pronoun, noun, and adjective. The third part (Units 11–15) describes the various forms of the verb and the fourth part (Units 16–21) describes irregular verb forms. The last units (Units 22–24) offer glimpses of other Aramaic texts together with very brief summaries of how the grammar of these texts differs from that of Biblical Aramaic.

From the beginning, extended passages in Aramaic are presented. The first text encountered in Units 1–3 is the story of the writing on the wall, from the book of Daniel, Chapter 5. Units 4–10 incorporate the story of Daniel's experience in the den of lions. The last exercise of each of these units involves a portion of the book of Daniel. In these exercises, the Aramaic sentences are translated twice, once in a word-for-word manner beneath each Aramaic word and the other in a standard running translation that follows the entire passage. The word-for-word translation is intended to give the learner an idea of how Aramaic sentences are constructed as well as to reinforce some common vocabulary. After Unit 9, the final exercise of each unit does not contain the word-for-word translation.

In general, the translations of Aramaic sentences and verses in this course tend to be rather literal; this is to make more obvious which Aramaic words correspond to which English words and how the words relate to each other. Where a more periphrastic translation is necessary a literal translation often follows in parentheses. More idiomatic translations of the Bible are, of course, easy to find. These include the New Revised Standard Version and that of the Jewish Publication Society.

Since Biblical Aramaic is no longer spoken, special care must be taken in scrutinizing the words for every detail they can give us. Despite careful analysis, some ambiguities will remain. But, such open endedness should not be disheartening. In fact, just the opposite. Our lack of understanding of certain phrases or constructions is an invitation to continue the work of rescuing these texts and their ideas from oblivion. Everyone has a part to play in this. Even the amateur linguist.

- **What you will learn** gives an overview of the main topics of each unit.
- **What you will read** identifies the biblical passage used to demonstrate the language taught in the unit.
- **Grammar** sections will explain three or four points of language usage. The more straightforward aspects of Aramaic grammar are presented in the early units, and more challenging material is presented in the second half of the book.
- **Practice** offers a variety of exercises, including comprehension and translation, to give you a change to see and understand words and phrases in context.
- **Reading sections** are intented to show the language in context and provide opportunities for translation, to improve your knowledge of the language.
- **Language insight** boxes aim to give you additional information about vocabulary, word usage and grammar points.
- **Cultural insight** boxes aim to give you additional information about Aramaic culture and history.
- **Test yourself** gives you some brief questions to test your understanding of the material in each unit.
- **Suggestions for further study** contains ideas for taking your learning further.
- **Self-check** gives an overview of what you should now be able to do after completing the work in each unit.
- The **Answer key** provides answers to all the exercises in each unit.
- The **Glossary of grammatical terms** offers a brief explanation of English and Aramaic grammatical terms.
- The **Verb tables** set out examples of verbs in all stems.
- The **Glossary** is a list of vocabulary in the course, in alphabetical order, although it is not exhaustive.

To help you through the course, a system of icons indicates the actions to take:

Figure something out

Check your progress

Learn to learn

Some readers enjoy learning lists of vocabulary and grammatical forms; others find it easier to learn how words function within a text. Most people learn best if they employ a variety of approaches, and so this course encourages you to do that. If you find some of the suggestions unhelpful or irrelevant you can simply ignore them, but you are advised at least to try them for a few weeks to see if they work for you.

Reading Aramaic depends on carefully working through each unit. The time spent may vary, but on average, each unit should take approximately nine hours of study. Some helpful ways for studying include

- repeating the exercises and double-checking your answers with the Answer key at the end of the course
- writing words and forms out on a separate sheet of paper and trying to do so by memory
- applying what you learn to your everyday life, for example, writing your name and the names of your friends in Aramaic.

Keep in mind that some confusion is inevitable. It is a necessary part of the learning process! When encountering confusion, slow down. Go over exercises and carefully look over the examples to find the mistakes. Once you feel comfortable with the relevant topic, move on to the next unit.

Guide to pronunciation

The precise pronunciation of ancient Aramaic is unknown. Study of its pronunciation can be guided by certain data, including ancient spellings, grammars written by medieval scribes, as well as certain universal principles of phonological development, but in the end how exactly ancient speakers articulated the consonants and vowels is beyond our knowledge. With this in mind, the reader should recognize that some words are pronounced by different people today in slightly different ways.

The pronunciation that is commonly used in today's classrooms to teach Biblical Aramaic is essentially the same as that used to teach Biblical Hebrew, which, in turn, is based on the pronunciation of contemporary Israeli Hebrew. Due to this tradition, many of the sounds that were once made in the pronunciation of both Aramaic and Hebrew are not typically articulated in modern classrooms. Knowing something about the ancient sounds is useful since it helps explain the distinctions between certain letters. It is sometimes useful for the purposes of memorization to make these sounds yourself in order to distinguish otherwise homophonous words.

The sounds of Official or Biblical Aramaic can be divided into consonantal and vocalic (or vowel) sounds. The consonants of Aramaic are mostly like those of contemporary English and can be grouped according to how they are articulated in the mouth:

b, **p**, **m**, **w** – bringing the lips together
d, **t**, **n** – tongue rising towards the front teeth
g, **k** – the back of the tongue rising towards the palate.

In addition, Aramaic has an **l** sound, an **h** sound (as in North American *hello*), as well as a **y** (as in *you*) and a **v** (as in *victory*) sound. Other sounds are less common in English and require closer attention.

A glottal stop is the silence that accompanies the halt of airflow through the larynx. This absence of sound was actually considered a consonant by Aramaic speakers and was, therefore, represented with its own letter (the **aleph**). The same sound is sometimes found in English, as in the rapid pronunciation of *atmosphere* (i.e. **a`-mos-feer**) or *atlas* (i.e. **a`-las**), though it is not considered a consonant in English.

A similar sound is that associated with the letter **'ayin**. Instead of halting all air, this sound is made by constricting the back of the throat in a manner not unlike the constriction felt while gagging. Today, this sound is commonly not pronounced in classrooms.

Another sound not commonly found in English is the sound of **ḥet**. In antiquity and the Middle Ages, this was pronounced as a heavy *h*, an h sound that involved a very slight constriction of the throat (*ħ* in the International Phonetic Alphabet). In later times and in modern classrooms the same letter is routinely pronounced as the raspy **ch** in the word *chutzpah* and in the Scottish pronunciation of *loch* (*x* in the International Phonetic Alphabet).

The three sounds associated with the letters **aleph**, **'ayin**, and **ḥet** are all gutturals, that is, sounds made toward the back of the mouth or throat. Another guttural is the **h** sound (like the *h* in *hello* in North American English). Similar to these sounds is **r**, which was likely close to the **r** heard in French and Israeli Hebrew today.

Aramaic also had different sibilant (i.e. *s*) sounds, **s** and **z** being the ones easiest for the English speaker to hear. Another sound shared between Aramaic and English is the **sh** sound (as in *shell*), which is represented in transliteration in this way: **š**. Another sound, unfamiliar to English speakers, is represented as **ś**. This is a sound between an *s* and an *l*. Imagine holding a piece of hard candy to the roof of your mouth with your tongue and pronouncing the word *slow*. The sound you make in pronouncing *sl-* is close to **ś**. By the time the book of Daniel was written, however, the **ś** was pronounced like plain *s*, as it still is today.

Another three sounds overlap with some of those already mentioned. These are called emphatic sounds. There was an emphatic *t*, represented as *ṭ*; an emphatic *k*, represented as **q** or as *ḳ*; and an emphatic *s*, represented as *ṣ*. In antiquity, these letters were pronounced like their corresponding normal, non-emphatic counterparts followed by a glottal stop or the sound of **'ayin**. Today, however, no distinction is made between **t** and *ṭ*, nor between **k** and **q**. In contemporary classrooms, the emphatic *ṣ* is pronounced like **ts** (as in *bets*).

As for the vowels, the earliest form of Aramaic probably had only three vowels that were distinguished by their quality. These were the **a** (pronounced like the vowel in the interjection *ah*); **i** (pronounced like the *i* in *latrine* or the *ee* in *see*); and **u** (pronounced like the *u* in *rule*). Each of these represented a distinct sound. In addition, the vowels were distinguished by the amount of time it took to pronounce them. They could be pronounced for a relatively short time or be held for a relatively long time. The result was that there were a total of six possible vowels: short **a**, short **i**, short **u**, and long **ā**, long **ī**, long **ū**.

LANGUAGE INSIGHT

Notice that in many contemporary English classrooms, the term long vowel refers to vowels that are not only pronounced for a longer time than short vowels, but that also have a different articulation, a different quality (cf. the short **a** of *cat* with the long **ā** of the name *Kate*). In Aramaic, by contrast, there is no distinction in quality between long and short vowels. They are distinguished only by the amount of time it takes to express them.

By the time of Official or Biblical Aramaic, three other vowels had developed: the vowel **ɛ** (pronounced like the vowel in the word *bed*); **e** (pronounced like *ey* in *convey* (this is what English teachers refer to as a long **ā** sound)); and **o** (pronounced like the vowel in the North American pronunciation of the interjection *oh*). Like the other vowels, these could generally be articulated for a short or long time, though the **ɛ** does not appear as a long vowel. The result is another three short vowels: **ɛ**, **e**, and **o**; and, another two long vowels: **ē** and **ō**.

The language also exhibits a muttered vowel, called **shewa**, that is represented as ə. This too is found in English, for example, the sound represented by *a* in *about*.

There are many other nuances to the ancient pronunciation of Aramaic, though these can be learned and studied at a later time. We have sufficient knowledge to begin our study.

Abbreviations

*	a historical form (reconstructed based on etymology and analogy)
**	a form that never would have existed
abs.	absolute
aph.	**aph'el**
BDB	Francis Brown, S.R. Driver, and Charles A. Briggs. *The Brown-Driver-Briggs Hebrew and English Lexicon: With an Appendix Containing the Biblical Aramaic*. Houghton, Mifflin, 1906.
BHS	*Biblia Hebraica Stuttgartensia*. 4th Edition. Eds. K Elliger, W. Rudolph. Stuttgart: Deutsche Bibelgesellschaft, 1997 (first ed. 1967–1977).
c.	common
CAL	*Comprehensive Aramaic Lexicon Project* (cal.huc.edu)
conj.	conjunction
cstr.	construct
COS	William W. Hallo and K. Lawson Younger. *The Context of Scripture, vol. 1*: Canonical Compositions (1997), vol. 2: Monumental Inscriptions (2000), vol.3: Archival Documents (2002). Leiden: Brill, 1997–2002.
det.	determined
DSS	Dead Sea Scrolls
du.	dual
Egypt.	Egyptian
f.	feminine
fem.	feminine
ha.	**haph'el**
HALOT	L. Koehler and M. Baumgartner. *Hebrew and Aramaic Lexicon to the Old Testament*. Trans. M.E.J. Richardson. 3rd ed. 5 vols. Leiden: Brill, 1994–2000.
hitpa.	**hitpa''al**
hitpə.	**hitpə'el**
hu./ho.	**huph'al/hoph'al**
impv.	imperative
itpa.	**itpa''al**
itpə.	**itpə'el**
juss.	jussive
KAI	Herbert Donner and Wolfgang Röllig. *Kanaanäische und aramäische Inschriften*. Vol. 1. 5th ed. Wiesbaden: Harrassowitz, 2002.

m.	masculine
p.	plural
pa.	**pa‘‘el**
pə.	**pə‘al**
pref.	prefix
prep.	preposition
s.	singular
suff.	suffix
TAD	Bezalel Porten and Ada Yardeni. *Textbook of Aramaic Documents from Ancient Egypt: Newly copied, edited, and translated into Hebrew and English*, vol. 1: Letters (1986), vol. 2: Contracts (1989), vol. 3: Literature, accounts, lists (1993), vol. 4: Ostraca and assorted Inscriptions (1999). Winona Lake, Ind.: Eisenbrauns, 1986–1999. See the note on text citations.

Text citations

Biblical verses are cited according to the verse numbers of *BHS*. The Correspondences of verses at the back of the book lists those cases where this verse numbering does not align with popular English translations of the Bible. The Dead Sea Scrolls are commonly identified with a sequence of numerals. For example, the label 1Q20 (the Genesis Apocryphon) indicates that this is the twentieth scroll from the first cave at Qumran. The label 4Q541 (The Apocryphon of Levi) implies that this is the 541st scroll from the fourth cave at Qumran. Aramaic texts from Egypt are commonly cited according to a letter and numeral after the abbreviation *TAD*. The letter A = volume 1 of *TAD*; letter B = volume 2; letter C = volume 3; letter D = volume 4. For example, the label *TAD* A2.3 implies that the text is from the first volume of Porten/Yardeni's work. Inscriptions are commonly cited according to their label in *KAI*.

1 Consonants and the alphabet

In this unit, you will learn how to:

- **recognize and pronounce the basic forms of Aramaic consonants**
- **recognize the forms of Aramaic consonants at the ends of words**
- **transliterate these consonants into Roman letters**

In this unit you will read:

- **Daniel 5:1–9**

Grammar

THE ARAMAIC ALPHABET

The Aramaic alphabet derives ultimately from a set of hieroglyphic Egyptian symbols and was used originally to represent only consonants. Vowels were not indicated in this alphabet. The forms of archaic Aramaic letters are actually quite close to the Phoenician letters borrowed by the Greeks and Etruscans (and eventually the Romans) to write their own languages. For this reason, the shape of archaic Aramaic letters is often quite similar to the shapes of those in the Roman alphabet, as used in English. During the course of the first millennium BCE, the Aramaic alphabet continued to develop. Eventually, due to the fact that Aramaic was used as a common language in the Persian empire, the alphabet was also adopted to write other languages like Hebrew and Arabic. In fact, the Hebrew letters we see on signs and in books are really based on the forms of Aramaic letters from antiquity. Arabic letters are also based originally on letter forms used to write Aramaic texts.

The fortunate aspect of this shared history is that even in their later forms, Aramaic letters still sometimes share traits of the Roman alphabet. The basic form of the letter is the reverse of English, reflecting the fact that Aramaic (like Hebrew and Arabic) is read from right to left. Based on this knowledge, consider the following list of Aramaic letters (reading from right to left).

א ב ג ד ה ו ז ח ט י כ ל

מ נ ס ע פ צ ק ר שׂ שׁ ת

LANGUAGE INSIGHT

A language's inventory of sounds is not identical to its alphabet. Often there are more sounds than symbols. The concept is easy to grasp if we consider the many values of the letter *c* in the Roman alphabet, by which we write the English language. For example, consider the two *c*'s of *concept*.

PRACTICE 1

1 **Write the two Aramaic letters that look most like the Roman uppercase *H*.**

2 **Write the Aramaic letter that looks like a (backward) lowercase *q*.**

3 **Write the Aramaic letter that looks most like a (backward) lowercase *r*. (Hint: look for a rounded corner.)**

4 **Write the Aramaic letter that looks most like a (backward) *C* (Hint: look for rounded corners.)**

The Aramaic letters that most resemble *H* represent two varieties of the sound h. The letter that looks like a backward *q* represents a k sound. The letter that looks like a backward *r* represents an r sound and the letter that looks like a backward *C* represents a k sound.

LANGUAGE INSIGHT

Another feature of the Aramaic letters helps us remember their values. The letter that represents l is akin to the Roman lowercase *l* in that the Aramaic letter has an ascender (a part of the letter that rises above the other letters): ל. It is the only Aramaic letter to have an ascender.

TRANSLITERATION, LETTER NAMES, AND PRONUNCIATION

The following are the Aramaic letters, their transliteration into the Roman alphabet, their respective names, and their pronunciations. The names of the letters are not revealed in early Aramaic texts and it is common to refer to them according to their Hebrew name, especially in the study of Biblical Aramaic. The Hebrew name of the letter is given together with its name in Syriac (a later dialect of Aramaic). Where the letter name is the same in both languages, the name is only listed once.

Aram.	Transl.	Name	Pronunciation in the contemporary classroom	
א	ʾ	**aleph/alaph**	–	(originally a glottal stop)
ב	**b**	**bet**	b	(or v)
ג	**g**	**gimmel/gamal**	g	
ד	**d**	**dalet**	d	
ה	**h**	**he**	h	
ו	**w**	**waw**	v	(though originally w)
ז	**z**	**zayin/zayn**	z	
ח	**ḥ**	**ḥet**	ch	(as in *chutzpah* and Scottish *loch*)
ט	**ṭ**	**ṭet**	t	(though originally an emphatic t)
י	**y**	**yod**	y	
כ	**k**	**kaph**	k	(or ch)
ל	**l**	**lamed/lamad**	l	

מ	m	**mem/mim**	m	
נ	n	**nun**	n	
ס	s	**samekh/semkat**	s	
ע	ʿ	**ʿayin/ʿe**	–	(though originally a gagging-like sound)
פ	p	**peh**	p	(or ph as in *phone*)
צ	ṣ	**ṣadeh**	tz	(though originally an emphatic s)
ק	q	**qoph**	k	(though originally an emphatic k)
ר	r	**reš**	r	
שׂ	ś	**śin**	s	(though originally a sound between s and l)
שׁ	š	**šin**	sh	
ת	t	**taw**	t	

In relation to the Aramaic letters, notice that the only distinction in shape between the **śin** and **šin** is the dot above the letter (**śin** = שׂ vs. **šin** = שׁ). Note also that **taw** (ת) resembles **ḥet** (ח), though the **taw** has a left leg that is bent, with a foot at the end. In handwriting, sometimes an **ʿayin** (ע) will look like a **ṣadeh** (צ).

LANGUAGE INSIGHT

A helpful way to remember the differences between **ʿayin** (ע) and **ṣadeh** (צ) is that the **ṣadeh** sounds like a German *z* (tz) and it looks vaguely like a backward *z*, with the top bar angled diagonally downward. The **ʿayin** (ע), on the other hand, is written a bit like a Roman lowercase *y*, though of course it is not pronounced as a *y*. In relation to the transliteration, the only distinction between **aleph** and **ʿayin** is the direction of the apostrophe.

The name of the letters in the Hebrew alphabet is very close to or identical with the Aramaic names listed. In fact, at least some of the names of the letters in the Hebrew alphabet come from Aramaic. Thus, the ר r in Hebrew is called **reš**, the Aramaic word for *head*. The letter is named this because its early form was that of a human head. If the name of the letter in Hebrew were really of Hebrew origin, then it would be called **roš**, since this is the Hebrew word for *head*. The Phoenicians presumably used the name **roš** for the letter, something we assume based on the fact that the Greeks, who adopted the alphabet from the Phoenicians, called the same letter **rho**.

There is another link shared between the Roman alphabet and the Aramaic sequence of letters: their basic order. Note the similarities here: *A* (א), *B* (ב), *C* (ג), *D* (ד), *E* (ה), *F*, *G*, *H* (ה), *I* (י), *J*, *K* (כ), *L* (ל), *M* (מ), *N* (נ), *O* (ע), *P* (פ), *Q* (ק), *R* (ר), *S* (שׁ), *T* (ת), *U*, *V*, *W*, *X*, *Y*, *Z*.

PRACTICE 2

1 Practise copying out the Aramaic alphabet and the corresponding transliteration. Then match the following Aramaic and Roman letters. Check your answers against the list given earlier.

א	h	he	ל	ʿ	ʿayin
ב	k	kaph	מ	ś	śin
ג	d	dalet	נ	s	samekh
ד	ṭ	ṭet	ס	n	nun
ה	ḥ	ḥet	ע	r	reš
ו	w	waw	פ	l	lamed
ז	b	bet	צ	š	šin
ח	y	yod	ק	p	peh
ט	g	gimmel	ר	t	taw
י	ʾ	aleph	שׁ	m	mem
כ	z	zayin	שׂ	ṣ	ṣadeh
			ת	q	qoph

2 Make flashcards for yourself. Each card should have an Aramaic letter on one side and the transliteration on the back. Go through them several times. Then match the following Aramaic and Roman letters.

ע	b	bet	ד	k	kaph
ק	n	nun	מ	t	taw
ו	r	reš	כ	s	samekh
ל	ṭ	ṭet	ס	z	zayin
שׁ	ḥ	ḥet	א	ś	śin
ר	w	waw	ת	y	yod
ח	l	lamed	י	d	dalet
ב	ʿ	ʿayin	ז	p	peh
ט	ṣ	ṣadeh	ג	h	he
צ	q	qoph	שׂ	m	mem
נ	š	šin	ה	g	gimmel
			פ	ʾ	aleph

3 Reflect on any mistakes you made in Exercises 1 and 2. Since the shapes of the letters will be unfamiliar, and there is a good deal of similarity between some of them, it is important to recognize the slight variations between similarly shaped letters.

4 Look carefully at the list of letters at the beginning of this section. Setting aside the pair of śin (שׂ) and šin (שׁ), there are several sets of letters that look similar to each other. Identify these and then copy them out, together with their names.

FINAL LETTER FORMS

In addition to the letters given, five letters have forms that occur only at the end of a word. These are often forms with a descender (a part of the letter that stretches beneath the other letters). Notice that only one regular letter has a descender: **qoph** (ק). The final forms of the letters are the following:

ךְ	**k**	**kaph**	Note the two dots that are often written with the final **kaph**. Note also how the final **kaph** looks remotely like an upside down Roman *k*.
ם	**m**	**mem**	
ן	**n**	**nun**	
ף	**p**	**peh**	Note how final **peh** looks like a backward lowercase Roman *p*.
ץ	**ṣ**	**ṣadeh**	

These letters are pronounced and transliterated in the same way that the initial/medial letter forms are. For instance, a **mem** that occurs at the end of a word is pronounced and transliterated as /m/, just like a **mem** at the beginning of a word.

LANGUAGE INSIGHT

The English language also used to use word final letters. The *j* started off as the word final form of *i* and was only later used to represent exclusively the sound we now associate with it.

PRACTICE 3

1 **What regular (initial/medial) letter is closest in appearance to final kaph (ךְ)? Write out the two letters and note what distinguishes them.**

2 **What regular letter is closest in appearance to final mem (ם)? Write out the two letters and note what distinguishes them.**

3 **What regular letter is closest in appearance to final nun (ן)? Write out the two letters and note what distinguishes them.**

Reading

DANIEL 5:1

Transliterate the following individual words. Note that although the Aramaic script is written and read from right to left (e.g. ךְ←ל←מ), the transliterated word in the Roman alphabet is written and read from left to right, as in English (e.g. *m→l→k*). The following sequence of Aramaic words make up Daniel 5:1: 'Belshazzar, the king, made a great feast for his thousand nobles and before the thousand he was drinking wine.'

Example: בלשאצר   blš'ṣr

a מלכא
b עבד
c לחם
d רב
e לרברבנוהי
f אלף
g ולקבל
h אלפא
i חמרא
j שתה

DANIEL 5:2

Match the Aramaic word with its transliteration. The sequence of words makes up the first half of Dan 5:2: 'Belshazzar commanded, under influence of the wine, to bring out the vessels of gold and silver which Nebuchadnezzar, his father, had removed . . .'

a	בלשאצר	1	wksp'
b	אמר	2	lhytyh
c	בטעם חמרא	3	blš'ṣr
d	להיתיה	4	nbwkdnṣr
e	למאני	5	dy hnpq
f	דהבא	6	'bwhy
g	וכספא	7	bṭ'm ḥmr'
h	די הנפק	8	dhb'
i	נבוכדנצר	9	'mr
j	אבוהי	10	lm'ny

DANIEL 5:3

Practise reading Aramaic letters by transliterating the following texts, according to the example.

Example: Daniel 5:2 (the second half)

מן היכלא די בירושלם
וישתון בהון מלכא
ורברבנוהי שגלתה ולחנתה

mn hykl' dy byrwšlm
wyštwn bhwn mlk'
wrbrbnwhy šglth wlḥnth

... from the temple which (was) in Jerusalem,
so that (lit. and) they might drink with them – the king
and his nobles, his consorts and his concubines.

a באדין היתיו מאני דהבא
b די הנפקו מן היכלא
c די בית אלהא די בירושלם
d ואשתיו בהון מלכא
e ורברבנוהי שגלתה ולחנתה

a *Then, the vessels of gold were brought in*
b *which had been removed from the temple*
c *which (was) the house of the God which (was) in Jerusalem*
d *they drank with them – the king*
e *and his nobles, his wives, and his concubines.*

DANIEL 5:4

Transliterate the following.

a אשתיו חמרא ושבחו לאלהי דהבא
b וכספא נחשא פרזלא אעא ואבנא

a *They drank the wine and praised the gods of gold*
b *and of silver, bronze, iron, wood, and stone.*

DANIEL 5:5

Transliterate the following.

a בה שׁעתה נפקו אצבען די יד אנשׁ
b וכתבן לקבל נברשׁתא
c על גירא די כתל היכלא די מלכא
d ומלכא חזה פס ידה די כתבה

a *In that moment, fingers of a human hand emerged*
b *and wrote, before the lamp,*
c *upon the plaster of the wall of the king's palace*
d *so that the king saw the palm of the hand that wrote.*

DANIEL 5:6

Transliterate the following individual words into Aramaic letters. The words comprise all of Daniel 5:6: 'Then, as for the king, his appearance changed upon him, his thoughts frightening him and the joints of his hips coming loose and his knees knocking against each other.'

a ’dyn

b mlk’

c zywhy

d šnwhy

e wr‘ynhy

f ybhlwnh

g wqṭry ḥrṣh

h mštryn

i w’rkbth

j d’ ld’ nqšn

DANIEL 5:7

Match the transliterated word with the Aramaic. The words comprise the first half of Daniel 5:7: ‘The king cried loudly to bring in the exorcists, Chaldeans, and the diviners. The king spoke up and said to the sages of Babel . . . ’

a	qr’	**1**	כשׂדיא
b	mlk’	**2**	ענה מלכא
c	bḥyl	**3**	לחכימי בבל
d	lh‘lh	**4**	לאשפיה
e	l’špyh	**5**	קרא
f	kśdy’	**6**	להעלה
g	wgzry’	**7**	ואמר
h	‘nh mlk’	**8**	מלכא
i	w’mr	**9**	בחיל
j	lḥkymy bbl	**10**	וגזריא

DANIEL 5:8

Practise writing Aramaic letters by transliterating the following from Roman letters into the Aramaic alphabet. Remember that k, m, n, p and ṣ have different forms at the end of a word.

Example: Daniel 5:7 (second half):

dy kl ’nš dy yqrh
ktbh dnh wpšrh yḥwnny
’rgwn’ ylbš whmwnk’ dy dhb’ ‘l ṣw’rh
wtlty bmlkwt’ yšlṭ

די כל אנש די יקרה
כתבה דנה ופשרה יחונני

ארגונא ילבש והמונכא די דהבא על צוארה
ותלתי במלכותא ישלט

Any person who can read
this writing and its interpretation tell me
will wear the purple (robes of office) and the golden necklace
(will be) over his neck,
and as the third (ruler), the kingdom he will rule.

a ʾdyn ʿllyn kl ḥkymy mlkʾ
b wlʾ khlyn ktbʾ lmqrʾ
c wpšrʾ lhwdʿh lmlkʾ

a *Then all the royal sages came*
b *but were not able to read the writing,*
c *nor its interpretation to make known to the king.*

DANIEL 5:9

Transliterate the following from Roman letters into the Aramaic alphabet.

1 ʾdyn mlkʾ blšʾṣr śgyʾ mtbhl
2 wzywhy šnyn ʿlwhy
3 wrbrbnwhy mštbšyn

1 *Then, the king, Belshazzar, became very alarmed,*
2 *his appearance changing upon him*
3 *and his nobles were confused.*

Test yourself

Transcribe the Aramaic letters in the following excerpt from the Aramaic translation (targum) of the Song of Hannah, which represents only a portion of the expanded version of 1 Sam 2:1 (from manuscript BL Or 2210).

a וצליאת חנה ברוח נבואה

b ואמרת כבר שׁמואל ברי

c עתיד למהוי נביא על ישׂראל

d ביומוהי יתפרקון מידא דפלשׁתאי

e ועל ידוהי יתעבדן נסין וגבורן

f בכין תקיף לבי

g בחולקא דיהב לי ייי

a *Hannah prayed in the spirit of prophecy*

b *and said 'Perhaps, Samuel (or Shemuel), my son,*

c *will be a prophet over Israel.*

d *In his days they will be rescued from the hand of the Philistines*

e *and by his hands miracles and wonders will be done.*

f *Therefore, my heart is made bold*

g *in the portion that the Lord has given me.'*

Suggestions for further study

Make flashcards for each letter. Then test yourself to see if you can recognize the Aramaic letters and write them.

SELF-CHECK

	I CAN...
●	recognize and pronounce the basic forms of Aramaic consonants
●	recognize the forms of Aramaic consonants at the ends of words
●	transliterate these consonants into Roman letters

2 Vowels, maters, and begadkephat letters

In this unit you will learn how to:

- **recognize and pronounce the Aramaic vowels**
- **recognize the Aramaic consonants that mark some long vowels**
- **recognize the six consonants called the begadkephat letters**

In this unit you will read:

- **Daniel 5:10–16**

Grammar

THE VOWELS

As outlined in Unit 1, there are eleven vowels in Official and Biblical Aramaic: six short vowels and five long vowels:

a	i	e	ɛ	u	o
ā	ī	ē		ū	ō

Reference to a vowel's brevity or length indicates how long the vowel is pronounced. Each corresponding pair of short/long vowels has a single sound or quality (e.g. both i and ī are articulated like the i in *latrine* or the ee in *see*; the long version, ī, is just held for longer than the short version). The sounds of the vowels can be characterized in the following manner:

a pronounced like the a in *father*
i pronounced like the i in *latrine* or the ee in *see*
e pronounced like the ey in *convey*
ɛ pronounced like the e in *pet*
u pronounced like the u in *rule*
o pronounced like the o in *role*

CONSONANTS USED TO MARK VOWELS: MATERS

Vowels were initially not indicated in the alphabet of Aramaic or those of many other early Semitic languages. One can easily imagine the ambiguities this produced. It should not be surprising, therefore, that in time, scribes developed a way of indicating at least some vowels, particularly long vowels at the ends of words. Instead of inventing new symbols, the scribes used the symbols of four consonants (aleph א, he ה, waw ו, yod י) to represent long vowels at the end of a word. For example the he (ה) was used to indicate a word-final long ā.

The spelling of the independent pronoun **אנה** *I* implies that the word ends with the long ā sound: ʾănā. The two letters waw (ו) and yod (י) were also used frequently to mark long vowels within words. For example, in the adverb **יתירה** *very much* the yod in the middle of the word implies the long ī while the final he implies the long ā sound: yattīrā. These four consonantal symbols, when used to mark vowels, are called *matres lectionis*, Latin for *mothers of reading*, since they help you pronounce and read the words more accurately. For the sake of simplicity, we call them maters.

In general, each mater is associated with a pair of long vowels that are naturally linked to the letter's consonantal value. For example, because the y sound represented by yod (י) is affiliated with the sound of i (consider the y of English *sunny*), a yod came to indicate a preceding long ī. The yod (י) is also used to represent ē (the sound of ey in English *convey*). Phonetically, the w sound, marked by waw (ו) in Aramaic, is close to the u and o sounds (consider English *new* and *sew*, as well as the spelling of the w sound with u in words like *suite*). Because of this, the letter waw (ו) is used to mark long ū and long ō vowels. The long ā at the end of a word was represented by a he (ה) (consider the spelling of the interjection *ah* and the spelling of the name *Sarah*), as well as by aleph (א). In addition, occasionally aleph (א) and he (ה) function as maters for a preceding ē vowel at the end of a word, and rarely for a preceding ō vowel.

LANGUAGE INSIGHT

That the yod is linked with the i vowel was something not lost on early Greek writers, who adopted the Phoenician version of yod to write their i sound, for which the symbol became **ι** and was named iota.

This system for marking long vowels was used for at least a millennium before Aramaic scribes, specifically those working in the Syriac dialect of Aramaic, began to include particular symbols above and below the letters to record all the vowel sounds of the words. Hebrew scribes followed suit and eventually the Aramaic portions of the Hebrew Bible/Old Testament were supplied with these vowel marks. These are the vowel marks that we are going to learn. As you will see, sometimes they are associated with maters and sometimes they are not. Because they were developed primarily to indicate vowels in the Hebrew language, the symbols have Hebrew names.

CULTURAL INSIGHT

Although Aramaic is almost exclusively found in alphabetic writing, at least once it was written in syllabic cuneiform (where each symbol represents a syllable). In around 200 BCE, an Aramaic incantation was written in cuneiform on a clay tablet in the Mesopotamian city of Uruk. Among the commands, adjusted to Biblical Aramaic vowels, are ḥăgīrtā rəhuṭī *Crippled one, run!* and ʾĕmar šāṭē qūm ḥărīš *Speak fool! Arise dumb-one!* (See Geller 1997–2000, 2006; Kaufman 1984). Another text (Papyrus Amherst 63), written in the cursive form of hieroglyphs called Demotic, comes from upper Egypt from around 300 BCE and mentions, among other things, soldiers coming from Samaria and Jerusalem, perhaps reflecting the origins of the Judean and Aramean mercenaries in Syene and Elephantine (see Steiner 2017, van der Toorn 2016, 2018). It is most famous, however, for containing an Aramaic version of the Hebrew Psalm 20.

VOWEL SYMBOLS

Here are the vowel signs and the consonants that sometimes accompany them. In this list, the vowel signs are represented beneath or above the letter mem; their transliterated form, name, and their pronunciation follow. In order to distinguish true consonants from maters, it is helpful to represent the maters as superscript letters in transliteration (e.g. the last part of mar'ā^{h} *vision*). In the case of a mater aleph (א), however, the transliteration (') is already so small that a superscript version of it will be hard to see. Therefore, if aleph is used as a mater, the vowel is indicated with a circumflex (i.e., â and ê), as at the end of malkâ *the king*.

Aram.	Transl.	Name	Pronunciation in the contemporary classroom
מַ	a	patach	like ah.
מָ	ā	qamets	like ah. Sometimes, especially at the end of a word, it is also represented as מָה or מָא (ā^{h}, â). The same symbol also marks a short o.
מֶ	ɛ	seghol	like the e in *bed*.
מֵ	e, ē	sere	like the ey in *convey*. Often the long vowel is represented at the end of a word with a mater (yod, aleph, or he): מֵי ē^{y}; מֵא ê, and מֵה ē^{h}. Distinguishing between the short and long e is often difficult. For the beginning student, it will be helpful to transliterate this symbol as ē if accompanied by a mater and e if not.
מִ	i	hiriq	like the i in *latrine* and the ee in *see*. Rarely the simple hiriq without mater can represent ī within a word.
מִי	ī^{y}	hiriq	like the i in *latrine* and the ee in *see*. Very rarely a hiriq with a yod mater marks a short i.
מָ	o	qamets-hatuf	like the vowel in the North American interjection *oh*. The same vowel is sometimes represented with a holem.

LANGUAGE INSIGHT

The reason that a single symbol (ָ) was used to represent both ā and o is that when these vowel symbols were invented and applied to the consonantal text (ca. 800 CE), there was not a clear distinction between the o and ā sounds. All the same, it is now conventional to distinguish these two vowels in transliteration and pronunciation. Such a distinction also reflects the earlier pronunciation of Aramaic and Hebrew in the time of the Dead Sea Scrolls (c. 100 BCE).

מֹ	o, ō	holem	like in the North American interjection *oh*. When the holem is written with the waw mater it usually represents long ō: מוֹ = ō^{w}; without the mater it is usually short o.
מֻ	u	qibbutz	like the u in *rule*. Rarely the symbol marks long ū.
מוּ	ū^{w}	shuruq	like the u in *rule*.
מְ	ə	shewa	like the a in *above*. The shewa symbol also marks the absence of a vowel. Determining which of these two alternatives the shewa symbol represents will sometimes prove difficult.

PRACTICE 1

The various vowels (excluding shewa) can be grouped into three categories: a-vowels (a and ā), i-vowels (ɛ, e, ē, i, ī), and u-vowels (o, ō, u, ū). What similarities are shared between the two symbols representing the a-vowels? What similarities are shared between the three symbols representing the i-vowels?

HATEPH VOWELS AND DIPHTHONGS

The following three symbols represent variations on the muttered shewa vowel.

אֲ	ă	hateph-patach
אֱ	ɛ̆	hateph-seghol
אֳ	ŏ	hateph-qamets

These three symbols represent ultra-short vowels, essentially like the murmured vowel in *nature*, but each having a slightly distinct quality. Typically these vowels appear under guttural consonants (i.e., א, ה ,ח, and ע; sometimes also before or after ג and ק and sometimes before ל, נ, and ר). Unlike the shewa, which only sometimes should be pronounced, these three symbols always represent a pronounced vowel.

מַי	ay	Occasionally, a vowel and consonant are pronounced together. The most common in Biblical Aramaic is the short a + yod, which is pronounced like the English word *eye*.

DISTINGUISHING MATERS AND OTHER CONCERNS

Distinguishing when an aleph (א), he (ה), waw (ו), or yod (י) is being used as a mater and when it is being used as a true consonant can be easy, once you get the hang of it. Follow these guidelines:

1. **An aleph (א) or he (ה) at the end of a word is usually a mater for a preceding long vowel, a qamets ā or sere ē. When a mappiq (or dot) appears in the middle of a he (הּ), then it is considered a true consonant, not a mater, and is transliterated accordingly as h.**
2. **A waw (ו) mater will either appear as וֹ = ō or וּ = ū. If it appears with any other vowel mark, then it is a consonant.**
3. **A yod (י) mater will never appear with a vowel symbol above or beneath it. Nor will it appear with a following וֹ = ō or וּ = ū. If a yod (י) appears with a vowel symbol above or beneath it (or is followed by a וֹ or וּ), then it is a true consonant.**

Several other matters should be addressed:

- Note that when a kaph appears last in a word it has this form: ךְ the shewa symbol after this letter always represents the absence of a vowel sound and is not transliterated.
- Also of importance: word stress, or 'tone' usually falls on the last syllable of a word. Occasionally it falls on the penultimate syllable, in which case in this course a mark appears above the first consonant of that syllable (ˋ): כְּתַ֫בוּ.
- A qamets followed by a hateph-qamets will have the value of a short o. Note the frequent preposition/conjunction לָקֳבֵל loqŏbel *because of, correspondingly, because.*

PRACTICE 2

1 Find the maters in the following words and phrases. Remember, only aleph (א), he (ה), waw (ו) and yod (י) are used as maters. Also, remember that the words have been simplified in their spelling. Their actual spelling is explained in Unit 3.

sages of	חַכִּימֵי	a
and they were not able	וְלָא כָהֲלִין	b
the writing	כְּתָבָא	c
to read	לְמִקְרֵא	d
to make known	לְהוֹדָעָה	e
many	שַׂגִּיא	f
about him	עֲלוֹהִי	g
words of	מִלֵּי	h
and she said	וַאֲמֶרֶת	i
forever	לְעָלְמִין	j
live	חֱיִי	k
let them disturb you	יְבַהֲלוּךְ	l
and in the days of	וּבְיוֹמֵי	m
illumination	נַהִירוּ	n
exorcists	אָשְׁפִין	o
great	יַתִּירָה	p
and solving	וּמְשָׁרֵא	q
let him expound	יְהַחֲוֵה	r
he spoke up	עָנֵה	s
exile	גָלוּתָא	t

2 Now, try transliterating the words and phrases in Exercise 1. Except in a final kaph ךְ, the shewa symbol always represents a muttered vowel and should, therefore, be transliterated with an ə. (In a final kaph ךְ the shewa is silent and not transliterated.) Furthermore, every qamets represents ā and should be transliterated as such. Every holem is accompanied by a waw mater and represents ō. Remember that Aramaic is read from right to left, though we transliterate into Roman letters from left to right.

Example: חַכִּימֵי ḥakī^{y}mē^{y} *sages of*

BEGADKEPHAT LETTERS

In ancient times, the six letters bet (ב), gimmel (ג), dalet (ד), kaph (כ), peh (פ), and taw (ת) could be pronounced in different ways. Each of these letters had a 'hard' pronunciation involving the brief halting of breath, as in the 'hard' pronunciation of the p in the English word *poke*, and a 'soft' pronunciation, where the breath is not completely halted, as in the pronunciation of ph in English *phone*. The same Aramaic letter (peh פ) could be pronounced in either way. The same applied for the other five letters of this set, which are collectively known by an acronym: the begadkephat letters.

Whether or not the letters were articulated in a 'hard' or a 'soft' way was determined based on one factor: the presence (or absence) of a preceding vowel. If the begadkephat letter was immediately preceded by a vowel then it was pronounced 'soft'. If it was not preceded by a vowel, then the begadkephat letter was pronounced 'hard'. Diphthongs, like ay, did not result in a following 'hard' pronunciation. Thus, we find the word *the house* spelled **בַּיְתָא** baytâ, where the taw is 'soft'.

LANGUAGE INSIGHT

Think of it in this way: If you are pronouncing a vowel, your mouth must remain open, emitting a breath; this physical necessity encourages the pronunciation of a following begadkephat letter with some of this 'extra' breath, which turns the hard sound soft.

When one of these letters is pronounced hard it is given a dagesh (or dot) in its centre. Thus, we have the expression **פִּשְׁרָא** pišrâ *the interpretation*. (For clarity, hard and soft pronunciations are noted in the transliteration, though this is not done elsewhere.) If the expression is preceded by the preposition **לְ** lə *for* then the peh is preceded by a vowel and is soft: **לְפִשְׁרָא** ləfišrā *for the interpretation*. In a similar way, bet (**ב**) is pronounced hard at the beginning of a word, as with the b of **בַּר** = bar *son*. When preceded by a vowel, it is pronounced v as in English *victory*, as in the Aramaic expression **לְבַר** ləvar *to a son*. The letter kaph (**כ**) is pronounced hard as k in **כֹּל** kol *all*. When pronounced soft, it sounds like the pronunciation of ḥet **ח** = ḥ, as in the ch of *chutzpah*; thus, **לְכֹל** *for all* is pronounced in the same way as **לְחֹל***. The other begadkephat letters are not articulated as soft consonants in the classroom today.

LANGUAGE INSIGHT

In antiquity and in the Middle Ages, however, these other begadkephat letters were pronounced in different ways. The soft gimmel (**ג**) sounded a bit like the Parisian French r; the soft dalet (**ד**) sounded like the th in English *this*. The soft taw (**ת**) sounded like the th in English *thin*.

The different pronunciations do not presuppose different meanings. Pronounced **בַּר** bar or **בַר** var, the word means *son*. Since the different pronunciations of the letters do not affect the meaning of the words, we do not indicate the hard or soft pronunciations in transliteration. Both **בַּר** and **בַר** are transliterated as bar.

LANGUAGE INSIGHT

In English, we sometimes pronounce the same basic sound in slightly different ways, though we often do not notice it. For example, note the subtle distinctions between the pronunciation of s in *base* and the pronunciation of the same letter in *safe*. In the former word, the *s* is held longer than in the latter.

Reading

THE QUEEN ADVISES BELSHAZZAR.

Practise reading Aramaic by transliterating the following texts, according to the model. Remember that although the Aramaic script is written and read from right to left (e.g. ךְ←לְ←מ), transliteration in the Roman alphabet is written and read from left to right, as in English (e.g. *m→l→k*). Also, remember the following points:

1 **We do not distinguish between hard and soft begadkephat letters in the transliteration.**

2 **The shewa symbol in the words of this exercise always represents a muttered vowel and should, therefore, be transliterated with a ə, except in the case of ךְ, as explained in Practice 2. (Elsewhere, we will learn that the same symbol sometimes also represents the absence of a vowel.)**

3 **The qamets represents ā in every word except its first occurrence in וְשָׂכְלְתָנוּ wəśokləṭānūʷ *and intelligence* as well as in וְחָכְמָה wəḥokmāʰ *and wisdom* and כְּחָכְמַת kəḥokmat *like the wisdom of*, all of which are found for the first time in Dan 5:11.**

4 **כֹּל = kol (The holem without mater represents a short /o/.)**

5 **The spelling of some words has been slightly simplified. The correct spelling will be indicated in the following unit.**

Example: Daniel 5:10, first part

מַלְכְּתָא לָקֳבֵל מִלֵּי מַלְכָּא וְרַבְרְבָנוֹהִי

לְבֵית מִשְׁתְּיָא עַלַּת

a malkətâ loqŏbel milēʸ malkâ wərabrəbānōhīʸ

b ləbēʸt mištəyâ ʻalat

a *The queen, because of the words of the king and his nobles,*

b *entered the banquet hall.*

DANIEL 5:10, SECOND PART

a עֲנָת מַלְכְּתָא וַאֲמֶרֶת

b מַלְכָּא לְעָלְמִין חֱיִי

c אַל יְבַהֲלוּךְ רַעְיוֹנָךְ

d וְזִיוָךְ אַל יִשְׁתַּנּוֹ

a *The queen responded and said:*

b *'O king, live forever!*

c *Do not let your thoughts disturb you,*

d *and may your appearance not be changed.'*

DANIEL 5:11

a אִיתַי גְּבַר בְּמַלְכוּתָךְ דִּי רוּחַ אֱלָהִין קַדִּישִׁין בֵּהּ

b וּבְיוֹמֵי אֲבוּךְ נַהִירוּ וְשָׂכְלְתָנוּ וְחָכְמָה

c כְּחָכְמַת אֱלָהִין הִשְׁתְּכַחַת בֵּהּ

d וּמַלְכָּא נְבֻכַדְנֶצַּר אֲבוּךְ

e רַב אָשְׁפִין כַּשְׂדָּאִין גָּזְרִין

f הֲקִימֵהּ אֲבוּךְ מַלְכָּא

a *'There is a man in your kingdom in whom is the spirit of the holy gods.*
b *In the days of your father, illumination, insight, and wisdom*
c *were found in him, like the wisdom of the gods.*
d *As for the king, Nebuchadnezzar, your father –*
e *captain of exorcists, of Chaldeans, of diviners –*
f *your father, the king, made him.*

DANIEL 5:12

a כֹּל קֳבֵל דִּי רוּח יַתִּירָה וּמַנְדַּע וְשָׂכְלְתָנוּ
b מְפַשַּׁר חֶלְמִין וַאַחֲוָיַת אֲחִידָן
c וּמְשָׁרֵא קִטְרִין הִשְׁתְּכַחַת בֵּהּ
d בְּדָנִיֵּאל דִּי מַלְכָּא שָׂם שְׁמֵהּ בֵּלְטְשַׁאצַּר
e כְּעַן דָּנִיֵּאל יִתְקְרֵי וּפִשְׁרָא יְהַחֲוֵה

a *because a great spirit, knowledge, and insight*
b *of one interpreting dreams and (insight) to declare riddles,*
c *(insight) of one solving difficult problems were (all) found in him,*
d *in Daniel, whom the king named Belteshazzar.*
e *Now, let Daniel be called so the interpretation he might declare.'*

DANIEL 5:13

a בֵּאדַיִן דָּנִיֵּאל הֻעַל קֳדָם מַלְכָּא
b עָנֵה מַלְכָּא וְאָמַר לְדָנִיֵּאל
c אַנְתְּ הוּא דָנִיֵּאל דִּי מִן בְּנֵי גָלוּתָא דִּי יְהוּד
d דִּי הַיְתִי מַלְכָּא אַבִי מִן־יְהוּד

a *Then, Daniel was brought before the king.*
b *The king spoke up and said to Daniel:*
c *'You are Daniel, who is from among the exiles* (lit. *the children of the exile*) *of Judah,*
d *whom the king, my father, brought from Judah.'*

DANIEL 5:14

Practise writing Aramaic letters by transliterating the following texts from Roman letters into the Aramaic alphabet and vowels.

Example: Daniel 5:14, first part

wəšimʿet ʿălāk dī^{y} rū^{w}ḥ ʾĕlāhī^{y}n bāk

וְשִׁמְעֵת עֲלָךְ דִּי רוּח אֱלָהִין בָּךְ

'I have heard about you that the spirit of the gods is in you.'

The King talks to Daniel.

a wənahī^{y}rū^{w} wəśoklətānū^{w}
b wəḥokmā^{h} yatī^{y}rā^{h} hištəkaḥat bāk

a *'And that illumination, and insight,*
b *and great wisdom is found in you.'*

DANIEL 5:15

a ū^{w}kə'an hu'alū^{w} qŏdāmay ḥakī^{y}mayâ 'āšəpayâ
b dī^{y} kətābā^{h} dənā^{h} yiqrō^{w}n
c ū^{w}pišreh ləhō^{w}dā'ū^{w}tanī^{y}
d wəlâ kāhălī^{y}n pəšar miltâ ləhaḥăwāyā^{h}

a *'And, now, the sages (and) the exorcists were brought before me*
b *so that they might read this writing*
c *and that its interpretation they should make known to me*
d *but they were not able to declare the interpretation of the thing.'*

DANIEL 5:16

a wa'ănā^{h} šim'et 'ălāk dī^{y} tī^{y}kū^{w}l
b pišrī^{y}n ləmipšar wəqiṭrī^{y}n ləmišrê
c kə'an hēn tī^{y}kū^{w}l kətābā^{h} ləmiqrê
d ū^{w}pišreh ləhō^{w}dā'ū^{w}tanī^{y}
e 'argəwānâ tilbaš wəhamnī^{y}kâ dī^{y} dahăbâ 'al ṣawərāk
f wətaltâ bəmalkū^{w}tâ tišlaṭ

a *'I have heard about you that you are able*
b *to give interpretations and to solve difficult problems.*
c *Now, if you are able to read the writing*
d *and to make known to me its interpretation,*
e *then, you will wear purple (robes of office) and the gold necklace (will be) around your neck*
f *and as the third (ruler) the kingdom you will rule.'*

CULTURAL INSIGHT

The dialect known as Yiddish is essentially a variety of German, but it is written with Aramaic/Hebrew letters. Any language can be written with the Aramaic alphabet, even English: יוּ כַּן סְפֶּל אֶנגְלִשׁ וֶרדס וִת אֲרָמַיִךְ לֶתֶּרס (*you can spell English words with Aramaic letters*).

Test yourself

Transliterate the Roman letters into Aramaic and insert in the blanks. Then, read the whole text out loud, checking against the transcription given. These lines conclude the expanded version of 1 Sam 2:1, the first verse of the Song of Hannah. (The Aramaic has been slightly altered from its original form to reflect some of the things learned in this lesson.)

a וְאַף הֵימָן בַּר יוֹאֵל ______________ שְׁמוּאֵל — bar bərī^{y}
b דַּעֲתִיד דִּיקוּם הוּא וְאַרְבְּעַת עֲסַר ______________ — bənō^{w}hī^{y}
c לְמִהְוֵי ______________ בְּשִׁירָא עַל יְדֵי נִבְלִין וְכִנָּרִין — 'āmərī^{y}n

d	עִם אֲחֵיהוֹן לֵיוָאֵי לְשַׁבָּחָא ________	bəbēʸt maqdəšâ
e	בְּכֵין רֵימַת ________ בְּמַתַּנְתָּא דְּמַנִּי לִי יְיָ	qarnīʸ
f	________ פּוֹרְעָנוּת נִסָּא דַּעֲתִיד לְמֶהֱוֵי בִּפְלִשְׁתָּאֵי	wə’ap ‘al
g	דַּעֲתִידִין דְּיַיְתוֹן יָת ________	’ărōʷnâ
h	בַּעֲגַלְתָּא חֲדַתָּא וְעִמֵּיהּ קֻרְבַּן ________	’ăšāmâ
i	בְּכֵין תֵּימַר כְּנִשְׁתָּא ________ אִתְפְּתַח פּוּמִי לְמַלָּלָא	dəyiśrā’el
j	רַבְרְבָן עַל ________ אֲרֵי חֲדִיתִי בְּפֻרְקָנָךְ	ba‘ălēʸ dəbābay

Transliteration and translation

a wə’ap hēʸmān bar yōʷ’el bar bərīʸ šəmūʷ’el
Also Heman, son of Joel, son of my son, Samuel

b da‘ătīʸd dīʸqūʷm hūʷ’ wə’arbə‘at ‘ăsar bənōʷhīʸ
who will arise, he and his 14 sons

c ləmihwēʸ ’āmərīʸn bəšīʸrâ ‘al yədēʸ niblīʸn wəkinārīʸn
to speak in song over harps and lyres,

d ‘im ’ăḥēʸhōʷn lēʸwā’ēʸ ləšabāḥâ bəbēʸt maqdəšâ
with his brothers, the Levites, to give praise in the holy temple.

e bəkēʸn rēʸmat qarnīʸ bəmatantâ dəmanīʸ līʸ yəyāy
Therefore, my horn is exalted in the gift that the Lord has assigned to me.

f wə’ap ‘al pōʷr‘ānūʷt nisâ da‘ătīʸd ləmihwēʸ biplištā’ēʸ
And also over the miraculous punishment that will be (executed) against the Philistines

g da‘ătīʸdīʸn dəyaytōʷn yāt ’ărōʷnâ
who will bring the ark

h ba‘ăgaltâ ḥădatâ wə‘imēʸh qurban ’ăšāmâ
with a new cart and with it a sacrifice of the guilt offering.

i bəkēʸn tēʸmar kəništâ dəyiśrā’el ’itpətaḥ pūʷmīʸləmalālâ
Therefore, the congregation of Israel will say my mouth was opened to speak

j rabrəbān ‘al ba‘ălēʸ dəbābay ’ărēʸ ḥădīʸtīʸ bəpurqānāk
great things against my enemies because I rejoiced in your deliverance.

Suggestions for further study

Writing English with Aramaic letters and vowels can be an entertaining way to learn the writing system. Begin by simply writing your name or a grocery list in this way and then moving on to more complicated phrases.

SELF-CHECK

	I CAN...
●	recognize and pronounce the Aramaic vowels
●	recognize the Aramaic consonants that mark some long vowels
●	recognize the six consonants called the begadkephat letters

3 Syllabification and shewa

In this unit you will learn how to:

- **distinguish between a shewa symbol that represents a murmured vowel and a shewa that represents the absence of a vowel**
- **break Aramaic words into syllables**
- **recognize when the dagesh represents doubling of a consonant**
- **recognize a silent aleph**

In this unit you will read:

- **Daniel 5:23–6:1**

Grammar

THE SHEWA SYMBOL

As already mentioned, the shewa symbol often represents a muttered vowel, though sometimes it indicates the absence of a vowel. In the words and exercises up to this point, almost every shewa has indicated a muttered vowel. Going forward, the shewa may also represent the absence of a vowel. Where it represents the absence of a vowel, it is not transliterated. The phrase *the king*, for example, is represented as מַלכָּא malkâ. There is no vowel symbol beneath the lamed. In the Bible, however, the same phrase is spelled מַלְכָּא malkâ where the shewa beneath the lamed indicates the absence of a vowel. Note, similarly, the spelling of the phrase *the queen* מַלכְּתָא malkətâ, which is spelled in the Bible מַלְכְּתָא malkətâ. The first shewa (under the lamed) represents the absence of a vowel, while the second represents a muttered vowel. This is a general rule; if two shewa symbols appear beneath consecutive consonants, then the first represents the absence of a vowel and the second represents a muttered vowel. Note some other examples of this from the last unit, with the words spelled correctly here with two consecutive shewas: וְרַבְרְבָנוֹהִי wərabrəbānō^{w}hī^{y} *and his nobles*, מִשְׁתְּיָא mištəyâ *the banquet* (Dan 5:10); הִשְׁתְּכַחַת hištəkaḥat *it was found* (5:11); יִתְקְרֵי yitqərē^{y} *let him read* (Dan 5:12).

> **LANGUAGE INSIGHT**
>
> In Aramaic and in Semitic languages in general, it is uncommon to find two or more consonants at the beginning of any syllable, as in English *state*, *school*, and *green*. Moreover, in Aramaic, there is only one case where a syllable begins with a vowel: the conjunction ū^{w} *and*, which attaches to the beginning of a word. In every other case, each syllable begins with a single consonant; this consonant is followed, in turn, by a single vowel.

How can someone predict whether or not to pronounce the shewa? In addition to the rule just mentioned, there are two general principles. First, if the shewa appears first in a word or phrase, it is pronounced: גְּבַר gəbar *man* and בְּמַלְכוּתָךְ bəmalkū^{w}tāk *in your kingdom* (Dan 5:11). Second, if the shewa is preceded by a short vowel (a ַ, e ֶ, i ִ, o ָ, or u ֻ), then the shewa is not pronounced. Conversely, if the shewa is preceded by a long vowel (ā ָ, ē ֵ, ī ִי, ō וֹ, ū וּ (and sometimes ֻ)), then the shewa is pronounced. Thus, in מַלְכָּא *the king*, the shewa should not be pronounced because the preceding vowel is short: malkâ. Similarly, in שִׁמְעֵת *I heard* the shewa beneath the mem is silent (šimʻet) because the preceding vowel is short. So also with רַעְיוֹנָךְ raʻyō^{w}nāk *your thoughts*, יִשְׁתַּנּוֹ yištanō^{w} *be changed* (Dan 5:10); מַלְכוּתָךְ malkū^{w}tāk *your kingdom*, כַּשְׂדָּאִין kaśdā’ī^{y}n *Chaldeans* (5:11); וּמַנְדַּע ū^{w}mandaʻ *and knowledge*, חֶלְמִין ḥɛlmī^{y}n *dreams*, קִטְרִין qiṭrī^{y}n *difficult problems*, וּפִשְׁרָא ū^{w}pišrâ *and the interpretation* (5:12). Conversely, notice that the shewa represents a muttered vowel when preceded by a long vowel: וּבְיוֹמֵי ū^{w}bəyō^{w}mē^{y} *and in the days of* (Dan 5:11) and וּמְשָׁרֵא ū^{w}məšārê *and one solving* (Dan 5:12).

Recall that the qamets represents two vowels, one long (ā) and one short (o). In cases where the shewa symbol is preceded by a qamets, then, it is unclear whether the shewa should be pronounced or not. The distinction is based on a word's etymology and history and a student needs to be told how the word should be pronounced. There are, however, some general tendencies that are consistent. In the previous unit, the words that are verbs (specifically participles) have the sequence qamets followed by a pronounced shewa: אָשְׁפִין ’āšəpī^{y}n *exorcists* and גָּזְרִין gāzərī^{y}n *diviners*. In such participles, the qamets always represents a long ā. In addition, the qamets is followed by a pronounced shewa in the common expression *forever* לְעָלְמִין ləʻāləmī^{y}n. In several other nouns, the qamets is followed by a shewa representing the absence of a vowel: וְשָׂכְלְתָנוּ wəśokləṭānū^{w} *and intelligence* and וְחָכְמָה wəḥokmā^{h} *and wisdom.*

PRACTICE 1

Transliterate the following words, being careful to distinguish where the shewa symbol represents the absence of a vowel (i.e., after a short vowel), and where it indicates a muttered sound (ə) (i.e., at the beginning of a word, after a silent shewa, and after a long vowel).

Example: הִתְרוֹמַמְתָּ hitrō^{w}mamtā *you have exalted yourself*

his temple (or *house*)	בַּיְתֵהּ	a
they were brought	הַיְתִיו	b
your nobles	רַבְרְבָנָךְ	c
(the sere = ē) *your wives*	שֵׁגְלָתָךְ	d
the wine	חַמְרָא	e
(the) silver	כַּסְפָּא	f
(the) iron	פַּרְזְלָא	g
(they) do not listen – a verb, participle	לָא שָׁמְעִין	h
(they) do not know – a verb, participle	לָא יָדְעִין	i
your breath	נִשְׁמְתָךְ	j
(the holem = ō) *your ways*	אֹרְחָתָךְ	k
and this writing	וּכְתָבָא דְנָה	l

this writing	דְּנָה כְּתָבָא	**m**
your rule (or *kingdom*)	מַלְכוּתָךְ	**n**
in the scales	בְמֹאזַנְיָא	**o**
(it) is divided	פְּרִיסַת	**p**
and (it) is hereby given	וִיהִיבַת	**q**

CULTURAL INSIGHT

The name shewa, sometimes also spelled sheva, is an English word, but is derived from either Hebrew or Aramaic. Because the symbol sometimes represents the absence of a vowel, it is commonly suggested that the word is a slight alteration of the Hebrew word שָׁוְא šāw' which means *emptiness, worthlessness*. Others, however, suggest that the word should instead be derived from šəwayyā, a word from Syriac, a dialect of Aramaic, that refers to a punctuation symbol made up of two dots, one on top of the other (See Khan).

SYLLABIFICATION

As mentioned earlier, Aramaic is consistent in the structure of its syllables. A syllable must begin with one (and only one) consonant. Each syllable has just one vowel. The only variable is whether or not a consonant ends the syllable. Thus, there are two options: consonant + vowel (called an 'open' syllable) or consonant + vowel + consonant (called a 'closed' syllable). In the phrase *the king*, מַלְכָּא, we have both kinds: mal + kâ. The first is a closed syllable (consonant + vowel + consonant) and the second is an open syllable (consonant + vowel). Notice that the mater aleph at the end of the second syllable is not considered a consonant since it is only a graphic means of indicating the preceding vowel. In the phrase *the queen*, מַלְכְּתָא, we also see both sequences: mal + kə + tâ.

There is one exception to this rule. The conjunction וּ ūʷ *and*, which stands as its own syllable, does not start with a consonant: וּבְיוֹמֵי ūʷ + bə + yōʷ + mēʸ *and in the days of* (Dan 5:11).

Two more characteristics of Aramaic syllables must be learned. First, recall that the stressed syllable of a word is usually the last in a word, unless marked with the symbol ˓in this course. All other syllables in a word are considered non-stressed. If a syllable is non-stressed, it must conform to one of three patterns:

1 consonant + long vowel

2 consonant + muttered vowel (i.e. shewa or hateph vowel)

3 consonant + short vowel + consonant

A non-stressed syllable can never contain the sequence consonant + short vowel. In the inflection of a word, if such a sequence were to appear, the short vowel becomes a muttered vowel or disappears entirely.

Phrased in another way: in a non-stressed syllable a long vowel or shewa will always be in an open syllable and a short vowel will always be in a closed syllable. A stressed syllable, on the other hand, may exhibit any sequence except consonant + muttered vowel.

Notice these patterns in the following transliteration from the last unit (Dan 5:14 – with all vowels noted now): וְשִׁמְעֵת עֲלָךְ דִּי רוּחַ אֱלָהִין בָּךְ wə-šim-'et 'ă-lāk dīʸ rūʷḥ 'ĕ-lā-hīʸn bāk '*(and) I have heard about you that the spirit of the gods is in you*'. In אֱלָהִין 'ĕ-lā-hīʸn *gods*, for example, the first two syllables are non-stressed. The first syllable (ʼĕ) contains the sequence consonant + muttered vowel, and in this case the muttered vowel is a hateph-seghol. The next syllable (lā) exhibits the sequence consonant + long vowel. Because a mater does not count as a consonant in syllabification, the last syllable (which is stressed: hīʸn) exhibits the sequence consonant + long vowel + consonant. This sequence is found primarily in stressed syllables.

There are exceptions to these patterns, though they are not numerous. Notice, first, that a cluster of syllables sometimes appears at the end of the masculine singular pronoun *you* **אַנְתְּ ʼant** and rarely at the end of the second masculine singular verbal forms, like **יְהַבְתְּ** yəhabt *you gave*. Second, in words like **נַהִירוּ** na-hīʸ-rūʷ *illumination*, the first syllable would seem to exhibit a sequence that is exceptional for non-stressed syllables, that is, consonant + short vowel. In truth, the pronunciation of this word in antiquity would have been more like *nah-hīʸ-rūʷ where the first syllable was closed and of the pattern consonant + short vowel + consonant. Similarly, in phrases like **דַּהֲבָא** da-hă-bâ *the gold*, the first syllable also seems to exhibit the pattern consonant + short vowel. Here again, the pronunciation in antiquity would have been more consistent with the patterns outlined: *dah-bâ.

Being familiar with these regular patterns will make it easier to inflect nouns and verbs and, so, it is important to commit them to memory.

LANGUAGE INSIGHT

In the example to Practice 1, **הִתְרוֹמַמְתָּ** *you have exalted yourself*, the third syllable is stressed. As explained, such a syllable may exhibit the sequence consonant + short vowel. Based on this fact, you might assume that the third syllable of the word is *ma. How does the dagesh in the taw at the end of the word make such an interpretation impossible? Or, expressed another way, why must the third syllable be mam, and that the whole word is expressed as hitrōʷmamtā? (Answer: The dagesh represents a hard taw. This implies that it is not preceded by a vowel. This, in turn, means that the shewa symbol under the second mem represents the absence of a vowel.)

PRACTICE 2

Write out the transliterations of the words from Practice 1, putting dashes between the syllables.

Example: **הִתְרוֹמַמְתָּ** hit-rōʷ-mam-tā

DAGESH REPRESENTING A DOUBLED CONSONANT

In the last unit, we learned that a dagesh (or dot) in a begadkephat letter indicates that it is hard, not soft. The dagesh can also be used in the other non-guttural letters (i.e., waw **ו**, zayin **ז**, ṭet **ט**, yod **י**, lamed **ל**, mem **מ**, nun **נ**, samekh **ס**, ṣadeh **צ**, qoph **ק**, śin **שׂ**, šin **שׁ**).

LANGUAGE INSIGHT

The guttural consonants (aleph **א**, heh **ה**, ḥet **ח**, ʻayin **ע**) and resh (**ר**) do not take the dagesh. Nevertheless, sometimes the three gutturals heh **ה**, ḥet **ח**, ʻayin **ע** were doubled in antiquity, leading to spellings such as **נַהִירוּ** (nahīʸrūʷ but reflecting an earlier *nahhīʸrūʷ) *illumination*. This is called ʻvirtual doublingʼ.

In cases where the dagesh appears in these non-guttural letters it represents doubling of the consonant (e.g. חַסִּיר ḥassīʸr *lacking*). Some words that we have encountered in the preceding exercises really do attest this dagesh, but in the preceding exercises, the dagesh was not written (in the interest of making the examples easier to understand). For instance, in the Reading section in Unit 2, we came across the expression מִלֵי milēʸ *words of*. Based on what we have just learned, the first syllable is not what we expect, since it is a non-stressed open syllable (consonant + short vowel: mi-). Such a syllable does not typically occur in Aramaic. In fact, in the Bible the word is written מִלֵּי, the dagesh in this instance representing a doubled lamed. Thus, the transliteration should be millēʸ and this conforms to our expectations of Aramaic syllable structure. Broken down into its syllables, the transliteration is mil-lēʸ. The first syllable is non-stressed and closed (consonant + short vowel + consonant). Other examples from Unit 2, spelled in the correct manner here with dagesh, include: חַכִּימֵי ḥakkīʸmēʸ *wise men of*, שַׂגִּיא śaggī *many*, קַדִּישִׁין qaddīʸšīʸn *holy*, יַתִּירָה yattīʸrāʰ *great*, מְפַשֵּׁר məpaššēr *interpreting*, דָּנִיֵּאל dāniyyēl *Daniel* (with a silent aleph), חַכִּימַיָּא ḥakkīʸmayyâ *the wise men*, and צַוְּארָךְ ṣawwərāk *your neck*. Notice that a doubled consonant always indicates a break between syllables: חַכִּימֵי ḥak-kīʸ-mēʸ and שַׂגִּיא śag-gī.

CULTURAL INSIGHT

The name דָּנִיֵּאל dāniyyēl *Daniel* was originally pronounced something closer to dānī'ēl or dān'ēl, as reflected in spellings of the name in Hebrew (e.g. דָּנִאֵל), where the yod is not doubled and the aleph is still pronounced like a true consonant. The name could be translated *El is my judge* or *El is (the) ruler*. Although the word *El* is a common word for *God* in Hebrew and Aramaic, it also frequently refers to the father figure of the West Semitic pantheon, *El* (or *Ilu*). Interestingly, the name *Dani'el* or *Dan'el* was likely chosen for these biblical stories based on an association of the name and wise people of the past. Daniel is the name of the human protagonist in the Epic of Aqhat, an early poetic text from north Syria in the Ugaritic language (which is linguistically close to Hebrew and Aramaic). The same name is mentioned with Job and Noah as a wise person in Ezek 14:14, 20. And, in Ezek 28:3, God states sarcastically 'You are wiser than Daniel!'

Sometimes, a begadkephat letter is also doubled. In these cases, the letter bears a dagesh and is pronounced 'hard'. Therefore, a hard begadkephat consonant that is singular and a hard begadkephat consonant that is doubled will look the same. How can you distinguish between the two types of dagesh in begadkephat letters? Look at the example of יַתִּירָה yattīʸrāʰ *great*. Why must the dagesh in the taw represent a doubled consonant and not just a single taw that is hard? The answer relates to our expectations for non-stressed syllables. (Answer: the first syllable is non-stressed and contains a short vowel, a patach. It must, therefore, be in a closed syllable (consonant + vowel + consonant).)

PRACTICE 3

Transliterate the following words, being sure to indicate where the dagesh represents doubling and where it indicates simply a hard bedgadkephat letter. Remember, a

syllable cannot begin or end with two consonants side-by-side; each syllable must begin with a consonant and end with a vowel or consonant.

Example: שְׁמַיָּא šəmayyâ *the heavens*

a	שַׁבַּחְתָּ	*you praised*
b	לָא הַדַּרְתָּ	*you did not honour*
c	פַּסָּא	*the palm*
d	מִלְּתָא	*the word*
e	תְּקִילְתָּה	*you have been weighed*
f	וְהִשְׁתְּכַחַת	*and you have been found*
g	חַסִּיר	*lacking*
h	שַׁלִּיט	*ruler*
i	קַבֵּל	*he took*
j	שִׁתִּין	*60*

SILENT ALEPH AND OTHER MATTERS

In this unit you have come across three words that have an aleph which is not transliterated. In some earlier form of Aramaic, perhaps in the early part of the first millennium BCE, the alephs in words like דָּנִיֵּאל, שַׂגִּיא, and צַוְּארָךְ were pronounced. For example, the name *Daniel* was likely pronounced dānī'ēl. By the middle of the first millennium BCE, however, the name was pronounced with a yod sound instead: dāniyyēl. Although the aleph of this and similar words was not pronounced, it was still written. The only place, in fact, that an aleph would normally be pronounced or heard in Official and Biblical Aramaic would be at the beginning of a syllable. This means that when an aleph comes at the end of a syllable you should not transliterate it. If it is functioning as the mater for a preceding long ā or ē, the vowels are transliterated with a circumflex: â and ê. Assume that every aleph at the end of a word, when preceded by a qamets or sere, is a mater. Since the aleph in the above three words is not functioning as a mater, the words can be transliterated without any indication of the aleph, dāniyyēl, śaggī, and ṣawwərāk. Alternatively, to indicate the correct spelling with aleph, the aleph can be put in parentheses: dāniyyē(')l, śaggī('), and ṣawwə(')rāk.

CULTURAL INSIGHT

Aleph, the name of the first letter of the alphabet is technically Hebrew, though the later Aramaic pronunciation is quite similar: alaph. The related verb, אלף, although occurring in Hebrew, is much more common in Aramaic, where it means *to learn* and *to teach*.

Frequently, words are linked in the medieval manuscripts with what looks, in essence, like a hyphen: דִּי־בַיְתֵהּ *of his house*. This is simply a way of indicating a connection between the words. There is no specific meaning attached to this symbol, which is called a maqqeph.

When an i or u vowel is followed at the end of a word by a guttural, a helping /a/ vowel (called a 'furtive patach') appears between the vowel and guttural, though this does not affect the syllabification of the words and often is not transliterated: רוּחַ reflects the pronunciation roo-ach, but the word is transliterated rūʷḥ *spirit*.

LANGUAGE INSIGHT

The reason that a patach appears under the final guttural of such words as רוּחַ is that this reflects the pronunciation of the medieval scribes.

Reading

THE WRITING ON THE WALL

Practise reading and translating Aramaic by transliterating the Aramaic verses and translating the words that have not been translated for you. The Aramaic words and their translations are found in Practice 1. Remember the following rules:

1. **A non-stressed syllable should have one of only three forms (cons. + long vowel; cons. + shewa/hateph; cons. + short vowel + cons.).**
2. **A dagesh in a non-begadkephat letter represents doubling.**
3. **An aleph followed by a vowel is a true consonant and is transliterated (with the symbol /'/); an aleph at the end of a word, when preceded by a qamets or sere, is a mater; an aleph without a following vowel within a word is commonly not transliterated.**

Example: Daniel 5:23, first part

וְעַל מָרֵא שְׁמַיָּא הִתְרוֹמַמְתָּ

wəʿal mārê šəmayyâ hitrōʷmamtā

(Daniel speaking) *And, against the lord of heaven you have exalted yourself.*

DANIEL 5:23, SECOND PART

a וּלְמָאנַיָּא דִּי־בַיְתֵהּ הַיְתִיו קָדָמָךְ
b וְאַנְתְּ וְרַבְרְבָנָךְ וְשֵׁגְלָתָךְ וּלְחֵנָתָךְ
c חַמְרָא שָׁתַיִן בְּהוֹן
d וְלֵאלָהֵי כַסְפָּא־וְדַהֲבָא נְחָשָׁא פַרְזְלָא אָעָא וְאַבְנָא
e דִּי לָא־חָזַיִן וְלָא־שָׁמְעִין וְלָא־יָדְעִין שַׁבַּחְתָּ
f וְלֵאלָהָא דִּי־נִשְׁמְתָךְ בִּידֵהּ וְכָל־אֹרְחָתָךְ לֵהּ לָא הַדַּרְתָּ

a *'The vessels of his temple* ______________________ *before you,*

b *and you and* ______________________, ______________________ *and your concubines*

c *drank* ______________________ *with them*

d *and the gods of* ______________________ *and gold, bronze,* ______________________, *wood and stone*

e *that do not see,* ______________________, *and* ______________________ *you praised.*

f *But, the god in whose power* (lit. *hand*) *is* ______________________ *and belonging to whom (are) all* ______________________ *you did not honour.'*

DANIEL 5:24

Transliterate the following and fill in the blanks.

a בֵּאדַ֫יִן מִן־קֳדָמ֫וֹהִי
b שְׁלִיַח פַּסָּא דִי יְדָא
c וּכְתָבָא דְנָה רְשִׁים

a *'Then, from before him (i.e., before God),*
b *the palm of the hand was sent*
c ______________________________ *was inscribed.'*

DANIEL 5:25

a וּדְנָה כְתָבָא דִּי רְשִׁים
b מְנֵא מְנֵא תְּקֵל וּפַרְסִין

a *'And this is* ______________________________ *which is inscribed,*
b mәne, mәne, tәqel, *and* pharsin.'

DANIEL 5:26

a דְּנָה פְּשַׁר־מִלְּתָא מְנֵא
b מְנָה אֱלָהָא מַלְכוּתָךְ וְהַשְׁלְמַהּ

a *'This is the interpretation of the word* mina (mәne)*:*
b *God has determined* ______________________________ *and brought it to completion.'*

DANIEL 5:27

a תְּקֵל תְּקִילְתָּה בְמֹאזַנְיָא
b וְהִשְׁתְּכַ֫חַתְּ חַסִּיר

a *'(As for) shekel* (tәqel)*, you have been weighed* ______________________________
b *and been found lacking.'*

DANIEL 5:28

a פְּרֵס פְּרִיסַת מַלְכוּתָךְ
b וִיהִיבַת לְמָדַי וּפָרָס

a *'(As for)* half-mina (pәres)*, your kingdom* ______________________________*,*
b ______________________________ *to the Medes and Persians.'*

CULTURAL INSIGHT

Notice that the word on the wall is פַּרְסִין and the word quoted in the verse in its interpretation is פְּרֵס. The first word is the plural form of the second. The link between the word on the wall and its interpretation is easy to see in Aramaic; both the noun פְּרֵס and the verb form פְּרִיסַת, which forms the central kernel of the interpretation are from the same root. In addition, note the phonetic link between this root and the etymologically unrelated gentilic noun פָּרָס *Persian(s)*. Linking a text with its interpretation through phonetically similar words is frequent in early biblical interpretations like those found in the Dead Sea Scrolls.

DANIEL 5:29

Transliterate the following texts from Roman letters into the Aramaic alphabet.

Example: Daniel 5:29 (first part)

bē$^{(’)}$dayin ’ămar bēləša$^{(’)}$ṣṣar

בֵּאדַיִן אֲמַר בֵּלְשַׁאצַּר

Then Belshazzar commanded . . .

a wəhalbišū^{w} lədāniyyē$^{(’)}$l ’argəwānâ
b wəhamnī^{y}kâ dī^{y} dahăbâ ‘al ṣawwə$^{(’)}$reh
c wəhakrizū^{w} ‘ălō^{w}hī^{y} dī^{y} lɛhĕwê šallī^{y}ṭ taltâ bəmalkū^{w}tâ

a *And Daniel was clothed with purple (robes)* (lit. *the purple*)
b *and the gold necklace (was set) around his neck.*
c *And, it was proclaimed about him that he would be the third ruler in the kingdom.*

DANIEL 5:30

Transliterate the following text from Roman letters into the Aramaic alphabet.

beh bəlē^{y}ləyâ qəṭī^{y}l bēlə$^{(’)}$šaṣṣar malkâ kaśdāyâ
In that (same) night, Belshazzar, king of the Chaldeans, was killed.

DANIEL 6:1

Transliterate the following texts from Roman letters into the Aramaic alphabet.

a wədārəyāwɛš mādāyâ qabbel malkū^{w}tâ
b kəbar šənī^{y}n šittī^{y}n wətartē^{y}n

a ‘*Darius the Mede took the kingdom,*
b *(when he was) about 62 years (old).*’

Test yourself

Read the following text out loud, checking against the transliteration in the Answer key. Then, circle all those shewas that represent the absence of a vowel. The text comprises the Aramaic translation (and expansion) of 1 Sam 2:8, also from the Song of Hannah. (The Aramaic has been slightly altered from its original form to reflect some of the things learned in this lesson; for the same text in a form closer to the original, see the Appendix.)

a מְקִים מֵעַפְרָא מִסְכֵּינָא מִקִּלְקְלְתָּא
b מְרִים חַשִּׁיכָא לְאָתָבוּתְהוֹן עִם צַדִּיקַיָּא רַבְרְבֵי עָלְמָא
c וְכֻרְסֵי יְקָרָא מַחְסֵין לְהוֹן
d אֲרֵי קֳדָם יְיָ גְּלַן עוֹבָדֵי בְּנֵי אֲנָשָׁא
e מִלְּרַע אַתְקֵין גֵּיהִנָּם לְרַשִׁיעַיָּא
f וְצַדִּיקַיָּא עָבְדֵי רְעוּתֵיהּ שַׁכְלֵיל לְהוֹן תֵּבֵל

a *The one raising from dust the poor from disgrace,*
b *the one lifting those in need to return them with the righteous, the nobles of the world.*
c *He gives them a glorious throne.*
d *Because before the Lord the deeds of humanity are revealed*
e *below he has established Gehenna for the wicked.*
f *And as for the righteous, those doing his will, he completed for them the world's lands.*

Suggestions for further study

Once you feel confident about the material in this unit, you can continue to practise what you have learned by going back over the texts covered in this unit, as well as those in Units 1 and 2. The verses are primarily from Daniel 5, which tells the story of the writing on the wall. The text in Units 1 and 2 has been simplified for pedagogical purposes, but you can now read the actual text to these same passages. You will find these passages from Daniel 5 in the Appendix, as they appear in the Bible. (Explanations to some of the scribal errors and idiosyncrasies in the text are included in the Appendix.)

SELF-CHECK

	I CAN...
●	distinguish between a shewa symbol that represents a murmured vowel and a shewa that represents the absence of a vowel
●	break Aramaic words into syllables
●	recognize when the dagesh represents doubling of a consonant
●	recognize a silent aleph

4 Independent pronouns, the root, and the prepositions בְּ, כְּ, and לְ

In this unit you will learn how to:
- **identify and use the independent pronouns**
- **identify Aramaic roots**
- **identify Aramaic prepositions בְּ, כְּ, and לְ**
- **identify and produce the demonstrative pronouns**

Grammar

INDEPENDENT PRONOUNS

Aramaic uses pronouns that are independent words in the same way that English uses subject pronouns like *I*. Where English uses *me*, *my*, and *mine*, Aramaic uses suffixed forms of the pronoun that attach directly to a noun, verb, or preposition. The suffixed forms of the pronouns are introduced in Unit 9. Here, the focus is on the pronouns that function as independent words. Also unlike English, Aramaic distinguishes in its second and third pronouns between masculine and feminine genders.

LANGUAGE INSIGHT

In English, there are three forms of each pronoun. For the first person singular, there are *I*, *me*, *mine*. *I* is always used as the subject of the verb (e.g. *I hit the ball*), while *me* is the object of the verb (e.g. *the ball hit me*) or follows a preposition (e.g. *to me*). *Mine* is used to mark that which is possessed (e.g. *the ball is mine*). In addition, the adjective *my* is used to mark possession with a following noun (e.g. *my ball*).

Singular			Plural		
1cs	*I*	אֲנָה	1cp	*we*	אֲנַ֫חְנָה
2ms	*you*	אַנְתְּ (also אַנְתְּה)	2mp	*you*	אַנְתּוּן
2fs	*you*	אַנְתִּי	2fp	*you*	אַנְתֵּן
3ms	*he, it*	הוּא	3mp	*they*	אִנּוּן + (Ezra: הִמּוֹ/Dan: הִמּוֹן)
3fs	*she, it*	הִיא	3fp	*they*	אִנִּין

The 2ms pronoun is most commonly spelled אַנְתְּה, reflecting two slightly different pronunciations of the pronoun. The consonants alone presuppose a pronunciation with a final long /ā/ vowel, ʼantā, while the vowels alone reflect the pronunciation ʼant. The 3mp pronouns הִמּוֹ (found in the book of Ezra) and הִמּוֹן (found in the book of Daniel) are unusual in that they are almost exclusively used as the object of verbs and are translated *them*.

CULTURAL INSIGHT

The Elchasites were a Mesopotamian religious group who spoke Aramaic. Their faith was a mixture of Christian and Jewish ideas. According to their theology (as reported in Greek by Epiphanius in Panarion 19.4.3), salvation was effected, in part, through the utterance of a magic palindrome at the centre of which is the 1cs pronoun: abar anid mōib nōchile daasim anē daasim nōchile mōib anid abar selam. To understand it, begin with the middle word anē, then read the letters backwards ēna = *I*; misaad (shd = *to testify*) = *witness*; elichōn = *to you* (m. pl.); biom = *in the day of*; dina = *the judgment*; raba = *great*. All together, it reads: *I testify to you in the day of the great judgment* and would be rendered in Biblical Aramaic **אֲנָה מְסַהֵד עֲלֵיכוֹן בְּיוֹם דִּינָא רַבָּא**. Perhaps not surprisingly, Epiphanius himself did not understand it as a palindrome, nor even as Aramaic and presented a contorted interpretation of the words.

PRACTICE 1

1 Complete the table with the correct Aramaic pronouns. Repeat the exercise until you are confident.

Singular			Plural		
1cs	*I*	________	1cp	*we*	________
2ms	*you*	________	2mp	*you*	________
2fs	*you*	________	2fp	*you*	________
3ms	*he, it*	________	3mp	*they*	________
3fs	*she, it*	________	3fp	*they*	________

2 Fill in the blanks based on the translation provided. Note that the verb *to be* is often not expressed in Aramaic.

a אֱלָהָא חַיָּא ________ — *he is the living God*

b ________ מְהֵימַן — *faithful is he = he is faithful*

c מִתְבְּנֵא ________ — *it* (masc.) *is being built*

d תְּקוּם לְעָלְמַיָּא ________ — *it* (fem.) *will stand forever*

e בָּבֶל ________ — *it* (fem.) *is Babylon*

f עֶזְרָא ________ — *you, Ezra*

g זָבְנִין ________ עִדָּנָא — *time you* (masc. pl.) *are buying = you are buying time*

h בְּנֵיהוֹן וּנְשֵׁיהוֹן ________ — *they* (masc.), *their children, and their wives* (Daniel 6:25)

i נְבוּכַדְנֶצַּר ________ — *I, Nebuchadnezzar* (Daniel 4:34)

j יָדְעֵת ________ — *I know* (Daniel 4:6)

THE ARAMAIC ROOT

Most Aramaic words are associated with a three consonant root. Due to the fact that most Aramaic words have only three consonants, identifying the root consonants is often rather easy. For example, the word מֶלֶךְ is from the root מלך. Being able to recognize the root of a word is important because it usually reveals the basic sense of the word and informs how the word's pronunciation will change when suffixes are added to it. Additionally, some dictionaries are organized by root and it is necessary to know the root of a noun or adjective in order to look it up. Sometimes words contain three root consonants and a mater. For example, the word דְּחִיל *fearsome* (root דחל) has a yod mater. Since the mater is being used to mark the preceding vowel as long, together with the fact that there are three other consonants in the word, it is clear that the yod should not be considered a root consonant. This also applies to forms that end in -ā^h. The word-final he is not a root consonant; it is only a mater. For example, in מַלְכָּה *queen*, the root is מלך. In those rare cases where the he is really a true final root consonant, it appears with a mappiq or dot in its centre, as in the word for *God*: אֱלָהּ.

PRACTICE 2

Identify the roots of the following words.

a קַבֵּל *he received*
b שְׁפַר *it was pleasing*
c נִשְׁמָה *breath*
d קֳדָם *before*
e נְזִק *damaged*
f מִנְחָה *offering*
g שַׁפִּיר *beautiful*
h קְיָם *edict*
i אֱלָהּ *God*
j עֲבִידָה *work, service*
k אֱנָשׁ *man, person*
l יַתִּיר *very much*
m עֲשִׁית *he thought*
n מַלְכוּ *kingdom*
o קַדִּישׁ *holy*

WEAK ROOTS

Let's consider the four most basic types of roots:

1 **strong – having three 'stable' consonants. In most cases, these consonants are: ב, ג, ד, ה, ז, ח, ט, כ, ל, מ, נ, ס, ע, פ, צ, ק, ר, שׂ, שׁ, ת.**

2 **first weak – having a 'weak' (א, ו, י, נ) consonant as the first root consonant.**

3 **middle weak – having a 'weak' (ו, י) consonant as the second root consonant.**

4 **final weak – having a 'weak' (א, ו, י) consonant as the third root consonant.**

The strong or stable roots consistently have the same three consonants in all their various forms. Some examples of these are found in Practice 2 (e.g. יַתִּיר *very much* and מִנְחָה *offering*). Often weak consonants will not appear in verbs and this makes their identification more difficult. For nouns and adjectives, however, only the middle weak roots offer real problems. In first weak and final weak nouns/adjectives the aleph, waw, yod and nun are usually expressed as true consonants, as with יְקָר *honour* (root יקר) and עֲוָיָה *iniquity* (root עוי). Still, it is important to mention some conventions. Almost all roots that might have originally had a ו as a first root consonant are realized as having first י as first root consonant in Aramaic and are listed this way in the dictionaries. Roots that were originally final א or final ו are all listed as final י in the dictionaries. This course follows these conventions.

For middle weak roots, note that some words express the middle-waw or yod as a true consonant (as with עֲוָיָה *iniquity*). For other words, follow these guidelines:

- If a word has only two obvious root consonants with a mater ו or י between them (e.g. דִּין *judgment*), then the mater likely reflects a ו or י root consonant. The word דִּין *judgment* is from the root דין and רוּחַ *spirit, wind* is from רוח. Contrast these with words like דְּחִיל *fearsome* and מַלְכוּ *kingdom* that contain three strong root consonants. In such words, the mater yod or waw is only a mater; it is not part of the root.
- If a word has only two consonants and a qamats between them (e.g. טָב *good*), then the word is likely from a middle weak root. The word טָב *good* is from the root טוב.
- By knowing just two root consonants, you will have difficulty determining whether the missing second consonant is ו or י. And, even where a yod is expressed in a word, it may be that the root is really middle-waw. The word קְיָם *edict* looks like it is from the root קים, but is instead from קום. Middle waw roots, on the whole, are more common than middle yod roots.

PRACTICE 3

Identify the root consonants in the following words. For roots with two root consonants and no mater, assume the middle root consonant is waw.

a יוֹם *day*
b טִין *clay*
c רוּחַ *spirit*
d קָל *voice, sound*
e סוֹף *end*
f אָת *sign*
g שִׂים *it was set*
h טוּר *mountain*

NOUNS WITH PREFIXED MEM

Some nouns and verbal forms exhibit an initial mem that is not part of the root. Usually, recognizing what the root consonants are is not difficult since words often contain three stable consonants in addition to the initial mem. In these cases, by a process of elimination, it is most likely that the three consonants that follow mem are the true root consonants. For example, the word מַדְבַּח *altar* exhibits four consonants, so one must be extraneous to the root; the root consonants must be דבח.

When a word starts with a mem and has only two clear root consonants, then the root itself might begin with mem (e.g. מַלְכָּה *queen*, root: מלך). As in the cases described, however, where a mater י or ו appears in the word and there are only two obvious root consonants, the mater can often be assumed to reflect an earlier י or ו root consonant, meaning that the mem is not part of the root. For example, in מָזוֹן *food*, the root is זון; the mem is not part of the root.

PRACTICE 4

Match these words with their root consonants. (NB: some words do have a mem as a first root consonant):

a	מִשְׁכַּן *abode*	1	אמר
b	מַעֲבַד *work*	2	מנח
c	מֵאמַר *command*	3	שׁכב
d	מַלְכָּה *queen*	4	דור
e	מַלְאַךְ *angel*	5	עבד
f	מְדוֹר *dwelling-place*	6	שׁכן
g	מַחְלְקָה *division*	7	דין
h	מִשְׁכַּב *bed*	8	חלק
i	מִנְחָה *offering*	9	מלך
j	מְדִינָה *province*	10	לאך

CULTURAL INSIGHT

Some words in Aramaic are of foreign origin and do not have clear root consonants. One of these words is הֵיכַל *temple, palace*. This word, also found in Hebrew, is derived ultimately from Sumerian, the language of southern Mesopotamia that is preserved in cuneiform tablets. In Sumerian, the word's pronunciation is unknown, though transliterated from cuneiform it is represented as e_2-gal. The first component, e_2, means *house* and the second, gal, *big*.

PREPOSITIONS בְּ, כְּ, AND לְ

These three prepositions are generally translated as follows:

בְּ	*in, with*
כְּ	*as, like*
לְ	*to, for*

But, sometimes the Aramaic prepositions do not match English prepositions (see Language insight). In addition to the translations given, the preposition בְּ can be used like English *due to* or *by means of*, as in מַצְלְחִין בִּנְבוּאַת חַגַּי *they were succeeding due to the prophecy of Haggai* . . . (Ezra 6:14). The preposition לְ often marks the direct object of a verb and in this use is left untranslated in English as in the phrase תִּסְגְּדוּן לְצֶלֶם דַּהֲבָה *you will worship the golden image*. The preposition can also be used to indicate possession, as in the expression גֻּבָּא לְדָנִיֵּאל *the den of Daniel* or *Daniel's den*. For more on the usage of this preposition, see Unit 9 and consult the Glossary.

It is an ancient graphic convention that these three prepositions are written directly before a following word, as though part of the word. For example, *in a kingdom* is בְּמַלְכוּ and *to a queen* is לְמַלְכָּה. In these cases, although the preposition + noun looks to be one word, the prepositions are still considered independent of the nouns that follow them. In these two examples, it should be clear that the root consonants are מלך. But, when one of these prepositions comes before a word with only two root consonants, it can be difficult to identify the word. That is, it is sometimes unclear whether an initial בְּ, כְּ, or לְ is a root consonant or a preposition. For example, the word *writing* is כְּתָב; the root consonants are

כתב. But, it would be conceivable for this to be an expression made up of the preposition כְּ followed by the participle תָּב *one who returns* (from the root תוב) to make the expression *as one who returns*. In such cases, it should first be assumed that the initial בְּ, כְּ, or לְ is part of the root and, if no appropriate word is found beginning with one of these consonants, it should then be assumed that such an initial consonant is a preposition.

Note also that the vowel under the preposition may change. If the following word would ordinarily begin with a consonant + (vocal) shewa, then the shewa of the preposition shifts to hiriq and the shewa of the word's first consonant is not pronounced (e.g. כִּנְמַר kinmar *like a leopard* from כְּ + נְמַר; note the further shift: -iʸ- > -īʸ- in לִיקָר *for honor* from לְ + יְקָר). If the word begins with a consonant + hateph vowel, then the shewa of the preposition becomes the full-vowel version of the hateph vowel (e.g. כֶּאֱנָשׁ kɛʼĕnāš *like a person* from כְּ + אֱנָשׁ).

LANGUAGE INSIGHT

The prepositions of one language do not exactly match the prepositions of another language. It should not be surprising, then, that the Aramaic prepositions described here can be translated by numerous English prepositions. Usually the exact nuance of the preposition will be clear from the context.

PRACTICE 5

Match the Aramaic word with its root, identifying along the way which of the following expressions exhibit an initial בְּ, כְּ, or לְ preposition.

a	כִּכְתָב	1	צדק
b	כְּסַף	2	לבשׁ
c	בִּרְגַז	3	בני
d	בְּשַׂר	4	יום
e	בְּצִדְקָה	5	כסף
f	בִּבְהִילוּ	6	טור
g	לְבוּשׁ	7	חיל
h	בְּיוֹם	8	רגז
i	בְּחַיִל	9	כתב
j	לְטוּר	10	בשׂר
k	לִשָּׁן	11	בהל
l	בִּנְיָן	12	לשׁן

DEMONSTRATIVE AND INTERROGATIVE PRONOUNS

Demonstrative pronouns are those that correspond to the English words *this, that, these,* and *those*. Aramaic has multiple demonstrative pronouns, though it does not distinguish between the near (*this, these*) and far (*that, those*) pronouns.

	Masculine	Feminine
singular (*this, that*)	דֵּךְ דִּכֵּן דְּנָה	דָּא דָּךְ דִּכֵּן
	Common	
plural (*these, those*)	אִלֵּין אִלֵּךְ	

The independent pronouns (**הוּא** *he* and **אִנּוּן** *they*) are sometimes used as demonstrative pronouns too (e.g. **מַלְכַיָּא אִנּוּן** *these kings*).

Aramaic has a set of interrogative pronouns that mark the beginning of questions: **מַן** *who?*; **מָה** *what?*; **אָן** *where?* The prepositions **עַל** and **לְ** can combine with **מָה** to make expressions **לְמָה** and **עַל־מָה** that ask *for what?* or *why?*

Although only a linguistic accident, the mismatch between English and Aramaic pronouns can help you to remember them: English *she* = Aramaic **הִיא**; English *he* = Aramaic **הוּא**; and English *who?* = *Aramaic* **מַן**.

Test yourself

Match the Aramaic pronouns with the correct English translation.

a	דָּא	**1**	*she*
b	אֲנָה	**2**	*this* (m.s.)
c	אַנְתְּה	**3**	*you* (f.s.)
d	דֵּךְ	**4**	*I*
e	אֲנַחְנָא	**5**	*these* (c.p.)
f	אִלֵּין	**6**	*this* (f.s.)
g	הִיא	**7**	*he*
h	דְּנָה	**8**	*we*
i	אַנְתְּי	**9**	*you* (m.s.)
j	הוּא	**10**	*this* (m.s.)

SELF-CHECK

	I CAN...
○	identify and use the independent pronouns
○	identify Aramaic roots
○	identify Aramaic prepositions בְּ, כְּ, and לְ
○	identify and produce the demonstrative pronouns

5 Nouns and adjectives

In this unit, you will learn how to:

- **recognize and produce the absolute state of the noun**
- **recognize and produce the construct state of the noun**
- **recognize and produce the determined state of the noun**
- **inflect Aramaic nouns and adjectives for gender, number, and state**

In this unit, you will read:

- **Daniel 6:2–4**

Grammar

GENDER AND NUMBER

In many Semitic languages, Aramaic among them, nouns and adjectives are very similar, sometimes overlapping in form and function. So, for example, adjectives often can be used like nouns and have the same morphological patterns as nouns. The adjective **חַכִּים** *wise* also means *a wise person, a sage*. Conversely, nouns can be used as adjectives, as with the noun קְשֹׁט *truth* in the phrase כָּל־מַעֲבָדוֹהִי קְשֹׁט *all his deeds are true* (literally, … *are truth*).

Nouns and adjectives have two genders: masculine and feminine. Usually, the basic form of a masculine noun/adjective has no particular type of ending. A feminine noun/adjective, on the other hand, is usually marked with a final -āʰ (ָה -) in its most basic form, as with the word for *offering* **מִנְחָה**. It is easy to compare the endings on adjectives: **טָב** *good* for the masculine and **טָבָה** *good* for the feminine.

Nouns and adjectives have three numbers: singular, dual (for things in pairs), and plural. The singular has no special ending or marking, as in **יַד** *hand*. The dual is uncommon and is usually used for body parts that naturally appear in pairs. It has the basic ending -ayin (ַיִן -) for both masculine and feminine words, as in יְדַיִן *two hands*. The plural has the basic ending -īn (ִין -) for masculine nouns/adjectives and -ān for feminine nouns/adjectives (ָן -). Note, for example, the plural nouns מַלְכִין *kings* and מַלְכָן *queens*. Compare the masculine and feminine plural forms of the adjective *good*: טָבִין and טָבָן.

> **LANGUAGE INSIGHT**
>
> It is especially common for Aramaic adjectives to be used like nouns. A similar thing happens in English, though it is less common. For instance, *evil* and *good* are adjectives but are also used as nouns. Similarly, *divine* is an adjective but can be used as a noun to mean a theologian or minister.

By applying the correct endings, you can inflect Aramaic adjectives and nouns. This is similar to the application of an *s* to make singular English nouns plural: *girl* > *girls*.

PRACTICE 1

Add the appropriate dual or plural ending (ַיִן- or ִין- or ָן-) to these words.

Example: *gifts* (a feminine noun) ____________ מַתְּנ → מַתְּנָן

- **a** *gods* (a masculine noun) ____________ אֱלָה
- **b** *two horns* ____________ קַרְנ
- **c** *sages* (a masculine noun) ____________ חַכִּימ
- **d** *two feet* ____________ רַגְל
- **e** *beasts* (a feminine noun) ____________ חֵיו
- **f** *days* (a masculine noun) ____________ יוֹמ
- **g** *open* (a fem. pl. adjective) ____________ פְּתִיח
- **h** *forever* (a masc. pl. noun) ____________ עָלְמ
- **i** *two sets of teeth* ____________ שִׁנּ
- **j** *greats* (a feminine adjective) ____________ רַבְרְב

For many masculine plural nouns/adjectives, you can reverse the process and subtract a final ִין- to find the singular form of a word: קָלִין *sounds* > קָל *sound*. Recall that the basic singular form of a feminine noun ends in -āʰ (ָה-), as in מִנְחָה *offering*. If you come across a plural feminine noun, to find its singular form, you must replace the final plural morpheme ָן- with the singular morpheme -āʰ (ָה-). So, מְדִינָן *provinces* is מְדִינָה *province* in the singular.

PRACTICE 2

Write the singular forms for the following plural nouns and adjectives.

Example: *gift* (a feminine noun) מַתְּנָן → מַתְּנָה

- **a** *strong* (as a masc. adj.) תַּקִּיפִין
- **b** *singers* (a masculine noun) זַמָּרִין
- **c** *sections* (a feminine noun) מַחְלְקָן
- **d** *ends* (a masculine noun) סוֹפִין
- **e** *many* (as a fem. adj.) שַׂגִּיאָן

THE ABSOLUTE, CONSTRUCT, AND DETERMINED STATES

In addition to the characteristics of gender (masculine, feminine) and number (singular, dual, plural), nouns and adjectives are also qualified according to their 'state'. Nouns and adjectives have three states: the absolute, the construct, and the determined state (also called the emphatic state). These are best explained by examples:

absolute:	קְיָם = *edict*
construct:	קְיָם = *edict of*
determined:	קְיָמָא = *the edict*

The absolute state marks the basic sense of the word. It exhibits the most basic form of a noun or adjective, the form listed in a dictionary entry. The construct state indicates a connection to a following word. So, **קְיָם** in the construct state might be followed by the word **מַלְכָּה** *queen* to give the expression **קְיָם מַלְכָּה** *an edict of a queen*, or *a queen's edict*. (Note that in the case of the word **קְיָם**, the absolute and construct states are identical in form and you can only differentiate them based on how they appear in a sentence.) The determined state implies that a speaker is referring to a specific thing. In simple terms, the final **ָא** of **קְיָמָא** is like English *the*.

CULTURAL INSIGHT

Sometimes the determined state in Aramaic is used to mark a vocative expression, that is, an expression indicating the addressee of a following statement or assertion. In Mark 5:41, Jesus is quoted in Aramaic, *Little girl, get up!* The original language of the New Testament is Greek so the Aramaic is transliterated into Greek letters, *ταλιθα κουμ*, which in turn would be represented in the Roman alphabet as talitha koum and **טְלִיתָא קוּם** following the Biblical Aramaic model. The /a/ vowel at the end of *ταλιθα* = talitha marks the determined state; Jesus uses the determined state here as a vocative to specify to whom he is speaking.

When a word in the construct state precedes another word in the absolute state, both words lack specificity and can be translated with the English *a* or *an*. When a word in the construct state precedes another in the determined state, both words carry this nuance of specificity and both can be translated with the English word *the*:

קְיָם מַלְכָּה	*an edict of a queen* or *a queen's edict*
קְיָם מַלְכְּתָא	*the edict of the queen* or *the queen's edict*

The absolute and construct states are identical for the word **קְיָם**, but this is not the case for other words, e.g. consider the word **מַלְכָּה** (*queen*, a feminine noun):

absolute:	**מַלְכָּה**	*queen*
construct:	**מַלְכַּת**	*queen of*
determined:	**מַלְכְּתָא**	*the queen*

INFLECTION OF THE NOUNS AND ADJECTIVES

Nouns and adjectives are inflected according to the following paradigm, illustrated here by the adjective **דְּחִיל** (*fearsome, frightful*):

singular	masc.	fem.
abs.:	דְּחִיל	דְּחִילָה
const.:	דְּחִיל	דְּחִילַת
det.:	דְּחִילָא	דְּחִילְתָּא (də-ḥīʸl-tâ)*
*(Note the irregularity: long ī in a closed, non-stressed syllable.)		

plural	masc.	fem.
abs.:	דְּחִילִין	דְּחִילָן
const.:	דְּחִילֵי	דְּחִילָת
det.:	דְּחִילַיָּא	דְּחִילָתָא

The distinctive endings of each of these forms are as follows:

singular	masc.	fem.
abs.:	–	דְּחִיל- ָה
const.:	–	דְּחִיל- ַת
det.:	דְּחִיל- ָא	דְּחִיל- ְתָא

plural	masc.	fem.
abs.:	דְּחִיל- ִין	דְּחִיל- ָן
const.:	דְּחִיל- ֵי	דְּחִיל- ָת
det.:	דְּחִיל- ַיָּא	דְּחִיל- ָתָא

Most Aramaic nouns and adjectives follow these patterns. And, by identifying an ending, you can usually identify the gender, number, and state of a noun or adjective. For instance, the ending -ē^{y} (- ֵי) almost always indicates that the noun or adjective to which it is attached is a masculine plural noun/adjective in construct with a following word. From this, you can also usually produce the other forms of the noun. If you encounter the form חַכִּימֵי *wise men of*, you can assume that the plural determined form would be חַכִּימַיָּא *the wise men.*

PRACTICE 3

1 Match the English phrases with the Aramaic, which stem from זַמָּר *singer* and מַתְּנָה *gift*. Then write down the distinctive ending (if any) on the Aramaic words.

a *singers of*	**1** מַתְּנָן
b *the singer*	**2** זַמָּרָא
c *gifts of*	**3** זַמָּר
d *gifts*	**4** זַמָּרֵי
e *the singers*	**5** מַתְּנָת
f *singer of*	**6** זַמָּרַיָּא

2 Give either the absolute or determined endings to these nouns and adjectives based on their translations. Notice that the first vowel of the ending goes under the last root consonant.

Example: *officials* (m. pl. absolute noun) ______________סָרַךְ → סָרְכִין

a *the officials* (m. pl. det. noun) ______________סָרַךְ

b *the writing* (m. sing. det. noun) ______________כְּתָב

c *fingers* (f. pl. abs. noun) ______________אֶצְבַּע

d the concubines (f. pl. det. noun) ________________ לְחֵנ
e the tongues (m. pl. det. noun) ________________ לִשָּׁנ
f strong (f. sing. abs. adjective) ________________ תַּקִּיפ
g the den (m. sing. det. noun) ________________ גֻּבּ
h the men (m. pl. det. noun) ________________ גֻּבְר
i the living (m. sing. det. adjective) ________________ חַיּ
j many (f. pl. abs. adjective) ________________ שַׂגִּיא

3 Give the construct endings to these nouns and adjectives in the following phrases based on their translations (the absolute forms are in parentheses).

Example: *the days of* (m. pl. יוֹמִין) *your father* — יוֹמֵי אֲבוּךְ → יוֹמ ____________ אֲבוּךְ
a *wisdom of* (f. sing. חָכְמָה) *gods* — חָכְמ ________________ אֱלָהִין
b *the gods of* (m. pl. אֱלָהִין) *silver and gold* — אֱלָהּ ________________ כַּסְפָּא־וְדַהֲבָא
c *the officials of* (m. pl. סָרְכִין) *the kingdom* — סָרְכ ________________ מַלְכוּתָא
d *the burning of* (f. sing. יְקֵדָה) *the fire* — יְקֵד ________________ אֶשָּׁא
e *the names* (f. pl. [in form] שְׁמָהָן) *of the men* — שְׁמָה ________________ גֻּבְרַיָּא
f *the riches of* (m. pl. נִכְסִין) *the king* — נִכְס ________________ מַלְכָּא
g *the work of* (f. sing. עֲבִידָה) *God* — עֲבִיד ________________ אֱלָהָא
h *the dedication of* (f. sing. חֲנֻכָּה) *the house of God* — חֲנֻכּ ________________ בֵּית־אֱלָהָא
i *the children of* (m. pl. בְּנִין) *Israel* — בְּנ ________________ יִשְׂרָאֵל
j *the types* (m. pl. זְנִין) *of music* — זְנ ________________ זְמָרָא

4 Fill in the table for masculine nouns/adjectives.

Noun/adj. abs./cstr. sing.	det. sing.	plural abs.	pl. cstr.	pl. det.
עַתִּיק *(old)*	עַתִּיקָא			
טָב *(good*, root: טוב*)*				
זְעֵיר zəʿēʸr *(little)*				
דִּין *(judgment*, root: דין*)*				
טוּר *(mountain)*				
חַכִּים *(wise)*				
לִשָּׁן *(tongue)*				
קָל *(voice*, root: קול*)*				
שְׁאָר *(remnant)*				

Notice that the two words with waw as a middle consonant of their root (טָב and קָל) have similar forms.

5 Fill in the table for feminine nouns/adjectives.

Noun/adj.sing. abs.	cstr. sing.	det. sing.	plural abs.	pl. cstr.	pl. det.
עַתִּיקָה (*old*)		עַתִּיקְתָּא			
טָבָה (*good*, root: טוב)		טָבְתָּא			
זְעֵירָה zəʻēʸrāh (*little*)		זְעֵירְתָא			
חֲבוּלָה (*crime*)		חֲבוּלְתָּא			
חֵיוָה (*animal*, root: חיי)		חֵיוְתָא			
חַכִּימָה (*wise*)					
תַּקִּיפָה (*strong*)					
חָכְמָה ḥokmāʰ (*wisdom*)					

Note the qamets of חָכְמָה represents a short o vowel: ḥokmāʰ and is not attested in the plural.

LANGUAGE INSIGHT

It should be apparent that there are certain consistencies between these words. For example, the words עַתִּיקָה, חַכִּימָה, and תַּקִּיפָה all have the same vowel pattern. Similarly, the words דְּחִילָה, זְעֵירָה, and חֲבוּלָה have similar forms, though the long middle vowel of each is different. Recognizing these patterns helps to make learning new words easier.

As explained in Unit 3, if a syllable is non-stressed, then a long vowel will stand in an open syllable and a short vowel in a closed syllable. It is important to notice one major exception to this rule in the words in Exercise 5. In a feminine singular determined noun, long ū, long ā, and long ī can appear in closed syllables, e.g. עַתִּיקְתָּא = ʻat-tīʸq-tâ. This does not happen with ē: זְעֵירְתָא zə-ʻēʸ-rə-tâ.

Note that some feminine words like מִלָּה *thing, word*, will inflect as though they were masculine: מִלִּין *things, words* and מִלַּיָּא *the things, the words*.

Note also that the pronunciation of the feminine adjective in the absolute state is identical to that of the masculine adjective in the determined state. The only difference in these forms above are their graphic representation, ָה- on the feminine adjective (the typical marker of femininity) and ָא- on the determined masculine noun. Because the difference between these two morphemes is only graphic, scribes often used them interchangeably; it is common to find feminine nouns with the ending ָא- and masculine determined nouns with the ending ָה-. For the purposes of pedagogy, the feminine absolute ending is rendered usually in this course with **he**, and the masculine determined form with an **aleph**.

SYNTAX OF ADJECTIVES AND DEMONSTRATIVE PRONOUNS

An adjective or demonstrative pronoun usually has one of three roles in an Aramaic sentence. First, it can function as a noun, similar to the English adjectives *evil* and *divine* or *this*. Consider these examples:

עַמִּיקָתָא	*the deep things* (adj. עַמִּיק *deep*)
עַתִּיק יוֹמַיָּא	*the one ancient of days* (adj. עַתִּיק *ancient*)
דְּנָה חֶלְמָא	*this is the dream*
כָּל־דְּנָה יְדַעְתְּ	*all of this you knew*

Second, an adjective or demonstrative can modify a noun. When an adjective modifies a noun it usually agrees with the noun in all its qualities (gender, number, and state i.e., absolute or determined). In the expression מֶ֫לֶךְ רַב *great king* the Aramaic adjective for *great* (רַב) is masculine, singular, and in the absolute state since it is modifying the word *king* (מֶ֫לֶךְ) which is also masculine, singular, and in the absolute state. Notice also that the adjective usually follows the noun. Similarly, in the expression אֱלָהִין קַדִּישִׁין *holy gods* the adjective *holy* (קַדִּישִׁין) follows the noun *gods*; both words are masculine, plural, and absolute. Demonstrative pronouns are similar to adjectives, though these do not inflect for state and can appear before or after the determined noun they modify: כְּתָבָא דְנָה *this writing*; אִלֵּין מַלְכְוָתָא *these kingdoms*.

Third, an adjective (less so a demonstrative) can act as a predicate in a clause. When an adjective functions as a predicate, it matches the subject of the clause in number and gender, but not in its state and the adjective can appear before the subject. In the clause יַצִּיב חֶלְמָא *the dream is certain*, the adjective יַצִּיב precedes the noun and agrees with it only in gender and number, not in its state (יַצִּיב is in the absolute and חֶלְמָא in the determined state).

PRACTICE 4

Compose the following phrases in Aramaic with the following vocabulary: חַכִּים *wise*; קַדִּישׁ *holy*; תַּקִּיף *strong*. Note that some adjectives are used to modify nouns while some are used as nouns themselves or as predicates. Where relevant, you will need to alter the adjectives according to the gender, number, and state of the respective nouns. Where an adjective is used as a noun assume that it is masculine. The English preposition *of* presumes that the preceding noun is in the construct state.

Example: a strong beast (חֵיוָה)(*beast* is fem. sing. abs.) חֵיוָה תַּקִּיפָה

- **a** *the strong beast* (חֵיוְתָא)
- **b** *the wise queen* (מַלְכְּתָא)
- **c** *the son* (בְּרָא) *is wise*
- **d** *the beasts* (חֵיוָתָא) *are strong*
- **e** *the sons* (בְּנַיָּא) *are wise*
- **f** *the holy ones of God* (lit. *the God* אֱלָהָא)
- **g** *the wise ones of the king* (מַלְכָּא)
- **h** *strong kings* (מַלְכִין)
- **i** *the wise queens* (מַלְכָתָא)
- **j** *the word* (מִלָּה) *of the officials* (סָרְכִין)

CULTURAL INSIGHT

The Persian king Darius, mentioned in Daniel 6, was a usurper who justified his rule, in part, through an inscription, called the Bisitun inscription, that is carved into the face of a cliff in what is today western Iran. The inscription, presented in three languages (Elamite, Akkadian, and Old Persian) explains in first person narration how and why Darius established his rule. The inscription was also translated into Aramaic, a copy of which was found in Egypt (which was once part of the Persian empire). The text frequently describes the help Darius received from Ahuramazda, the divinity: **בטלה זי אהורמזד חילא זילי קטלו למרדיא**. Assuming a vocalization somewhat like Biblical Aramaic, we would pronounce this: **בְּטַלֵּהּ דִּי אֲהוּרְמַזְד חֵילָא דִּילִי קְטַלוּ לְמָרָדַיָּא** *thanks to the assistance of Ahuramazda, my army killed the rebels*. In a later passage, he seems to warn future rulers to be honest and forthright, adding: **הודע איך זי עביד אנת ואיך הלכתך** (assuming Biblical Aramaic pronunciation: **הוֹדַע אֵיךְ דִּי עֲבִיד אַנְתְּ וְאֵיךְ הִלְכְתָךְ**) *Make known how you are made and how (is) your habit.*

Reading: Daniel 6:2–4

Identify the noun/adjective endings in the parenthetical words drawn from Daniel 6. In this and some subsequent units the passages from the Bible are laid out with a literal translation under the Aramaic words and a more idiomatic translation following this. This two-fold translation is intended to help the reader understand the manner in which Aramaic words fit together to make sentences.

DANIEL 6:2

a שְׁפַר קֳדָם דָּרְיָוֶשׁ וַהֲקִים עַל־מַלְכוּתָא
over the kingdom ← to establish ← Darius ← before ← it pleased

b לַאֲחַשְׁדַּרְפְּנַיָּא מְאָה וְעֶשְׂרִין
and twenty ← one hundred ← satraps

c דִּי לֶהֱוֺן בְּכָל־מַלְכוּתָא
throughout all of the kingdom ← they might be ← so that

a *It pleased Darius* (lit. *it was pleasing before Darius*) *to establish* (lit. *and he established*) *over the kingdom* (**מַלְכוּתָא** → **תָא-** fem. sing. det. ending on **מַלְכוּ**)

b *one hundred and twenty* (**עֶשְׂרִין**) *satraps* (**אֲחַשְׁדַּרְפְּנַיָּא**)

c *that they might be throughout all of the kingdom.*

DANIEL 6:3

a וְעֵלָּא מִנְּהוֹן סָרְכִין תְּלָתָה דִּי דָנִיֵּאל חַד־מִנְּהוֹן
one of them ← Daniel ← who ← three ← officials ←above them

b דִּי לֶהֱוֺן אֲחַשְׁדַּרְפְּנַיָּא אִלֵּין יָהֲבִין לְהוֹן טַעְמָא
the report ← to them ← give ← these ← satraps ← would ← who

c וּמַלְכָּא לָא לֶהֱוֵה נָזִק
(need to) bother ← would ← not ← so the king

a *Above them (were) three officials* (**סָרְכִין**), *one of whom was Daniel,*

b *to whom these satraps would give the report* (**טַעְמָא**)

c *so the king* (**מַלְכָּא**) *would not need to bother (with it).*

DANIEL 6:4

a אֱדַ֫יִן דָּנִיֵּאל דְּנָה הֲוָה מִתְנַצַּח
distinguished himself ← this ← Daniel ← then

b עַל־ סָרְכַיָּא וַאֲחַשְׁדַּרְפְּנַיָּא כָּל־קֳבֵל דִּי רוּחַ יַתִּירָה בֵּהּ
in him ← great ← spirit ← because ← and the satraps ← the officials ← above

c וּמַלְכָּא עֲשִׁית לַהֲקָמוּתֵהּ עַל־כָּל־ מַלְכוּתָא
the kingdom ← over all of ← to appoint him ← thought ← and the king

a *Then, this Daniel distinguished himself*
b *above the officials* (סָרְכַיָּא) *and the satraps because a great* (יַתִּירָה) *spirit was in him;*
c *and the king* (מַלְכָּא) *thought to appoint him over all of the kingdom* (מַלְכוּתָא).

Test yourself

Identify the number, gender, and state of the underlined nouns in the following text based on their endings. The text is the Aramaic translation and expansion of Judg 4:4–5.

a וּדְבוֹרָה אִתְּתָא נְבִיאֲתָא אִתַּת לַפִּידוֹת
b הִיא דָּיְנָא יָת יִשְׂרָאֵל בְּעִדָּנָא הַהוּא
c וְהִיא יָתְבָא בְּקַרְתָּא בְּעַטְרוֹת
d דְּבוֹרָה מִתְפַּרְנְסָא דִּילַהּ
e לַהּ דִּקְלִין בִּירִיחוֹ פַּרְדֵּיסִין בְּרָמְתָא
f זֵיתִין עָבְדִין מְשַׁח בְּבִקְעֲתָא בֵּית שְׁקְיָא בְּבֵית אֵל
g עֲפַר חִיוָּר בְּטוּר מַלְכָּא
h וְסָלְקִין לְוָתַהּ בְּנֵי יִשְׂרָאֵל לְדִינָא

a *Now, Deborah, a <u>prophet</u>* (נְבִיאֲתָא) *woman, wife of Lapidot,*
b *she was judging Israel at that <u>time</u>* (עִדָּנָא).
c *She was dwelling in the city, in Atarot.*
d *Deborah was supporting herself from what was hers;*
e *she had <u>date-palms</u>* (דִּקְלִין) *in Jericho, gardens in Rama,*
f *<u>olive trees</u>* (זֵיתִין) *making oil in <u>the valley</u>* (בִּקְעֲתָא)*, irrigated land in Beth-El,*
g *white soil in Tur-<u>Malka</u>* (מַלְכָּא) *(lit. Mountain of <u>the King</u>).*
h *So the <u>children of</u>* (בְּנֵי) *Israel would go up toward her for <u>judgment</u>* (lit. *the judgment* (דִּינָא)).

SELF-CHECK

	I CAN...
○	recognize and produce the absolute state of the noun
○	recognize and produce the construct state of the noun
○	recognize and produce the determined state of the noun
○	inflect Aramaic nouns and adjectives for gender, number, and state

6 Participles

In this unit you will learn how to:

- **recognize and produce active participles**
- **recognize and produce passive participles**
- **apply the rules of vowel reduction**

In this unit you will read:

- **Daniel 6:5–6**

Grammar

ACTIVE PARTICIPLES

The participles in Aramaic have forms and inflections similar to those of nouns and adjectives. There are active and passive participles. Both types of participle are used as nouns / adjectives or as verbs. Active participles are more common and are described first.

As nouns, active participles often are used to express a person or thing that does the action of the verb. For example, כָּתֵב (the active participle from the root כתב *to write*) can be translated as a noun *one who writes*. Note, for example, the definite participles in Daniel 4:4: אָשְׁפַיָּא ... וְגָזְרַיָּא *the exorcists ... and the diviners*. As adjectives, participles can modify nouns that immediately precede them. The active participle דָּלִק (from the root דלק *to burn*) appears in the phrase נוּר דָּלִק *burning fire*.

As verbs, active participles can indicate an action in the past, present, or future. Participles usually represent an action that is done repeatedly or without cessation. This may be an act of mentation (e.g. יָדַע אֲנָה *I know*) or emotion (e.g. דָּחֲלִין *they were afraid*). In other cases the act that the participle represents is one done once but by multiple people; note the participle (עָלְלִין from the root עלל *to come*) in Daniel 4:4 בֵּאדַיִן עָלְלִין חַרְטֻמַיָּא אָשְׁפַיָּא ... ... וְגָזְרַיָּא *Then, the magicians, the exorcists ... and the diviners each came ...*

Notice that although the act represented by the Aramaic participle is something that occurs repeatedly or continuously this is not always represented by the bare form of the English verb. That is, we do not translate יָדַע אֲנָה as *I am knowing* or דָּחֲלִין as *they were being afraid* since this seems less idiomatic in English than *I know* and *they were afraid*. In the case of עָלְלִין, in another context the same participle might imply a continuous movement of people and be translated *were coming*. But, in Daniel 4:4 the participle seems instead to represent the individual approach of multiple groups of soothsayers. The participle specifies that the action of *coming* was done repeatedly by different groups; the magicians came at a different time than the exorcists, etc. A translation should ideally reflect the idiom of the target language, in this case English. The translation *each came* indicates the sense of the participle, though the Aramaic contains no separate word equivalent to *each*.

Some participles seem to be used to indicate a simple past tense. This is especially the case with the verbs **אמר** *to say* and **ענה** *to answer, speak up*, which often occur together to preface direct speech.

Outside of these exceptional cases, the tense of the participle is determined by context. Therefore, if a participle appears in the context of the past, the participle should be translated with the English past tense, but if the context is the present, then it should be translated with the English present. Note the sequence of three participles in Daniel 2:8, where the participles are underlined in the word-by-word translation:

וְעָנֵה מַלְכָּא וְאָמַר מִן־יַצִּיב יָדַע אֲנָה

אֲנָה	יָדַע	מִן־יַצִּיב	אָמַר	וְ	מַלְכָּא	עָנֵה	וְ
I ←	*<u>know</u>* ←	*with certainty* ←	*<u>say</u>* ←	*and*	← *the king*	← *<u>answer</u>*	← *and*

and the king answered and said: 'with certainty I know . . .'

The first two participles (**אָמַר** and **עָנֵה**) are translated in the past tense since they are part of the past-tense narrative. On the other hand, when the king is speaking he is describing his present knowledge and the participle **יָדַע** is translated with the present tense.

LANGUAGE INSIGHT

English exhibits two types of participles too, but these are the past and present participles. Past participles often end with *-ed* and present participles with *-ing*. The latter are also used as nouns, often as verbal nouns that represent the abstract idea *knowing*, *buying*, etc. By contrast, in Aramaic neither the active nor the passive participle is used to describe the abstract verbal idea. Instead, the infinitive is used to express this sense. When the Aramaic participle is used as a noun, it has the sense *one who does X*.

The inflection of the participle can be exemplified with the root for writing:

singular	**masc.**	**fem.**
abs.	כָּתֵב	כָּתְבָה
const.	כָּתֵב	כָּתְבַת
det.	כָּתְבָא	כָּתִבְתָּא

plural	**masc.**	**fem.**
abs.:	כָּתְבִין	כָּתְבָן
const.:	כָּתְבֵי	כָּתְבָת
det.:	כָּתְבַיָּא	כָּתְבָתָא

Notice that the active participle always has a long /ā/ vowel under its first consonant. In the masculine singular, the sere vowel here represents a short /e/ **כָּתֵב** kāteb. In some cases the second vowel is a hiriq **נָחִק** nāḥiq *one going forth*. Verbs with hiriq inflect exactly like verbs with sere. In fact, as is seen in later units, the two vowels /e/ and /i/ are alternatives to each other; one can appear for the other in the same verbal form without any distinction in meaning.

The most important forms to know are the absolute forms, since these will often be used as verbs in Aramaic. These forms exhibit good examples of vowel reduction.

VOWEL REDUCTION

The stress of a word is typically on the last syllable. When a word is inflected, a syllable is often added to the end of the word and this usually results in a shift in stress. Often, what is a closed syllable becomes an open syllable and what is a short vowel becomes a muttered vowel or disappears entirely. The shift from a full short vowel to a muttered vowel or the loss of the vowel entirely is called vowel reduction. Only short vowels reduce, especially a ַ, e ֶ, i ִ, and u ֻ. (Long vowels like ā ָ, ī ִי, ē ֵי, /ū וּ are stable and do not reduce or change.) Furthermore, the short vowels only reduce in syllables that are, or would be, open (consonant + vowel). Short vowels cannot occur in open, non-stressed syllables.

So, in the inflection of the active participle, the short e of the masculine singular absolute (כָּתֵב kāteb) can be described as reducing to a muttered vowel in the three other absolute forms. (An asterisk indicates an intermediary, hypothetical form.)

f.s.	כָּתְבָה	kāteb + ā^h	=	*kātebā^h	→	kātəbā^h
m.p.	כָּתְבִין	kāteb + ī^{y}n	=	*kātebī^{y}n	→	kātəbī^{y}n
f.p.	כָּתְבָן	kāteb + ān	=	*kātebān	→	kātəbān

This vowel reduction reflects the rule that a non-stressed open syllable (i.e. consonant + vowel) cannot have a short vowel.

Vowel reduction will also be found in other nominal and verbal forms described throughout this course and is one of the features that gives Aramaic its distinctive rhythm and cadence. It typically affects short vowels in the pre-stress syllable of a word, which will often (but not always) be the penultimate syllable of a word.

LANGUAGE INSIGHT

Vowel reduction appears in other languages too. In English, a similar phenomenon is found in the pronunciation of the participle *listening*. It can either be pronounced with three syllables (/li-se-ning/) or two (/lis-ning/).

PRACTICE 1

1 Add the correct vowels to these participles based on their translations and maters (verbs are indicated in parentheses).

a מַלְכָּא שׁאל — *The king is asking* (שׁאל).

b אֲחַשְׁדַּרְפְּנַיָּא אִלֵּין יהבין לְהוֹן טַעְמָא — *These satraps would give* (יהב) *the report to them.*

c לָא־יכלין לְהַשְׁכָּחָה — *They were not able* (יכל) *to find.*

d מַלְכָּא חָזֵה פַּס יְדָא דִּי כתבה — *The king was watching the palm of the hand which was writing* (כתב).

e אַרְכֻּבָתֵהּ דָּא לְדָא נקשן — *His knees were knocking* (נקשׁ) *one against the other.*

f אַרְבַּע חֵיוָן רַבְרְבָן סלקן — *Four great beasts were coming up* (סלק) *(from the sea).*

g ידעי דָּתֵי אֱלָהָךְ — *Those who know of* (ידע) *the laws of your God* (lit. *the knowers of the laws of your God*).

h שְׁאָרָא בְּרַגְלַיהּ רפסה — (The fourth beast) was trampling (רפס) the rest with its feet.

i יהב חָכְמְתָא לְחַכִּימִין — He gives (יהב) wisdom to sages.

j נוּרָא יקדתא — The burning (יקד) fire. (*Fire* is fem., though it looks masc.)

2 **Fill out the following table, which isolates the forms most important for the participle.**

root	m.s. abs.	f.s. abs.	m. pl. abs.	f. pl. abs.
אבד (*to perish*)				
שׁאל (*to ask for* or *request*)				
נפק (*to go out*)				
סלק (*to go up*)				
עבד (*to do, make*)				

Some participles have a patach (ַ) under the second root consonant instead of a sere (ֵ) when the following consonant is a guttural (א, ה, ח, and ע) or resh (ר). For example, אָמַר *to say*; פָּלַח *to serve, pay reverence to*; שָׁלַח *to send*; יָדַע *to know*.

SYNTAX OF PARTICIPLES

Participles, when they are used as predicates or verbs, match their subject in gender and number, but not in their state: וְעָנֵה מַלְכָּא *and the king answered*. (Normally the subject is in the determined state and the predicative participle is in the absolute state.)

Unlike in English, in Aramaic the subject of the verb can follow it in the sentence. This has already been seen twice in the sample sentence from Daniel 2:8. It is also possible, however, for the subject to precede the participle, as in many of the examples in Practice 1, where the participle is last in the clause.

When the participle is used as a verb and the subject is clear from the context, then there does not need to be an independent pronoun. The plural form אָמְרִין might occur on its own, without a pronoun, but be translated into English as *they said*. It is not uncommon, however, to find an independent pronoun before or after the participle explicitly indicating its subject: הוּא בָּרֵךְ *he was kneeling*, אַנְתְּה פָּלַח *you serve*, and יָדַע אֲנָה *I know*.

PRACTICE 2

1 **Parse the Aramaic participles (i.e., identify their gender, number, and state) based on their vowel patterns.**

a אָמַר אֲנָה — *I said* (אמר).

b יָהֵב חָכְמְתָא לְחַכִּימִין — *He gives* (יהב) *wisdom to sages.*

c שָׁמְעִין כָּל־עַמְמַיָּא קָל קַרְנָא — *All the peoples were listening* (שׁמע) *to the sound of the horn.*

d וְעָבֵד אָתִין וְתִמְהִין — *And he makes* (עבד) *signs and wonders.*

e וְקַרְנָא דִכֵּן עָבְדָה קְרָב עִם־קַדִּישִׁין — *And this horn made* (עבד) *war with holy ones.*

f פָּלְחֵי בֵּית אֱלָהָא — *Those who serve* (פלח) *in the temple of God* (lit. *the servers of the house of God*).

g דָּבְחִין דִּבְחִין — *They sacrifice* (דבח) *sacrifices.*

h לָא־כָהֲלִין כְּתָבָא לְמִקְרֵא — *They were not able* (כהל) *to read the writing.*

i אַרְבַּע חֵיוָן סָלְקָן מִן־יַמָּא — *Four beasts were coming up* (סלק) *from the sea.*

j כָּל־יָדְעֵי דָּתֵי אֱלָהָךְ — *All those knowing* (ידע) *the laws of your God* (lit. *all those knowers of the laws of your God*).

2 Translate these English sentences into Aramaic based on the preceding exercise. Pay close attention to render English words with *the* in the determined state and English words without *the* in the absolute state. Nouns are listed in the singular absolute in parentheses.

a *Wisdom* (חָכְמָה) *said* (fem. sing. absolute of אמר).

b *He hears* (masc. sing. absolute of שמע) *the horn* (קֶרֶן (see 1c)).

c *She makes* (fem. sing. absolute of עבד) *signs* (אָת) *and wonders* (תְּמַהּ (see 1d)).

d *They know* (masc. pl. absolute of ידע) *sacrifices* (דְּבַח (see 1g)).

e *They serve* (fem. pl. absolute of פלח) *the God* (אֱלָהּ).

CULTURAL INSIGHT

As described in the introduction, Aramaic was a language of many empires, the Assyrian, the Babylonian, the Persian, even the Greek and the Roman. It is no wonder, then, that many tales of court life are preserved in Aramaic. The most famous of these are certainly those found in the book of Daniel, though in antiquity, the story of Aḥiqar (some of which is presented in Unit 24) may have been equally well known. In addition to these, there are several fragmentary texts known from the Dead Sea Scrolls that are set at the Babylonian or Persian court. The 'Proto-Esther' text (also called 'Tales of the Persian Court' 4Q550) describes various events and conflicts at the court of Darius and Xerxes that make one think of the Hebrew story of Esther. In the 'Prayer of Nabonidus' (4Q242), the eponymous king recounts his healing by a Judean and his declaration of the power of God.

PASSIVE PARTICIPLE

The passive participle is not as common as the active, but is essentially used in a similar manner. Whereas the active participle is translated by the English active voice *one who knows* or *I know* the passive participle is translated by the passive voice: *what is known* or *it was known*.

The form of the passive participle most often appears with a long /ī/ vowel between the second and third root consonants and so has the form of an adjective, like דְּחִיל *fearsome*.

The full inflection of the participle is shown with the root for writing, though the most common forms are the absolute forms:

singular	masc.	fem.
abs.	כְּתִיב	כְּתִיבָה
const.	כְּתִיב	כְּתִיבַת
det.	כְּתִיבָא	כְּתִיבְתָּא

plural	masc.	fem.
abs.	כְּתִיבִין	כְּתִיבָן
const.	כְּתִיבֵי	כְּתִיבָת
det.	כְּתִיבַיָּא	כְּתִיבָתָא

PRACTICE 3

Provide the vowels to the unvocalized passive participles. Notice the way that they are used.

a *And he said: '(May) their God be blessed.'* וְאָמַר בריך אֱלָהֲהוֹן

b *A kingdom (will be) divided.* מַלְכוּ פליגה

c *And it will be raised.* וזקיף

d *They were not thought of.* לָא חשיבין

e *And windows* (fem. noun, though masc. in appearance) *(were) open.* וְכַוִּין פתיחן

Reading

Identify and parse the participles and identify the noun / adjective endings of those words in parentheses from the following passage of Daniel 6.

DANIEL 6:5

a אֱדַיִן סָרְכַיָּא וַאֲחַשְׁדַּרְפְּנַיָּא הֲווֹ בָעַיִן

sought ← and the satraps ← the officials ← so

b עִלָּה לְהַשְׁכָּחָה לְדָנִיֵּאל מִצַּד מַלְכוּתָא

the kingdom ← concerning ← against Daniel ← to find ← a pretext

c וְכָל־עִלָּה וּשְׁחִיתָה לָא־ יָכְלִין לְהַשְׁכָּחָה

to find ← they were able ← not ← or fault ← but any pretext

d כָּל־קֳבֵל דִּי מְהֵימַן הוּא

he ← trustworthy ← on account of the fact that

e וְכָל־ שָׁלוּ וּשְׁחִיתָה לָא הִשְׁתְּכַחַת עֲלוֹהִי

against him ← was found ← not ← or fault ← inadvertent error ← so any

a *So, the officials and satraps sought*

b *to find against Daniel a pretext* (עִלָּה) *concerning the kingdom* (מַלְכוּתָא)

c *but they were not able* (part.: יָכְלִין) *to find any pretext or fault* (part.: שְׁחִיתָה, a passive participle, lit. '*thing that is corrupted*')

d *on account of the fact that he was trustworthy.*

e *So, no inadvertent error or fault was found against him.*

DANIEL 6:6

a אֱדַיִן גֻּבְרַיָּא אִלֵּךְ אָמְרִין

said ← these ← men ← then

b דִּי לָא נְהַשְׁכַּח לְדָנִיֵּאל דְּנָה כָּל־עִלָּה
any pretext ← this ← against Daniel ← we will find ← not ← '

c לָהֵן הַשְׁכַּחְנָא עֲלוֹהִי בְּדָת אֱלָהֵהּ
'his God ← in the law of ← against him ← we find ← unless

a *Then, these men* (גֻּבְרַיָּא) *said* (part.: אָמְרִין):

b *'We will not find any pretext against this Daniel,*

c *unless, we find (it) against him in the law of his God.'*

Test yourself

Translate the English into Aramaic using the independent pronouns and the appropriate participial forms for the following verbs: אזל to go, ידע to know, יתב to dwell, נחת to go down, סלק to go up, פלח to serve. Follow the word order of the English phrases.

a You (f.s.) are going.

b We are going up and going down. (Here, you may choose to use the m.p. or f.p. participle.)

c They (m.p.) know.

d One (f.s.) who knows understanding (בִּינָה). (The phrase is more literally 'one knowing of understanding'; use the construct form of the participle.)

e You (m.s.) are dwelling.

f He is serving.

g They (m.p.) are the ones serving the house of God (בֵּית אֱלָהָא). (The phrase is more literally '… ones serving of the house of God'; use the construct form of the participle.)

h We go. (Here, you may choose to use the m.p. or f.p. participle.)

i Knowers (f.p. cstr.) of song (זְמָר).

j The dwellers (m.p. cstr.) of the earth (אַרְעָא).

SELF-CHECK

	I CAN...
○	recognize and produce active participles
○	recognize and produce passive participles
○	apply the rules of vowel reduction

7 More complex noun patterns

In this unit you will learn how to:

- **inflect nouns and adjectives of the types like כְּסַף and אִגְּרָה**
- **inflect more complex nouns of the type like מַלְכוּ**
- **identify geminate and other types of nouns**

In this unit you will read:

- **Daniel 6:7–9**

Grammar

MORE COMPLEX NOUNS AND ADJECTIVES

Some of the most common nouns in Aramaic are composed of just two root consonants (in contrast to the usual three). In nouns of this type, the singular absolute and construct are identical; it is the singular determined form that exhibits vowel reduction (that is the reduction of a short vowel in an open, pre-stress syllable (in this case to a muttered vowel): e.g. *barâ → **bərâ** = בְּרָא).

	בַּר *son, child*	יַד *hand, power*	חַד *one*
singular			
abs.	בַּר	יַד	חַד
cstr.	בַּר	יַד	חַד
det.	בְּרָא	יְדָא	חֲדָא

Note that the plural of בַּר is (irregular): בְּנִין; and יד occurs (outside the singular) only in the dual: יְדַ֫יִן. The word *one* has no plural form.

Many other nouns and adjectives in Aramaic witness changes in their inflection more complex than these nouns and more complex than the participles just described. These changes are most easily explained based on the etymology of the words.

It is relatively common to find masculine nouns with the vowel pattern ə-a in both the singular absolute and construct, but another pattern in the singular determined and in the plural forms. The words for *gold* (דְּהַב), *silver* (כְּסַף), *book* (סְפַר), *wall* (כְּתַל), and *man* (גְּבַר) exemplify these types of words, though every form of each noun is not attested in Biblical Aramaic.

	דְּהַב *gold*	כְּסַף *silver*	סְפַר *book*	כְּתַל *wall*	גְּבַר *man*
singular					
abs.	דְּהַב	כְּסַף	סְפַר	כְּתַל	גְּבַר
const.	דְּהַב	כְּסַף	סְפַר	כְּתַל	גְּבַר
det.	דַּהֲבָא	כַּסְפָּא	סִפְרָא	כֻּתְלָא	גֻּבְרָא
plural					
abs.	דַּהֲבִין	כַּסְפִּין	סִפְרִין	כֻּתְלִין	גֻּבְרִין
const.	דַּהֲבֵי	כַּסְפֵּי	סִפְרֵי	כֻּתְלֵי	גֻּבְרֵי
det.	דַּהֲבַיָּא	כַּסְפַּיָּא	סִפְרַיָּא	כֻּתְלַיָּא	גֻּבְרַיָּא

The differences between the nouns are explained by their etymological bases. The singular absolute of *gold* began as *dahab; after the short vowel in the pre-stress syllable reduced (to a muttered vowel) it was dəhab. Similarly, the singular determined form began as *dahabâ, with two short a vowels, but vowel reduction affected the second a vowel such that it reduced to a hateph vowel ă (since he is a guttural consonant) and was pronounced dahăbâ. The plural absolute developed similarly: *dahabī^{y}n became dahăbī^{y}n.

In the case of the three nouns *silver* (כְּסַף), *book* (סְפַר), and *wall* (כְּתַל), the form of the singular absolute and construct originally had only one vowel after the first root consonant: *kasp-, *sipr-, and *kutl-. Although this vowel was lost and/or displaced in these forms by the time of Biblical Aramaic, the singular determined and plural forms all still reflect this historical vowel of the first syllable. In essence the historical form of the singular determined *kutlâ is the same as in Biblical Aramaic: כֻּתְלָא. Note that for words like כְּתַל, sometimes the vowel of the singular determined is a short o instead of u, as with תָּקְפָּא (toqpâ) *the strength* (the singular determined form of תְּקַף).

LANGUAGE INSIGHT

Sometimes etymology offers conflicting evidence. From other dialects of Aramaic, we would expect *man* to be inflected like כְּסַף, i.e., in the singular determined גַּבְרָא* and in the plural absolute גַּבְרִין*. In the case of this noun, the etymological a may have shifted to u in Biblical Aramaic due to the following bet consonant.

PRACTICE 1

1 Many Aramaic nouns/adjectives exhibit an inflection like כְּסַף. Complete the following table for these words that follow the pattern of כְּסַף.

sing. abs./cstr.	sing. det.	pl. abs.	pl. cstr.	pl. det.
חֲמַר *wine (of)*				
תְּרַע *gate (of)*				

2 **Identify the singular absolute form to the following nouns. Infer the number and state of the nouns from the translation. (Note: not all nouns exhibit vowel reduction or alteration like those in כְּסַף and סְפַר.)**

a *the interpretation* פִּשְׁרָא
b *the land* אַרְעָא
c *prefects and the prefects* סִגְנִין and סִגְנַיָּא
d *the province of Babel* מְדִינַת בָּבֶל
e *the sages of Babel* חַכִּימֵי בָבֶל
f *riddles* אֲחִידָן
g *problems* קִטְרִין
h *the writing* כְּתָבָא
i *the honour* יְקָרָא
j *the majesty* הַדְרָא

3 **Write the following sentences in Aramaic, using the independent pronouns learned in Unit 4 where appropriate, the participial forms learned in Unit 6, and the vocabulary of the last exercise. Put the Aramaic words in the same order as the English.**

a *You* (f.s.) *speak* (אמר) *the interpretation.*
b *The sages of Babel are hearing* (שׁמע) *the riddles.*
c *It* (f.s.) *is consuming* (אכל) *the land.*
d *I am writing* (m.s. or f.s. כתב) *to* (לְ) *the prefects.*
e *He is coming forth* (נפק) *from* (מִן) *the province.*

CULTURAL INSIGHT

The three words salaam (also written salām) from Arabic, שְׁלָם from Aramaic, and שָׁלוֹם from Hebrew all *mean well-being* or *peace* and are used as greetings in all three languages. All derive from a common origin, which was pronounced similar to the realization in Arabic (i.e. in the common ancestor to all these languages it would be *salām). In both Aramaic and Hebrew the original s sound turned into sh. Notice also that the Aramaic word exhibits vowel reduction (a to ə) while the Hebrew exhibits just the opposite: vowel lengthening (a to ā). In Old Aramaic the word would have been pronounced šalām, but after vowel reduction it was pronounced as in Biblical Aramaic: שְׁלָם.

Many Aramaic nouns that otherwise follow the pattern of כְּסַף or סְפַר have an *e* (ֵ) vowel in the singular absolute, like בְּעֵל *master* and תְּקֵל *shekel* (a weight measure).

4 **Complete the following table for these words that otherwise follow the pattern of כְּסַף and סְפַר. The hateph vowel in בַּעֲלָא and the plural is due to the ʿayin guttural. The plural of עֲבֵד exhibits a spirantized (i.e., soft) dalet.**

sing. abs./cstr.	sing. det.	pl. abs.	pl. cstr.	pl. det.
בְּעֵל *master (of)*, like כְּסַף	בַּעֲלָא	בַּעֲלִין	בַּעֲלֵי	בַּעֲלַיָּא
צְלֵם *image (of)*, like כְּסַף				
עֲבֵד *slave (of)*, like כְּסַף		עַבְדִין		
תְּקֵל *shekel (of)*, like סְפַר				

Other nouns of this general type exhibit other vowel patterns in the singular absolute and construct, but attest a similar tendency for a short vowel in a closed syllable in the singular determined, dual, and plural forms.

	מֶ֫לֶךְ **king**	קֶ֫רֶן **horn**	עַ֫יִן **eye**	בַּ֫יִת **house**	חֵ֫לֶם **dream**	קְשֹׁט **truth**
singular						
abs.	מֶ֫לֶךְ	קֶ֫רֶן	עַ֫יִן	בַּ֫יִת	חֵ֫לֶם	קְשֹׁט
const.	מֶ֫לֶךְ	קֶ֫רֶן	עֵין	בֵּית	חֵ֫לֶם	קְשֹׁט
det.	מַלְכָּא	קַרְנָא	עַיְנָא	בַּיְתָא	חֶלְמָא	קֻשְׁטָא* or קָשְׁטָא*
dual						
abs.		קַרְנַ֫יִן				
const.		קַרְנֵי				
det.		קַרְנַיָּא				
plural						
abs.	מַלְכִין	קַרְנָן	עַיְנִין	בָּתִּין	חֶלְמִין	קֻשְׁטִין* or קָשְׁטִין*
const.	מַלְכֵי	קַרְנָת	עַיְנֵי	בָּתֵּי	חֶלְמֵי	קֻשְׁטֵי* or קָשְׁטֵי*
det.	מַלְכַיָּא	קַרְנָתָא	עַיְנַיָּא	בָּתַּיָּה	חֶלְמַיָּא	קֻשְׁטַיָּא* or קָשְׁטַיָּא*

The dual is found among these nouns only with קֶ֫רֶן *horn*, a feminine noun (though it looks masculine in the singular); the plural forms of this noun are explicitly feminine. The word *eye* appears only in the singular and plural (though one imagines it appeared in the dual too in an earlier variety of Aramaic). The singular construct is the only form of עַ֫יִן to show the shift in the diphthong of ay to ē. The word **בַּ֫יִת** *house* exhibits the same shift and has an irregular plural form (with a long vowel in a closed, non-stressed syllable, e.g. bāttī^{y}n).

In words formed like קְשֹׁט *truth* (historical *qušṭ), the historical short u has not only shifted to after the second consonant (*qəšuṭ), but it has also shifted to o (qəšoṭ). Sometimes the original u is realized as short o in the determined state, as with **נָגְהָא** (noghâ) *the light*. The exact realization of קְשֹׁט in the singular determined and plural forms is not known but would have had either u or o in the first syllable.

LANGUAGE INSIGHT

Since the singular absolute is the form listed in the glossary or in a dictionary, it is important to be able to infer it from other forms. This is sometimes straightforward as with nouns like לִשָּׁן *tongue*, where the determined and plural forms have the same vowels as the absolute (e.g. לִשָּׁנָא *the tongue*). But, if the determined or plural form of a noun like כְּסַף *silver*, בְּעֵל *master*, or מֶ֫לֶךְ *king* is encountered while reading and the word is unfamiliar, it is impossible to know what the singular absolute would be. For example, if you found קַרְנָא and did not know its singular absolute form already, it would be unclear whether its absolute form was קְרַן*, קְרֵן*, or קֶ֫רֶן. Usually, the language has only one noun of this type and so identifying it in the glossary or dictionary is not too difficult. Also, it is important to recognize that some words exhibit alternative singular absolute/construct forms like אֲלַף *thousand* which has a construct form אֶ֫לֶף. The word צְלֵם *image* has two construct forms: צְלֵם and צֶ֫לֶם. Similarly, the noun טְעֵם *taste, decree, judgment* has two construct forms: טְעֵם and טַ֫עַם. This means that when looking up a word, it is important to recognize various possible forms a masculine singular absolute noun may take.

Vowel reduction of a historical short vowel in a pre-stress syllable is also reflected in some of these nouns listed in the preceding table, especially the first, מֶ֫לֶךְ *king*. Although this noun had just one vowel in the singular, *malk-, the plural had two: *malak-. Thus, the plural absolute began as *malakī^{y}n and then developed into malkī^{y}n (where the second a vowel reduced completely). The development is analogous to that of *dahabī^{y}n → dahăbī^{y}n (דַּהֲבִין). That there was a second vowel in מַלְכִין is suggested by the soft kaph, which presumes a vowel preceded it at some point in its history. The fact that it is soft, though not preceded by a vowel in Biblical Aramaic implies that the softening (or spirantization) of begadkephat letters took place before the reduction of vowels; i.e., (where k̲ = soft kaph) 1 *malakī^{y}n → 2 *malak̲ī^{y}n (spirantization) → 3 malk̲ī^{y}n (vowel reduction).

5 Give the Biblical Aramaic plural form of the following nouns and adjectives based on their historical forms. First, write the word in transliteration and then in Aramaic letters. Vowel reduction affects short vowels that appear in open syllables, most commonly where the open syllable is just before the stressed syllable (that is, in most cases, a penultimate syllable that is open). NB: Some of the following words do not experience vowel reduction.

Example: *birakī^{y}n → birkī^{y}n בִּרְכִין (sing. בְּרַךְ *knee*)

a *garamī^{y}n → ______________ (sing. גְּרַם *bone*)

b *dayyānī^{y}n → ______________ (sing. דַּיָּן *judge*)

c *naharī^{y}n → ______________ (sing. נְהַר *river*)

d *ḥabirī^{y}n → ______________ (sing. חֲבַר *companion*)

e *yaraḥī^{y}n → ______________ (sing. יְרַח *month*)

f *dibaḥī^{y}n → ______________ (sing. דְּבַח *sacrifice*)

g *zammārī^{y}n → ______________ (sing. זַמָּר *musician*)

h *ḥadatī^{y}n → ______________ (sing. חֲדַת *new*)

i *siganī^{y}n → ______________ (sing. סְגַן *prefect*)

j *liššānī^{y}n → ______________ (sing. לִשָּׁן *tongue*)

Vowel reduction can also explain the inflection of various feminine nouns.

	צִדְקָה ***righteousness***	אִגְּרָה ***letter***	מַלְכָּה ***queen***
singular			
abs.	צִדְקָה	אִגְּרָה	מַלְכָּה
const.	צִדְקַת	אִגְּרַת	מַלְכַּת
det.	צִדְקְתָא	אִגַּרְתָּא	מַלְכְּתָא
plural			
abs.	צִדְקָן	אִגְּרָן	מַלְכָן
const.	צִדְקָת	אִגְּרָת	מַלְכָת
det.	צִדְקָתָא	אִגְּרָתָא	מַלְכָתָא

The (simplified) historical form of צִדְקָה had a short a vowel after the dalet, *ṣidaqa-. In the singular absolute and construct, that vowel (a short vowel in a pre-stress syllable) reduced:

*ṣidaqa- → ṣidqā^{h} and *ṣidaqat → ṣidqat

The initial vowel was preserved because it was left in a closed syllable. In the singular determined form, the pre-stress vowel also reduced; however, this was not the a after the dalet, but the a after the qoph *ṣidaqatâ → *ṣidaqtâ. In addition, the initial vowel of the word also reduced (in this case to a murmured vowel) since in this form it was in an open, non-stressed syllable: *ṣidaqtâ → ṣədaqtâ. The middle a vowel was preserved because it was in a closed syllable. A similar process explains the variations in the paradigm of אִגְּרָה. In the singular absolute, *ʾiggara- became ʾiggərā^{h} through vowel reduction. The singular determined form began as *ʾiggaratâ before experiencing vowel reduction and becoming ʾiggartâ. (NB: We would have expected the taw of the singular determined forms to be soft (or spirantized) given the preceding historical vowel.)

Both צִדְקָה and אִגְּרָה began with three vowels. The singular of מַלְכָּה *queen*, on the other hand, had only two *malka-. The initial vowel never reduced because it was always in a closed syllable (e.g. the singular determined: *malkatâ → malkətâ). That there was never a vowel after the lamed is suggested by the hard (non-spirantized) kaph. The plural forms of מַלְכָּה *queen* also can be explained as due to vowel reduction. The original plural absolute had two short a vowels *malakān before experiencing vowel reduction and becoming malkān. The soft kaph of מַלְכָן again implies a preceding vowel was present when the process of spirantization was underway.

Remember, a vowel does not reduce if it is a long vowel (e.g. ◌ִי , וֹ , ◌ָ) or if it is in a closed syllable, that is, a syllable that ends with a consonant. Therefore, the qamets vowel of the word יְקָם *edict* does not reduce because ◌ָ here represents a long vowel (ā). In the adjective עַתִּיק (ʿattī^{y}q) *old*, neither vowel reduces; the patach (short a) does not reduce because it is in a closed syllable and the hiriq (ī) in the second does not reduce because it is long.

6 Supply the correct vowels to the following nouns based on the translations and the information provided in the glossary. English *of* presumes the construct form. The singular absolute forms are given in parentheses.

a	*The image* (צְלֵם) *(is) great.*	צלמא רַב
b	*These gave* (m.p. part. of יהב) *the decree* (טְעֵם) *to them.*	אִלֵּין יהבין לְהוֹן טעמא
c	*All the servants* (עֲבֵד) *of Pharaoh went up with him.*	סְלִקוּ עִמֵּהּ כֹּל עבדי פַּרְעֹה
d	*The king* (מֶלֶךְ) *spoke up and said* (m.s. part. of אמר) …	עָנֵה מלכא וְאמר
e	*Lo, (there were) eyes* (עַיִן) *like human eyes* (lit. *the eyes of the human*)	אֲלוּ עינין כְּעיני אֲנָשָׁא
f	*The work* (עֲבִידָה) *on the house* (בַּיִת) *of God* (אֱלָהּ) (lit. *the work of the house of God*)	עבידת בית אלהא
g	*If you are able to tell the dream* (חֵלֶם) *and the interpretation* (פְּשַׁר) …	הֵן חלמא ופשרא תְּהַחֲוֹן

h *Those acting* (m.p. part. constr. of עבד) *righteously* (צִדְקָה) (lit. *those doing of the charity*) … — עבדי צדקתא

i *Jehu wrote letters* (אִגְּרָה) *and sent (them) away* … — כְּתַב יֵהוּא אגרן וְשַׁדַּר

j *The queen* (מַלְכָּה) *entered the house* (בַּיִת) *of banqueting.* — מלכתא לְבית מִשְׁתְּיָא עַלַּלת

CULTURAL INSIGHT

The image of Nebuchadnezzar driven from his court for seven years, eating grass like oxen, and ultimately recognizing the Most High as sole ruler of the world (as found in Daniel 4) seems to reflect stories associated with a later Babylonian king, Nabonidus, who spent at least ten years in the city of Tema in what is today northern Saudia Arabia. Away from his capital Babylon, Nabonidus neglected the traditional worship of that city's god, Marduk. His sojourn in Tema, located at the crossroads of various trade routes, was perhaps related to his devotion to the moon god Sin, whom he characterized in inscriptions as the supreme god, rivalling all others, including Marduk. His singular devotion to the moon god was a stock element in later Persian propaganda that denigrated Nabonidus and portrayed Cyrus (the Persian king) as the one to restore Marduk to his proper place in Babylonian worship. Nabonidus's son is Belshazzar, who features in other stories in the book of Daniel.

OTHER NOUN/ADJECTIVE PATTERNS

Some feminine nouns have an absolute form like the word for *kingdom*, מַלְכוּ. Note that what is a vowel ū in the singular corresponds with a waw consonant in the plural. This correspondence is common for this and similar nouns (like חַשְׁחוּ *need*).

singular	fem.	
abs.:	מַלְכוּ	malkū^{w}
const.:	מַלְכוּת	malkū^{w}t
det.:	מַלְכוּתָא	malkū^{w}tâ

plural		
abs.:	מַלְכְוָן	malkəwān
const.:	מַלְכְוָת	malkəwāt
det.:	מַלְכְוָתָא	malkəwātâ

N.B. The shewa under the lamed in this word indicates the absence of a vowel, though the kaph is unexpectedly pronounced soft. What rule suggests that the shewa under the lamed indicates the absence of a vowel and not a murmured vowel?

The related word נַהִירוּ *illumination* is from the root נהר; it is interesting because the initial short vowel is not reduced. This is due to the following ה, which is virtually doubled. In other words, although the ה is not marked as doubled by a dagesh (dot), it acts as if it were and this prevents the short a vowel from reducing. In historical terms, it is likely that the he was doubled in pronunciation (nahhī^{y}rū^{w}) until relatively late, close to the time of the Dead Sea Scrolls.

Most nouns that have a final ū represent abstract or non-tangible entities: בְּעוּ *request*, גָּלוּ *exile*, רְבוּ *greatness*. These three nouns are all from III-aleph/waw/yod roots. Such roots are usually listed as having a yod as a third root consonant or a heh, depending on the lexicon. The dictionary BDB lists בְּעוּ under the root בעה, but the CAL categorizes it from the root בעי. They are identified as III-yod in this grammar. The inflection of these nouns is analogous to that of מַלְכוּ and חַשְׁחוּ.

singular	fem.	fem.
abs.:	רְבוּ	בָּעוּ
const.:	רְבוּת	בָּעוּת
det.:	רְבוּתָא	בָּעוּתָא

Other feminine nouns from III-aleph/waw/yod roots sometimes exhibit a singular absolute form with a waw (e.g. חֶדְוָה *joy*); such nouns inflect normally (חֶדְוַת *joy of* and חֶדְוְתָא *the joy* (plural not attested, but presumably abs. חֶדְוָן; cstr. חֶדְוָת; det. חֶדְוָתָא)). In still other cases no remnant of the last root consonant is found in the singular absolute, but instead the noun ends with a feminine morpheme -t or -āʰ; however, a waw does appear in the inflected forms: כְּנָת *associate* is a singular absolute noun from the root כני; the final -t is the feminine singular morpheme. The plural form, כְּנָוָן *associates*, however does exhibit a III-waw root consonant. The word פֶּחָה *governor* is similar. It is from פחי but no remnant of the final root consonant appears in the singular; the final -āʰ is the feminine morpheme as is the final -at in the singular construct form פַּחַת *governor of*. In the plural, however, there is a III-waw, as in the determined form, פַּחֲוָתָא *the governors*.

Note too the singular נְבִזְבָּה *reward* and the plural determined form נְבָזְבְּיָתָא.

Masculine nouns from III-aleph/waw/yod roots are somewhat less common, but also occur. In the singular absolute, they exhibit a final ē; this is represented by an aleph or he mater in Biblical Aramaic (like מָרֵא *lord* and מִשְׁתֵּא *banquet*), but by a yod mater in Targumic Aramaic (מִשְׁתֵּי *banquet*). In the singular determined state, the final root consonant is usually yod in both Biblical Aramaic (מִשְׁתְּיָא *the banquet*) and Targumic Aramaic. The plural forms are poorly attested, but presumably also attested a final yod consonant (cf. the participle בָּנַיִן *those building* m.p. of בני). On the other hand, dual and plural forms with suffixes (see Unit 9) do not attest a final yod or waw root consonant.

There are several other irregular patterns illustrated in the following table, each word exhibiting a waw or yod at the end of its stem in some parts of the paradigm:

	throne	*lion*
sing. abs.	כָּרְסֵא (korsê)	אַרְיֵה
sing. cstr.	כָּרְסֵא*	אַרְיֵה
sing. det.	כָּרְסְיָא	אַרְיְוָא
pl. abs.	כָּרְסְוָן	אַרְיָוָן
pl. cstr.	כָּרְסְוָת	אַרְיָוָת
pl. det.	כָּרְסְוָתָא	אַרְיָוָתָא

CULTURAL INSIGHT

In 2 Kings 18, an Assyrian official, called the Rab Shakeh, comes to Jerusalem to warn Hezekiah and the people of Jerusalem of the threat posed by not submitting to Sennacherib. The title Rab Shakeh, sometimes rendered *cupbearer*, is an Assyrian term, referring to a royal official or administrator. The phrase is made up of the word rab (רַב), which means *overseer* (or *great* as an adjective), and the participle shakeh (שָׁקֵה), meaning *the one who serves drinks*. The cognate term for shakeh in Aramaic is, in the determined state, שָׁקְיָא *the server*, and is also used as the title for a court official cupbearer (e.g. in Targum Onqelos to Gen 40:1). The same Aramaic title has been found on a jar from near the Sea of Galilee, dating to ca. 850 BCE, in the (unvocalized) expression לשקיא *belonging to the official*. The exact identity of this official is unknown. (See Mazar.)

PRACTICE 2

Translate the following words, looking up the absolute forms in the glossary where necessary. Be sure to translate determined nouns with *the* and construct nouns with a following *of*.

a מַלְכַיָּא (sing. abs. מֶ֫לֶךְ)
b סָלְקָן (i.e. the feminine plural absolute active participle of סלק; m.s. abs. is סָלֵק)
c נַהִירוּת (sing. abs. נַהִירוּ)
d כְּתְלִין (sing. abs. כְּתַל)
e יָהֲבִין (i.e. masculine plural absolute active participle of יהב; m.s. abs. is יָהֵב)
f בְּהִילוּת (sing. abs. בְּהִילוּ)
g כָּתְבָה (i.e. feminine singular absolute active participle of כתב; m.s. abs. is כָּתֵב)
h עַבְדָּא (sing. abs. עֲבֵד)
i תַּרְעֵי (sing. abs. תְּרַע)
j חַשְׁחוּת (sing. abs. חַשְׁחוּ)
k בֵּית (sing. abs. בַּ֫יִת)
l רְבוּתָא (sing. abs. רְבוּ)
m צְבוּת (sing. abs. צְבוּ)
n גֻּבְרַיָּא (sing. abs. גְּבַר)
o גָּלוּתָא (sing. abs. גָּלוּ)

GEMINATE NOUNS AND ADJECTIVES

Nouns and adjectives that have the same second and third root consonants, like רַב rab *great* (from רבב) and גֹּב gob *pit, den* (from גבב), exhibit just two consonants in the masculine singular absolute and construct, but all three consonants in the other forms, including in all feminine forms. These are called geminate nouns and adjectives since the last consonant in the singular is doubled or geminated when it bears a suffixed morpheme. In the plural, the initial two root consonants sometimes reduplicate and nouns that are feminine sometimes exhibit the endings normally associated with masculine nouns. Note the following:

	רַב great		עֵז she-goat	מִלָּה word	גֹּב cave	אֻמָּה nation
	masc.	fem.	masc.	fem.	masc.	fem.
singular						
abs.	רַב	רַבָּה	עֵז	מִלָּה	גֹּב	אֻמָּה
cstr.	רַב	רַבַּת	עֵז	מִלַּת	גֹּב or גָּב־	אֻמַּת
det.	רַבָּא	רַבְּתָא	עִזָּא	מִלְּתָא	גֻּבָּא	אֻמְּתָא
plural						
abs.	רַבְרְבִין	רַבְרְבָן	עִזִּין	מִלִּין	גֻּבִּין	אֻמִּין
cstr.	רַבְרְבֵי	רַבְרְבָת	עִזֵּי	מִלֵּי	גֻּבֵּי	אֻמֵּי
det.	רַבְרְבַיָּא	רַבְרְבָתָא	עִזַּיָּא	מִלַּיָּא	גֻּבַּיָּא	אֻמַּיָּא

Other examples include **גַּף** *wing* in the plural absolute **גַּפִּין** and the adjective **חַי** *alive, living* which occurs in the singular determined **חַיָּא**, the plural construct **חַיֵּי**, and plural determined **חַיַּיָּא**. In its plural forms it can be used as an adjective *alive* or as a noun with the sense *life*. The word **שֵׁן** *tooth* occurs in the dual, **שִׁנַּיִן**, with the sense *two (rows of) teeth*. The word **בַּר** *field* (originally *barr-) exhibits compensatory lengthening in the singular determined form **בָּרָא** *the field*. (Contrast this noun with the singular determined noun **בְּרָא** *the son*.) The word **עַם** *people* has the singular determined form **עַמָּא** and the plural determined form **עַמְמַיָּא** *the peoples*.

As with nouns like **מַדְבַּח** *altar* and **מָזוֹן** *food* encountered in Unit 4, sometimes nouns of geminate roots exhibit an initial mem. In these cases, the doubling of the root consonant is indicated with a dagesh. Thus, **מְגִלָּה** *scroll* is from the root **גלל**. The inflection is normal (**מְגִלַּת** *scroll of*; **מְגִלְּתָא** *the scroll* (plural unattested)).

The word **כֹּל** *all, every* is an irregular geminate noun of the **גֹּב** and **אֻמָּה** type, but instead of attesting a u vowel when endings are added, the o remains: **כֹּלָּא**. Notice that the stress is over the syllable with the o vowel. In the construct, the word often carries a qamets, also representing a short o vowel **כָּל־** *all of*.

PRACTICE 3

Write the following expressions in Aramaic. Absolute singular forms for other nouns are given in parentheses.

- **a** *the great words*
- **b** *the great nation*
- **c** *the living God* (אֱלָהּ)
- **d** *in* (בְּ) *the land of* (אֲרַע) *the living* (lit. *those alive*)
- **e** *all of* (כֹּל) *the peoples, and the nations, and the tongues* (לִשָּׁן)

WORDS WITH -Āʰ (OR -Â), -ĀN, -Ōʷ N, -Īʸ AND -ĪʸT SUFFIXES

Some nouns exhibit a word-final **-āʰ** (or **-â**), **-ān**, **-ōʷn** , **-īʸ** and **-īʸt** suffix. These are not part of the root of the word; nor are they expressive of feminine gender or plurality. The final -āʰ/-â marks a word as an adverb. It is distinct from the feminine singular ending since the adverbial -āʰ/-â is not usually stressed: עֵ֫לָּא *over, above*, יַתִּ֫ירָא *exceedingly*, כֹּ֫לָּא *entirely*. Where יַתִּיר appears as a feminine adjective, there is stress on the last syllable and usually a he mater (רוּחַ יַתִּירָה *a great spirit* and רְבוּ יַתִּירָה *surpassing greatness*), though not always (רוּחַ יַתִּירָא *a great spirit*).

Due to the similarity with the ending on masculine singular nouns in the determined state, it seems that sometimes the adverbial -āʰ/-â suffix was, however, stressed: יַצִּיבָא *certainly*. A reverse confusion may have led to the determined form of כֹּל being pronounced כֹּ֫לָּא *the entirety*, identical to the adverbial expression; we would have expected the noun to inflect like גֹּב *den* and be כֻּלָּא* (stress on the last syllable).

Usually, nouns with -ān or -ōʷn endings appear in the singular and are abstractions: חָזוֹן (root חזי) *vision*, פָּלְחָן (root פלח) *worship*, רַעְיוֹן (root רעי) *thought*, שָׁלְטָן (root שׁלט) *dominion*, שִׁלְטוֹן (root שׁלט) *ruler*. Neither -ān nor -ōʷn alter in the inflection of these nouns so the forms are entirely predictable (e.g. רַעְיוֹנִין *thoughts*). However, there is ambiguity in some cases, as with פָּלְחָן *worship*, which could also be the feminine plural active participle *those worshipping*.

The final -īʸ and -īʸt endings often indicate a location, as with אַרְעִית *bottom* (related to אֲרַע *earth*), אַחֲרִית *end*, עִלִּית *upper chamber*. Other examples include שְׁרֹשִׁי *corporal punishment* and נְוָלִי *dung, rubbish heap*.

IRREGULAR NOUNS

Some words are simply irregular and need to be learned separately. These include many nouns relating to family members like *son*, which is בַּר in the singular absolute (singular determined: בְּרָא) but בְּנִין in the plural absolute (determined: בְּנַיָּא). The masculine noun *father* is אַב in the singular absolute (singular determined would be: אַבָּא) but has a feminine ending (with an extra he) in the plural, the absolute presumably being אֲבָהָן (based on other plural forms) and אֲבָהָתָא in the determined state. The word שֻׁם *name* is similar: שְׁמָהָן *names*. The singular form of *woman, wife* might be אִנְתָּה (based on comparative evidence from other Aramaic dialects, though it is unattested in Biblical Aramaic), while the plural form is נְשִׁין. The singular of *house* is בַּ֫יִת but the plural is בָּתִּין. The word יוֹם *day* exhibits a plural form with a masculine type ending and another with a feminine type ending יוֹמִין *days* and יוֹמָת *days of*. The noun שָׁעָה *moment* appears in the determined form with different vowels: שַׁעֲתָא *the moment*.

PRACTICE 4

Write the following forms in Aramaic. The singular absolute is given in parentheses, together with the singular determined where necessary. Assume that all words follow the patterns outlined in this and the last unit.

- **a** *the kings* (מֶ֫לֶךְ; det. מַלְכָּא)
- **b** *ones going forth* (feminine plural absolute active participle of נפק; m.s. abs. is נָפֵק)
- **c** *the illumination* (נַהִירוּ)
- **d** *the eye* (עַיִן)
- **e** *ones able to* or *they are able* (masculine plural absolute active participle of יכל; m.s. abs. is (יָכֵל)

f *tastes* or *judgments* (טְעֵם; det. טַעְמָא)
g *exile of* (גָּלוּ)
h *blessed one* (feminine singular absolute passive participle of ברך; m.s. abs. is בְּרִיךְ)
i *the wisdom* (חָכְמָה)
j *the interpretations* (פְּשַׁר; det. פִּשְׁרָא)
k *need of* (חַשְׁחוּ)
l *words of* (מִלָּה)
m *the house* (בַּיִת)
n *the peoples* (עַם; det. עַמָּא)
o *the writing* (כְּתָב)
p *times* (עִדָּן)
q *the province* (מְדִינָה)
r *they were open* (feminine plural absolute passive participle of פתח; m.s. abs. is פְּתִיחַ)
s *the will* (רְעוּ)
t *the priests* (כָּהֵן)

CULTURAL INSIGHT

Although it is not attested in Biblical Aramaic, in later vocalized dialects of Aramaic, the noun *father* in the determined state appears as אַבָּא *the father*. It is this form that is borrowed into Greek and then into Latin as *abbat*; eventually it is realized in English as the word *abbot*.

Reading

Identify the number (singular, dual, plural) and state (absolute, construct, determined) of the nouns from the following verses. Then, define the words by looking up the singular absolute form in the glossary and fill in the blanks to complete the translation.

DANIEL 6:7

a אֱדַיִן סָרְכַיָּא וַאֲחַשְׁדַּרְפְּנַיָּא הַרְגִּשׁוּ עַל־ מַלְכָּא

________ ← *around* ← *gathered hectically* ← *and the satraps* ← ________ ← *then*

b וְאָמְרִין לֵהּ דָּרְיָוֶשׁ מַלְכָּא לְ עָלְמִין חֱיִי

live! ← ________ ← *for* ← ________ ← *O, Darius* ← *to him* ← ________

a *Then the* ______________________ *and the satraps gathered hectically around the* ______________________

b *and they* ______________________ *to him: 'O, Darius,* ______________________ (more literally, *the* ______________________), *live for* ______________________*!'*

סָרְכַיָּא
מַלְכָּא
אָמְרִין
עָלְמִין

DANIEL 6:8

a אִתְיָעַטוּ כֹּל סָרְכֵי מַלְכוּתָא
_______ ← _______ ← all ← advised

b סִגְנַיָּא וַאֲחַשְׁדַּרְפְּנַיָּא הַדָּבְרַיָּא וּפַחֲוָתָא
the governors ← the counsellors ← the satraps ← ___________

c לְקַיָּמָה קְיָם מַלְכָּא
________ ← ________ ← to establish

d וּלְתַקָּפָה אֱסָר דִּי כָל־ דִּי־ יִבְעֵה בָעוּ
a request ← request ← who ← all ← that ← ________ ← and to make severe

e מִן־ כָּל־ אֱלָהּ וֶאֱנָשׁ עַד־ יוֹמִין תְּלָתִין
← 30 ← days ← within ← and person ← god ← any ← to

f לָהֵן מִנָּךְ מַלְכָּא יִתְרְמֵא לְגֹב אַרְיָוָתָא
the lions ← to the _______ of ← will be thrown ← O king ← from you ← except

a *All the ______________________________ of the ______________________________*
b *– the ______________________________, and the satraps, the counsellors, and the governors advised*
c *to establish the ______________________________ of the ______________________________*
d *and to make severe ______________________________ that anyone who prays a prayer* (lit. *who requests a request*)
e *to any god or person, within 30 days*
f *except to you, O king, will be thrown to the ______________________________ of the lions.*

סָרְכֵי
מַלְכוּתָא
סִגְנַיָּא
קְיָם
מַלְכָּא
אֱסָר
גֹּב

DANIEL 6:9

a כְּעַן מַלְכָּא תְּקִים אֱסָרָא וְתִרְשֻׁם כְּתָבָא
______ ← and you should sign ← ______ ← you should establish ← O king ← now

b דִּי לָא לְהַשְׁנָיָה
to change ← not ← so that

c כְּ דָת־ מָדַי וּפָרַס דִּי לָא תֶעְדֵּה

it be revoked ← not ← that ← and Persian(s) ← Mede(s) ← ______ ← according to

a *'Now, O king, may you establish the __________ and you should sign the __________*
b *so that no one will change it,*
c *according to the __________ of the Medes and Persians, that it not be revoked.*

אֱסָרָא

כְּתָבָא

דָת

Test yourself

Supply the correct vowels to the nouns, adjectives, and participles, based on the translation and the following vocabulary: גַּף *wing* (גַּפָּא det.), דמי *to be like*, חֵיוָה *beast*, יַם *sea* (יַמָּא det.), סלק *to come up*, עֲלַע *rib* (עִלְעָא det.), רַב (m.p. abs. רַבְרְבִין). The text is based on Daniel 7:3–6.

a	אַרְבַּע חיון רברבן סלקן מִן־ימא	*Four great beasts were coming up from the sea*
b	קַדְמָיְתָא כְאַרְיֵה וְגפין דִּי נְשַׁר לַהּ	*The first was like a lion, and it had wings of an eagle*
c	וַאֲרוּ חיוה אָחֳרִי תִנְיָנָה דמיה לְדֹב	*And, lo, another, second beast was like a bear*
d	וּתְלָת עלעין בְּפֻמַּהּ	*and three ribs were in its mouth*
e	וַאֲרוּ אָחֳרִי כִּנְמַר וְאַרְבְּעָה רֵאשִׁין לְחיותא	*And, lo, another was like a leopard and the beast had four heads*
f	וַאֲרוּ חיוה רְבִיעָיָה	*And, lo, a fourth beast*
g	וְהִיא מְשַׁנְּיָה מִן־כָּל־חיותא דִּי קָדָמַיהּ	*and it was different from all the beasts which were before it*

Suggestions for further study

Take the words from the Reading section that are listed after each verse and try to produce all the forms of each word (the singular absolute, singular construct, etc.). Then, memorize the meaning of these words as well as the meaning of the words in the other exercises from this unit.

SELF-CHECK

I CAN...

- inflect nouns and adjectives of the types like כְּסַף and אִגְּרָה
- inflect more complex nouns of the type like מַלְכוּ
- identify geminate and other types of nouns

8 The suffix conjugation of the strong root

In this unit you will learn how to:

- **describe the basic structure of the Aramaic verbal system**
- **recognize the suffix-conjugation verb**
- **recognize and produce the pə ʿal, paʿʿel, haphʿel suffix-conjugation verbal forms for strong roots**

In this unit you will read:

- **Daniel 6:10–13**

Grammar

THE VERBAL SYSTEM

As described in Unit 5, each Aramaic noun and adjective can usually be associated with a three-consonant root. Verbs are no different. Like other Semitic languages, Aramaic communicates certain verbal meanings through the alteration of vowels around and between a given root's three consonants. A single Aramaic root can be expressed in one of at least nine different stems, each with a slightly different meaning. The three most common stems are the **pəʿal**, the **paʿʿel**, and the **haphʿel**. The different vowel patterns presuppose different basic senses. For example, consider the senses of the root שׁני:

LANGUAGE INSIGHT

The names of the stems are derived from the form of the root פעל in each stem, though this root is only rarely found in Aramaic. The names of each stem can be used as a mnemonic for the vowel pattern characteristic of the suffix conjugation in each stem. For example, the pə ʿal is characterized by the vowel sequence ə-a in the suffix conjugation of this stem, as in כְּתַב *he wrote*. The paʿʿel is characterized by the sequence a-e (כַּתֵּב) and the haphʿel by the sequence ha-e (הַכְתֵּב). Weak verbs have a different pattern as exhibited by the verb שׁני (**pə ʿal** שְׁנָה; **paʿʿel** שַׁנִּי; and **haphʿel** הַשְׁנִי).

PRACTICE 1

Identify the stem (pəʿal, paʿʿel, or haphʿel) of the following verb forms based solely on their vowel patterns in their most basic forms (the 3rd masculine singular suffix conjugation).

a יְהַב *he gave*
b פַּקֵּד *he commanded*
c עֲבַד *he made*

d הַנְפֵּק *he brought forth*
e יְדַע *he knew*
f קְצַף *he grew angry*
g הַלֵּךְ *he walked*
h הַשְׁלֵט *he caused to rule*
i שְׁלַח *he sent*
j הַנְעֵל *he brought in*

In the pəʿal (פְּעַל) stem, the most basic form of the verb **שׁני** would be **שְׁנָה** (with final he mater); it would be translated *he was different* or *he changed* (in an intransitive sense). The pəʿal is the most common verbal stem and usually conveys a verb's primary sense. We have already learned the active and passive participles of the pəʿal (e.g. **כָּתֵב** *one who writes* or *he writes* and **כְּתִיב** *what is written* or *it is written*).

In the paʿʿel (פַּעֵל) stem, the verb's most basic form would be **שַׁנִּי** and could be translated *he made (something) be different*. The paʿʿel in general indicates the transformation of a person's or a thing's state. Consider Dan 4:13: **לִבְבֵהּ מִן־אֲנָשָׁא יְשַׁנּוֹן**; translated most literally, this would be: *his heart from a human (heart) they will make different* (paʿʿel of **שׁני**), though more idiomatically this becomes *his mind was altered from being a human mind*. With other verbs, the paʿʿel can indicate the repetition or intensification of a given action, as with the verb **קטל**, which has the sense *kill* in the pəʿal and *slay* in the paʿʿel.

In the haphʿel (הַפְעֵל) stem, the same verb **שׁני** would appear in its most basic form as **הַשְׁנִי** and could be translated *he caused (something) to change*, where again the verb is transitive. The haphʿel usually conveys a notion of causation, where the subject of the verb causes the object of the verb to perform the verbal action. For example, Dan 2:21 (**הוּא מְהַשְׁנֵא עִדָּנַיָּא וְזִמְנַיָּא**) can be translated: *he causes times and seasons to change*. In some cases the haphʿel can take two direct objects, as is commonly the case with the haphʿel of **ידע** *to know*: **הוֹדְעָךְ מָה־דִי לֶהֱוֵא** *he has caused you to know what will be* (Dan 2:29), where both *you* and *what will be* are the direct objects. In these cases, it is sometimes preferable to avoid the English verb *cause* and so translate somewhat less literally: *he has made known to you what will be*.

The pəʿal, paʿʿel, and haphʿel are the three fundamental stems of Aramaic. Although abstractly representing different things, it often happens that the differences between the paʿʿel and haphʿel stems are subtle and may not be perceived in more idiomatic, free translations. For example, in Dan 3:28 the paʿʿel of **שׁני** might be translated *disobey*, though its literal sense is to make something different: **מִלַּת מַלְכָּא שַׁנִּיו** *they disobeyed the word of the king* (lit. *they made the word of the king different*). The literal sense is close to the more literal sense of the haphʿel of **שׁני** in Dan 6:16: **... דִּי־כָל־אֱסָר וּקְיָם דִּי־מַלְכָּא יְהָקֵים לָא לְהַשְׁנָיָה** *... that every injunction or edict that the king establishes cannot be changed* or more literally ... one should not *cause to change*.

However, a given verb will usually be attested in only the paʿʿel or the haphʿel, not both. So, for example, the root **בטל** appears in the pəʿal with the sense *cease* and in the paʿʿel with the sense *make cease*. The root **אבד**, on the other hand, has the sense *perish* in the pəʿal and the sense *make perish* or *destroy* in the haphʿel.

There are also passive stems that correspond to these three fundamental stems:
The pəʿīl (פְּעִיל), the passive of the pə ʿal
The *puʿʿal (פֻּעַל*), the passive of the paʿʿel
The huphʿal (הֻפְעַל), the passive of the haphʿel

Of these, the pəʿīl is the most important, the most commonly used, and the puʿʿal is not attested in Biblical Aramaic but appears in other dialects.

In addition, there are three t-prefix stems, each corresponding to one of the three active stems, each usually expressing a reflexive notion or a passive notion. This means that there are technically three ways to create a passive verbal form:

1 **through a pəʿal passive participle**
2 **through the passive stems (pəʿīl, puʿʿal, huphʿal)**
3 **through the t-prefix stems**

The hitpəʿel (הִתְפְּעֵל)
The hitpaʿʿal (הִתְפַּעַל)
The *hittaphʿal (הִתַּפְעַל*)

Of these, only the hitpəʿel and hitpaʿʿal stems are found in Biblical Aramaic, while the hittaphʿal is found in other dialects.

In addition to these more regular stems, Aramaic attests a few rarer stems that involve the reduplication of one or more root consonants. These often are restricted to II-waw/yod and geminate roots (i.e. those whose second and third root consonants are identical, like עלל) and so are treated in the units dealing with these root types. But, rarely one encounters a strong root in such a stem, such as נְעַרְבֵּב *let us confuse*, the paʿlel stem of ערב. Usually stems involving reduplication are used in place of the paʿʿel and related stems.

Each of the stems mentioned so far has a suffix conjugation (which is characterized by suffixes to the base form of the verb), as well as participles. The active stems (pə ʿal, paʿʿel, and haphʿel) and the t-stems also attest a prefix conjugation (characterized by prefixes to the base form of the verb), imperatives, and infinitives. In addition to the participle, which has already been introduced, the two most important verbal forms are the suffix and prefix conjugations. The suffix conjugation usually expresses events or actions as complete, often translated by the English past or present tenses. The prefix conjugation is like the participle in that it expresses events or actions that are not fixed or complete, which happen repeatedly or continuously. The prefix conjugation can also express what is wished for or what is obligatory (as do English constructions with *can*, *could*, *may*, *must*, and *should*).

First the suffix conjugation is learned. The third masculine singular (3ms) form is the most important since it is the form of the verb sometimes listed in dictionary entries and is the basis for most of the other forms in the suffix-conjugation paradigm.

CULTURAL INSIGHT

The Aramaic alphabet had wide-ranging influences. In cities like Petra, the Nabateans spoke Arabic, but wrote their inscriptions in an Aramaic dialect. The distinctive way they wrote Aramaic letters eventually led to the Arabic alphabet. At the beginning or in the middle of a word, the Nabatean he, for example, looks like the he with which we are familiar (ה). But, at the end of a word it is written more like a closed circle, a form that would influence the form of the corresponding Arabic letter ha (ه).

Pəʿal suffix conjugation

The following paradigm isolates the distinctive features of each form of the suffix conjugation.

3ms	כְּתַב	--	kətab
3fs	כִּתְבַת	כִּתְב ַת	kitbat
2ms	כְּתַבְתָּ / כְּתַבְתְּ	כְּתַבְ תָּ/כְּתַבְ תְּ	kətabt/kətabtā
2fs	כְּתַבְתִּי	כְּתַבְ תִּי	kətabtīʸ
1cs	כִּתְבֵת	כִּתְב ֵת	kitbet
3mp	כְּתַבוּ	כְּתַב וּ	kətabūʷ
3fp	כְּתַבָה	כְּתַב ָה	kətabāʰ
2mp	כְּתַבְתּוּן	כְּתַבְ תּוּן	kətabtūʷn
2fp	כְּתַבְתֵּן	כְּתַבְ תֵּן	kətabten
1cp	כְּתַבְנָא	כְּתַבְ נָא	kətabnâ

Notice that the vowels within the root consonants are the same throughout the paradigm except for the 3fs (*she*) and 1cs (*I*) forms.

LANGUAGE INSIGHT

The 3fs and 1cs forms are counter-intuitive from a historical perspective. Their etymological form is *katabat and *katabtu. Based on these forms, we would expect the first vowel to be a not i. Note, however, that the vowel is a in roots that begin with a guttural consonant. E.g. אֲמַרֵת *I said*, עַבְדֵת *I made*, etc. In two instances, the 3fs forms have unusual vowels: אֲמֶרֶת *she said* and בְּטֵלַת *it stopped.*

Practice 2

Write out the paradigm of כְּתַב until it is memorized. Then, supply the appropriate vowels to the following words based on the accompanying translations. The verbs exhibit the same vowel patterns as כְּתַב, though recall that a guttural as a first root consonant will exhibit a hateph patach instead of a regular shewa (e.g. אֲמַר he said).

Example: *he was angry* בנס → בְּנַס

- **a** *he went* אזל
- **b** *they* (mp) *ate* אכלו
- **c** *they* (mp) *fell* נפלו

d *I lifted* נטלת
e *you* (ms) *did* עבדתּ
f *they* (fp) *went forth* נפקה
g *I heard* שׁמעת
h *she grew strong* תּקפת
i *we sent* שׁלחנא
j *it* (fs) *came up* סלקת

THE PA''EL AND HAPH'EL SUFFIX CONJUGATION

The sequence of vowels for each stem are relatively stable and are usually found throughout a verb's paradigm. For strong roots, the pə'al usually has the sequence ə-a. The pa''el and the haph'el have the sequence a-e or alternatively a-i. (The e vowel and the i vowel seem to be interchangeable in the verbs.) In addition, the pa''el is characterized by the doubling of the second root consonant and the haph'el by a prefixed he (ה). An alternative form of the haph'el is the aph'el which is otherwise the same as the haph'el but has either no prefix or a prefixed aleph instead of a he. It is much more common in later dialects of Aramaic, like those reflected in the targums.

Forming the suffix conjugation of the pa''el and haph'el is usually no more difficult than adding the same suffixes to the stock base of the stem.

The 2fp suffix תֵּן + the base of the pa''el כַּתֵּב = כַּתֵּבְתֵּן *you made written*

The 1cp suffix נָא + the base of the haph'el הַכְתֵּב = הַכְתֵּבְנָא *we caused to write*

The same applies to the other stems, like the pə'īl and the hitpa''al:

The 3fs suffix ַת + the base of the pə'īl כְּתִיב = כְּתִיבַת *it* (fs) *was written*

The 3mp suffix וּ + the base of the hitpa''al הִתְכַּתַּב = הִתְכַּתַּבוּ *they were made written*

In the following table, the vowel e (represented by sere ֵ) could also be realized as i (represented by hiriq ִ). This has only been indicated in the first form (3ms) of the pa''el and haph'el so as not to overburden the student with different forms. In general, wherever you see e you can expect an alternative pronunciation with i. There is no difference in sense.

	pə'al	pa''el	haph'el
3ms	כְּתַב	כַּתֵּב or כַּתִּב	הַכְתֵּב or הַכְתִּב
3fs	כִּתְבַת	כַּתְּבַת	הַכְתְּבַת
2ms	כְּתַבְתְּ or כְּתַבְתָּ	כַּתֵּבְתְּ or כַּתֵּבְתָּ	הַכְתֵּבְתְּ or הַכְתֵּבְתָּ
2fs	כְּתַבְתִּי	כַּתֵּבְתִּי	הַכְתֵּבְתִּי
1cs	כִּתְבֵת	כַּתְּבֵת	הַכְתְּבֵת
3mp	כְּתַבוּ	כַּתִּבוּ	הַכְתִּבוּ
3fp	כְּתַבָה	כַּתִּבָה	הַכְתִּבָה
2mp	כְּתַבְתּוּן	כַּתֵּבְתּוּן	הַכְתֵּבְתּוּן
2fp	כְּתַבְתֵּן	כַּתֵּבְתֵּן	הַכְתֵּבְתֵּן
1cp	כְּתַבְנָא	כַּתֵּבְנָא	הַכְתֵּבְנָא

LANGUAGE INSIGHT

Note the two 1cp forms כַּתֵּבְנָא and הַכְתֵּבְנָא. While both pa‘‘el and haph‘el contain the sequence -תֵּב--, it represents something slightly different in each case. The dagesh (i.e. dot) in the taw in the pa‘‘el indicates that the middle consonant is doubled (–tteb–). In the haph‘el form, the dagesh in the taw indicates only that it is pronounced hard (–teb–). The above pa‘‘el form would be transliterated kattebnâ, while the haph‘el form would be transliterated haktebnâ.

PRACTICE 3

Write out the paradigms of כְּתַב in the pa‘‘el and haph‘el until they are memorized. Then, identify the following suffix-conjugation forms and fill in the blanks to complete the translations.

Example: שְׁפַר → pə‘al 3ms suffix conjugation *it was pleasing*

a עֲבַדוּ → ______________ *made*

b הֲוַיִת ______________ *were*

c יְהַב ______________ *gave*

d אֲכַלוּ ______________ *ate*

e שַׁבְּחֵת ______________ *praised*

f קַבֵּל ______________ *received*

g הַנְפֵּק ______________ *brought out*

h הַשְׁפֵּלְתְּ ______________ *humbled*

i הַרְגִּזוּ ______________ *angered*

j הַכְרִזוּ ______________ *proclaimed*

CULTURAL INSIGHT

In Iranian languages like Parthian and Middle Persian (from the mid-first millennium CE), whole Aramaic words are used as ideograms (or heterograms). For example, the sequence of letters מלכא was read not as malkâ (*the king*) or something similar, but instead as šāh (= *shah*). Similarly, שמיא was not read šəmayyâ (*the heavens*) but rather as asman (= *heaven*); אחי was not read ’aḥīʸ (*my brother*) but rather as brād (= *brother*). Even whole verbal forms are used; עבדו ‘ăbadūʷ *they made* is used to represent karānd *they shall make* (See Nyberg et al. and Skjærvø 1996.)

GUTTURAL CONSONANTS AND IRREGULAR ROOTS

Certain verbs appear in the pə‘al with a hiriq (i) and/or sere (e) where כְּתַב *he wrote* and other verbs have patach (a). Thus, *he worshipped* is סְגִד; and *they went up* is סְלִקוּ. Sometimes there is alternation between sere and hiriq: *he approached* is קְרֵב but *they approached* is קְרִבוּ or even sometimes with a mater קְרִיבוּ, though the i is short even with a mater. As mentioned, hiriq also sometimes replaces a sere in the pa‘‘el: קַטִּל *it slayed*.

In verbs where a guttural or resh (i.e. ר, ע, ח, ה, א) is the first root consonant, the 3fs and 1cs exhibit a patach (a) instead of hiriq (i). Thus, you find in the pəʿal עַבְדֵת *I made*. The form looks almost like a paʿʿel form with the initial a vowel. However, if this were a paʿʿel verb, then it would have a dagesh in the middle root consonant representing its doubling: עַבְּדֵת*.

When a paʿʿel verb has a guttural (including resh) as a middle root consonant, the doubling is not evidenced directly in the orthography. In the case of he and ḥet (and sometimes ʿayin), the guttural sound was likely doubled in the dialect of the biblical writers, but was not indicated by a dagesh by the medieval scribes since they did not double these consonants in their own pronunciation (e.g. we would expect בַּהֲלְתּוּן baheltūʷn *you* (m.p.) *frightened*, though earlier it was bahheltūʷn). However, even the biblical writers did not double aleph or resh (and sometimes not ʿayin either). This resulted in the preceding vowel being lengthened (e.g., a > ā). So, in the paʿʿel, the 1cs suffix conjugation of the root ברך would have been pronounced בָּרְכֵת bārəket instead of בַּרְּכֵת** **barrəket.

In verbs with a guttural or resh as a third root consonant, the sere or hiriq that would normally appear in the paʿʿel, as in כַּתֵּב (or כַּתִּב), and in the haphʿel, as in הַכְתֵּב is instead a patach: שַׁבַּ֫חוּ *they praised*, and בַּקַּ֫רוּ וְהַשְׁכַּ֫חוּ *they searched* and *they found*. This reflects the same tendency for patach to replace sere in active participles with a final guttural consonant, as in אָמַר (see Unit 7). For these verbs, the 3fs and 1cs have a sequence of two patachs and look identical: הַשְׁכַּ֫חַת could be either *she found* or *I found*. You must infer from the context the correct translation.

PRACTICE 4

Produce the paʿʿel and haphʿel suffix conjugations from the English translations and Aramaic roots.

- **a** *he promoted* (haphʿel of צלח)
- **b** *I praised* (paʿʿel of שׁבח)
- **c** *they praised* (paʿʿel of שׁבח)
- **d** *we found* (haphʿel of שׁכח)
- **e** *they* (m.p.) *found* (haphʿel of שׁכח)
- **f** *they* (m.p.) *searched* (paʿʿel of בקר)
- **g** *you* (m.s.) *honoured* (paʿʿel of הדר)
- **h** *you* (m.s.) *humbled* (haphʿel of שׁפל)
- **i** *you* (f.s.) *praised* (paʿʿel of שׁבח)
- **j** *I honoured* (paʿʿel of הדר)
- **k** *they slayed* (paʿʿel of קטל)
- **l** *he took out* (haphʿel of נפק)
- **m** *they* (m.p.) *ceased* (paʿʿel of בטל)
- **n** *he established* (paʿʿel of שׁכן)
- **o** *they* (m.p.) *humbled* (haphʿel of שׁפל)
- **p** *they* (f.p.) *searched* (paʿʿel of בקר)
- **q** *they* (m.p.) *proclaimed* (haphʿel of כרז)
- **r** *we praised* (paʿʿel of שׁבח)

s *they* (m.p.) *rushed together quickly* (haph'el of רגשׁ)
t *she honoured* (pa''el of הדר)

> **LANGUAGE INSIGHT**
>
> Although there is sometimes ambiguity, it is often the case that a given sequence of vowels and/or vowels and consonants will be particular to a given verb form. So, for example, the sequence qamets-sere, (presented with the root כתב for the sake of illustration) כָּתֵב, is typical of pə'al m.s. absolute participles. The sequence qamets-shewa-qamets, כָּתְבָה, is typical of pə'al f.s. absolute participles. On the other hand, the sequence hiriq-shewa-patach-taw, כִּתְבַת, is typical of pə'al 3fs suffix-conjugation verbs and hiriq-shewa-sere-taw, כִּתְבֵת, is typical of the 1cs. Being familiar with such vowel patterns will greatly enhance your ability to read Aramaic.

Reading

Provide the correct forms to the words in the blanks in the Aramaic texts using the information provided in the translation to help.

DANIEL 6:10

כָּל־קֳבֵל דְּנָה מַלְכָּא דָּרְיָוֶשׁ ____(רשׁם)_____ כְּתָבָא וֶ _____ (אֱסָר)_____

the prohibition← and ← the decree ← he signed ← Darius ← the king ← this ← because of

Because of this, the king, Darius, ____________________ *signed*
____________________ (pə'al 3ms suff. conj. רשׁם) *the decree and*
____________________ *the prohibition* ____________________ (אֱסָר m.s. det.)

DANIEL 6:11

a וְדָנִיֵּאל כְּדִי ____________________ (ידע) ____________________
he knew ← although ← Now, Daniel

b דִּי רְשִׁים _________ (כְּתָב)____________ עַל לְבַיְתֵהּ
his house ← he entered ← the decree ← was signed ← that

c וְכַוִּין _______ (פתח) _______ לֵהּ בְּעִלִּיתֵהּ נֶ֫גֶד יְרוּשְׁלֶם
Jerusalem ← before ← in the upper chambers ← belonging to it ← were open ← windows

d וְזִמְנִין תְּלָתָה בְּ _______ (יוֹם) _______ הֲוָה בָּרֵךְ עַל־ בִּרְכ֫וֹהִי
his knees ← over ← he would bend ← the day ← in ← three ← times

e וּמְצַלֵּה וּמוֹדֵה קֳדָם אֱלָהֵהּ
his God ← before ← and give thanks ← and pray

f כָּל־קֳבֵל דִּי־הֲוָה ____________(עבד)____________ מִן־קַדְמַת דְּנָה
this ← before ← he used to do ← as

a *Now, Daniel, although* ____________________ *he knew*
____________________ (pə'al 3ms suff. conj. of ידע)

b *that* ____________________ *the decree* ____________________ (כְּתָב m.s. det.) *was signed, he entered his house.*

c *Its* (i.e. the house's) *windows in the upper chambers* ____________________ *were open* ____________________ (pə ʽal f.p. passive part. abs. **פתח**) *before Jerusalem.*

d *Three times in* ____________________ *the day* ____________________ (**יום** m.s. det.) ____________________ *he would bend over his knees*

e *and pray and give thanks before his God*

f *as* ____________________ *he used to do* ____________________ (pə ʽal m.s. part. abs. **עבד**) *before this.*

DANIEL 6:12

a אֱדַיִן גֻּבְרַיָּא אִלֵּךְ ____________ (רגשׁ)____________

← then ← men ← these … *came hectically*

b וְ ____________ (שׁכח)________ לְדָנִיֵּאל בָּעֵה וּמִתְחַנַּן קֳדָם אֱלָהֵהּ

his God ← before ← and seeking favour ← praying ← Daniel ← they found ← and

a *Then, these men* ____________________ *came hectically* ____________________ (haph'el 3mp suff. conj. **רגשׁ**)

b *and* ____________________ *they found* ____________________ (haph'el 3mp suff. conj. **שׁכח**) *Daniel praying and seeking favour before his God.*

DANIEL 6:13

a בֵּאדַיִן__________ (קרב)__________ וְ__________ (אמר)__________

said ← and ← they approached ← then

b קֳדָם־ מַלְכָּא עַל־ אֱסָר מַלְכָּא

the king ← injunction of ← concerning ← the king ← before

c הֲלָא אֱסָר __________ (רשׁם)__________ דִּי

so that ← you signed ← a prohibition ← is it not

d כָּל־ אֱנָשׁ דִּי יִבְעֵה מִן־ כָּל־ אֱלָהּ וֶאֱנָשׁ

or person ← god ← any ← to ← will pray ← who ← person ← any

e עַד־__________ (יום)__________ תְּלָתִין לָהֵן מִנָּךְ מַלְכָּא

O king ← to you ← except ← 30 ← days ← for

f יִתְרְמֵה לְגוֹב אַרְיָוָתָא

the lions ← to the den of ← will be thrown

g עָנֵה מַלְכָּא וְ__________ (אמר)__________

said ← and ← the king ← answered

h יַצִּיבָא __________ (מִלָּה)__________

the word ← is accurate

i כְּדָת מָדַי וּפָרַס דִּי־ לָא תֶעְדֵּא

be revoked ← not ← which ← and Persian(s) ← Mede(s) ← according to the law of

a *After that,* ____________________ *they approached* ____________________ (pə'al 3mp suff. conj. **קרב**) *and* ____________________ *and they said* ____________________ (pə'al m.p. part. abs. of **אמר**)

b *before the king, concerning the injunction of the king:*

c *Did you not* ____________________ *sign* ____________________ (pəʿal 2ms suff. conj. **רשם**) *the injunction so that*

d *any person who will pray to any god or person*

e *for 30* ____________________ *days* ____________________ (**יוֹם** m.p. abs.) *except to you, O king,*

f *will be thrown to the den of the lions?*

g *The king answered and* ____________________ *said* ____________________ (pəʿal m.s. part. abs. **אמר**):

h ____________________ *the word* ____________________ (**מִלָּה** f.s. det.) *is accurate,*

i *according to the law of the Medes and Persians, which cannot be revoked.*

Test yourself

1. What distinguishes the pəʿal conjugation in its form from the paʿʿel?
2. What distinguishes the three conjugations in terms of their meanings?
3. Write the following paradigms:
   - **a** The pəʿal suffix conjugation of **אזל** *to go*
   - **b** The paʿʿel suffix conjugation of **קטל** *to kill* (paʿʿel *to slay*)
   - **c** The haphʿel suffix conjugation of **שפל** *to be low* (haphʿel *to humble, make or bring low*)

Suggestions for further study

Try writing the Aramaic verses out on a separate sheet of paper and then translating as much of each verse as possible before consulting the translation. Commit the vocabulary of the exercises to memory.

SELF-CHECK

	I CAN...
●	describe the basic structure of the Aramaic verbal system
●	recognize the suffix-conjugation verb
●	recognize and produce the pəʿal, paʿʿel, haphʿel suffix-conjugation verbal forms for strong roots

9 Prepositions and nouns with pronominal suffixes

In this unit you will learn how to:

- **recognize and produce pronominal suffixes on prepositions and nouns**
- **identify and use pronominal suffixes on nouns**

In this unit you will read:

- **Daniel 6:17–20**

Grammar

PREPOSITIONS WITH SUFFIXES

As described in Unit 4, the prepositions בְּ *in, with*, כְּ *as, like*, and לְ *to, for* attach directly to the word that follows them (לְמַלְכָּה *to a queen*). Where a pronoun follows בְּ or לְ the pronoun takes the form of a suffix, not the independent form of the pronoun. Therefore, you never find the expression *to me* expressed as the preposition לְ followed by the independent form of the pronoun, אֲנָה *I*. Instead, you find לְ followed by the first common singular pronominal suffix -ִי: לִי *for me* or *to me*. This phrase appears as an independent word, not attached to any other word. Note that Aramaic has four forms of the second person suffix: masculine singular and feminine singular, masculine plural and feminine plural.

PRACTICE 1

Note the form of the suffixes on לְ and then complete the column for just the preposition בְּ *in, with*.

	לְ	בְּ	מִן	עִם	עַל	קֳדָם
1cs	לִי		מִנִּי		עֲלַי	קֳדָמַי
2ms	לָךְ		מִנָּךְ		עֲלָיךְ	קֳדָמָיךְ
2fs	לֵ֫כִי			עִמֵּ֫כִי	עֲלַ֫יכִי	קֳדָמַ֫יכִי
3ms	לֵהּ		מִנֵּהּ		עֲל֫וֹהִי	קֳדָמ֫וֹהִי
3fs	לַהּ			עִמַּהּ	עֲלַיהּ	קֳדָמַיהּ
1cp	לַ֫נָא		מִנַּ֫נָא		עֲלַ֫ינָא	קֳדָמַ֫ינָא
2mp	לְכֹם			עִמְּכֹם	עֲלֵיכֹם	קֳדָמֵיכֹם
2fp	לְכֵן			עִמְּכֵן	עֲלֵיכֵן	קֳדָמֵיכֵן
3mp	לְהֹם		מִנְּהֹם		עֲלֵיהֹם	קֳדָמֵיהֹם
3fp	לְהֵן		מִנְּהֵן		עֲלֵיהֵן	קֳדָמֵיהֵן

Some peculiarities should be mentioned. First, the stress usually falls on the last syllable, with the exception of the 2fs and 1cp pronominal suffixes. Second, the dot or mappiq in the final he of the 3ms and 3fs suffix indicates that this he is actually pronounced as a consonant and is distinct from the mater he that marks the feminine singular noun (e.g. מַלְכָּה *queen*). Third, the 2mp pronoun כֹם- frequently appears as כוֹן- while the 3mp pronoun הֹם- appears as הוֹן-. The form with mem and no mater is the earlier.

LANGUAGE INSIGHT

The distribution of linguistic features can sometimes suggest a relative time frame for when a work was written. For instance, the Aramaic of Ezra most often uses the כֹם- and הֹם- suffixes, while Daniel uses only the כוֹן- and הוֹן- suffixes. Together with other features (like the greater number of verbs that appear in the aph'el in Daniel than in Ezra), the distribution of possessive suffixes suggests that the Aramaic of Ezra is earlier than that of Daniel.

PRACTICE 2

Match the English with the Aramaic (using the pe'al suffix-conjugation verb forms from Unit 8: כִּתְבֵת *I wrote* and כְּתַבוּ *they* [m.p.] *wrote*).

a	*I wrote to him*	**1**	כִּתְבֵת בַּהּ
b	*they wrote to you* (f.s.)	**2**	כִּתְבֵת לָךְ
c	*I wrote with it* (f.s.)	**3**	כְּתַבוּ לַהּ
d	*they wrote to me*	**4**	כִּתְבֵת לֵהּ
e	*I wrote to them* (m.p.)	**5**	כְּתַבוּ לִי
f	*they wrote to us*	**6**	כִּתְבֵת לְכֵן
g	*I wrote to you* (m.s.)	**7**	כְּתַבוּ לֵכִי
h	*they wrote to her*	**8**	כְּתַבוּ לַנָא
i	*I wrote to you* (f.p.)	**9**	כִּתְבֵת לְהֵן
j	*I wrote to them* (f.p.)	**10**	כִּתְבֵת לְהֹם

As mentioned in Unit 4, the preposition לְ *to, for* can also be used to indicate the direct object of the verb and to express possession. These uses are also found where the preposition has a pronominal suffix: as in לֵהּ פְּלַחוּ *they served him* and כָּל־אָרְחָתֵהּ לֵהּ *all ways are his* (i.e. are God's). Notice first that the preposition can come first or last in its clause. In the latter example, the prepositional phrase could also be translated *all ways (belong) to him*. Similar phrases can even be translated with the English verb *to have* as in עַיְנִין לַהּ *she has eyes*. Since the Aramaic does not express a verb analogous to *are*, *belong*, or *have*, and since the preposition לְ can be understood in many different ways, it is sometimes difficult to be sure how to translate such phrases. One should become familiar with recognizing forms like לַהּ and לֵהּ as possibly expressing *are hers/his, belong to her/him*, or *she/he has*. The preposition לְ can also be used in a way that approximates English *according to* (e.g. לְמִנְיָן שִׁבְטֵי יִשְׂרָאֵל *according to the number of tribes of Israel* Ezra 6:17) and *at* (e.g. לִקְצָת יוֹמַיָּא *at the end of the days* Dan 4:31 (Leningrad Codex has יוֹמַיָּה)).

PRACTICE 3

Match the English to the Aramaic. For consistency the English sentences are presented in the past tense, though the Aramaic could just as easily be translated with the present or future. Consult the following vocabulary: אַרְבַּע *four*, בַּ֫יִת *house*, גְּבַר (det. גֻּבְרָא) *man*, גַּף (pl. גַּפִּין) *wing*, דִּי *of*, כַּוָּה (pl. כַּוִּין) *window* (a fem. noun), נְשַׁר *eagle*, פתח *to open*, שְׁלָם *peace*.

a	כַּוִּין פְּתִיחָן לַהּ	**1**	*you had peace*
b	גַּפִּין דִּי נְשַׁר לְהֹם	**2**	*it had four wings*
c	לַהּ גַּפִּין אַרְבַּע	**3**	*the man Micah had a house*
d	שְׁלָם לָךְ	**4**	*it had opened windows*
e	גֻּבְרָא מִיכָה לֵהּ בַּ֫יִת	**5**	*they had wings of an eagle*

CULTURAL INSIGHT

In the Bible, the history of the patriarchs is closely tied with Aram and the Arameans. Abraham comes from Ur of the Chaldees, the Chaldees (or Chaldeans) being commonly associated with the Arameans. He moves to Haran, a city in northern Mesopotamia, which has a long association with Arameans. Isaac married Rebekah, the daughter of Bethuel, the Aramean and sister of Laban, the Aramean. Later generations are to remember this ancestry and Abraham's wanderings. Deut 26:5 presents what one should say (in Hebrew) when offering first-fruits: *My ancestor was a lost Aramean and went down to Egypt and sojourned there …* The word *lost* in Hebrew, **אֹבֵד**, often translated *wandering*, is unusual in this passage; usually the verb means *to perish, die, disappear.* Curiously, many of the ancient translations seem to downplay this admission of Aramean ancestry. In later Aramaic translations of the passage, the word **אֹבֵד** is interpreted as referring to what Laban did to Abraham (not who Abraham was), *Laban, the Aramean, sought to destroy* (haph'el of **אבד**) *(our) ancestor, so he (Abraham) went down to Egypt.*

The prepositions **מִן** *from* and **עִם** *with* are similar to each other in that they both actually have a doubled second consonant (i.e. minn- and 'imm-), something that is only indicated in the orthography when they are accompanied by a suffix (e.g. **מִנִּי** *from me* and **עִמַּהּ** *with her*). The suffixes that attach to these prepositions are identical to those on **בְּ** and **לְ**.

Note that the preposition **מִן** can be used in several different ways. In addition to being used like English *from*, it can also indicate agency, like English *by*. It occurs in this way in the phrase **מִנִּי שִׂים טְעֵם** *by me a decree was set* (which is translated more idiomatically into English *I set a decree*). The preposition also indicates the cause of something (English *due to*): **מִן־רְבוּתָא דִּי … יְהַב־לֵהּ … כֹּל עַמְמַיָּא … הֲווֹ זָאְעִין** *Due to the greatness that he gave him … all the peoples … were trembling …* (Dan 5:19). The preposition can also indicate a partitive sense and be translated *some*, as in **רַגְלוֹהִי מִנְּהֵן** *(as for) its feet, some of them …* (Dan 2:33). The preposition can additionally be used in comparative expressions where it is translated *than* or *more than*, as in **חָכְמָה דִּי אִיתַי בִּי מִן־כָּל־חַיַּיָּא** *wisdom that is in me more than all (other) living things* (Dan 2:30).

PRACTICE 4

Fill in the blanks in the earlier table for the two prepositions מִן *from* and עִם *with*.

The prepositions עַל *over, to, about* and קֳדָם *before* both take another set of pronominal suffixes, as illustrated in the earlier table. A yod appears as part of each suffix, except for in the 3ms suffix. This yod is pronounced only in the 1cs suffix as part of the dipthong ay; it is not pronounced in the other forms.

The same peculiarities found with the suffixes that attach to לְ also occur in relation to these suffixes. Note in particular that the 2mp pronoun כֹם- can also appear as כוֹן- while the 3mp pronoun הֹם- can also appear as הוֹן-. In addition, some spellings imply two separate pronunciations (cf. the two pronunciations presumed by the spelling of the 2ms independent pronoun אַנְתְּה (*'ant* vs. *'antā*), as explained in Unit 4). The consonants of the 2ms suffix (e.g. עֲלָיךְ *over you*) may imply a pronunciation like -ayik (e.g. עֲלַ֫יִךְ*), while the vowel symbols presuppose -āk (e.g. עֲלָךְ*); similarly the consonants of עֲלַיהּ may presuppose עֲלַ֫יְהָ* (or, alternatively, עֲלֵיהָ*), though the vowels reflect עֲלַהּ. As for the preposition קֳדָם, it sometimes appears with a full qamets under the qoph: קָדָמַי *before me* and קָדָמ֫וֹהִי *before him*. There is no distinction in meaning. Note also that in Ezra 4:12, 18; 5:17 the form עֲלֶ֫ינָא appears for what we would have expected to be עֲלַ֫ינָא*.

PRACTICE 5

Write the following sentences in Aramaic using the prepositional phrases above and the following pəʿal suffix-conjugation verb forms: אֲמַר *he said*; אֲמַרְתְּ *you* (m.s.) *said*; אֲמַ֫רְנָא *we said*; שִׁמְעֵת *I heard*; and שִׁמְעַת *she heard*.

- **a** *he said before them* (m.p.)
- **b** *I heard about her*
- **c** *you* (m.s.) *said before me*
- **d** *we said before you* (m.s.)
- **e** *she heard about it* (m.s.)
- **f** *you* (m.s.) *said before him*
- **g** *he said before me*
- **h** *I heard about you* (m.s.)
- **i** *she heard about it* (m.s.)
- **j** *you* (m.s.) *said before her*

PRONOMINAL SUFFIXES ON SINGULAR NOUNS

Instead of using independent words to indicate possession (as in English *my, your, her*), Aramaic uses suffixal pronouns on nouns. The phrase *my scribe* therefore is expressed as a combination of the word *scribe* (סָפַר) and the suffix *my* (ִי-), that is, סָפְרִי *my scribe*. The suffix -īʸ (ִי-) is the same suffix used on the preposition לְ *to, for* (and other prepositions). In fact, all the suffixes used with לְ *to, for* are also used with singular nouns (both masculine and feminine) as well as with feminine plural nouns. The suffixes used with עַל *over* and קֳדָם *before* are those that appear on masculine plural nouns.

The addition of pronominal suffixes to nouns follows rather simple principles of vowel reduction, as described in earlier Units 6 and 7. If a noun cannot experience vowel reduction because it has only long vowels and/or short vowels in closed syllables (like לִשָּׁן liššān *tongue*), then the vowels do not change (i.e. לִשָּׁנִי liššānīʸ *my tongue*). In many other nouns like סָפַר (sāpar) *scribe*, when a pronominal suffix like ־ִי (-īʸ) *my* is added, the second syllable would contain a short vowel in an open syllable (i.e. סָפַרִי* *sāparīʸ *my scribe*); since this is not allowed in Aramaic pronunciation, the short a reduces to a muttered vowel: סָפְרִי sāpərīʸ *my scribe*. It is sometimes hard to predict how vowels reduce and change in certain types of nouns like מֶ֫לֶךְ *king* and אִגְּרָה *letter* without a knowledge of the early history of Aramaic.

Nevertheless, you can usually predict the form of the noun if you have memorized the noun's inflectional forms, that is, the construct and determined forms. For most pronominal suffixes, you can take the determined form of the singular noun and subtract the ־ָא ending (or the ־ַיָּא ending for masculine plural nouns) and then supply the appropriate suffix.

the scribe	סָפְרָא → סָפְר־* → סָפְרִי	*my scribe*
the letter	אִגַּרְתָּא → אִגַּרְת־* → אִגַּרְתָּךְ	*your* (m.s.) *letter*
	סָפְרַיָּא → סָפְר־* → סָפְר֫וֹהִי	*his scribes*

This same technique also works with the 2mp, 2fp, 3mp, and 3fp suffixes on nouns like מֶ֫לֶךְ (from *malk-) that had only one vowel originally. However, this technique does not work for most other nouns in relation to the 2mp, 2fp, 3mp, and 3fp suffixes. Before these suffixes, the construct form of the noun usually appears. Contrast, for example, אִגַּרְתָּךְ *your* (m.s.) *letter* with אִגְּרַתְכֹם *your* (m.p.) *letter.*

	ms noun סָפַר ***scribe***	**ms noun** לִשָּׁן ***tongue***	**ms noun** מֶ֫לֶךְ ***king***	**fs noun** אִגְּרָה ***letter***	**fs noun** מַלְכוּ ***kingdom***
const./det. form	סָפְרָא / סָפַר	לִשָּׁנָא / לִשָּׁן	מַלְכָּא / מֶ֫לֶךְ	אִגַּרְתָּא / אִגְּרַת	מַלְכוּתָא / מַלְכוּת
1cs *my* ־ִי	סָפְרִי	לִשָּׁנִי	מַלְכִּי	אִגַּרְתִּי	מַלְכוּתִי
2ms *your* ־ָךְ	סָפְרָךְ	לִשָּׁנָךְ	מַלְכָּךְ	אִגַּרְתָּךְ	מַלְכוּתָךְ
2fs *your* ־ֵ֫כִי	סָפְרֵ֫כִי	לִשָּׁנֵ֫כִי	מַלְכֵּ֫כִי	אִגַּרְתֵּ֫כִי	מַלְכוּתֵ֫כִי
3ms *his* ־ֵהּ	סָפְרֵהּ	לִשָּׁנֵהּ	מַלְכֵּהּ	אִגַּרְתֵּהּ	מַלְכוּתֵהּ
3fs *her* ־ַהּ	סָפְרַהּ	לִשָּׁנַהּ	מַלְכַּהּ	אִגַּרְתַּהּ	מַלְכוּתַהּ
1cp *our* ־ַ֫נָא	סָפְרַ֫נָא	לִשָּׁנַ֫נָה	מַלְכַּ֫נָא	אִגַּרְתַּ֫נָה	מַלְכוּתַ֫נָה
2mp *your* ־כֹם	סָפַרְכֹם	לִשָּׁנְכֹם	מַלְכְּכֹם	אִגְּרַתְכֹם	מַלְכוּתְכֹם
2fp *your* ־כֵן	סָפַרְכֵן	לִשָּׁנְכֵן	מַלְכְּכֵן	אִגְּרַתְכֵן	מַלְכוּתְכֵן
3mp *their* ־הֹם	סָפַרְהֹם	לִשָּׁנְהֹם	מַלְכְּהֹם	אִגְּרַתְהֹם	מַלְכוּתְהֹם
3fp *their* ־הֵן	סָפַרְהֵן	לִשָּׁנְהֵן	מַלְכְּהֵן	אִגְּרַתְהֵן	מַלְכוּתְהֵן

As with the preceding suffixes on prepositions, ־כוֹן sometimes appears for ־כֹם and ־הוֹן for ־הֹם. Note that the 2mp, 2fp, 3mp, and 3fp pronouns include a shewa that represents the absence of a vowel when the preceding vowel is short (סָפַרְכֹם sāparkōm and מִלַּתְכֹם millatkom), and a murmured vowel when the preceding vowel is long (אֱלָהֲכֹם ʾĕlāhăkom) or when another shewa that represents the absence of a vowel comes right before it (**מַלְכְּכֹם** malkəkom and **אַרְעֲכֹם** ʼarʻăkom). Whether or not the shewa represents the absence of a vowel, the following kaph is always spirantized or pronounced soft.

> **CULTURAL INSIGHT**
>
> The status and mythology of the Aramaic language in early Judaism is reflected in various post-biblical writings. It was generally argued that Hebrew was the first language of the world, as reflected for example in the Aramaic translations of Gen 11:1, including that of Targum Neofiti: *All the dwellers of the earth had one tongue* (לשן = liššān) *and one speech, and were conversing in the language of the holy temple* (i.e. Hebrew) *because in it the world was created at the beginning*. Another competing view was that Aramaic was the original language of humanity, as expressed in the Babylonian Talmud (b. San. 38b), where a Jewish authority from Babylon (where Aramaic was the dominant language) claims that Adam spoke Aramaic, suggesting this is to be inferred from Ps 139:17 which contains words that could almost be construed as Aramaic (though they are really Hebrew): *how precious to me are your thoughts, o God*. Debate also concerned many other facets of linguistic usage, including whether or not angels spoke or understood Aramaic (with some affirming and others denying the possibility). (See Fraade.)

PRACTICE 6

Write out the column containing the word סָפַר *scribe* from the earlier table until the pronominal suffixes become familiar. Then, match the following English phrases to the Aramaic, which requires identifying the person, number, and gender of the suffix. This exercise uses the following vocabulary: אֱלָהּ *God*; גְּשֵׁם (det. גִּשְׁמָא) *body*; מַלְאַךְ *angel*; רֵאשׁ *head*; שְׁלָם *peace*.

a	*your* (m.s.) *God*	**1**	גִּשְׁמַהּ
b	*its* (f.s.) *body*	**2**	רֵאשִׁי
c	*their* (m.p.) *God*	**3**	גִּשְׁמַ֫נָא
d	*my God*	**4**	שְׁלָמְכוֹן
e	*her angel*	**5**	מַלְאֲכִי
f	*your* (m.p.) *peace*	**6**	אֱלָהָךְ
g	*my head*	**7**	אֱלָהִי
h	*her God*	**8**	שְׁלָמְהֵן
i	*your* (f.s.) *head*	**9**	אֱלָהַ֫נָא
j	*their* (f.p.) *peace*	**10**	שְׁלָמֵהּ
k	*our body*	**11**	אֱלָהֲהֹם
l	*my angel*	**12**	מַלְאֲכַהּ
m	*his peace*	**13**	רֵאשֵׁ֫כִי
n	*our God*	**14**	מַלְאֲכֵהּ
o	*his angel*	**15**	אֱלָהַהּ

PRONOMINAL SUFFIXES ON PLURAL NOUNS

For feminine plural nouns, you find the same pronominal suffixes as on לְ and singular nouns. As with singular nouns, take the determined form and subtract the אָ- ending and then supply the appropriate suffix (even with the 2m/fp and 3m/fp suffixes).

the letters	אִגְּרָתָא	→	*אִגְּרָת	→	אִגְּרָתַהּ	*her letters*
the kingdoms	מַלְכְוָתָא	→	*מַלְכְוָת	→	מַלְכְוָתֵהּ	*his kingdoms*

	fp noun אִגְּרָן	fp noun מַלְכְוָן
const./det. form	אִגְּרָתָא / אִגְּרַת	מַלְכְוָתָא / מַלְכְוַת
1cs *my* ִי-	אִגְּרָתִי	מַלְכְוָתִי
2ms *your* ָךְ-	אִגְּרָתָךְ	מַלְכְוָתָךְ
2fs *your* ֵכִי-	אִגְּרָתֵ֫כִי	מַלְכְוָתֵ֫כִי
3ms *his* ֵהּ-	אִגְּרָתֵהּ	מַלְכְוָתֵהּ
3fs *her* ַהּ-	אִגְּרָתַהּ	מַלְכְוָתַהּ
1cp *our* ַנָא-	אִגְּרָתַ֫נָא	מַלְכְוָתַ֫נָא
2mp *your* כֹם-	אִגְּרָתְכֹם	מַלְכְוָתְהֹם
2fp *your* כֵן-	אִגְּרָתְכֵן	מַלְכְוָתְכֵן
3mp *their* הֹם-	אִגְּרָתְהֹם	מַלְכְוָתְהֹם
3fp *their* הֵן-	אִגְּרָתְהֵן	מַלְכְוָתְהֵן

Note that when a shewa is preceded by a long vowel it is pronounced, as in אִגְּרָתְכֹם ʾiggərātəkom. As with the preceding suffixes on prepositions and singular nouns, כוֹן- sometimes appears for כֹם- and הוֹן- for הֹם-.

PRACTICE 7

Identify the plural feminine noun in each pair of words, then identify the person, gender, and number of the suffixes by translating both words (distinguishing the number and gender of second person suffixes).

a אִגְּרָתָךְ   אִגַּרְתָּךְ
b מַלְכוּתַהּ   מַלְכְוָתַהּ
c אִגַּרְתִּי   אִגְּרָתִי
d מַלְכוּתְהֹם   מַלְכְוָתְהֹם
e אִגְּרָתַ֫נָא   אִגַּרְתַּ֫נָה

Masculine plural nouns take the suffixes that appear on the prepositions עַל *over, to, about* and קֳדָם *before* (note the patach in the 1cp). The yod is pronounced only in the 1cs suffix. In the other forms, the yod functions as a graphic marker that the word is a plural word. The nouns with suffixes are formed by taking the determined form (e.g. מַלְכַ֫יָּא), subtracting the ending (e.g. -מַלְכ), and then adding the suffix (e.g. מַלְכַי *my kings*).

	mp noun סָפְרִין	mp noun לִשָּׁנִין	mp noun מַלְכִין
const./det. form	סָפְרַ֫יָּא / סָפְרֵי	לִשָּׁנַ֫יָּא / לִשָּׁנֵי	מַלְכַ֫יָּא / מַלְכֵי
1cs *my* ַי-	סָפְרַי	לִשָּׁנַי	מַלְכַי
2ms *your* ָיךְ-	סָפְרָיךְ	לִשָּׁנָיךְ	מַלְכָיךְ

2fs *your* -ַ֫יכִי	סָפְרַ֫יכִי	לִשָׁנַ֫יכִי	מַלְכַ֫יכִי
3ms *his* -ו֫הִי	סָפְר֫וֹהִי	לִשָׁנ֫וֹהִי	מַלְכ֫וֹהִי
3fs *her* -ַיהּ	סָפְרַיהּ	לִשָׁנַיהּ	מַלְכַיהּ
1cp *our* -ַ֫ינָא	סָפְרַ֫ינָא	לִשָׁנַ֫ינָה	מַלְכַ֫ינָא
2mp *your* -ֵיכֹם	סָפְרֵיכֹם	לִשָׁנֵיכֹם	מַלְכֵיכֹם
2fp *your* -ֵיכֵן	סָפְרֵיכֵן	לִשָׁנֵיכֵן	מַלְכֵיכֵן
3mp *their* -ֵיהֹם	סָפְרֵיהֹם	לִשָׁנֵיהֹם	מַלְכֵיהֹם
3fp *their* -ֵיהֵן	סָפְרֵיהֵן	לִשָׁנֵיהֵן	מַלְכֵיהֵן

As with the preceding suffixes, -כוֹן sometimes appears for -כֹם and -הוֹן for -הֹם.

LANGUAGE INSIGHT

Notice that the only difference between the singular and plural of some nouns will be the type of suffix. For instance, סָפְרִי *my scribe* and סָפְרַי *my scribes* are differentiated only on the basis of the suffix. For this reason, it is particularly important to know the suffixes well. In the case of סָפְרַהּ *her scribe* and סָפְרַיהּ *her scribes*, the singular and plural forms sound identical: sāfərah; the only difference between them is in the spelling, the unpronounced yod in the suffix on the plural noun.

PRACTICE 8

1 Copy out the first column from the previous table until you are familiar with the forms. Then, translate and identify the following suffixes on masculine plural nouns. Following this, write the same noun with the same suffix, but in the singular. The vowels of most of the following nouns are the same in the absolute singular and plural; usually only the suffix changes (the exceptions being h–j).

Example: אֱלָהָיךְ → *your gods* → 2nd masc. sing. // אֱלָהָךְ *your god*

a סָרְכ֫וֹהִי ______________________ *commanders*

b יוֹמֵיהוֹן ______________________ *days*

c אֱלָהַי ______________________ *gods*

d חַבְר֫וֹהִי ______________________ *companions*

e קַרְצֵיהוֹן ______________________ *morsels*

f עָרָיךְ ______________________ *enemies*

g זִיוָיךְ ______________________ *face* (lit. *faces*)

h עַבְדַי ______________________ *servants* (sing. abs. is עֲבֵד and det. עַבְדָּא)

i עַבְד֫וֹהִי ______________________ *servants* (sing. abs. is עֲבֵד and det. עַבְדָּא)

j בְּנ֫וֹהִי ______________________ *children* (sing. abs. is בַּר and det. בְּרָא)

2 Identify the plural nouns from the singular by circling the plural, then identify the absolute form by looking up the word in the glossary or dictionary.

Example: עַבְדֵּהּ עַבְד֫וֹהִי *his slave(s)* pl. עַבְד֫וֹהִי → absolute sing.: עֲבֵד

a בְּנַיהּ בְּרַהּ *her son(s)*

b מַלְכַ֫ינָא מַלְכַּנָא *our king(s)*

c חַבְרֵהּ חַבְר֫וֹהִי *his companion(s)*

d	מַלְכוּתְהֹם	מַלְכְוָתְהֹם	*their kingdom(s)*
e	מִלַּי	מִלְּתִי	*my word(s)* (hint: the pl. has the form of a masc. noun)
f	מְדִינְתָךְ	מְדִינָתָךְ	*your* (m.s.) *province(s)*
g	חֲבוּלָתְכֵן	חֲבוּלָתְכֵן	*your* (f.p.) *crime(s)*
h	אָתֵהּ	אָתוֹהִי	*his sign(s)*
i	אֱלָהָיךְ	אֱלָהָךְ	*your God(s)*
j	זִיוֹהִי	זִיוֵהּ	*its brightness* (sing.) *and his appearance* (pl.)

IRREGULAR NOUNS WITH SUFFIXES

The noun אַב *father* in the singular exhibits a long ū before pronominal suffixes (אֲבוּךְ *your* (m.s.) *father*), though not with the 1cs (אַבִי *my father*). Where a vowel usually comes before the consonant of the suffix (e.g. -eh *his* and -ah *her*), with אַב the vowel of the suffix follows the consonant (e.g. אֲבוּהִי *his father* and אֲבוּהָ *her father*). The plural form of *father* is irregular, אֲבָהָן, though suffixes attach to this form according to the expected pattern (e.g. אֲבָהָתִי *my fathers*).

The word אַח *brother* in the singular is not attested in Biblical Aramaic but would show the same type of inflection as אַב, something suggested by spellings in the Dead Sea Scrolls and in later Aramaic. The plural for אַח *brother* has the following form with the 2ms pronoun: אֶחָיךְ.

As explained in Unit 7, the noun כֹּל *all, every* appears with a holem (without mater) representing short o in the determined state (כֹּלָּא). With the 3mp suffix, the word appears with a qamets representing short o: כָּלְהוֹן *all of them.*

Nouns from III-aleph/waw/yod roots with suffixes usually do not attest the last root consonant. In מָרִאי *my lord* the vowels reflect mārīʸ. Two dual nouns occur with suffixes: חֲדוֹהִי *its breasts* and מְעוֹהִי *its stomach.*

CULTURAL INSIGHT

In 1 Cor 16:22, you will find another Aramaic phrase (transliterated into Greek letters): **μαραν αθα** = maran atha *our Lord, come!* The first word is מָרֵא *Lord* with the 1cp suffix. Apparently, in the dialect that this reflects, the 1cp suffix was not -anā, but simply -an, as it is in Targum Neofiti.

Reading

Vocalize the Aramaic words without vowels, using the information provided in the translation to help. See hints at the end of each verse.

DANIEL 6:17

a בֵּאדַיִן מלכא אמר וְהַיְתִיו לְדָנִיֵּאל
Daniel ← and they brought ← (he) said ← the king ← then

b וּרמו לְגֻבָּא דִּי אַרְיָוָתָא
the lions ← of ← to the den ← and they threw him

c ענה מלכא וְאמר לְדָנִיֵּאל
to Daniel ← and he said ← the king ← and (he) spoke up

d אלהך דִּי אַנְתְּ פלח־ לֵהּ בִּתְדִירָא הוּא יְשֵׁיזְבִנָּךְ
(he) will deliver you ← he ← constantly ← him ← serve ← you ← who ← your God

a *Then,* ______________________ (the determined form of מֶ֫לֶךְ *the king*) ______________________ (pəʿal 3ms suffix conjugation of אמר *said*) *and they brought Daniel.*
b *They threw (him) to the den of lions.*
c ______________________ (the determined form of מֶ֫לֶךְ *the king*) ______________________ (pəʿal m.s. active participle of ענה *spoke up*) *and* ______________________ (pəʿal m.s. active participle of אמר *said*) *to Daniel:*
d ______________________ (אֱלָהּ followed by the 2ms pron. suffix *your God*) *whom you serve* ______________________ (pəʿal m.s. active participle of פלח) *continually will save you.*

DANIEL 6:18

a וְהֵיתָיִת אֶ֫בֶן חֲדָה וְשֻׂמַת עַל־ פֻּם גֻּבָּא
the den ← the mouth of ← over ← and was set ← one ← stone ← was brought

b וְחַתְמַהּ מלכא בְּעִזקתה וּבְעִזקת רברבנוהי
his nobles ← and with the signet rings of ← with his signet ring ← the king ← he sealed it

c דִּי לָא־ תִשְׁנֵא צְבוּ בְּדָנִיֵּאל
with Daniel ← matter ← changed ← not ← so that

a *A stone was brought and set over the mouth of the den*
b *and* ______________________ (the determined form of מֶ֫לֶךְ *the king*) *sealed it with* ______________________ (עִזְקָה followed by the 3ms pron. suffix = *his signet ring*) *and with* ______________________ (עִזְקָה in the plural construct *the signet rings*) *of* ______________________ (רַבְרְבָן in the plural with the 3ms pron. suffix: *his nobles*)
c *so that no matter changed with regard Daniel.*

Hint: The determined form of עִזְקָה is עִזְקְתָא.

DANIEL 6:19

a אֱדַ֫יִן אזל מלכא לְהיכלה
to his palace ← the king ← (he) went ← then

b וּבָת טְוָת וְדַחֲוָן לָא־ הַנְעֵל קדמוהי
before him ← were brought ← not ← things ← fasting ← (he) spent the night

c וְשִׁנְתֵּהּ נַדַּת עלוהי
over him ← (it) fled ← his sleep

a *Then,* ______________________ (the determined form of מֶ֫לֶךְ *the king*) ______________________ (pəʿal 3ms suffix conjugation of אזל *went*) *to* ______________________ (הֵיכַל followed by the 3ms suffix *his palace*)
b *and spent the night fasting and no things* (דַּחֲוָן unclear meaning) *were brought* ______________________ (קֳדָם followed by 3ms suffix *before him*)

c *and his sleep fled (from)* ______________________ (עֲל followed by 3ms suffix *over him*)

Hint: In the first line, the subject of the verb follows the verb in the Aramaic, but the subject should precede the verb in the English translation.

DANIEL 6:20

a בֵּאדַ֫יִן מלכא בִּשְׁפַּרְפָּרָא יְקוּם

arose ← at dawn ← the king ← then

b בְּנָגְהָא וּבְהִתְבְּהָלָה לְגֻבָּא דִּי־ אַרְיָוָתָא אזל

he went ← lions ← of ← to the den of ← and in haste ← in the daylight

a *Then,* ______________________ (the determined form of מֶ֫לֶךְ *the king*) *arose at dawn;*
b *in the daylight and in haste* ______________________ (pəʿal 3ms suffix conjugation of אזל *he went*) *to the den of the lions.*

Hint: In the last line, note that the verb comes last in the sentence in Aramaic, but it is translated in English before the prepositional phrase *to the den of the lions.*

Test yourself

1 Match the Aramaic with the correct English translation (consulting the glossary where necessary) and then supply the form of the Aramaic word (or words) in the singular without suffix.

a	מִנִּי	**1**	*your God*
b	בְּמַלְכוּתִי	**2**	*the king*
c	כָּהֲנ֫וֹהִי	**3**	*from me* (or, *by me*)
d	עִמָּךְ	**4**	*in your hand*
e	מַלְכָּא	**5**	*his counsellors*
f	יָעֲטֹהִי	**6**	*their God*
g	אֱלָהָךְ	**7**	*his dwelling place*
h	בִּידָךְ	**8**	*in my kingdom*
i	מִשְׁכְּנֵהּ	**9**	*with you*
j	אֱלָהָהֹם	**10**	*his priests*

2 Translate the following (Ezra 7:13–15) using this vocabulary: אֱלָהּ God, בְּ *in*, דְּהַב *gold*, דִּי *that, who*, דָּת (cstr. דָּת) *law*, הִתְנַדַּ֫בוּ *have volunteered, donated*, וְ (or וּ) *and*, טְעֵם *decree*, יַד *hand*, יְהוּד *Yehud, Judah*, יְהָךְ *he may go*, יָעֵט counselor, יְרוּשְׁלֶם *Jerusalem*, יִשְׂרָאֵל *Israel*, כָּהֵן *priest*, כֹּל (cstr. כָּל) *all, anyone*, כָּל־קֳבֵל דִּי *because, for*, כְּסַף *silver*, לְ *to*, לְבַקָּרָא *to search* (לְ prep. + בַּקָּרָה pa‘‘el inf.), לְהֵיבָלָה *to bring* (לְ prep. + הֵיבָלָה haph‘el inf.), לֵוָיֵא *the Levites*, לְמְהָךְ *to go* (לְ prep. + מְהָךְ pəʿal inf.), מִן *from, by*, מִשְׁכַּן *dwelling*, מִתְנַדַּב *who volunteer*, עַל *over, about*, עַם *people* (det.), עִם *with*, קֳדָם *before*, שִׂים *was set*, שִׁבְעַת *seven*, שְׁלִיחַ *was sent*. The עַמָּא passage purports to be a decree given by Artaxerxes, king of the Persian empire, to Ezra. The spelling has only slightly been changed for consistency.

13 a מִנִּי שִׂים טְעֵם

b דִּי כָל־מִתְנַדַּב בְּמַלְכוּתִי מִן־עַמָּא יִשְׂרָאֵל

c וְכָהֲנ֫וֹהִי וְלֵוָיֵא לִמְהָךְ לִירוּשְׁלֶם עִמָּךְ יְהָךְ

14 a כָּל־קֳבֵל דִּי מִן־קֳדָם מַלְכָּא וְשִׁבְעַת יָעֲטֹהִי

b שְׁלִיחַ לְבַקָּרָה עַל־יְהוּד וְלִירוּשְׁלֶם

c בְּדָת אֱלָהָךְ דִּי בִידָךְ

15 a וּלְהֵיבָלָה כְּסַף וּדְהַב

b דִּי מַלְכָּא וְיָעֲטוֹהִי הִתְנַדַּבוּ

c לֶאֱלָהּ יִשְׂרָאֵל דִּי בִירוּשְׁלֶם מִשְׁכְּנֵהּ

Suggestions for further study

Practise looking up the nouns in the following phrases and then write down their singular absolute forms, as listed in the glossary.

לְגֻבָּא listed as גֹּב

אֶבֶן

וְדַחֲוָן

וְשִׁנְתֵּהּ

בִּשְׁפַרְפָּרָא

בִּנְגְהָא

SELF-CHECK

	I CAN...
○	recognize and produce pronominal suffixes on prepositions and nouns
○	identify and use pronominal suffixes on nouns

10 The syntax of dīʸ and the existential particle ʾīʸtay

In this unit you will learn how to:

- **recognize the existential particle ʾīʸtay *there is (are, was, were)***
- **identify the genitive use of the particle dīʸ *of***
- **identify the relative use of the particle dīʸ *who, whose, whom, which, where***
- **identify the conjunctive use of the particle dīʸ *that***

In this unit you will read:

- **Daniel 6:21–3**

Grammar

EXISTENTIAL PARTICLE ʾĪʸTAY

The Aramaic particle **אִיתַי** is often used to express existence or (with the negative adverb **לָא** *not*) non-existence. For example, note **בְּרַם אִיתַי אֱלָהּ בִּשְׁמַיָּא** *nevertheless, there is a God in the heavens* and **אִיתַי גֻּבְרִין יְהוּדָאִין** *there are Judean men* … It sometimes appears with an accompanying participle or adjective, functioning like the verb *to be*. In these cases, sometimes **אִיתַי** has a pronominal suffix that indicates the grammatical subject of the clause. The suffixes are the same as those which occur on masculine plural nouns: **הַאִיתָיךְ כָּהֵל** *are you able …?* and **לֵאלָהַי לָא אִיתֵיכוֹן פָּלְחִין** *you are not serving my gods* (lit. *my gods you are not serving*). (In these cases the final diphthong -ay- found in the un-suffixed form has been lost.)

THE GENITIVE USE OF THE PARTICLE DĪʸ

A genitive expression is one in which one noun modifies another. We have already encountered many genitive expressions before, especially with words in the construct state. Typically the genitive relationship between nouns is indicated in English with the preposition *of*, as in *a son of a king*. In Aramaic, the construct state forms just one type of genitive expression. One can also use the particle **דִּי** to express the same sense. Thus, the expression *a son of a king* might be expressed with either:

the construct state: **בַּר מֶ֫לֶךְ**
or
the particle **דִּי** *of*: **בַּר דִּי מֶ֫לֶךְ**

LANGUAGE INSIGHT

The syntax of the second type of genitive expression with דִּי is closer to the English equivalent in the sense that the Aramaic, like the English, uses a particle to express the relationship between nouns and because each noun is in the same state.

PRACTICE 1

Match the Aramaic to the English expression, using the following vocabulary: אָע *wood*, גַּף *wing*, דְּהַב *gold*, חֲסַף *clay*, נִדְבָּךְ *row*, נְהַר *river*, נוּר *fire*, נְשַׁר *eagle*, פֶּחָר *potter*, צְלֵם *image*.

a נְהַר דִּי נוּר
b גַּפִּין דִּי־נְשַׁר
c חֲסַף דִּי־פֶחָר
d צְלֵם דִּי־דְהַב
e נִדְבָּךְ דִּי־אָע

1 *image of gold*
2 *row of wood*
3 *river of fire*
4 *clay of a potter*
5 *wings of an eagle*

In these examples, the noun preceding דִּי is not in the determined state. In fact, the expression בְּרָא דִּי מַלְכָּא* would be unexpected. For the sense *the son of the king*, the construct state can be used, בַּר מַלְכָּא. Alternatively, another construction exists (quite common in later varieties of Aramaic, but also appearing in Biblical Aramaic): the word before דִּי bears a third person possessive suffix, agreeing in number and gender with the determined word that follows דִּי. This seems redundant to the English reader, but makes good Aramaic.

בְּרֵהּ דִּי מַלְכָּא — *the son of the king* (lit. *his son of the king*)

The construction is not used when the word following דִּי is in the absolute state. In the example, the 3ms suffix on בַּר agrees in number and gender with the following word *king*. If the expression had *queen* instead of *king*, then the suffix on *son* would be the 3fs: בְּרַהּ דִּי מַלְכְּתָא *the son of the queen*. Note the similar expressions where the gender of the pronoun depends on the noun following דִּי.

אִגַּרְתֵהּ דִּי מַלְכָּא — *the letter of the king*
אִגַּרְתַהּ דִּי מַלְכְּתָא — *the letter of the queen*

Note that the more literal translations of such phrases (e.g. *his letter of the king*; *her letter of the queen*; etc.) are not idiomatic in English and should be avoided.

PRACTICE 2

Supply the correct suffix to the following nouns.

a עַבְד______ דִּי־אֱלָהָא — *the servant of God* (lit. *the God*)
b שְׁמ______ דִּי־אֱלָהָא — *the name of God* (lit. *the God*)
c אֱלָהּ______ דִּי־שַׁדְרַךְ מֵישַׁךְ וַעֲבֵד נְגוֹ — *the God of Shadrach, Meshach, and Abednego*
d שָׁרְשׁ______ דִּי אִילָנָא — *the root of the tree*
e אֱלָה______ דִּי־דָנִיֵּאל — *the God of Daniel*

Consider the forms where one of the nouns is in the plural.

1 *the sons* (or *children*) *of the king:*

בְּנֵי מַלְכָּא

בְּנ֫וֹהִי דִּי מַלְכָּא

2 *the sons* (or *children*) *of the kings:*

בְּנֵי מַלְכַיָּא

בְּנֵיהֹם דִּי מַלְכַיָּא

3 *the son of the kings*

בַּר מַלְכַיָּא

בְּרְהֹם דִּי מַלְכַיָּא (?) (This form of *son* is unattested; cf. Syriac: berhōn.)

PRACTICE 3

Translate the following construct phrases into the expanded form of the genitive construction in Aramaic with the particle דִּי. In order to produce the form of the word with suffix, you may have to consult the glossary and find its form in the determined state.

Example: שֻׁם מַלְכָּא *the name of the king* → שְׁמֵהּ דִּי־מַלְכָּא

a בַּר מַלְכְּתָא *the son of the queen*

b מִלַּת אֱלָהָא *the word of God* (lit. *the God*)

c יוֹמֵי מַלְכַיָּא *the days of the kings*

d אִגְּרַת מַלְכָתָא *the letter of the queens*

e עַבְדֵי אֱלָהָא *the servants of God* (lit. *the God*)

LANGUAGE INSIGHT

Words that exhibit vowel changes in their inflection are presented in the glossary in the absolute and determined states. From the vowels of the determined state, it is possible to predict the form of a noun with suffix.

CULTURAL INSIGHT

The city of Haran (also spelled Harran and Ḥaran), located in northern Mesopotamia along a major east-west trade route, was home to many Arameans at least as far back as the 600s BCE when the Assyrians took a kind of census of the town (taking account of names, family ties, and sometimes the height of individuals). According to it, approximately 60 per cent of the residents had Aramaic names, 20 per cent had Assyrian names (see Brock, *Hidden Pearl*, 1:95). According to the Bible, the same city was where Abraham and his family stopped on their way to Canaan from Ur. In antiquity, the city was most famously associated with the worship of the moon god, called Śehr (in Aramaic) or Sin (in Assyrian). The popularity of this god is reflected in numerous ways. Nabonidus, the Babylonian monarch, was a devotee and his mother a priestess of the god. Haran continued to be associated with moon-worship well into the Islamic era (the last references to it being about a thousand years ago).

THE RELATIVE USE OF THE PARTICLE DĪ[Y]

The particle דִּי also functions as a relative pronoun, translated into English as *who, whose, whom, which, that, that which, where*, depending on the context. For example, note the following usages from the single verse of Daniel 2:11:

מִלְּתָא דִי־מַלְכָּא שָׁאֵל יַקִּירָה	*The matter* (lit. *word*) *which the king requests (is) hard.*
וְאָחֳרָן לָא אִיתַי דִּי יְחַוִּנַּהּ קֳדָם מַלְכָּא	*Another there is not who can explain it before the king,*
לָהֵן אֱלָהִין דִּי מְדָרְהוֹן עִם־בִּשְׂרָא לָא אִיתוֹהִי	*except gods whose dwellings are not among mortals.*

The English word *who*, when used as a relative pronoun, usually is used as the subject of a following verb. In Aramaic, דִּי can function in a similar way: כָּל־אֱנָשׁ דִּי יִשְׁמַע קָל קַרְנָא *any person who will hear the sound of the horn* …

The English word *whose* usually denotes a possessive or genitive relationship. Notice that in Aramaic such a relationship is often indicated by דִּי + noun + possessive suffix: דִּי ← מְדָר- ← הוֹן *whose dwellings*. This is redundant and awkward if rendered literally in English (cf. . . . *gods who their dwellings are not among mortals*). But, this is good Aramaic.

The English *whom* as a relative pronoun often functions as the grammatical object of the verb within a relative clause. For instance, in the clause אַרְיוֹךְ דִּי מַנִּי מַלְכָּא *Arioch, whom the king had appointed*, the Aramaic דִּי and English *whom* refer to Arioch, and both דִּי and *whom* are the object of the verb *appoint*. Like clauses where דִּי is translated *whose*, in these clauses there is usually a pronominal suffix that ends the דִּי-phrase. Note, for example, Dan 3:12 where the particle יָת marks the direct object: אִיתַי גֻּבְרִין יְהוּדָאיִן דִּי־מַנִּיתָ יָתְהוֹן *There are Judean men whom you have appointed* … (More literally and unidiomatically this could be rendered in English: *There are Judean men whom you have appointed them.*)

Where דִּי is translated as *which* or *that* it can function either as the subject of the verb in the relative clause or its object. For example, in the short phrase אִילָנָא דִּי חֲזַיְתָ דִּי רְבָה וּתְקִף *the tree that you saw, that grew great and strong* (Dan 4:17), both דִּי pronouns refer back to the tree (אִילָנָא). But, the first דִּי functions as the object of the immediately following verb חֲזַיְתָ *you saw* and the second דִּי functions as the subject of the last two verbs רְבָה *grew great* and תְקִף *(grew) strong.*

The particle also combines with the interrogative pronouns מַן *who?* and מָה *what?* to create the expanded relative pronouns מַן־דִּי *who, whom* (or *whoever, whomever*) and מָה־דִּי *what* (or *whatever*), as in הוֹדַע לְמַלְכָּא מָה־דִי לֶהֱוֵא *he made known to the king what would be.*

Rarely, the relative דִּי will function as the subject of a verb in the relative clause and refer to a second person pronoun. In these cases, the verbs that follow within the relative clause are also in the second person, though in English we would express the same verbs in the third person. For example, note Dan 4:19: אַנְתְּה־הוּא מַלְכָּא דִּי רְבַית וּתְקֵפְתְּ *It is you, O king, who has grown* (lit. *you have grown*) *and become strong* (lit. *you have become strong*).

In both earlier and later Aramaic, the particle דִּי combines with the lamed preposition and a suffixed pronoun to create expressions like דִּילִי that express possession *which (is) mine*. When combined with a preceding noun, the expression can be translated with just the English possessive adjective: בְּעִירָא דִּילִי *my livestock*, יַמִּינָא דִּילָךְ *your right hand*, כָּהֲנָא דִּילֵהּ *his priest*. In other cases, it can function as the predicate of a non-verbal sentence, as in דִּילִי כֹּל אַרְעָא *all the earth (is) mine*.

> **CULTURAL INSIGHT**
>
> The Aramean ruler Bar Rakib of Sam'al (many miles to the west of Haran) is pictured in an inscription seated beneath a crescent moon superimposed on a disc (presumably the full moon). On one side of the crescent/full moon symbol it reads: mr'y b'l ḥrn (with Biblical Aramaic vowels and pronunciation: מָרְאִי בְּעֵל חָרָן) *my master (is) Lord of Ḥaran*; on the other side of the symbol it reads: 'nh brrkb br pnm(w) (אֲנָה בַּרְרָכִב בַּר פנמו) *I (am) Bar Rakib, son of Panamuwa* (vocalization unclear). The implication, of course, is that Bar Rakib worshipped Śehr, the moon god.

CONJUNCTIVE AND OTHER USES OF THE PARTICLE DĪʸ

In addition, דִּי can be used as a conjunction to connect phrases together, especially after verbs of knowing, saying, or perception, like English *that* in *I know that you are buying time*, or *I said that I would find it*, the former of which is a direct quotation from Daniel 2:8: יָדַע אֲנָה דִּי עִדָּנָא אַנְתּוּן זָבְנִין *I know that you are buying time.*

The particle can also indicate a notion of purpose or result and be translated *so that*, as in:

וּמָה חַשְׁחָן ... לֶהֱוֵא מִתְיְהֵב לְהֹם ... דִּי לֶהֱוֹא מְהַקְרְבִין נִיחוֹחִין	*and whatever is needed … let it be given to them … so that they may make soothing offerings.*

Sometimes the particle also indicates cause and can be translated *because* or *because of*, as in Dan 2:20, where דִּי is used also as a genitive marker (*of*) and as a relative pronoun (*which*):

לֶהֱוֵא שְׁמֵהּ דִּי־אֱלָהָא מְבָרַךְ מִן־עָלְמָא וְעַד־עָלְמָא דִּי חָכְמְתָא וּגְבוּרְתָא דִּי לֵהּ־הִיא

Let the name of God (lit. *the God*) *be blessed forever and ever* (lit. *from the eternity until the eternity*) *because of the wisdom and the power which are his.*

Note the similar expression in Dan 2:23:

לָךְ אֱלָהּ־אֲבָהָתִי מְהוֹדֵא וּמְשַׁבַּח אֲנָה דִּי חָכְמְתָא וּגְבוּרְתָא יְהַבְתְּ לִי
You, God of my fathers, I thank and praise because of the wisdom and power you have given to me.

The particle also combines with prepositions to form conjunctions, as in כְּדִי *when, as soon as*; מִן־דִּי *because*; עַד דִּי *until*; כָּל־קֳבֵל דִּי *because* or *in as much as*.

The extremely versatile particle דִּי can also indicate direct speech, especially when it follows a verb for speaking. In these cases it is not translated, as in אֱדַיִן גֻּבְרַיָּא אִלֵּךְ אָמְרִין דִּי לָא נְהַשְׁכַּח *Then, these men said 'we will not find …'* (Dan 6:6). Because it can also mean *that* after verbs of speaking, there is sometimes ambiguity as to whether the particle is indicating direct or indirect speech.

In summary, דִּי can be used like a preposition and translated *of*, like a relative pronoun and translated *that, which, who (whose, whom), where*, and like a conjunction and translated *so that, because*. It also can mark direct speech and so be left untranslated.

PRACTICE 4

Translate דִּי in the following sentences.

Example:	אֱלָהָךְ דִּי אַנְתְּ פָּלַח לֵהּ	*your God whom you serve* (lit. *you serve him*)
a	וְכָל־חֲבָל לָא־הִשְׁתְּכַח	*no harm was found* (lit. *every harm was not found*)
	בֵּהּ דִּי הֵימִן בֵּאלָהֵהּ	*in him* ______________________ *he trusted in his God.*
b	וְהַיְתִיו גֻּבְרַיָּא אִלֵּךְ	*bring these men*
	דִּי־אֲכַלוּ קַרְצוֹהִי דִּי־דָנִיֵּאל	______________________ *slandered Daniel* (lit. *ate the morsels of Daniel*)
c	אֲמַר לֵהּ דִּי־הַשְׁכַּחַת גְּבַר	*he said to him 'I have found a person*
	מִן־בְּנֵי גָלוּתָא דִּי יְהוּד	*from the exiles* ______________________ *Judah*
	דִּי פִשְׁרָא לְמַלְכָּא יְהוֹדַע	______________________ *will make known the interpretation to the king'*
d	שְׁמָהָתְהוֹן שְׁאֵלְנָא ... דִּי נִכְתֻּב	*their names we asked ...* ______________________ *we might write*
	שֻׁם גֻּבְרַיָּא דִּי בְרָאשֵׁיהֹם	*the names of the men* ______________________ *were in charge* (lit. *in their heads*)
e	אֱלָהָא דִּי־נִשְׁמְתָךְ בִּידֵהּ	*and God* (lit. *the God*), *in* ______________________ *hand (is) your breath*
f	וְלֵאלָהֵי כַסְפָּא־וְדַהֲבָא ...	*and the gods of silver and gold ...*
	דִּי לָא חָזַיִן וְלָא־שָׁמְעִין	______________________ *do not see and do not hear*
	וְלָא יָדְעִין שַׁבַּחְתָּ	*and do not know you have praised*
g	הֲלָא דָא־הִיא בָּבֶל רַבְּתָא	*is this not great Babel*
	דִּי־אֲנָה בֱנַיְתַהּ	______________________ *I built* (lit. *I built it*)?
h	לָא אִיתַי דִּי יְחַוִּנַּהּ	*there is not one* ______________________ *can describe it*
i	דָּנִיֵּאל דִּי שְׁמֵהּ בֵּלְטְשַׁאצַּר	*Daniel* ______________________ *name was Belteshazzar*
j	וְהוֹדַעְנָא לְמַלְכָּא דִּי יְבַקַּר	*we made known to the king* ______________________ *he might search*

CULTURAL INSIGHT

The homeland of the Arameans (i.e. where they first appear in the historical record), in northern Mesopotamia and western Syria, was the location of several semi-independent kingdoms in the 900s–700s BCE. Inscriptions from these sites tell us something of the rulers and their conflicts with each other and the nearby superpowers. While initially submitting to Assyrian suzerainty, many of the kingdoms periodically rebelled. Eventually the Assyrians conquered them and killed or deported their inhabitants. The kingdoms (and their cities) are mentioned in the Bible when the Rab-shakeh of Sennacherib speaks to the people of Jerusalem at the time of Hezekiah (see 2K 18:34, 19:12–13; Isa 36:19, 37:12–13). The people of Beth-Eden, Gozan, Hamath, Arpad, Haran are presented as the epitome of the conquered. In various ways, the Rab-shakeh asks 'Where are these people?' and 'Where are the gods of these peoples?' and 'Have the gods of these peoples stopped the hand of the Assyrians?' The question 'Where are they?' likely implies that the Aramean peoples had been deported to another part of the empire; something similar was happening to the northern Israelite tribes at the time the Rab-shakeh was speaking or shortly after.

THE PARTICLE QŎBEL

The word **קֳבֵל** combines with different particles to form compound prepositions and conjunctions. With a preceding lamed preposition it has the form **לָקֳבֵל** and is used as a preposition *opposite, according to, due to* (e.g. **וְכָתְבָן לָקֳבֵל נֶבְרַשְׁתָּא** *they (the fingers) wrote before the lamp* Dan 5:5; **מַלְכְּתָא לָקֳבֵל מִלֵּי מַלְכָּא … עַלַּלַת** *the queen, due to the words of the king …, entered* Dan 5:10). This compound preposition can, itself, be preceded by the preposition **כְּ** to form **כָּל־קֳבֵל** which is usually translated *because of* or *inasmuch as* (e.g. **כָּל־קֳבֵל דְּנָה בֵּהּ זִמְנָא קְרִבוּ גֻּבְרִין** *because of this, at that time men approached* Dan 3:8). It has a similar translation when it is followed by **דִּי** and used as a conjunction (e.g. **כָּל־קֳבֵל דִּי רוּחַ יַתִּירָה … הִשְׁתְּכַחַת בֵּהּ** *because a great spirit … was found in him* Dan 5:12). In other contexts it can be translated *although* or *despite* (e.g. **לָא הַשְׁפֵּלְתְּ לִבְבָךְ כָּל־קֳבֵל דִּי כָל־דְּנָה יְדַעְתָּ** *you did not lower your heart* (i.e. *humble yourself*) *despite all you knew* Dan 5:22). (Note that the first part of **כָּל־קֳבֵל** is not the word *all* but rather the kaph and lamed prepositions.)

Reading

Identify the words not translated for you and look these up in the glossary (using the notes below each verse) and then supply the correct translations in the blanks. Identify the singular absolute form of nouns/adjectives and the root consonants for verbs.

DANIEL 6:21

a וּכְמִקְרְבֵהּ לְגֻבָּא לְדָנִיֵּאל
b בְּקָל עֲצִיב זְעִק
c עָנֵה מַלְכָּא וְאָמַר לְדָנִיֵּאל
d דָּנִיֵּאל עֲבֵד אֱלָהָא חַיָּא
e אֱלָהָךְ דִּי אַנְתְּה פָּלַח לֵהּ בִּתְדִירָא
f הַיִכִל לְשֵׁיזָבוּתָךְ מִן־אַרְיָוָתָא

a *And when he* (i.e. the king) *approached to the* ______________________ *of Daniel*
b *with a despairing* ______________________ *he* (i.e. the king) *cried out*
c ______________________ ______________________ *and* ______________________ *to* ______________________
d '______________________, ______________________ *of the living* ______________________,
e *your* ______________________ *whom you* ______________________ *continuously*
f *is he able to save you* ______________________ ______________________?'

Note that in line b the adjective **עֲצִיב** *despairing* modifies the preceding noun. In line c, the two verb forms **עָנֵה** and **אָמַר** are participles but are translated as if they were suffix-conjugation forms. In line e, the phrase **בִּתְדִירָא** is made up of the preposition bet followed by the word **תְּדִירָא** but is used like the English adverb *continuously*.

DANIEL 6:22

a אֱדַיִן דָּנִיֵּאל עִם־מַלְכָּא מַלִּל
b מַלְכָּא לְעָלְמִין חֱיִי

a ______________________, ______________________ spoke
______________________ ______________________:

b 'O king, for ______________________ live!'

DANIEL 6:23

a אֱלָהִי שְׁלַח מַלְאֲכֵהּ
b וּסְגַר פֻּם אַרְיָוָתָא
c וְלָא חַבְּלוּנִי
d כָּל־קֳבֵל דִּי קֳדָמוֹהִי
e זָכוּ הִשְׁתְּכַחַת לִי
f וְאַף קֳדָמָיךְ מַלְכָּא
g חֲבוּלָה לָא עַבְדֵת

a 'My ______________________ ______________________ his ______________________

b and he ______________________ the ______________________ of the ______________________

c and they did not injure me

d since ______________________ ______________________

e ______________________ was accredited to me (lit. was found to me)

f and also ______________________ ______________________, O king,

g a ______________________ I did not commit.'

In line d, the sequence of particles כָּל־קֳבֵל דִּי is translated *since*. The blank spaces correspond to the preposition plus pronominal suffix קֳדָמוֹהִי.

Test yourself

Write the underlined English phrases in Aramaic, filling in the blanks of the Aramaic text (Dan 2:8–9). Use the particle דִּי (= that) and the words in parentheses, inflecting the words according to the context. English *the* presupposes the Aramaic determined state. Nouns and adjectives whose inflection is ambiguous in the absolute state are also presented in the determined state. Pay attention to the word order of the Aramaic and how it differs from the English translation.

a וְעָנֵה מַלְכָּא וְאָמַר מִן־יַצִּיב יָדַע אֲנָה
b ______________________ אַנְתּוּן זָבְנִין
c כָּל־קֳבֵל דִּי חֲזֵיתוֹן דִּי אַזְדָּא מִנִּי ______________________
d ______________________ לָא תְהוֹדְעֻנַּנִי
e חֲדָה־הִיא דָתְכוֹן

f וּמִלָּה ______________ וּ ______________ הִזְ מִנְתּוּן

(= הִזְדְּמִנְתּוּן) לְמֵאמַר קָדָמַי

g עַד דִּי ______________ יִשְׁתַּנֵּא

h לָהֵן ______________ אֱמַ֫רוּ לִי

i וְאִנְדַּע ______________ תְּהַחֲוֻ֫נַּנִי

- **a** *And, the king answered and said: With certainty I know*
- **b** *<u>that</u> you are buying <u>time</u>* (literally, *<u>that the time</u>* (**עִדָּן**) *you are buying*)
- **c** *for, you have seen that I am assured over <u>the matter</u>* (literally, *assured by me (is) <u>the matter</u>* (**מִלָּה**))
- **d** *<u>that if the dream</u> (if =* **הֵן**; *dream =* **חֵ֫לֶם** (det. **חֶלְמָא**)) *you cannot make known*
- **e** *there is one verdict for you* (literally, *one is your verdict*)
- **f** *A <u>deceitful</u>* (**כְּדַב** (det. **כִּדְבָא**)) *and <u>corrupt</u>* (**שְׁחִית**) *word you have conspired to speak before me*
- **g** *until circumstances change* (lit. *until <u>the time</u>* (**עִדָּן**) *is changed*).
- **h** *Therefore, <u>the dream</u>* (**חֵ֫לֶם** (det. **חֶלְמָא**)) *speak to me*
- **i** *so I may know <u>that its interpretation</u>* (**פְּשַׁר** (det. **פִּשְׁרָא**)) *you are able to tell me.*

Suggestions for further study

Memorize the words you looked up in the Reading exercises. Review the words and forms you have learned so far and attempt to read as much of Daniel 6 as you can from the Reading exercises before looking at the translations.

SELF-CHECK

I CAN...
recognize the existential particle ʾīʸtay *there is (are, was, were)*
identify the genitive use of the particle dīʸ *of*
identify the relative use of the particle dīʸ *who, whose, whom, which, where*
identify the conjunctive use of the particle dīʸ *that*

11 Pə ʿal prefix conjugation, imperative, infinitive and identifying the direct object

In this unit you will learn how to:
- **translate the prefix conjugation, imperative, and infinitive**
- **recognize and produce the form of these same verb forms in the pəʿal**
- **find the direct object of the verb**

In this unit you will read:
- **Daniel 3:8–12**

Grammar

REVIEW OF THE SUFFIX CONJUGATION

As described in Unit 8, the suffix conjugation expresses events or actions in the past or present. The conjugation is marked by suffixes to a basic root. The suffixes are almost always the same. At the same time, a single verb can appear in different stems (e.g. the pəʿal, paʿʿel, haphʿel) with slightly different senses. For example, the verb **קטל** may appear in the pəʿal as a 2ms: **קְטַלְתְּ** *you killed*; in the paʿʿel 2ms: **קַטֵּלְתְּ** *you killed many*; and in the haphʿel: **הַקְטֵלְתְּ** *you caused (someone else) to kill*. The different verbal forms are fairly consistent throughout the paradigm (e.g. the base **-קְטַל** is found for most pəʿal forms); the primary exceptions are the 3fs and 1cs forms: **קִטְלַת** *she killed* and **קִטְלֵת** *I killed*.

PRACTICE 1

Write the following phrases in Aramaic, using the following words אֲמַר *to say*, לְ *to*, מִלָּה *word*, מַלְכָּה *queen*, שְׁלַח *to send*, שְׁמַע *to hear*.

Example: *he heard the word* → שְׁמַע מִלְּתָא

- **a** *they* (m.p.) *heard the word*
- **b** *I heard the word of the queen*
- **c** *the queen said to them (m.p.)*
- **d** *you* (m.s.) *sent to us a word*
- **e** *we said to them (f.p.) a word*
- **f** *I sent a word to the queen*
- **g** *you* (m.p.) *said to the queen a word*
- **h** *I said to her*

i *you (f.s.) sent a word to him*
j *we heard the word*

THE MEANING OF THE PREFIX CONJUGATION

The prefix conjugation can communicate a future event or action (e.g. **וּפִשְׁרָא נְחַוֵּא** *and the interpretation we will declare* Dan 2:4). In addition, it can indicate what is wished for, possible, or obligatory (i.e. what is communicated with English constructions with *can, could, may, must*, and *should*, as in **דִּי־פְשַׁר חֶלְמָא יְהוֹדְעֻנַּנִי** *so that the interpretation of the dream they might/could make known to me* Dan 4:3). The prefix conjugation can also imply that events or actions are generally true, as in the final verb of Dan 4:14: **לְמַן־דִּי יִצְבֵּא יִתְּנִנַּהּ** *to whomever he wishes, he gives it*. (The first verb, **יִצְבֵּא**, might be translated more literally, but also more awkwardly, *he should wish*, the verb form here implying possibility).

In the book of Daniel especially, the prefix conjugation can, like the participle, also indicate actions done repeatedly or continuously, even in the past. Note that this is not always reflected explicitly by the English verb alone. In Dan 4:2, the verb **דחל** is in the prefix conjugation though the context clearly indicates the past: **חֵלֶם חֲזֵית וִידַחֲלִנַּנִי** *a dream I saw and it frightened me*. Although not reflected in the English translation, the implication of the Aramaic verb would seem to be that Nebuchadnezzar's dream was scaring him all the time. The translation may be nuanced with an adverb . . . *it frightened me continuously*, though even this seems somewhat awkward in English and an even more periphrastic translation can be imagined . . . *it frightened me and I could not cease thinking of it*. For pedagogical purposes, translations in this grammar will attempt to be simple (e.g. *frightened me*) and to indicate the nuance of such verbs in parentheses, as in . . . *it frightened me* (lit. *it was frightening me*). However, where the prefix conjugation occurs in what seems to be a subordinate clause, it is easier in English to convey its continuous sense, as with the verb **בהל** in Dan 4:16: **אֱדַיִן דָּנִיֵּאל . . אֶשְׁתּוֹמַם כְּשָׁעָה חֲדָה וְרַעְיֹנֹהִי יְבַהֲלֻנֵּהּ** *Then Daniel . . . was dumb-founded for one moment, his thoughts terrifying him.*

Some exceptional uses do occur. For example, in rare cases, the prefix conjugation appears where we would expect the suffix conjugation, as in **יְקוּם . . . אֲזַל** (*the king*) *arose* (pref. conj. of **קום**) . . . *(and) went* (Dan 6:20).

CULTURAL INSIGHT

Dreams and dream interpretation figure prominently in the book of Daniel (especially the Aramaic chapters 2 and 4). Similar motifs also seem to appear frequently in other Aramaic literature, including the Genesis Apocryphon (some of which is presented in Unit 23) and another, earlier inscription from a place just east of the Jordan river, called Deir Alla. The Deir Alla inscription represents portions of the **ספר בלעם בר בער** (according to Biblical Aramaic pronunciation **סְפַר בִּלְעָם בַּר בְּעֹר**) the book of Bal'am, son of Be'or. The same figure features in the book of Numbers (from the Bible) where he makes prophecies. In the Deir Alla inscription, whose language seems to be a mixture of Hebrew and Aramaic, Bal'am is described as a **חזה** (in Biblical Aramaic **חָזֵה**) *seer* to whom is revealed in a night vision the future destruction of the world by the Shaddayin, a group of deities. The singular form of this name, Shaddai (Hebrew **שַׁדַּי**), refers to God in the Bible (e.g. Exod 6:3), where it is often translated into English as *Almighty*.

THE Pəʿ AL PREFIX CONJUGATION

The form of the prefix conjugation is characterized by a combination of prefixes and suffixes. Predicting the correct forms of the verb in the various stems is relatively uncomplicated if you know the root, the theme vowel, and the series of prefixes/suffixes for each person/number/gender.

The theme vowel is the vowel that appears in the last syllable of the 3ms form. For the paʿʿel and haphʿel stems, every root has the same theme vowel e (ֵ), which alternates with i (ִ). If the third consonant is a guttural (א ,ה ,ח ,ע) or ר, the theme vowel is a (ַ), in accordance with the phonological rules of Aramaic (see Units 6 and 8).

In the pə ʿal, the theme vowel is less predictable. The most common is the short u vowel. This is found with roots like **כתב** (*to write*). Other roots have a short a, especially where the third root consonant is a guttural as in the roots connected to hearing (**שמע**) and speaking (**אמר**), but the theme vowel is a in other roots as well, like the one that indicates dressing (**לבשׁ**), or the root indicating wielding power (**שׁלט**). Usually, roots with a suffix conjugation like **שׁלט** with e (ֵ) as the second vowel (e.g. **שְׁלֵט**), have prefix conjugation forms with an a theme vowel (e.g. **יִשְׁלַט**).

Considering the following paradigms, wherever **כתב** has a u, verbs like **אמר** and **שׁלט** take a. They are otherwise completely analogous to **כתב**. A very few irregular roots, like **נפל** (*to fall*) and **נתן** (*to give*), have a theme vowel of e (ֵ) in the pəʿal; on **נפל** and **נתן**, see the following unit on I-weak roots.

The following paradigm isolates the distinctive suffixes and prefixes of each form of the prefix conjugation as well as the forms of verbs with an a theme vowel.

	כתב	distinctive features	שמע	שׁלט	נתן
3ms	יִכְתֻּב	י כְתֻּב	יִשְׁמַע	יִשְׁלַט	יִנְתֵּן
3fs	תִּכְתֻּב	תִּ כְתֻּב	תִּשְׁמַע	תִּשְׁלַט	תִּנְתֵּן
2ms	תִּכְתֻּב	תִּ כְתֻּב	תִּשְׁמַע	תִּשְׁלַט	תִּנְתֵּן
2fs	תִּכְתְּבִין	תִּ כְתְּב ִין	תִּשְׁמְעִין	תִּשְׁלְטִין	תִּנְתְּנִין
1cs	אֶכְתֻּב	אֶ כְתֻּב	אֶשְׁמַע	אֶשְׁלַט	אֶנְתֵּן
3mp	יִכְתְּבוּן	י כְתְּב וּן	יִשְׁמְעוּן	יִשְׁלְטוּן	יִנְתְּנוּן
3fp	יִכְתְּבָן	י כְתְּב ָן	יִשְׁמְעָן	יִשְׁלְטָן	יִנְתְּנָן
2mp	תִּכְתְּבוּן	תִּ כְתְּב וּן	תִּשְׁמְעוּן	תִּשְׁלְטוּן	תִּנְתְּנוּן
2fp	תִּכְתְּבָן	תִּ כְתְּב ָן	תִּשְׁמְעָן	תִּשְׁלְטָן	תִּנְתְּנָן
1cp	נִכְתֻּב	נִ כְתֻּב	נִשְׁמַע	נִשְׁלַט	נִנְתֵּן

The prefix vowel is the vowel of the prefix. In the pəʿal it is usually i as in the examples. Where the first root consonant is a guttural (א ,ה ,ח ,ע) or ר, the prefix vowel is different. With aleph it is ē as in **יֵאמַר** *he will say*. Where the first consonant is he, the vowel is ɛ as in **תֶּהֱוֵה** *she will be*. With ḥet the prefix vowel is a as in **יַחְלְפוּן** *they will pass*, though in other verbs it might have been ɛ (e.g. **יֶחֱדֵא*** *he will rejoice* and **תֶּחֱזֵא*** *you* (m.s.) *will live*). With ʿayin, it is either ɛ as in **יֶעְדֵּה** *it will pass away* or a as in **תַּעֲבֵד** *you will do*. In both **תֶּהֱוֵה** *she will be* and **תַּעֲבֵד** *you will* *do*, the guttural itself is followed by a hateph-vowel for euphonic purposes and reflects a later pronunciation; likely in the language of the writers the words had just two syllables. In the forms with suffixed morphemes, this hateph-vowel becomes a full vowel, as with תַּעַבְדוּן *you will do*; this again is a later phenomenon and for earlier readers, this form was likely pronounced תַּעְבְּדוּן*.

PRACTICE 2

Write out the paradigm to the verb כתב several times until it becomes familiar. Then, identify the person, number, and gender of each prefix conjugation form by simply looking at the prefixes and suffixes. Finally, identify the verb, look it up in the glossary and list its definition.

Example: תִּלְבַּשׁ → 3fs or 2ms לבשׁ *to wear*

a תִּשְׁלְחָן
b יִסְגֻּד
c יִפְלְחוּן
d אֶסְבַּר
e תִּשְׁפְּרִין
f נִסְגֻּד
g תִּסְגְּדוּן
h נִשְׁפַּר
i יִקְטְלוּן
j תִּלְבְּשׁוּן

The 2fs, 3m/fp, and 2m/fp forms of the prefix conjugation also occur with a full vowel after the second root consonant and without their final nun.

תִּכְתֻּ֫בִי	*may you write*
יִכְתֻּ֫בוּ	*let them write*
*יִכְתֻּ֫בָה	*let them write*
תִּכְתֻּ֫בוּ	*may you write*
*תִּכְתֻּ֫בָה	*may you write*

In these cases the prefix conjugation is called the jussive and explicitly conveys the speaker's wish or will. The jussives are usually translated *may you* . . . or *let him* . . . The other prefix conjugation forms (e.g. יִכְתֻּב and תִּכְתֻּב) can also be considered jussives translated in an analogous way (*let him* . . . or *let her* . . . etc.), if they convey the speaker's will or wish. But, these do not exhibit a special form. With the exception of the 2fs, the singular jussives cannot be formally distinguished from the regular prefix conjugation since they have the same graphic and phonetic form. Nevertheless, when the verb is preceded by a negative adverb (i.e. *not*), it is easy to discriminate between the jussive and regular prefix conjugation: the jussive will use the negative adverb אַל and the regular prefix conjugation will use the adverb לָא. With אַל the jussive usually has the sense of a negative imperative (e.g. לְחַכִּימֵי בָבֶל אַל־ תְּהוֹבֵד *do not destroy the sages of Babel*).

CULTURAL INSIGHT

In around 800 BCE, the king of Hamath, Zakkur, made an inscription in Aramaic, dedicated to בעל שמין *lord of heavens*, describing how various neighbouring kings had attacked him. In his plight, trapped in his own city, Zakkur says that he raised his hands to בעל שמין (in Biblical Aramaic בְּעֵל שְׁמַיִן) *and B'el-Shmayin answered me . . . through seers and diviners . . . (saying): 'Do no fear . . . I will deliver you'*. The penultimate phrase (*do not fear*) contains a jussive verb: **אל תזחל**, though it would be written differently in Biblical Aramaic, **אַל תִּדְחַל**.

PRACTICE 3

Write the following phrases in Aramaic, using the following vocabulary: הֵיכַל *palace*; לְ *to*; מֶ֫לֶךְ (det. מַלְכָּא) *king*; סגד *to worship*; פִּתְגָם *answer*; קטל *to kill*; שׁלח *to send*; שׁמע *to listen*. The prefix conjugation verbs without gutturals take the u theme vowel, while those with a guttural take a. Be sure to distinguish the regular (or indicative) form of the verb from the jussive and use אַל + jussive for negative commands (e.g. *do not . . .*) and לָא + regular prefix conjugation for other negative statements.

- **a** *Do not kill* (m.s.).
- **b** *You* (m.p.) *will not worship.*
- **c** *Do not listen* (f.s.).
- **d** *They* (m.p.) *will not send an answer to the king.*
- **e** *I will serve in the palace.*

THE PəʿAL IMPERATIVE

All the stems have imperatives, whose function is largely analogous to the imperative's function in English, that is, commands.

The forms of the imperatives are usually based on the 2nd-person forms of the jussive verb. Essentially, they are shortened versions of these forms. Therefore, from the pəʿal 2fs jussive form **תִּכְתֻּ֫בִי** we get the pəʿal f.s. imperative **כְּתֻ֫בִי** *write!* The taw prefix has been eliminated. Compare the prefix conjugations forms with the jussive and imperatives for the following verbs:

	כתב			שׁמע			שׁלט		
	prefix	jus.	imv.	prefix	jus.	imv.	prefix	jus.	imv.
m.s.	תִּכְתֻּב	תִּכְתֻּב	כְּתֻב	תִּשְׁמַע	תִּשְׁמַע	שְׁמַע	תִּשְׁלַט	תִּשְׁלַט	שְׁלַט
f.s.	תִּכְתְּבִין	תִּכְתֻּ֫בִי	כְּתֻ֫בִי	תִּשְׁמְעִין	תִּשְׁמַ֫עִי	שְׁמַ֫עִי	תִּשְׁלְטִין	תִּשְׁלַ֫טִי	שְׁלַ֫טִי
m.p.	תִּכְתְּבוּן	תִּכְתֻּ֫בוּ	כְּתֻ֫בוּ	תִּשְׁמְעוּן	תִּשְׁמַ֫עוּ	שְׁמַ֫עוּ	תִּשְׁלְטוּן	תִּשְׁלַ֫טוּ	שְׁלַ֫טוּ
f.p.	תִּכְתְּבָן	תִּכְתֻּ֫בָה	כְּתֻ֫בָה	תִּשְׁמְעָן	תִּשְׁמַ֫עָה	שְׁמַ֫עָה	תִּשְׁלְטָן	תִּשְׁלַ֫טָה	שְׁלַ֫טָה

PRACTICE 4

Distinguish the imperatives from the suffix conjugations by circling the imperative. For consistency, the English translations are presented in the order of the finite verb/imperative, irrespective of the order of Aramaic forms.

a	כְּתַ֫בוּ	כְּתֻ֫בוּ	*they wrote/write!*
b	אֲכַ֫ל	אֱכֻ֫ל	*he ate/eat!*
c	סְגִ֫דָה	סְגֻ֫דָה	*they bowed down/bow down!*
d	אֲכַ֫לְתְּ	אֱכֻ֫לִי	*you ate/eat!*
e	שְׁבַ֫קוּ	שְׁבֻ֫קוּ	*they left (it alone)/leave (it alone)!*

Notice that those roots with a guttural (or resh) as a third root consonant often have suffix-conjugation and imperatival forms that are identical or very similar: **שְׁמַ֫עוּ** *they heard* or *hear!* and **אֲמַ֫רוּ** *they said* vs. **אֱמַ֫רוּ** *say!*

THE Pəʿal INFINITIVE

In English, the infinitive is the verbal noun that often appears after the preposition *to* and which is listed at the head of dictionary entries, like *be*. The expression *to be* is composed of the preposition *to* followed by the infinitive *be*. In Aramaic, as in English, the infinitive is preceded by a preposition, often the preposition לְ *to*, though this is not always grammatically necessary. The infinitive, also as in English, can function syntactically as a noun.

Each stem in Aramaic has its own infinitive form. In the pəʿal, the infinitive has an initial mem prefixed to the root. The vowel within the root is usually a. So, the infinitive of **כתב** is **מִכְתַּב** *to write*. Where the verb is from a III-aleph/waw/yod root, the vowel is ē, as in **מִגְלֵא** *to reveal*. As with other nouns, the infinitive can take a pronominal suffix. The suffix can either express the subject of the verb's action or its object. Compare these two expressions (the latter of which is drawn from Targum Onqelos, though presented with the vowels of Biblical Aramaic):

כְּמִקְרְבֵהּ לְגֻבָּא	*when he drew near to the den* – suffix marks the subject
לְמִקְטְלִי	*to kill me* – suffix marks the object

PRACTICE 5

Identify the infinitives (and their roots) in the following phrases and then translate the entire phrases, looking up words you do not recognize in the glossary.

a מַלְכָּא שְׁלַח לְמִכְנַשׁ סְגְנַיָּא

b יְכֵלְתָּ לְמִגְלֵא רָזָא דְנָה

c מָה טָב לְמֶעְבַּד תַּעַבְדוּן

d לָא־כָהֲלִין כְּתָבָא לְמִקְרֵא

e כְּמִצְבְּיֵהּ עָבֵד בְּחֵיל שְׁמַיָּא

IDENTIFYING THE DIRECT OBJECT

The item that receives the action of a verb is called the direct object. In the sentence *The queen wrote the book*, *the book* is the direct object. *The queen* is the subject. In Aramaic, word order is freer than in English and the direct object can come before or after the verb. There are several ways that a direct object may appear in a sentence. In Biblical Aramaic, if the direct object is a noun or noun phrase, it may either appear without any marker or after the preposition lamed. Where it appears after lamed, the preposition is not translated.

כְּתָבָא אֶקְרֵא
I will read ← the writing
I will read the writing

לָא־ יִפְלְחוּן לְכָל־ אֱלָהּ
god ← (to) any ← they will serve ← not
they will not serve any god

In addition, in other dialects of Aramaic, the particle יָת is used before a direct object, as in Targum Onqelos to Gen 1:1: בְּרָא יוי יָת שְׁמַיָּא *The Lord made the heavens*. If a direct object is a pronoun, then the pronoun can appear in a suffixed form attached directly to the verb (as in סַתְרֵהּ *he destroyed it*); after the preposition lamed (as in לֵהּ יִפְלְחוּן *they will serve him*); or after the particle יָת (as in מַנִּיתָ יָתְהוֹן *you appointed them*). In addition, the 3mp independent object pronoun הִמּוֹ *them* and its variant הִמּוֹן appear as direct objects without a preceding preposition or particle, as in תְּקָרֵב הִמּוֹ *you will offer them*.

PRACTICE 6

Match the translation to the Aramaic, paying close attention to the direct objects. Look up the words you do not recognize in the glossary.

a	*The king made an image of gold.*	**1**	לָא חַבְּלוּנִי
b	*They did not harm me.*	**2**	אַנְתְּ פָּלַח־לֵהּ
c	*Daniel blessed the God of heaven.*	**3**	מַלְכָּא עֲבַד צְלֵם דִּי־דְהַב
d	*You serve him.*	**4**	תִּשְׁמְעוּן קָל קַרְנָא
e	*You will hear the sound of the horn.*	**5**	דָּנִיֵּאל בָּרִךְ לֶאֱלָהּ שְׁמַיָּא

Reading

Translate the following passage from Daniel 3:8–12, looking up the words you do not know in the glossary and using the notes that follow the text.

DANIEL 3:8

בֵּהּ־זִמְנָא קְרִבוּ גֻּבְרִין כַּשְׂדָּאִין וַאֲכַלוּ קַרְצֵיהוֹן דִּי יְהוּדָיֵא

DANIEL 3:9

עֲנוֹ וְאָמְרִין לִנְבוּכַדְנֶצַּר מַלְכָּא מַלְכָּא לְעָלְמִין חֱיִי

DANIEL 3:10

a אַנְתְּ מַלְכָּא שָׂמְתָּ טְעֵם דִּי כָל־אֱנָשׁ דִּי־יִשְׁמַע קָל קַרְנָא
b מַשְׁרֹקִיתָא קַיתְרֹס שַׂבְּכָא פְסַנְתֵּרִין וְסוּפֹּנְיָה
c וְכֹל זְנֵי זְמָרָא יִפֵּל וְיִסְגֻּד לְצֶלֶם דַּהֲבָא

DANIEL 3:11

וּמַן־דִּי־לָא יִפֵּל וְיִסְגֻּד יִתְרְמֵא לְגוֹא־אַתּוּן נוּרָא יָקִדְתָּא

DANIEL 3:12

a אִיתַי גֻּבְרִין יְהוּדָאִין דִּי־מַנִּיתָ יָתְהוֹן עַל־עֲבִידַת מְדִינַת בָּבֶל שַׁדְרַךְ מֵישַׁךְ וַעֲבֵד נְגוֹ
b גֻּבְרַיָּא אִלֵּךְ לָא־שָׂמוּ עֲלָיךְ מַלְכָּא טְעֵם
c לֵאלָהָיךְ לָא פָלְחִין וּלְצֶלֶם דַּהֲבָא דִּי הֲקֵימְתָּ לָא סָגְדִין

Daniel 3:8

בֵּהּ־זִמְנָא – *in that time* The initial two words form a temporal expression, though it might be more literally rendered *in it, the time*. This kind of redundant use of pronominal suffixes is typical of Aramaic (similar to the expanded genitive expressions with **דִּי** as in **אִגַּרְתֵּהּ דִּי מַלְכָּא** *the letter of the king*).

כַּשְׂדָּאִין – *Chaldeans* The word is the absolute plural of **כַּשְׂדָּי.** It is a gentilic noun, a type of noun treated in greater depth in Unit 15.

וַאֲכַלוּ קַרְצֵיהוֹן דִּי יְהוּדָיֵא – In Aramaic, *to eat someone's morsels* is an idiom meaning *to slander someone*.

Daniel 3:9

עֲנוֹ – This is the pəʿal 3mp suffix conjugation of the verb **ענה**.

אָמְרִין – The participle of this verb should be translated in the past. It seems to be used in an analogous fashion to the suffix conjugation.

מַלְכָּא מַלְכָּא – The repetition is not a mistake. The first instance of the noun is in apposition to the preceding name. In the second instance, the noun is used as a vocative *O, . . .*

חֱיִי – *live!* This is the pəʿal m.s. imperative of **חיה**.

Daniel 3:10

a

שָׂמְתָּ – The verb is a pəʿal 2ms suffix conjugation of the verb **שׂים**.

דִּי . . . דִּי – *that . . . who* The first **דִּי** should be translated *that* and the second one *who*.

b

מַשְׁרֹקִיתָא קִיתְרֹס שַׂבְּכָא פְסַנְתֵּרִין וְסוּפֹּנְיָה – . . . *the pipe, lute, the lyre, harps, or a trumpet* It is unclear what exactly the last term refers to, but it is related to the English word *symphony*, and is spelled with a mem before the peh later in this same text.

c

יִפֵּל – The verb is a pəʿal 3ms prefix conjugation of the verb **נפל**. It takes as subject the phrase **כָּל־אֱנָשׁ** from line a.

Daniel 3:11

מַן־דִּי־ – The combination of the interrogative **מַן** *who* and the relative is translated simply as anyone who. The sentence is not a question. In Aramaic, as in English, the same pronoun is used both as an interrogative as well as a relative.

יִפֵּל – See 3:10 line c.

יִתְרְמֵא – . . . *will be thrown* The verb is a hitpəʿel 3ms prefix conjugation of the verb **רמי** and should be translated passively.

אַתּוּן נוּרָא יָקִדְתָּא – The first word is in construct with the second. The third word is a pəʿal f.s. determined participle; in this phrase, it functions as an adjective modifying the second word.

Daniel 3:12

a מַנִּיתָ *you appointed*. This is the paʿʿel 2ms suffix conjugation of מני.

שַׁדְרַךְ מֵישַׁךְ וַעֲבֵד נְגוֹ – *Shadrach, Meshach, and Abed-Nego*

b

לָא־שָׂמוּ עֲלָיךְ מַלְכָּא טְעֵם – *(they) do not pay heed to your decree, O king* The idiom of שׂים with the preposition עַל implies *showing* (or *not showing*) *attention to something*, in this case the king's decree.

c הֲקֵימְתָּ *you set up*. This is the haphʿel 2ms suffix conjugation of קום.

Test yourself

Write the following phrases in Aramaic (based on verses from Daniel 2), using the following vocabulary and notes in parentheses: אֱלָהּ *God*, בַּיִת (cstr. בֵּית) *house*, דְּהַב (det. דַּהֲבָא) *gold*, דִּי *that*, כֹּל *all*, כְּנַשׁ *to gather*, מְדִינָה *province*, סגד *worship* (+ lamedh prep.), עֲבִידָה *work*, עִדָּן *time*, פלח *serve*, צְלֵם *image*, שׁבק *to leave alone*, שׁלח *to send*, שָׁלְטָן *dominion*, שִׁלְטוֹן *ruler*, שׁמע *to hear*. Words preceded by *the* should be in the construct or determined state, while words with *a* or *an* should be in the absolute; English *of* presupposes a construct phrase.

- **a** *In the time that you hear* (pəʿal prefix conj. 2mp) . . .
- **b** *You will worship* (pəʿal prefix conj. 2mp) *the image of gold* (literally *the image of the gold*).
- **c** *All of the dominions will serve* (pəʿal prefix conj. 3mp) *him* (lamedh + 3ms suff.).
- **d** *He sent to gather all of the rulers of the provinces.*
- **e** *Leave alone* (pəʿal m.p. imperative) *the work of the house of God* (literally *the God*).

Suggestions for further study

Memorize the vocabulary you had to look up in the Reading exercises. For the strong root verbs you looked up, try putting these into the prefix conjugation and imperative (looking up the theme vowel in the glossary when necessary).

SELF-CHECK

	I CAN...
●	translate the prefix conjugation, imperative, and infinitive
●	recognize and produce the form of these same verb forms in the pəʿal
●	find the direct object of the verb

12 *Pa‘‘el prefix conjugation, imperative, participle, infinitive and impersonal constructions with the plural verb*

In this unit you will learn how to:

- **produce the form of the pa‘‘el prefix conjugation, imperative, participle, and infinitive**
- **identify impersonal constructions**

In this unit you will read:

- **Daniel 3:13–16**

Grammar

REVIEW OF THE PA‘‘EL SUFFIX CONJUGATION: THE STRONG AND MIDDLE GUTTURAL ROOTS

The pa‘‘el stem is typically characterized by the vowel pattern a-e (or a-i) and the doubling of the middle root consonant, as in the 2ms suffix-conjugation form: קַטֵּלְתְּ *you slayed*. As explained in Unit 8, the pa‘‘el indicates the act of bringing something into a state, e.g. שַׁנִּי *he made (something) be different*. In addition, it can represent an act done repeatedly or intensely, as in the case of *slay*.

An aleph or resh (or sometimes ‘ayin) as a middle root consonant in the pa‘‘el will result in the preceding vowel lengthening: בָּרְכֵת bārəket instead of בַּרְּכֵת* *barrəket. The he and ḥet as middle root consonants do not usually trigger this type of lengthening.

As in the pə‘al, when the last root consonant is a guttural or resh what would be an e or i vowel after the second root consonant is instead a patach, as in בַּקַּ֫רוּ *they searched*. There is no lengthening that occurs due to this guttural or resh.

> **LANGUAGE INSIGHT**
>
> The lengthening of a preceding vowel due to the loss of doubling is a broad phenomenon in Aramaic and is termed ‘compensatory lengthening’. This is seen, for example, in the case of roots that begin with aleph: מֵאמַר *to say* (the infinitive of אמר) instead of מְאְמַר*.

THE PA‘‘EL PREFIX CONJUGATION AND IMPERATIVE

The prefix conjugation is characterized by the same features as the suffix conjugation. In addition, the prefix consonant typically is followed by a muttered vowel. The following table illustrates the forms of the paradigmatic verb **כתב** *to write* and a verb with a final resh root consonant, which attracts the a theme vowel in place of the usual e or i.

	prefix conj. of כתב *to write*	jussive of כתב	imperative of כתב	prefix conj. of בקר *to search*	prefix conj. of ברך *to bless*
3ms	יְכַתֵּב	יְכַתֵּב		יְבַקַּר	יְבָרֵךְ
3fs	תְּכַתֵּב	תְּכַתֵּב		תְּבַקַּר	תְּבָרֵךְ
2ms	תְּכַתֵּב	תְּכַתֵּב	כַּתֵּב	תְּבַקַּר	תְּבָרֵךְ
2fs	תְּכַתְּבִין	תְּכַתִּ֫בִי	כַּתִּ֫בִי	תְּבַקְּרִין	תְּבָרְכִין
1cs	אֲכַתֵּב			אֲבַקַּר	אֲבָרֵךְ
3mp	יְכַתְּבוּן	יְכַתִּ֫בוּ		יְבַקְּרוּן	יְבָרְכוּן
3fp	יְכַתְּבָן	יְכַתִּ֫בָה		יְבַקְּרָן	יְבָרְכָן
2mp	תְּכַתְּבוּן	תְּכַתִּ֫בוּ	כַּתִּ֫בוּ	תְּבַקְּרוּן	תְּבָרְכוּן
2fp	תְּכַתְּבָן	תְּכַתִּ֫בָה	כַּתִּ֫בָה	תְּבַקְּרָן	תְּבָרְכָן
1cp	נְכַתֵּב			נְבַקַּר	נְבָרֵךְ

Note that the m.s. and m./f.p. imperatives are identical to the 3ms and 3m/fp suffix conjugation forms.

The jussive is particularly rare in the pa‘‘el and occurs only with suffixes: e.g. אַל־יְבַהֲלוּךְ *may they not terrify you.*

PRACTICE 1

Write out the prefix conjugation of כתב in the pa‘‘el several times. Then, write the following phrases in Aramaic, using the following vocabulary: בהל pa‘‘el *to frighten*, בקר pa‘‘el *to search, enquire*, הִמּוֹ *them*, חבל pa‘‘el *to destroy*, מַלְכָּה *queen*, עַל *about*, קִרְיָה *city*, רַעְיוֹן *thought*. Use the pa‘‘el prefix conjugation, the jussive, or the imperative where relevant.

a *The thoughts of the queen will frighten them.*
b *The queen will enquire about the city.*
c *Destroy (m.s.) the city! Do not destroy them!*
d *I will enquire about your (m.s.) thoughts.*
e *You (f.s.) will not frighten them.*

PA‘‘EL PARTICIPLES AND INFINITIVE

Recall that Aramaic has two basic types of participles: active and passive. Both types are used as nouns/adjectives or as verbs. Pa‘‘el participles function in exactly the same way as pəʿal participles, but of course have the sense peculiar to the verb in the pa‘‘el stem.

Pa‘‘el participles are marked not only by the characteristic features of the stem (the a-e or a-i vowel sequence and doubling of the middle root consonant) but also by an initial mem prefix: מְהַלֵּךְ *one who walks back and forth*. As with the prefix conjugation, the vowel following the prefixed mem is a muttered vowel and the vowel after the first root consonant will exhibit compensatory lengthening if the middle root consonant is a guttural or resh, as in מְבָרֵךְ *one who blesses*.

The passive pa‘‘el participle is formally indistinguishable from the active, except in the masculine singular where the only difference is in the last vowel: a instead of e: מְבָרַךְ *one who is blessed*.

	active participle	passive participle	active participle	passive participle
m.s.	מְכַתֵּב	מְכַתַּב	מְבָרֵךְ	מְבָרַךְ
f.s.	מְכַתְּבָה		מְבָרְכָה	
m.p.	מְכַתְּבִין		מְבָרְכִין	
f.p.	מְכַתְּבָן		מְבָרְכָן	

The pa‘‘el infinitive exhibits a different vowel pattern from that of the other verb forms. In addition, unlike the pəʻal infinitive (e.g. **מִכְתַּב** *to write*), the pa‘‘el exhibits no initial mem:

כַּתָּבָה *to make written*
בָּרָכָה *to bless*

LANGUAGE INSIGHT

The sequence of two long ā vowels in the infinitive is characteristic of the infinitives of all the stems except the pəʻal.

CULTURAL INSIGHT

Biblical texts together with inscriptions depict various figures from the kingdom of Aram-Damascus, one of the most famous being Hazael. In 1Kings 19:15, Elijah, the Israelite prophet, is commanded by God to anoint Hazael as king over Aram-Damascus. Elijah does not do this, but instead his successor, Elisha, goes to Damascus, where Hazael appears to be a prince or a court official. The current king of Aram-Damascus, who is ailing, tells Hazael to go and meet Elisha and ask if his sickness will be fatal. Elisha responds by saying to Hazael that he (Hazael) should tell the king you will surely recover, though Elisha adds he will surely die. The biblical text recounts how Hazael returned to his king, told him he would recover, then dipped a blanket in water and smothered him, Hazael then becoming king himself. Although the historical reality of these incidents is impossible to prove, it is the case that Hazael is described in Assyrian inscriptions as a usurper (literally, mār lā mammāna *a son of a nobody*). The same Hazael is also recorded as resisting the Assyrians in numerous campaigns and attacking and subjugating the Israelites. In the Tel Dan Stele, written in Old Aramaic, the speaker (presumably Hazael) claims that he has killed a king who belonged to the **ביתדוד** *the house of David*. (See Younger.)

PRACTICE 2

1 Parse the following forms, identifying the stem, conjugation or form, and root (as well as person, number, gender where relevant). Then, look the verb up in the glossary and translate it:

Example: תְּקַבְּלוּן → pa‘‘el 2mp pref. conj. קבל *you will receive*

a יְטַעֲמוּן
b קַטָּלָה
c מְעָרַב
d מְהַלֵּךְ

e הַדֲּרְתָּ
f נַסָּכָה
g בַּטִּלוּ
h תְּקָרֵב
i מְצַבְּעִין
j כַּפִּתָה

2 **Give the vowels to the unvocalized pa‘‘el forms in the following sentences. Then, parse the verb forms and translate the sentences into English using the glossary. Remember that word order is very flexible and unpredictable in Aramaic.**

a לָךְ אֱלָהּ משבח אֲנָה
b שְׁמֵהּ דִּי־אֱלָהָא מברך מִן־עָלְמָא וְעַד־עָלְמָא
c בדרו אִנְבֵּהּ
d לְחַי עָלְמָא שבחת (1cs)
e לֵאלָהֵי כַסְפָּא וְדַהֲבָא שבחו
f בֵּאדַיִן דָּנִיֵּאל עִם־מַלְכָּא מלל
g יבקר בִּסְפַר־דָּכְרָנַיָּא
h אֲמַר לבטלה גֻּבְרַיָּא אִלֵּךְ
i וֵאלָהָא דִּי שכן שְׁמֵהּ תַּמָּה ימגר כָּל־מֶלֶךְ

IMPERSONAL CONSTRUCTIONS WITH PLURAL VERBS

In Aramaic it is very common to encounter active verbs though these lack a clear grammatical subject. In particular, 3mp suffix and prefix conjugations and m.p. participles often are used in an impersonal way. So, for instance, you might find כְּתַבוּ לַהּ and assume it should be translated *they wrote it*. But, if there is no clear antecedent to *they*, then the verb may have an impersonal sense. If so, the verbs are translated by the English passive voice. In the case of כְּתַבוּ לַהּ, you would translate with the English passive *it was written*. Often what is the object of the verb in a literal translation must become the subject of the verb in the English translation. Here are three examples from a single verse from Daniel 4:22:

וְלָךְ טָרְדִין מִן־אֲנָשָׁא . . . וְעִשְׂבָּא כְתוֹרִין לָךְ יְטַעֲמוּן וּמִטַּל שְׁמַיָּא לָךְ מְצַבְּעִין

Literally: *And they will drive you away* (pəʿal m.p. part.) *from humanity* (lit. *from the humanity*) . . . *and grass like oxen they will feed* (pa‘‘el 3mp prefix conj.) *you and from the dew of* (מִטַּל = טַל + מִן) *heaven they will drench* (pa‘‘el m.p. part.) *you.*

However, the context does not provide a clear antecedent to the *they*. So, it is assumed that the active verbs are being used impersonally and are translated with the English passive: *You will be driven away . . . and you will be fed . . . and you will be drenched . . .*

In other cases, you must use the word *this* or *these* as the subject of the verb in English, as in the following example from Daniel 7:5.

וַאֲרוּ חֵיוָה אָחֳרִי תִנְיָנָה דָּמְיָה לְדֹב וְלִשְׂטַר־חַד הֳקִמַת וּתְלָת עִלְעִין בְּפֻמַּהּ בֵּין שִׁנַּיהּ וְכֵן אָמְרִין לַהּ קוּמִי . . .

Literally: *And, lo, another, second beast resembled a bear, and it was lifted on its side, and three ribs (were) in its mouth, between its teeth, and thus they said to it: ‘Arise!. . .’* Again, there is no clear antecedent to *they* in the last sentence and so the phrase is understood impersonally and translated into the English passive *and thus, this was said to it: 'Arise! . . .'*

Reading

Translate the following passage from Daniel 3, looking up the words you do not know in the glossary and using the notes that follow the text.

DANIEL 3:13

a בֵּאדַ֫יִן נְבוּכַדְנֶצַּר בִּרְגַז וַחֲמָה אֲמַר
b לְהַיְתָיָה לְשַׁדְרַךְ מֵישַׁךְ וַעֲבֵד נְגוֹ
c בֵּאדַ֫יִן גֻּבְרַיָּא אִלֵּךְ הֵיתָ֫יוּ קֳדָם מַלְכָּא

DANIEL 3:14

a עָנֵה נְבוּכַדְנֶצַּר וְאָמַר לְהוֹן
b הַצְדָּא שַׁדְרַךְ מֵישַׁךְ וַעֲבֵד נְגוֹ
c לֵאלָהַי לָא אִיתֵיכוֹן פָּלְחִין וּלְצֶ֫לֶם דַּהֲבָא דִּי הֲקֵ֫ימֶת לָא סָגְדִין

DANIEL 3:15

a כְּעַן הֵן אִיתֵיכוֹן עֲתִידִין דִּי בְעִדָּנָא דִּי־תִשְׁמְעוּן קָל קַרְנָא
b מַשְׁרֹקִיתָא קַיתְרֹס שַׂבְּכָא פְּסַנְתֵּרִין וְסוּמְפֹּנְיָה
c וְכֹל זְנֵי זְמָרָא תִּפְּלוּן וְתִסְגְּדוּן לְצַלְמָא דִּי־עַבְדֵת
d וְהֵן לָא תִסְגְּדוּן בַּהּ־שַׁעֲתָא תִתְרְמוֹן לְגוֹא־אַתּוּן נוּרָא יָקִדְתָּא
e וּמַן־הוּא אֱלָהּ דִּי יְשֵׁיזְבִנְכוֹן מִן־יְדָי

DANIEL 3:16

a עֲנוֹ שַׁדְרַךְ מֵישַׁךְ וַעֲבֵד נְגוֹ וְאָמְרִין לְמַלְכָּא נְבוּכַדְנֶצַּר
b לָא־חַשְׁחִין אֲנַחְנָה עַל־דְּנָה פִּתְגָם לַהֲתָבוּתָךְ

Daniel 3:13

b

לְהַיְתָיָה – *to bring* This is the prep. לְ + haph'el infinitive of **אתי** *to come.*

c

הֵיתָ֫יוּ – *were brought* This is the huph'al/hoph'al 3mp suffix conjugation of **אתי** *to come.*

Daniel 3:14

a

עָנֵה . . . וְאָמַר – *spoke up . . . and said* Although both participles, these are translated as suffix-conjugation verbs.

b

הַצְדָּא – *is it true?* This is an adverbial expression made up of the interrogative particle הֲ and the word **צְדָא**.

c

אִיתֵיכוֹן – *you* This is the particle of existence, אִיתַי (which is explained in Unit 10), followed by the 2mp pronominal suffix.

הֲקֵימֶת – *I erected* This is the haph'el 1cs suffix conjugation of קום *to arise*.

Daniel 3:15

a

דִּי . . . דִּי – *(it will be the case) that . . . when* The verse is composed as an *if/then* conditional sentence. The protasis (the *if* clause) begins at the start of the verse. The apodosis (the *then* clause) likely begins with the first דִּי particle. The actual verb *to be*, as often in Aramaic, is not expressed.

b

מַשְׁרֹקִיתָא קִיתְרֹס שַׂבְּכָא פְסַנְתֵּרִין וְסוּמְפֹּנְיָה – . . . *the pipe, lute* (presumably pronounced קַתְרֹס), *the lyre, harps, trumpet*. See Unit 11.

c

תִּפְּלוּן – The verb is a pə'al 2mp prefix conjugation of the verb נפל.

d

תִתְרְמוֹן – *you will be thrown* This is the hitpə'el 2mp prefix conjugation of רמי *to throw*.

אַתּוּן נוּרָא יָקִדְתָּא – The first word is in construct with the second. The third word is a pə'al f.s. determined participle; in this phrase, it functions as an adjective modifying the second word.

e

הוּא – *is* The 3ms independent pronoun functions in place of the verb *to be*.

יְשֵׁיזְבִנְכוֹן – *will deliver you* This is the 3ms prefix conjugation of שׁיזב *to save, deliver*. Historically, this verb is really a shaphel stem, another version of the haphel found prominently in other Semitic languages, but not in Aramaic.

יְדָי – This is the pausal form that occurs at verse-end and would otherwise be written and pronounced: יְדַי.

Daniel 3:16

a

עֲנוֹ – The pə'al 3mp suffix conjugation of ענה.

אָמְרִין – The participle is translated like a suffix conjugation.

b

חָשְׁחִין – This is the pə'al m.p. part. of חשח. In the Leningrad Codex it is spelled incorrectly with a patach instead of a qamets.

פִּתְגָם לַהֲתָבוּתָךְ – *to return you an answer* The first word is the noun *answer* and is the object of the following infinitive phrase, made up of the preposition לְ + haph'el infinitive of תוב *to return* and the 2ms pronominal suffix.

Test yourself

1. Read the following verses and identify each *pə ʿal / paʿʿel* verb according to the following example: **כְּתַב** *pə ʿal* 3ms suffix-conj. and **תְּכַתֵּב** paʿʿel 3fs prefix-conj. Then, turn each pəʿal verb into a *paʿʿel* and each paʿʿel into a *pə ʿal*, re-translating them according to this new stem. The verses come from the Aramaic translations of the Bible, called targums; generally the targums use more maters than in Biblical Aramaic and sometimes have slightly different spelling from Biblical Aramaic. The spelling of vowels is also slightly different from Biblical Aramaic, but for the purposes of this exercise, the vowels are indicated as they would be in Biblical Aramaic.

Example:

מִלֵּי זְעֵירָא כְּרַבָּא תִּשְׁמְעוּן לָא תִּדְחֲלוּן

The words of the small like the great you will hear; you will not fear.

Answer: **תִּשְׁמְעוּן** *pə ʿal* 2mp prefix-conj.; *paʿʿel*: **תְּשַׁמְּעוּן** *you will sing*

תִּדְחֲלוּן *pə ʿal* 2mp prefix-conj.; *paʿʿel*: **תְּדַחֲלוּן** *you will (not) frighten*

1 יַחֲשֵׁב בְּלִיבֵּיהּ

(If) he will plot in his heart . . .

2 וְיִתְקַף רוּגְזִי . . . בְּעִדָּנָא הַהוּא

My rage will grow strong in that time.

3 וְלָא יִקְרְבוּן עוֹד בְּנֵי יִשְׂרָאֵל לְמַשְׁכַּן זִמְנָא

The children of Israel will not again approach toward the tent of assembly

4 עַד אִמַּתִי מְסָרֵיב [= מְסָרֵב] אַתְּ לְאִתְכְּנָעָא [= לְאִתְכְּנָעָה] מִן־קֳדָמַי שַׁלַּח עַמִּי

How long will you refuse to humble yourself before me? Release my people!

5 וְאַפִּילוּ יַחְמְכוּן כִּזְעֵיר

Even if they are a little wise (lit. . . . *are wise as a little*). . .

2. Vocalize and translate this short passage from the second of the Samaria Papyri. Use the vowel symbols typical of Biblical Aramaic, looking up words you do not recognize in the glossary. The papyri preserve deeds of sale for slaves from the mid-300s BCE. They were found in a cave among many human bones. It is commonly assumed that the owners of the slaves (and perhaps the slaves themselves) perished together at the hands of Alexander the Great's soldiers. At this period of time, due to a conservative spelling practice, the m.s. demonstrative **דְּנָה** *this* was spelled with an initial *zayin*, **זנה**, though it was likely pronounced according to the Biblical Aramaic spelling: *dənā*[h]. Hint: The word **מקבל** is a verbal form.

וכספא זנה לא מקבל אנה מנכי

The phrase is from the last part of the document and represents part of one of the contingency or "if . . . then . . ." clauses. The preceding part of the sentence is not preserved, but would have said something like "If I, the seller (of this slave), say to you: ' . . .'" The "I" in this and the above clause is the person selling the slave. Although very short, the passage does reveal something about the social/economic life of women among these Aramaic speakers. What is it?

Suggestions for further study

Memorize the vocabulary from this unit's preceding exercises and compose a short Aramaic text of your own using the vocabulary you have learned so far.

SELF-CHECK

	I CAN...
○	produce the form of the pa''el prefix conjugation, imperative, participle, and infinitive
○	identify impersonal constructions

13 Haph'el/Aph'el suffix conjugation, prefix conjugation, imperative, participle, infinitive

In this unit you will learn how to:

- **produce the haph'el and aph'el prefix conjugation, imperative, participle, and infinitive**

In this unit you will read:

- **Daniel 3:17–20**

Grammar

REVIEW OF THE HAPH'EL/APH'EL SUFFIX CONJUGATION

The haph'el stem and its alternative, the aph'el, typically convey a causative notion. The haph'el is characterized by the prefixed he and the vowel pattern a-e (or a-i), as in the 2ms suffix-conjugation form הַשְׁפֵּלְתְּ *you humbled*. The aph'el has instead a prefixed aleph or no prefix at all, but it has the same vowel pattern (e.g. אַשְׁפֵּלְתְּ*). The haph'el is more common in Biblical Aramaic, but is replaced by the aph'el in later texts.

HAPH'EL/APH'EL PREFIX CONJUGATION AND IMPERATIVE

The gutturals and resh as third root consonants change what would be an e vowel to an a vowel.

	haph'el prefix conj. of כתב *to write*	haph'el jussive	aph'el prefix conj. of כתב	imperative	haph'el prefix conj. of שְׁכַח *to find*
3ms	יְהַכְתֵּב	יְהַכְתֵּב	יַכְתֵּב		יְהַשְׁכַּח
3fs	תְּהַכְתֵּב	תְּהַכְתֵּב	תַּכְתֵּב		תְּהַשְׁכַּח
2ms	תְּהַכְתֵּב	תְּהַכְתֵּב	תַּכְתֵּב	הַכְתֵּב and אַכְתֵּב	תְּהַשְׁכַּח
2fs	תְּהַכְתְּבִין	תְּהַכְתִּ֫בִי	תַּכְתְּבִין	הַכְתִּ֫בִי and אַכְתִּ֫בִי	תְּהַשְׁכְּחִין
1cs	אֲהַכְתֵּב		אַכְתֵּב		אֲהַשְׁכַּח
3mp	יְהַכְתְּבוּן	יְהַכְתִּ֫בוּ	יַכְתְּבוּן		יְהַשְׁכְּחוּן
3fp	יְהַכְתְּבָן	יְהַכְתִּ֫בָה	יַכְתְּבָן		יְהַשְׁכְּחָן
2mp	תְּהַכְתְּבוּן	תְּהַכְתִּ֫בוּ	תַּכְתְּבוּן	הַכְתִּ֫בוּ and אַכְתִּ֫בוּ	תְּהַשְׁכְּחוּן
2fp	תְּהַכְתְּבָן	תְּהַכְתִּ֫בָה	תַּכְתְּבָן	הַכְתִּ֫בָה and אַכְתִּ֫בָה	תְּהַשְׁכְּחָן
1cp	נְהַכְתֵּב		נַכְתֵּב		נְהַשְׁכַּח

Not infrequently the haph'el/aph'el exhibits a hiriq where a sere might be expected. Therefore, תַּכְתֵּב would not be an unexpected alternative to the 3fs prefix conjugation. Note that the m.s. and m./f.p. imperatives are identical to the 3ms and 3m/fp suffix-conjugation forms.

LANGUAGE INSIGHT

Note that the aph'el has the opposite sequence of vowel symbols to the pa''el in the prefix conjugation. The pa''el has a shewa in the prefix and a patach (a) after the first root consonant (e.g. יְכַתֵּב), while the aph'el has a patach in the prefix and a shewa representing the absence of a vowel after the first root consonant (e.g., יַכְתֵּב).

HAPH'EL PARTICIPLES AND INFINITIVE

Just like the pa''el participle, the haph'el exhibits an active and a passive form, both with a prefixed mem. Again, the m.s. is the only form that can be distinguished as active or passive.

PRACTICE

Copy out the paradigm of the haph'el of כתב several times until it becomes familiar. Then, fill in the correct vowels and dageshes to the following forms. Look up words unfamiliar to you in the glossary.

- **a** פלחין *those serving* – the pə'al m.p. participle of פלח
- **b** נסגד *we will worship* – the pə'al 1cp prefix conjugation of סגד
- **c** יהשׁפל *he will bring low* (or *vanquish*) – the haph'el 3ms prefix conjugation of שׁפל
- **d** הנפק *he brought forth* – the haph'el 3ms suffix conjugation of נפק
- **e** יבהל *it* (masc.) *will terrify* – the pa''el 3ms prefix conjugation of בהל
- **f** הרגזו *they angered* – the haph'el 3mp suffix conjugation of רגז
- **g** יחסנון *they will possess* – the aph'el 3mp prefix conjugation of חסן
- **h** מפשׁר *to interpret* – the pə'al infinitive of פשׁר
- **i** כפתה *to bind* – the pa''el infinitive of כפת
- **j** השׁפלת *you brought low* (or *vanquished*) – the haph'el 2ms suffix conjugation of שׁפל
- **k** מהחצפה *one urgent* – the haph'el f.s. passive participle of חצף
- **l** השׁלט *he caused to rule* – the haph'el 3ms suffix conjugation of שׁלט
- **m** מהדר *one glorifying* – the pa''el m.s. participle of הדר
- **n** נהשׁכח *we will find* – the haph'el 1cp prefix conjugation of שׁכח
- **o** השׁפלה *to bring low* – the haph'el infinitive of שׁפל
- **p** מחצפה *one urgent* – the aph'el f.s. passive participle of חצף
- **q** השׁמדה *to destroy* – the haph'el infinitive of שׁמד
- **r** מהקרבין *they will offer* – the haph'el m.p. participle of קרב
- **s** יצבה *to make certain* – the pa''el infinitive of יצב
- **t** השׁכחה *to find* – the haph'el infinitive of שׁכח

	haph'el		aph'el	
	active participle	passive participle	active participle	passive participle
m.s.	מְהַכְתֵּב	מְהַכְתַּב	מַכְתֵּב	מַכְתַּב
f.s.	מְהַכְתְּבָה		מַכְתְּבָה	
m.p.	מְהַכְתְּבִין		מַכְתְּבִין	
f.p.	מְהַכְתְּבָן		מַכְתְּבָן	

The haph'el infinitive has the form הַכְתָּבָה and the aph'el אַכְתָּבָה. When these are in construct with following nouns, the final -āh becomes -at, as in הַנְזָקַת *to the harming of…*

CULTURAL INSIGHT

In the vicinity of Aleppo, an inscription was found that records in brief the life of Si'gabbar (spelled שאגבר in Old Aramaic), a priest of the moon god Śehr (or Sin in Assyrian). The inscription states that *in return for my righteousness before him* (with Biblical Aramaic vowels: בְּצִדְקְתִי קֳדָמוֹהִ), *Śehr/Sin gave me a good name and lengthened my days* (שָׂמַנִי שֻׁם טָב וְהַאֲרֵךְ יוֹמַי). (Note the haph'el of ארך.) The inscription goes on to state his longevity: *With my eyes I saw (my) fourth generation…* (בְּעַיְנַי מְחַזֵה אֲנָה בְּנֵי רִבַּע). (Note that the verb *to see*, חזי, is in the pa''el in Old Aramaic, whereas in most other dialects it is in the pə'al).

Reading

Translate the following passage from Daniel 3 using the glossary and the notes that follow the text.

DANIEL 3:17

a הֵן אִיתַי אֱלָהַנָא דִּי־אֲנַחְנָא פָלְחִין יָכִל

b לְשֵׁיזָבוּתַנָא מִן־אַתּוּן נוּרָא יָקִדְתָּא וּמִן־יְדָךְ מַלְכָּא יְשֵׁיזִב

DANIEL 3:18

a וְהֵן לָא יְדִיעַ לֶהֱוֵא־לָךְ מַלְכָּא דִּי לֵאלָהָיךְ לָא־אִיתַינָא פָלְחִין

b וּלְצֶלֶם דַּהֲבָא דִּי הֲקֵימְתָּ לָא נִסְגֻּד

DANIEL 3:19

a בֵּאדַיִן נְבוּכַדְנֶצַּר הִתְמְלִי חֱמָא . . . עָנֵה וְאָמַר לְמֵזֵא לְאַתּוּנָא

b חַד־שִׁבְעָה עַל דִּי חֲזֵה לְמֵזְיֵהּ

DANIEL 3:20

a וּלְגֻבְרִין גִּבָּרֵי־חַיִל דִּי בְחַיְלֵהּ אֲמַר לְכַפָּתָה לְשַׁדְרַךְ מֵישַׁךְ וַעֲבֵד נְגוֹ

b לְמִרְמֵא לְאַתּוּן נוּרָא יָקִדְתָּא

Daniel 3:17

a

אִיתַי אֱלָהַנָא . . . יָכִל – *our God is able* The particle of existence, אִיתַי, occurs in conjunction with the participle at the end of the line; it functions in place of the verb *to be*.

b

לְשֵׁיזָבוּתַנָא – *to deliver us* This is the infinitive of **שׁיזב** with a 1cp pronominal suffix.

מַלְכָּא – *O, king* This is the vocative use of the determined noun.

יְשֵׁיזִב – *he will deliver us* This is the 3ms prefix conjugation of the verb **שׁיזב**.

Daniel 3:18

a

יְדִיעַ לֶהֱוֵא – *let it be known* This is the pəʿal passive participle m.s. of **ידע** followed by the pəʿal 3ms jussive of **היה** *to be*. The jussive and prefix conjugation of this verb are unusual in that they use a prefixed lamed instead of yod.

b

הֲקֵימְתָּ – *you erected* This is the haphʿel 2ms suffix conjugation of **קום** *to arise*.

Daniel 3:19

a

הִתְמְלִי חֱמָא – *was filled with rage* The first word is the hitpəʿel 3ms suffix conjugation of **מלי** *to fill*. The second word is the feminine noun *rage* and should be written חֱמָה.

לְמֵזֵא – *to heat up* The preposition לְ + the pəʿal infinitive of **אזי** *to heat*.

b

חַד־שִׁבְעָה עַל דִּי חֲזֵה לְמֵזְיֵהּ – *seven times above (the temperature) to which it was normally heated* The phrase would be more literally translated *seven times over that which was seen to heat it*. חֲזֵה is the pəʿal m.s. passive participle. The first word, **חַד** *time*, is also the numeral one. The last word is the preposition לְ + the pəʿal infinitive of **אזי** *to heat* and the 3ms pronominal suffix.

Daniel 3:20

a

לְכַפָּתָה – This is the preposition לְ + the paʿʿel infinitive of **כפת**.

b

לְמִרְמֵא – *to throw* This is the preposition לְ + the pəʿal infinitive of **רמי**.

Test yourself

Produce the following phrases with verbal forms in the haphʿel or aphʿel using the following vocabulary: **אֱלָהּ** *God*, **דִּי** *that*, **כֹּל** *all, every*, **מָאן** (pl. det. **מָאנַיָּא**) *vessel*, **מְרָד** *rebellious*, **נִיחוֹחַ** *incense-offering*, **נפק** in ha. *to bring forth*, **סְפַר** *a document*, **עַל** *against*, **קֳדָם** *before*, **קרב** ha. *to offer*, **קִרְיָה** *city*, **שׁכח** ha. *to find*, **שׁלם** ha. *to deliver*.

a *They* (m.p.) *will bring forth against you* (f.s.) *a document.*
b *I will offer before him incense-offerings.*
c *Every document that you* (f.p.) *will find . . .*
d *The vessels deliver* (m.s.) *before God!*
e *You* (m.s.) *will find that the city is a rebellious city.*

Suggestions for further study

After memorizing the new vocabulary you had to look up from the Reading exercises, go back through the exercises and try to read as much of them as possible without looking at the translations or notes.

SELF-CHECK

	I CAN...
●	produce the haph'el and aph'el prefix conjugation, imperative, participle, and infinitive

14 The internal passive stems: pə ʿīl, pu``al, huph ʿal/hoph ʿal suffix conjugation and numerals

In this unit you will learn how to:

- **produce the pəʿīl stem**
- **produce the pu``al stem**
- **produce the huphʿal/hophʿal stem**
- **recognize cardinal and ordinal numerals**

In this unit you will read:

- **Daniel 5:24–8**
- **Daniel 3:21–4**

Grammar

THE INTERNAL PASSIVE STEMS

The three passive stems, the pəʿīl (פְּעִיל), pu``al (פֻּעַל), huphʿal (הֻפְעַל) or hophʿal (הָפְעַל), correspond respectively to these three active stems: the pəʿal, the pa``el, and the haphʿel. These three passive stems are referred to as internal passive stems since they differ from their active counterparts only internally, that is, with their vowels. Of these three, the pəʿīl is the most common and the pu``al is not attested (though appears in other dialects). The pəʿīl commonly occurs with a yod mater טְרִיד *he was driven away* but it sometimes occurs without the yod: כְּפִתוּ *they were bound*. This means that sometimes the passive pəʿīl verbs will look like active pəʿal verbs that have an i theme vowel, like סְלִק *he went up* and יְכִל *he was able*. However, verbs like טְרִיד and כְּפִת have an a vowel in their active forms (טְרַד and כְּפַת) and verbs like סְלִק and יְכִל do not occur in the pəʿīl.

For these stems, only the suffix conjugation and participles are attested. The participles for the pəʿīl stem are identical to the passive participles already described for the pəʿal in Unit 6.

The huphʿal stem is sometimes articulated with an initial short o vowel, instead of short u. For this reason, it is sometimes referred to as the hophʿal. In later dialects especially it appears without the initial he, in which case it is called the uphʿal/ophʿal.

THE Pəʿ ĪL, PUʿʿAL, AND HUPHʿAL/HOPHʿAL SUFFIX CONJUGATION

	pəʿīl suffix conj.	puʿʿal suffix conj.	huphʿal/hophʿal suffix conj.
3ms	כְּתִיב	כֻּתַּב*	הָכְתַּב and הֻכְתַּב
3fs	כְּתִיבַת	כֻּתְּבַת*	הֻכְתְּבַת
2ms	כְּתִיבְתְּ and כְּתִ֫יבְתָּ	כֻּתַּבְתְּ* and כֻּתַּ֫בְתָּ*	הֻכְתַּבְתְּ and הֻכְתַּ֫בְתָּ
2fs	כְּתִ֫יבְתִּי	כֻּתַּ֫בְתִּי*	הֻכְתַּ֫בְתִּי
1cs	כְּתִיבֵת	כֻּתְּבֵת*	הֻכְתְּבֵת
3mp	כְּתִ֫יבוּ	כֻּתַּ֫בוּ*	הֻכְתַּ֫בוּ
3fp	כְּתִ֫יבָה	כֻּתַּ֫בָה*	הֻכְתַּ֫בָה
2mp	כְּתִיבְתּוּן	כֻּתַּבְתּוּן*	הֻכְתַּבְתּוּן
2fp	כְּתִיבְתֵּן	כֻּתַּבְתֵּן*	הֻכְתַּבְתֵּן
1cp	כְּתִ֫יבְנָא	כֻּתַּ֫בְנָא*	הֻכְתַּ֫בְנָא

LANGUAGE INSIGHT

Note that the second vowel of the puʿʿal and huphʿal/hophʿal stems is not the e like in the active form, but a short a. This pattern is also found in the participles: מְכֻתַּב* (puʿʿal) vs. מְכַתֵּב (paʿʿel) and מְהֻכְתַּב (huphʿal/hophʿal) vs. מְהַכְתֵּב (haphʿel).

With passive verbs, agency can be expressed with the min preposition, especially in the phrase מִנִּי שִׂים טְעֵם *by me a decree was issued* (or, *set*). Since this expression is awkward in English, this phrase is commonly rendered in the active voice: *I issued a decree.*

PRACTICE

One of the highest concentrations of pəʿīl verb forms is found in the passage containing the famous episode of the writing on the wall. Vocalize the words not vocalized for you in this passage from Daniel 5:24–8 and translate the text using the glossary and the notes:

24: בֵּאדַ֫יִן מִן־קֳדָמ֫וֹהִי שליח פַּסָּא דִי־יְדָא וּכְתָבָא דְנָה רשים
25: וּדְנָה כְתָבָא דִּי רשים מְנֵא מְנֵא תְּקֵל וּפַרְסִין
26: דְּנָה פְּשַׁר־מִלְּתָא מְנֵא מְנָה־אֱלָהָא מַלְכוּתָךְ והַשְׁלְמַהּ
27: תְּקֵל תקילתה בְמֹאזַנְיָא וְהִשְׁתְּכַ֫חַתְּ חַסִּיר
28: פְּרֵס פריסת מַלְכוּתָךְ וִיהיבת לְמָדַי וּפָרָס

v. 25: מְנֵא מְנֵא תְּקֵל וּפַרְסִין The enigmatic words that are explained in the following verses would be translated more literally: *mina, mina, shekel, and half-minas*. The *half-mina, mina*, and *shekel* represented different weight measurements.

v. 27: תקילתה This is the pəʿīl 2ms suffix conjugation of תקל. Note the unusual presence of the final he mater. הִשְׁתְּכַ֫חַתְּ This is the hitpaʿʿal 2ms suffix conjugation of שׁכח and is translated *and you were found.*

v. 28: יהיבת and פריסת Both these verbs are pəʿīl 3fs suffix-conjugation forms.

CARDINAL NUMERALS

Numerals can be divided into two sets: those used for counting and indicating quantity (e.g. one, two, three, etc.) and those that indicate position or rank (e.g. first, second, third, etc.). The first set are described as cardinal numerals and the second as ordinal. The cardinal numerals in Aramaic are only rarely used in the construct. (These forms are indicated in the following table in parentheses, if they occur in Biblical Aramaic.)

	Cardinal numerals 1–10	
	used with masc. nouns	used with fem. nouns
1	חַד	חֲדָה
2	תְּרֵין (cstr. תְּרֵי)	תַּרְתֵּין
3	תְּלָתָה	תְּלָת
4	אַרְבְּעָה	אַרְבַּע
5	חַמְשָׁה	חֲמֵשׁ
6	שִׁתָּה	שִׁת or שֵׁת
7	שִׁבְעָה (cstr. שִׁבְעַת)	שְׁבַע
8	תְּמָנְיָה	תְּמָנֵה
9	תִּשְׁעָה	תְּשַׁע
10	עַשְׂרָה	עֲשַׂר

One curiosity that Aramaic shares with other Semitic languages is that the numerals 3–10 that are masculine in form modify feminine nouns; numerals that are feminine in form, modify masculine nouns. Therefore, to express *seven kings* you would write: **שִׁבְעָה מַלְכִין** or **מַלְכִין שִׁבְעָה** (the numeral can come either before or after the noun it modifies). But, to express *seven queens* you would write: **שְׁבַע מַלְכָן** or **מַלְכָן שְׁבַע**. Notice that in all these instances the item that is counted is in the plural, often in the absolute. Although the cardinal numerals are like adjectives, in that they modify nouns, they do not occur in the emphatic/determined state and only rarely appear in the construct state before the item counted.

Among the cardinal numerals from 11–19, only one appears in Biblical Aramaic: **תְּרֵי עֲשַׂר** 12. The numerals like 20, 30, 40, etc. have the form of absolute masculine plural nouns **עֶשְׂרִין** 20, **תְּלָתִין** 30. The word for 100 is **מְאָה**. In its dual form, **מָאתַיִן**, it means 200. The word for 1000 is **אֲלַף** and for 10,000 **רִבּוֹ**. The latter two numerals also appear in the plural where they express large numbers: **אֶלֶף אַלְפִין** one thousand thousands (i.e. one million) and **רִבּוֹ רִבְוָן** ten thousand ten thousands (i.e. one hundred million).

CULTURAL INSIGHT

Numerous documents, contracts, and wills written in Aramaic have been recovered from the south of Egypt, at the first cataract (which formed a border with lands further to the south), from the twin cities of Syene and Elephantine. There, the Persian empire (in the 400s BCE) positioned Judean and Aramean soldiers. The exact cultural affiliations of these people is difficult to know since the same person could call himself Judean in one document and Aramean in another. Furthermore, the names of specific individuals reveal a complex cultural fabric. For example, Pakhnum son of Besa, whose name is Egyptian, enters into a contract with Anani son of Haggai, a Judean. Pakhnum, despite his name, is identified in the contract as an Aramean of Syene (ארמי זי סון, which would be in later Aramaic אֲרַמָּי דִּי סְוֵן) and he is, like Anani, part of a military unit led by a person with an Akkadian name, Nabukudurri. (See Porten, *COS* 3.81 = *TAD* B3.13). The -āy ending on the word אֲרַמָּי *Aramean* is an adjectival ending typically found on gentilic labels and on ordinal numerals.

ORDINAL NUMERALS

The ordinals appear not only in the absolute state, but also in the determined state. The ordinal numerals are identified by a consistent -āy suffix added to the stem of the numeral (except for second תִּנְיָן (in m.s.) and תִּנְיָנָה (f.s.)). The usual feminine and plural morphemes (e.g. -āh for the feminine singular absolute, -īʸn for the masculine plural absolute) follow this -āy suffix. Especially in later Aramaic the -āy suffix is realized instead as -ā' where it is followed by one of the word-final morphemes. These alternative forms are listed to the right of the forms with yod.

	first			
	masculine		feminine	
sing. abs.	קַדְמָי		קַדְמָיָה	קַדְמָאָה
sing. det.	קַדְמָיָא	קַדְמָאָא	קַדְמָיְתָא	קַדְמֵיתָא
pl. abs.	קַדְמָיִין	קַדְמָאִין	קַדְמָיָן	קַדְמָאָן
pl. det.	קַדְמָיֵא	קַדְמָאֵא	קַדְמָיָתָא	קַדְמָאָתָא

The singular absolute forms of the ordinals from second to tenth are as follows:

	masculine	feminine	
second	תִּנְיָן	תִּנְיָנָה	
third	תְּלִיתָי	תְּלִיתָיָה	תְּלִיתָאָה
fourth	רְבִיעָי	רְבִיעָיָה	רְבִיעָאָה
fifth	חֲמִישָׁי	חֲמִישָׁיָה	חֲמִישָׁאָה
sixth	שְׁתִיתָי	שְׁתִיתָיָה	שְׁתִיתָאָה
seventh	שְׁבִיעָי	שְׁבִיעָיָה	שְׁבִיעָאָה
eighth	תְּמִינָי	תְּמִינָיָה	תְּמִינָאָה
ninth	תְּשִׁיעָי	תְּשִׁיעָיָה	תְּשִׁיעָאָה
tenth	עֲשִׂירָי	עֲשִׂירָיָה	עֲשִׂירָאָה

Reading

Translate the following passage from Daniel 3 using the glossary and the notes that follow the text.

DANIEL 3:21

a בֵּאדַ֫יִן גֻּבְרַיָּא אִלֵּךְ כְּפִ֫תוּ בְּסַרְבָּלֵיהוֹן פַּטְּשֵׁיהוֹן וְכַרְבְּלָתְהוֹן וּלְבֻשֵׁיהוֹן

b וּרְמִיו לְגוֹא־אַתּוּן נוּרָא יָקִדְתָּא

DANIEL 3:22

a כָּל־קֳבֵל דְּנָה מִן־דִּי מִלַּת מַלְכָּא מַחְצְפָה וְאַתּוּנָא אֵזֵה יַתִּ֫ירָא

b גֻּבְרַיָּא אִלֵּךְ דִּי הַסִּ֫קוּ לְשַׁדְרַךְ מֵישַׁךְ וַעֲבֵד נְגוֹ קַטִּל הִמּוֹן שְׁבִיבָא דִּי נוּרָא

DANIEL 3:23

a וְגֻבְרַיָּא אִלֵּךְ תְּלָתֵּהוֹן שַׁדְרַךְ מֵישַׁךְ וַעֲבֵד נְגוֹ נְפַ֫לוּ

b לְגוֹא־אַתּוּן־נוּרָא יָקִדְתָּא מְכַפְּתִין

DANIEL 3:24

a אֱדַ֫יִן נְבוּכַדְנֶצַּר מַלְכָּא תְּוַהּ וְקָם בְּהִתְבְּהָלָה
b עָנֵה וְאָמַר לְהַדָּבְרוֹהִי הֲלָא גֻבְרִין תְּלָתָא רְמֵ֫ינָא לְגוֹא־נוּרָא מְכַפְּתִין
c עָנַיִן וְאָמְרִין לְמַלְכָּא יַצִּיבָא מַלְכָּא

Daniel 3:21

b

רְמִיו – *they were thrown* This is the pəʿīl 3mp suffix conjugation of **רמי** *to throw*.

אַתּוּן נוּרָא יָקִדְתָּא – The first word is in construct with the second. The third word is a pəʿal f.s. determined participle; in this phrase, it functions as an adjective modifying the second word.

Daniel 3:22

a

כָּל־קֳבֵל דְּנָה מִן־דִּי – *As a consequence of this, because . . .* The sequence of the kaph preposition followed by the lamed preposition and the particle **קֳבֵל** often occurs in Biblical Aramaic followed by the demonstrative pronoun **דְּנָה** *this*. Here, the phrase indicates that the following event (i.e. the killing of the king's servants) was precipitated by their having thrown Shadrach, Meshach, and Abed-Nego into the furnace. The compound particle מִן־דִּי *because* indicates the immediate cause of the servants' death, namely the urgency with which the king ordered the three to be thrown into the furnace (and, by extension, the haste with which it must have been done) and the degree to which the furnace had been heated.

מַחְצְפָה – *urgent* This is the haphʿel f.s. passive participle of **חצף**. The haphʿel means *to insist on something* and the passive means more literally *to be made urgent*.

אֵזֵה – *heated* This is an unusual form of the pəʿal passive/pəʿīl participle of the root **אזי** *to heat*.

b

In this sentence, גֻּבְרַיָּא אִלֵּךְ is the object of the verb קַטִּל, whose subject is **שְׁבִיבָא דִּי נוּרָא**. The pronoun הִמּוֹן refers back to גֻּבְרַיָּא אִלֵּךְ.

הַסִּ֫קוּ – *(they) lifted* This is the haphʿel 3mp suffix conjugation of the irregular root **סלק** *to go up*.

Daniel 3:23

a

תְּלָתֵּהוֹן – *the three of them* This is the fem. numeral three with the 3mp pronominal suffix. Note its pronunciation: təlāttēhōn and the two taws before the suffix. The first is part of the root (**תלת**) and the second is the feminine morpheme.

b

מְכַפְּתִין – This is the paʿʿel passive participle of **כפת** and describes the condition in which Shadrach, Meshach, and Abed-Nego entered the furnace.

Daniel 3:24

a

קָם בְּהִתְבְּהָלָה – he arose *in alarm* (more literally *in being alarmed*). The first word is the 3ms pe'al suff. conj. of **קום**; the second is the bet preposition followed by the hitpə'el infinitive of **בהל** *to be alarmed*

b

רְמֵ֫ינָא – *we threw* This is the pə'al 3mp suffix conjugation of **רמי** *to throw.*

מְכַפְּתִין – see note to 3:23b

c

עָנַיִן – *they answered* This is the pə'al m.p. participle of **עני** *to answer* but used in the manner of a suffix conjugation.

מַלְכָּא – This is the determined form used as a vocative.

Test yourself

1 Turn the pə'īl suffix conj. verbs in the Practice section (Daniel 5:24–8) into the corresponding pə'al suffix conj. forms, looking up the theme vowel for each verb in the glossary; then translate the verbal forms.

2 Vocalize the following numerals, looking up in the glossary any words you are unfamiliar with.

a	ארבע חֵיוָן רַבְרְבָן	*four great beasts*
b	קדמיתא כְאַרְיֵה	*the first was like a lion*
c	חֵיוָה אָחֳרִי תנינה דָּמְיָה לְדֹב	*another second beast was like a bear*
d	ארבעה רֵאשִׁין לְחֵיוְתָא	*the beast had four heads*
e	חֵיוָה רביעיה דְּחִילָה	*a fourth terrifying beast*
f	תלת מִן־קַרְנַיָּא קדמיתא אֶתְעֲקַ֫רָה	*three of the first horns were plucked out*
g	הוּא יִשְׁנֵא מִן־קדמיא	*it will be different from the first ones*
h	ותלתה מַלְכִין יְהַשְׁפִּל	*and it will bring down three kings*

Suggestions for further study

Memorize the vocabulary from the exercises of this unit and attempt to give the inflection of the nouns from the preceding exercise. Review the noun patterns described in Unit 7.

SELF-CHECK

	I CAN...
●	produce the pə'īl stem
●	produce the pu''al stem
●	produce the huph'al/hoph'al stem
●	recognize cardinal and ordinal numerals

15 *Hitpə ʿel and hitpa ʿʿal stems and gentilic nouns*

In this unit you will learn how to:

- ▶ **produce the hitpə ʿel stem**
- ▶ **produce the hitpa ʿʿal stem**
- ▶ **recognize gentilic nouns and adjectives**

In this unit you will read:

- ▶ **Daniel 3:25–8**

Grammar

THE HITPəʿEL (הִתְפְּעֵל) AND HITPAʿʿAL (הִתְפַּעַּל) STEMS

The two stems are similar in form and sense. They are sometimes referred to as t-stems since the taw of the prefix always appears after another prefixal element (after a he in the suffix conjugation and imperative, after a yod or other prefix element in the prefix conjugation, and after a mem in the participle). As explained in Unit 8, each of these stems corresponds with an active stem, the hitpəʿel with the pəʿal and the hitpaʿʿal with the paʿʿel. A third t-stem, the hittaphʿal (הִתַּפְעַל* from an earlier hithaphʿal הִתְהַפְעַל*) exists in some dialects of Aramaic, corresponding to the haphʿel, but is not attested in Biblical Aramaic.

In Aramaic in general and in Biblical Aramaic in particular, the t-stems usually express a reflexive notion or a passive notion.

THE SUFFIX AND PREFIX CONJUGATIONS OF THE HITPəʿEL AND THE HITPAʿʿAL

	Suffix conjugation		Prefix conjugation	
Stems	**hitpə ʿel**	**hitpa ʿʿal**	**hitpə ʿel**	**hitpa ʿʿal**
3ms	הִתְכְּתֵב	הִתְכַּתַּב	יִתְכְּתֵב	יִתְכַּתַּב
3fs	הִתְכַּתְבַת	הִתְכַּתְּבַת	תִּתְכְּתֵב	תִּתְכַּתַּב
2ms	הִתְכְּתֵבְתְּ	הִתְכַּתַּבְתְּ	תִּתְכְּתֵב	תִּתְכַּתַּב
2fs	הִתְכְּתֵ֫בְתִּי	הִתְכַּתַּ֫בְתִּי	תִּתְכַּתְבִין	תִּתְכַּתְּבִין
1cs	הִתְכַּתְבֵת	הִתְכַּתְּבֵת	אֶתְכְּתֵב	אֶתְכַּתַּב
3mp	הִתְכְּתִ֫בוּ	הִתְכַּתַּ֫בוּ	יִתְכַּתְבוּן	יִתְכַּתְּבוּן
3fp	הִתְכְּתִ֫בָה	הִתְכַּתַּ֫בָה	יִתְכַּתְבָן	יִתְכַּתְּבָן
2mp	הִתְכְּתִבְתּוּן	הִתְכַּתַּבְתּוּן	תִּתְכַּתְבוּן	תִּתְכַּתְּבוּן
2fp	הִתְכְּתִבְתֵּן	הִתְכַּתַּבְתֵּן	תִּתְכַּתְבָן	תִּתְכַּתְּבָן
1cp	הִתְכְּתֵ֫בְנָא	הִתְכַּתַּ֫בְנָא	נִתְכְּתֵב	נִתְכַּתַּב

There are slight variations in these patterns. The attested examples of 3fs suffix-conjugation forms all have a guttural (or resh) as third root consonant and so exhibit a peculiar vowel pattern (e.g. **הִתְגְּזֶרֶת** *it was cut* and **הִשְׁתְּכַחַת** *it was found*). Sometimes you find a hiriq (i) vowel in place of a sere (e) in these verbal forms: e.g. **יִתְעֲבִד** *let it be done*. The same rules relating to gutturals in the active stems also apply to these stems. So, in the hitpəʿel the gutturals will precipitate a patach (a) instead of a sere (e): **יִתְנְסַח** *it will be torn*. In addition, in the hitpaʿʿal a guttural as a middle root consonant will result in the lengthening of the patach (/a/) to a qamets (/ā/) due to compensatory lengthening: e.g. **מִתְעָרַב** *it will be mixed*.

In rare cases (though more commonly in later Aramaic dialects) the prefix to the suffix conjugation is not **-הִתְ** but instead **-אִתְ** (or even **-אֶת**), as in **אִתְיָעַטוּ** *they deliberated*, and in these cases the stems are commonly referred to as the itpəʿel and the itpaʿʿal. There is no distinction in meaning with this prefix.

The prefixed taw of these stems switches places with the first root consonant when the first root consonant is a sibilant (i.e. zayin **ז**, samekh **ס**, sadeh **צ**, śin **שׂ**, or shin **שׁ**). This shift in consonants is called metathesis. For example, in the root **שׁכח** *to find*, the shin switches places with the prefixed taw and the verb in the hitpəʿel suffix conjugation is **הִשְׁתְּכַח** *he was found* (the patach a after the kaph is due to the final ḥet). Note too the ambiguous 3fs/1cs form **הִשְׁתְּכַחַת** *she/I was found*. When sadeh **צ** is the first root consonant, the sadeh metathesizes with the taw and the taw becomes tet **ט**. (Technically, the taw assimilates to the emphatic pronunciation of sadeh.) Thus, the root **צבע** *to wet* is in the hitpaʿʿal prefix conjugation **יִצְטַבַּע** *he will be drenched*. A similar transformation pertains to words whose first root consonant is zayin **ז**. In these cases, the taw becomes dalet. The hitpəʿel of the root **זמן** would be **הִזְדְּמֵן** *he conspired*. This is the only verb that experiences this shift in Biblical Aramaic and it is misspelled in the Leningrad Codex as **הִזְ‍מִנְתּוּן** *you conspired* (Dan 2:9). If a root has an initial dalet, in the t-stem the taw assimilated into the dalet, as in **נִדָּרֵא** (also spelled **נִדָּרֵי**) *we will be scattered*, the itpaʿʿal 1cp prefix conjugation of **דרי**. In this case, the patach (or short a) that would have appeared under the dalet is lengthened due to compensatory lengthening since the resh, which should double, cannot double.

The other verbal forms can be predicted due to their prefix and their consistent vowel patterns. In fact, the imperative forms are not attested in Biblical Aramaic, though their forms may be reconstructed based on analogy to other verbs and dialects of Aramaic. Note that the m.s. and m./f.p. imperatives are identical to the 3ms and 3m/fp suffix-conjugation forms.

	Imperative		Participle	
Stems	**hitpəʿel**	**hitpaʿʿal**	**hitpəʿel**	**hitpaʿʿal**
ms	הִתְכְּתֵב	הִתְכַּתַּב	מִתְכְּתֵב	מִתְכַּתַּב
fs	הִתְכְּתִ֫בִי	הִתְכַּתַּ֫בִי	מִתְכַּתְבָה	מִתְכַּתְּבָה
mp	הִתְכְּתִ֫בוּ	הִתְכַּתַּ֫בוּ	מִתְכַּתְבִין	מִתְכַּתְּבִין
fp	הִתְכְּתִ֫בָה	הִתְכַּתַּ֫בָה	מִתְכַּתְבָן	מִתְכַּתְּבָן

The infinitives to these stems are poorly attested, but again their regularity makes predicting their forms simple: **הִתְכְּתָבָה** hitpəʿel and **הִתְכַּתָּבָה** hitpaʿʿal. The forms that are attested are

הִתְקְטָלָה *to be killed* (hitpəʿel); הִתְבְּהָלָה *being alarmed* (hitpəʿel); and **הִתְנַדָּבוּת** *the contributing of*... (hitpaʿʿal in construct). The latter form is in construct with what follows and exhibits a final -ūʷt ending that is more common with infinitives followed by pronominal object suffixes (see Unit 20).

PRACTICE

1 Translate the following clauses using this basic vocabulary list: אָע *wood*, בַּיִת *house*, הרך *to singe*, חבל *to destroy*, חֵיוָה *beast*, חָכְמָה *wisdom*, יהב *to give*, יַתִּיר *great*, לְבַב *heart*, מַלְכוּ kingdom נסח *to tear*, רֵאשׁ *head*, שְׂעַר *hair*, שׁכח *to find*.

a לְבַב חֵיוָה יִתְיְהִב לַהּ

b חָכְמָה יַתִּירָה הִשְׁתְּכַחַת בָּךְ

c יִתְנְסַח אָע מִן־בַּיְתֵהּ

d מַלְכוּתֵהּ דִּי־לָא תִתְחַבַּל

e שְׂעַר רֵאשְׁהוֹן לָא הִתְחָרַךְ

2 Translate the following clauses into Aramaic using this basic vocabulary list: אֱדַיִן *then*, אֱלָהּ *God*, אִלֵּךְ *these*, בְּ *in*, גְּבַר (pl. גֻּבְרִין) *people, men*, דִּי *which*, דָּנִיֵּאל *Daniel*, חֲסַף (det. חַסְפָּא) *clay*, טַל *dew*, טְעֵם *decree*, יהב to give, כֹּל *all*, לְ *to*, לָא not, מִן *from*, נִפְקָה (det. נִפְקְתָא) *expense*, נצח *to distinguish*, סָרֵךְ *official*, עבד *to do*, עַל *above*, עִם *with*, ערב *to mix*, פַּרְזֶל (det. פַּרְזְלָא) *iron*, צבע *to drench*, שְׁמַיִן *heavens*. Follow the word order of the English. A word in parentheses is not translated, but understood from context. Remember that English *of* presumes a preceding word in the construct state.

a *All which (is) from the decree of the God of the heavens will be done* (hitpə. 3ms pref. conj.).

b *The expense will be given* (hitpə. f.s. part.) *to these people.*

c *Then Daniel* (דָּנִיֵּאל) *distinguished himself* (hitpa. m.s. part.) *above the officials.*

d *The iron is not mixed* (hitpa. m.s. part. – remember compensatory lengthening) *with clay.*

e *In the dew of the heavens he will be drenched* (hitpa. 3ms pref. conj. – remember metathesis and assimilation of taw to tet).

GENTILIC NOUNS/ADJECTIVES

In addition to the many other types of nouns and adjectives discussed in the previous units, Aramaic has a category of words that frequently is used to identify groups of people, the so-called gentilic nouns/adjectives. The forms of these words differ, but they have consistent endings, characterized by the suffixal component -āy or -āʾ followed by the regular noun/adjective morphemes. The -āy or -āʾ suffixes are like those on the ordinal numerals.

	masculine		feminine	
singular absolute	-āy		-āyāʰ	-āʾāʰ
construct singular	-āy		-āyat	-āʾat
singular determined	-āyâ	-āʾâ	-āyətâ	-āʾətâ> -ēʸtâ
absolute plural	-āyīʸn	-āʾīʸn	-āyān	-āʾān
construct plural	-āyēʸ	-āʾēʸ	-āyāt	-āʾāt
determined plural	-āyê	-āʾê	-āyātâ	-āʾātâ

The realization of these endings is illustrated with the gentilic word for *Judean*.

	Judean **masculine**		**feminine**	
singular absolute	יְהוּדָי		יְהוּדָיָה	יְהוּדָאָה
construct singular	יְהוּדָי		יְהוּדָיַת	יְהוּדָאַת
singular determined	יְהוּדָיָא	יְהוּדָאָא	יְהוּדָיְתָא	יְהוּדֵיתָא
absolute plural	יְהוּדָיִין	יְהוּדָאִין	יְהוּדָיָן	יְהוּדָאָן
construct plural	יְהוּדָיֵי	יְהוּדָאֵי	יְהוּדָיָת	יְהוּדָאָת
determined plural	יְהוּדָיֵא	יְהוּדָאֵא	יְהוּדָיָתָא	יְהוּדָאָתָא

LANGUAGE INSIGHT

Even more commonly than in English, in Aramaic adjectives can be used as nouns and nouns as adjectives. The overlap in English is especially apparent in gentilic names, where *Judean* can be used to describe another noun or can be used as a noun itself.

CULTURAL INSIGHT

The complex cultural interactions in the twin cities of Syene-Elephantine in southern Egypt are well represented by the conflict that arose in relation to two temples on the island of Elephantine, one dedicated to the Egyptian god Khnum (pictured as a ram-headed human), the other to the Judean God Yaho (the abbreviated name of Yahweh). The dispute is known from several documents (including two copies of an Aramaic letter (*TAD* A4.7, A4.8 = *COS* 3.51, 52) describing the conflict sent to the Persian governor of Judah). The priests of Khnum, in collusion with the local Persian officials, are said to have destroyed the temple of the Judeans who seek permission to rebuild the temple as it was formerly. In their letter, the Judeans say they will provide burnt (animal) offerings as well as other types of (non-animal) sacrifices in the name of the governor in return for a favourable response. The letter also mentions that a similar letter had been sent to the high priest of the temple in Jerusalem without a response. The governor of Judah apparently did respond. In a record of an apparent verbal communication (*TAD* A4.9), he (together with the governor of Samaria who was also contacted) agrees to the rebuilding of the Elephantine temple but implicitly declines to support burnt sacrifices, either due to the possible tensions this would cause with the Jerusalem temple (which Deuteronomy 12 claims should be the exclusive place for sacrifice to the Judean God) and/or due to the tensions sacrificing rams (as burnt offerings) might cause with the neighbouring temple of Khnum.

Reading

Translate the following passage from Daniel 3 using the glossary and the notes that follow the text.

DANIEL 3:25

a עָנֵה וְאָמַר הָא־אֲנָה חָזֵה גֻּבְרִין אַרְבְּעָה שְׁרַ֫יִן מַהְלְכִין בְּגוֹא־נוּרָא

b וַחֲבָל לָא־אִיתַי בְּהוֹן וְרֵוֵהּ דִּי רְבִיעָיָא דָּמֵה לְבַר־אֱלָהִין

DANIEL 3:26

a בֵּאדַ֫יִן קְרֵב נְבוּכַדְנֶצַּר לִתְרַע אַתּוּן נוּרָא יָקִדְתָּא
b עָנֵה וְאָמַר שַׁדְרַךְ מֵישַׁךְ וַעֲבֵד נְגוֹ עַבְדוֹהִי דִּי־אֱלָהָא עִלָּיָא פֻּ֫קוּ וֶאֱתוֹ
c בֵּאדַ֫יִן נָפְקִין שַׁדְרַךְ מֵישַׁךְ וַעֲבֵד נְגוֹ מִן־גּוֹא נוּרָא

DANIEL 3:27

a וּמִתְכַּנְּשִׁין אֲחַשְׁדַּרְפְּנַיָּא סִגְנַיָּא וּפַחֲוָתָא וְהַדָּבְרֵי מַלְכָּא
b חָזַ֫יִן לְגֻבְרַיָּא אִלֵּךְ דִּי לָא־שְׁלֵט נוּרָא בְּגֶשְׁמְהוֹן
c וּשְׂעַר רֵאשְׁהוֹן לָא הִתְחָרַךְ וְסָרְבָּלֵיהוֹן לָא שְׁנוֹ
d וְרֵיחַ נוּר לָא עֲדָת בְּהוֹן

DANIEL 3:28

a עָנֵה נְבוּכַדְנֶצַּר וְאָמַר בְּרִיךְ אֱלָהֲהוֹן דִּי־שַׁדְרַךְ מֵישַׁךְ וַעֲבֵד נְגוֹ
b דִּי־שְׁלַח מַלְאֲכֵהּ וְשֵׁיזִב לְעַבְדוֹ֫הִי דִּי הִתְרְחִצוּ עֲלוֹהִי

Daniel 3:25

a

עָנֵה וְאָמַר – participles translated as though suffix-conjugation forms.

שְׁרַ֫יִן – *unbound* This is the pəʿal passive/pəʿīl m.p. participle of **שרי**.

מַהְלְכִין – This is vocalized as an aphʿel participle, though it is likely supposed to be a paʿʿel.

Daniel 3:26

b

פֻּ֫קוּ וֶאֱתוֹ – *come out, come!* These are two pəʿal m.p. imperatives, the first from **נפק** and the second **אתי**.

Daniel 3:27

a

אֲחַשְׁדַּרְפְּנַיָּא סִגְנַיָּא וּפַחֲוָתָא וְהַדָּבְרֵי מַלְכָּא – *the satraps, the prefects, the governors, and the counsellors of the king*

b

חָזַ֫יִן – *they were watching* This is the pəʿal m. p. participle of **חזי** *to see, watch.*

דִּי לָא־שְׁלֵט נוּרָא בְּגֶשְׁמְהוֹן – The initial relative particle seems to have as antecedent the noun גֻּבְרַיָּא. You could translate this relative, together with the phrase בְּגֶשְׁמְהוֹן at the end of the clause together as in *whose body* or more idiomatically in English in *whose bodies*. However, with the verb **שלט** the prepositional phrase should more likely be translated *over whose bodies.*

c

לָא שְׁנוֹ – *were not changed or . . . altered* This is the negative particle followed by the pəʿal 3mp suffix conjugation of **שׁני** *to change.*

d

עֲדָת – *it did (not) pass = it did (not) touch* This is the pəʿal 3fs suffix conjugation of **עדי** *to pass (over).*

Daniel 3:28

a

אֱלָהֲהוֹן דִּי־שַׁדְרַךְ מֵישַׁךְ וַעֲבֵד נְגוֹ – *the God of Shadrach, Meshach, and Abed-Nego*

b

שֵׁיזִב – *he delivered* This is the 3ms suffix conjugation of the irregular verb **שׁיזב** *to deliver, save.*

Test yourself

Many individual verbal forms are homophones and can be interpreted in two or more different ways, as with the 3fs prefix conj. (e.g. in the pəʿal **תִּכְתֻּב** *she will write*) which is always pronounced the same way as the 2ms prefix conj. (e.g. **תִּכְתֻּב** *you will write*), even in other stems (e.g. **תְּהַכְתֵּב** is the 3fs and 2ms prefix conj. in the haphʿel *she/you will cause to write*). Each of the following verbal forms can be interpreted in two different ways. Indicate both by giving two parsings for each.

a הִתְכְּתֵב
b הַכְתֵּב
c הִתְכַּתַּ֫בוּ
d כַּתִּ֫בוּ
e הִתְכַּתַּב

2 Looking at just the consonants of a verbal form allows for even more possible interpretations. Consider that without vowels these two forms, **הִתְכְּתֵב** and **הִתְכַּתַּב**, would look identical: **התכתב**. Determining what the correct vowels are depends on various factors like the attestation of a given verb in a vocalized tradition of Aramaic (like Biblical Aramaic or Targumic Aramaic). All dictionaries will indicate the stems in which verbs occur. Usually a single dialect (like Biblical Aramaic) will attest a verb only in one of two similar stems (e.g. in the hitpəʿel and not the hitpaʿʿal or vice versa). Being able to quickly identify the different possible interpretations for a simple verbal form greatly enhances your ability to read Aramaic. Apply the vowels to the vowel-less forms in the following phrases, looking up the words in the glossary to determine what stem they appear in.

a נִפְקְתָא תֶּהֱוֵא מתיהבה לְגֻבְרַיָּא אִלֵּךְ
The expense will be given to these men.

b פַּרְזְלָא לָא מתערב עִם־חַסְפָּא
Iron (lit. *the iron*) *is not mixed with clay* (lit. *the clay*).

c אֱדַ֫יִן מַלְכָּא בֵּלְשַׁאצַּר שַׂגִּיא מתבהל
Then, the king, Belshazzar, was very alarmed.

d חָכְמָה יַתִּירָה השתכחת בָּךְ
Great wisdom has been found in you.

e נִפְקְתָא מִן־בֵּית־מַלְכָּא יתיהב
The expense will be given from the house of the king.

f מַלְכוּ דִּי לְעָלְמִין לָא תתחבל
A kingdom that will never (lit. *that for eternity will not*) *be destroyed.*

g בְּעוֹ דָּנִיֵּאל וְחַבְרוֹהִי לְהתקטלה
Daniel and his companions were about (lit. *sought*) *to be killed.*

h מִטַּל שְׁמַיָּא גִּשְׁמֵהּ יצטבע
From the dew of heaven his body will be drenched.

i אֱדַיִן דָּנִיֵּאל דְּנָה הֲוָה מתנצח
Then, this Daniel distinguished himself.

j הֲוָה משתדר לְהַצָּלוּתֵהּ
He was struggling to save him.

SELF-CHECK

I CAN...
produce the hitpəʻel stem
produce the hitpaʻʻal stem
recognize gentilic nouns and adjectives

16 *I-weak verbs*

In this unit you will learn how to:
- **form I-nun verbs**
- **form I-aleph verbs**
- **form I-waw/yod verbs**

In this unit you will read:
- **Ezra 4:11–14**

Grammar

I-WEAK VERBS

As mentioned in Unit 4, verbs with an initial aleph, waw, yod, or nun sometimes are hard to recognize due to their unusual forms. Recall also that a historical I-waw will usually appear as a I-yod in Biblical Aramaic and so will be listed in this manner in the dictionary. However, a memory of this historical waw is sometimes exhibited in the paradigms of these roots where, for example, a waw will appear as a mater, as in **הוֹדַע** *he caused to know*, the haph'el 3ms suffix conjugation of **ידע**.

I-NUN VERBS

Verbs with a nun as a first root consonant have regular participial and suffix-conjugation forms in the pə'al (**נָפְקִין** *they were going forth*; **נְפַק** *he went forth*; **נְפַקוּ** *they went forth*). But, in the pə'al prefix conjugation, imperatives, and infinitive, the nun often assimilates into the second root consonant. For example, the earlier form *yinpel (the prefix conjugation) becomes yippel = **יִפֵּל**. The same process occurs wherever the verb bears a prefix, as in the suffix conjugation of the haph'el as well as the prefix conjugation of the haph'el (and by association the imperative) as well as the participle and infinitive.

LANGUAGE INSIGHT

The process of assimilation may be familiar from English and other languages. In the Latin word corresponding to English *assimilation*, for example, the combination of the prefix *ad-* with the stem *similare* results in the *d* of *ad-* assimilating into the following letter such that the word has a double *s*: *assimilare*.

Since the form of the imperative is related to that of the prefix conjugation, the imperative of the pə'al lacks any indication of the initial nun (e.g. **פֶּל** *fall!* and **פֻּקוּ** *come out!*). The following table is made up largely of reconstructed forms in order to demonstrate the different verb types that might be encountered when reading extra-biblical texts.

	נפל *to fall*		נפק *to go or come out*		נתן *to give*
	pəʿal		**pəʿal**		**pəʿal**
	prefix	**imperative**	**prefix**	**imperative**	**prefix**
3ms	יִפֵּל		יִפֵּק		יִנְתֵּן
3fs	תִּפֵּל		תִּפֵּק		תִּנְתֵּן
2ms	תִּפֵּל	פֵּל	תִּפֵּק	פֵּק	תִּנְתֵּן
2fs	תִּפְּלִין	פִּ֫לִי	תִּפְּקִין	פֻּ֫קִי	תִּנְתְּנִין
1cs	אֶפֵּל		אֶפֵּק		אֶנְתֵּן
3mp	יִפְּלוּן		יִפְּקוּן		יִנְתְּנוּן
3fp	יִפְּלָן		יִפְּקָן		יִנְתְּנָן
2mp	תִּפְּלוּן	פִּ֫לוּ	תִּפְּקוּן	פֻּ֫קוּ	תִּנְתְּנוּן
2fp	תִּפְּלָן	פִּ֫לָה	תִּפְּקָן	פֻּ֫קָה	תִּנְתְּנָן
1cp	נִפֵּל		נִפֵּק		נִנְתֵּן

Sometimes the nun of the root seems not to assimilate, but be preserved (e.g. in the pəʿal יִנְתֵּן *he will give* above and in the haphʿel הַנְפֵּק *he took out* and הַנְפִּ֫קוּ *they took out* in the following table). Nevertheless, this nun reflects a secondary process of nasalization. It is not uncommon in Aramaic for a geminated (or doubled) consonant (e.g. -pp-) to become a nun plus a regular consonant (e.g. -np-). This is what is called nasalization. So, in the example of יִנְתֵּן *he will give*, although it looks as though the nun of the root never assimilated, it is actually better to construe the nun as secondary. The nun of the root, in fact, did assimilate initially (יִתֵּן yitten as seen sometimes in Biblical Aramaic) but the nun reappeared through nasalization as יִנְתֵּן yinten. We suspect this development since nasalization is also found with I-yod verbs (e.g. אִנְדַּע ʾindaʿ *I will know* (from ידע) and תִּנְדַּע tindaʿ *it will know*) and other roots that never contained a nun root consonant.

The following table illustrates the alternative realizations of the root **נפק** in the haphʿel/aphʿel. Assimilation (without nasalization) seems to be more common in later varieties of Aramaic (where you find the aphʿel) while the forms exhibiting nasalization seem more common in Biblical Aramaic and Official Aramaic (where you tend to find the haphʿel).

	נפק *to go or come out*					
	aphʿel			**haphʿel**		
	suffix	**prefix**	**imperative**	**suffix**	**prefix**	**imperative**
3ms	אַפֵּק	יַפֵּק		הַנְפֵּק	יְהַנְפֵּק	
3fs	אַפְּקַת	תַּפֵּק		הַנְפְּקַת	תְּהַנְפֵּק	
2ms	אַפֵּקְתְּ	תַּפֵּק	אַפֵּק	הַנְפֵּקְתְּ	תְּהַנְפֵּק	הַנְפֵּק
2fs	אַפֵּקְתִּי	תַּפְּקִין	אַפִּ֫קִי	הַנְפֵּקְתִּי	תְּהַנְפְּקִין	הַנְפִּ֫קִי
1cs	אַפְּקֵת	אַפֵּק		הַנְפְּקֵת	אֲהַנְפֵּק	
3mp	אַפִּ֫קוּ	יַפְּקוּן		הַנְפִּ֫קוּ	יְהַנְפְּקוּן	
3fp	אַפִּ֫קָה	יַפְּקָן		הַנְפִּ֫קָה	יְהַנְפְּקָן	
2mp	אַפֵּקְתּוּן	תַּפְּקוּן	אַפִּ֫קוּ	הַנְפֵּקְתּוּן	תְּהַנְפְּקוּן	הַנְפִּ֫קוּ
2fp	אַפֵּקְתֵּן	תַּפְּקָן	אַפִּ֫קָה	הַנְפֵּקְתֵּן	תְּהַנְפְּקָן	הַנְפִּ֫קָה
1cp	אַפֵּ֫קְנָא	נַפֵּק		הַנְפֵּ֫קְנָא	נְהַנְפֵּק	

In these aph‘el forms note that the dagesh represents a doubling (**אַפֵּק** ’appeq), but in the haph‘el, the dagesh represents the hard (non-spirantized) pe (**הַנְפֵּק** hanpeq). Sometimes the haph‘el/aph‘el exhibits a hiriq where a sere might be expected. Therefore, **תְּהַנְפִּק** would not be an unexpected alternative to the 3fs prefix conjugation. Note that the m.s. and m./f.p. imperatives are identical to the 3ms and 3m/fp suffix-conjugation forms.

The participles and infinitives would exhibit the following forms:

	נפק	
	aph‘el	**haph‘el**
participle		
m.s.	מַפֵּק	מְהַנְפֵּק
f.s.	מַפְּקָה	מְהַנְפְּקָה
m.p.	מַפְּקִין	מְהַנְפְּקִין
f.p.	מַפְּקָן	מְהַנְפְּקָן
infinitive		
	אַפָּקָה	הַנְפָּקָה

There are relatively few aph‘el forms from I-nun roots attested in Biblical Aramaic and most of them exhibit irregular vowels: **מַצִּל** *one who delivers* (aph‘el m.s. part. from **נצל** *to deliver*); **אֲחֵת** (for an expected **אַחֵת**) *deposit!* (aph‘el m.s. impv. from **נחת** *to go down*); **תַּחֵת** *you will deposit* (aph‘el m.s. pref. conj. from **נחת** *to go down*).

Another irregular verb should be mentioned here, **סלק** *to go up*. When the verb appears with a prefix element (in the prefix conjugation or in the haph‘el *to bring up*), the lamed assimilates backwards into the samekh and the resulting form often looks like a first nun verb. The verb appears with this assimilation (and subsequent nasalization) only three times in Biblical Aramaic, but it is quite frequent in other dialects of the language, so it is important to know the verb and its inflection. In Biblical Aramaic we find the haph‘el suffix conjugation **הַסִּקוּ** *they brought up*, the infinitive **הַנְסָקָה** *to bring up*, and the hoph’al/huph’al suffix conjugation **הֻסַּק** *it was brought up*. In later writings like the targums, you find spellings which reflect **יִסַּק** yissaq *he will go up* and **נִסַּק** nissaq *we will go up*.

PRACTICE 1

Copy the paradigm for the pə‘al prefix conjugation of נפל and the haph‘el suffix and prefix conjugations of נפק. Then, produce the following sentences using the vocabulary provided: בַּ֫יִת (det. בַּיְתָא) *house*, דָּת *decree* (fem. noun), כְּסַף (det. כַּסְפָּא) *silver*, מֶ֫לֶךְ (det. מַלְכָּא) *king*, מִן *from*, נטל *to lift* (pref.יִטֵּל), נפק pə‘al *to go out* (pref. יִפֵּק), haph‘el *to bring out*, עַ֫יִן *eye*.

a *They will go out* (pə‘al 3mp pref.) *from the house.*
b *I have brought out* (haph‘el 1cs suff. conj.) *the silver from his house.*
c *The decree went out* (pə‘al 3fs suff. conj.) *from the king.*
d *You will lift* (pə‘al 2fs pref. conj.) *your* (2fs) *eyes.*
e *We will lift* (pə‘al 1cp pref. conj.) *my house.*

I-ALEPH VERBS

Roots with an aleph as their first consonant have verbal forms that are only slightly different from those of the strong verb. As with first-nun roots, the differences appear primarily when prefixes are added to the root. For the pəʿal stem, the result is that the regular short i of the prefix in the prefix conjugation transforms into ē. That is, the earlier *yiʾmar becomes yēmar = **יֵאמַר** *he will say*. In the case of these verbs, the aleph does not assimilate to the following consonant, but instead it elides in pronunciation and in compensation for the loss of a consonant, the preceding vowel lengthens. This also happens with the pəʿal infinitive: **מֵאמַר** *to say*. In these cases the aleph is usually retained in the spelling, though it is sometimes also lost: **מֵמַר** *to say*. In neither case was it preserved in pronunciation as a glottal stop.

In the haphʿel, the initial aleph is often replaced by a waw or yod. The most commonly occurring verb forms are the following:

	haphʿel suff. conj. of אבד	**haphʿel pref. conj. of אבד**	**haphʿel imperat. of אבד**
3ms	הוֹבֵד	יְהוֹבֵד	
3fs	הוֹבְדַת	תְּהוֹבֵד	
2ms	הוֹבֵדְתְּ	תְּהוֹבֵד	הוֹבֵד
2fs	הוֹבֵ֫דְתִּי	תְּהוֹבְדִין	הוֹבֵ֫דִי
1cs	הוֹבְדֵת	אֲהוֹבֵד	
3mp	הוֹ֫בְדוּ	יְהוֹבְדוּן	
3fp	הוֹ֫בְדָה	יְהוֹבְדָן	
2mp	הוֹבֵדְתּוּן	תְּהוֹבְדוּן	הוֹבֵ֫דוּ
2fp	הוֹבֵדְתֵּן	תְּהוֹבְדָן	הוֹבֵ֫דָה
1cp	הוֹבֵ֫דְנָא	נְהוֹבֵד	

The participle (e.g. **מְהוֹבֵד**) and infinitive (**הוֹבָדָה**) exhibit the same shift to waw. Another important verb, **אתי** *to come*, is introduced in a following unit on III-yod verbs. The hophʿal/huphʿal is attesetd in **הוּבַד** *it was destroyed* (3ms suffix conjugation of **אבד**). For the anomalous forms **הֵיתָ֫יִת** and **הֵיתָ֫יוּ** (huphʿal/hophʿal of **אתי**), see the following unit on III-aleph/waw/yod verbs.

In other verbs, the aleph is replaced by a yod mater, as in **הֵימִן** *he believed*, the haphʿel 3ms suffix conjugation of **אמן**.

CULTURAL INSIGHT

The religious worship in the Elephantine Yaho temple is unexpected in more ways than one. In addition to its simple existence (which seems to violate the Deuteronomic stipulation that there should be a single temple in Jerusalem), the records of payments to the temple, preserved in Aramaic (*TAD* C3.15, lines 126–8), suggest the worship of more than one deity at the Elephantine temple: Yaho, Eshembethel, and Anathbethel. While Yaho is easily identifiable as Yahweh, the other two are less familiar. Both incorporate the divine name Bethel, a deity mentioned in numerous other inscriptions and perhaps to be interpreted as another name of Yaho (see van der Toorn 2016). Eshembethel is also mentioned in the Aramaic text in Demotic script (Papyrus Amherst 63). Anatbethel also incorporates the divine name Anat, a goddess known from Ugaritic texts from ca. 1200 BCE and who is closely affiliated with the storm god Baʿl. Presumably, in the context of the Elephantine temple, she was understood to be the consort of Bethel and/or Yaho.

I-YOD VERBS

Roots with a historical waw have generally transformed into I-yod roots. Roots with a yod as first root-consonant exhibit patterns like other verbs studied in this unit, in that peculiarities in their forms emerge only with the application of prefixes to their root. The pəʿal and paʿʿel suffix conjugations to these verbs are, therefore, analogous to strong verbs.

For the pəʿal prefix conjugation, there are two basic patterns, depending on the specific verb/root; both patterns are similar to those of I-nun roots. One pattern exhibits assimilation of the yod to the second root consonant (just like the I-nun root **נפל** (e.g. **יִפֵּל** *he will fall*)). Note, for example, **יִכֻּל** *he will be able*, the pəʿal 3ms prefix conjugation of **יכל**. The second pattern exhibits assimilation of the yod with subsequent nasalization (like **נתן** (e.g. **יִנְתֵּן** *he will give*)). Note **יִנְדַּע** *he will know*, the pəʿal 3ms prefix conjugation of **ידע**. For the haphʿel, the dominant pattern exhibits an ō vowel in the prefix, instead of a. These paradigms are illustrated in the following table. (Paʿʿel prefix conjugation forms are too rare to warrant discussion.)

	pəʿal prefix conj. of יכל	pəʿal prefix conj. of ידע	pəʿal imperative	haphʿel suff. conj. of ידע	haphʿel pref. conj. of ידע
3ms	יִכֻּל	יִנְדַּע		הוֹדַע	יְהוֹדַע
3fs	תִּכֻּל	תִּנְדַּע		הוֹדְעַת	תְּהוֹדַע
2ms	תִּכֻּל	תִּנְדַּע	דַּע	הוֹדַעְתְּ	תְּהוֹדַע
2fs	תִּכְלִין	תִּנְדְּעִין	דַּעִי	הוֹדַעְתִּי	תְּהוֹדְעִין
1cs	אִכֻּל	אֶנְדַּע		הוֹדְעֵת	אֲהוֹדַע
3mp	יִכְלוּן	יִנְדְּעוּן		הוֹדַעוּ	יְהוֹדְעוּן
3fp	יִכְלָן	יִנְדְּעָן		הוֹדַעָה	יְהוֹדְעָן
2mp	תִּכְלוּן	תִּנְדְּעוּן	דַּעוּ	הוֹדַעְתּוּן	תְּהוֹדְעוּן
2fp	תִּכְלָן	תִּנְדְּעָן	דַּעָה	הוֹדַעְתֵּן	תְּהוֹדְעָן
1cp	נִכֻּל	נִנְדַּע		הוֹדַעְנוּ	נְהוֹדַע

The pəʿal infinitive also exhibits the assimilation of the first root consonant (and sometimes secondary nasalization).

haphʿel participle:

מְהוֹדַע
מְהוֹדְעָה
מְהוֹדְעִין
מְהוֹדְעָן

pəʿal infinitive: **מִנְדַּע**
haphʿel infinitive: **הוֹדָעָה**

The haphʿel of **יְדַע** exhibits an a vowel where we would otherwise expect e (ֵ); this is due to the influence of the guttural ʿayin. Thus, we have **הוֹדַע** instead of **הוֹדֵע***. Some roots, like **יבל** *to bring* (and **ירת** *to inherit* in other dialects of Aramaic), deviate from the expected pattern and make the haphʿel with a prefixed **-הֵי** (hēʸ-) in the suffix conjugation (e.g. 3ms suffix conjugation: **הֵיבֵל** *he brought*). The prefix conjugation is not attested for these verbs.

LANGUAGE INSIGHT

The ō vowel of the prefix in the haph'el is usually marked with a waw mater (e.g. הוֹדַע) and this reflects the fact that many of these verbs were historically I-waw. Where the prefix vowel is instead ē and marked with a yod mater (e.g. הֵיבֵל), the verbs were historically I-yod. In both cases, the prefix vowels (ō and ē) derive from the resolution of earlier diphthongs (i.e. hawda' became hō^{w}da' = הוֹדַע; and *haybel became hē^{y}bel = הֵיבֵל).

One of the side effects of these similarities between the I-nun and I-yod roots is that it is sometimes difficult, when reading Biblical Aramaic, to recognize the root from which a given verb form derives. This, in turn, makes it difficult to look up the meaning of the verb. It is often necessary to go through a dictionary looking up the various possible roots from which a given verbal form may derive.

PRACTICE 2

Copy out the paradigms for the root נפל in the pə'al, for the root אבד in the haph'el, and for ידע in the pə'al and haph'el. Then, parse the participial, infinitive, and suffix/prefix conjugation verb forms, making sure to indicate the possible root and verb stem. Confirm your answer by looking up the different possible roots in the glossary and then translate the word.

Example: מְהֵימַן → haph'el m.s. part. (abs.) of the root אמן or ימן (it is אמן) *one who believes* or *he believes*

a תְּהוֹדְעוּן
b תִּפְּלוּן
c תְּהַנְזִק
d מְהוֹדְעִין
e הֵימִן
f אָמְרִין
g מְהַנְזְקָה
h יָכְלִין
i הוֹתֵב
j נְחִת
k הֵיבְלָה
l תִּנְדַּע
m נֵאמַר
n תַּחֵת
o הַצְלָה
p מְהַחֲתִין
q הֵיבֵל
r יְאבַד
s יִתֵּב
t נָפְלִין

CULTURAL INSIGHT

The Aramaic text in Demotic script, Papyrus Amherst 63, contains an Aramaic version of Psalm 20. You can compare the Aramaic text (as interpreted by Steiner 2017) and the Hebrew of verse 5. The Demotic symbols (col. XI, lines 14–15) seem to reflect the following Aramaic words **ימתן (ינתן) אלן מר כבלבן**, the first word bearing a mistake of mem for nun. The amended text would be rendered in Biblical Aramaic pronunciation something like יִנְתֵּן אֱלַן מָר כִּבְלִבַּן *May (my) Lord give to us according (to what) is in our heart.* Note the preposition אֱל *to,* which is an Egyptian Aramaic variation of עַל; note too מָר, the abbreviated form of מָרֵא (*Lord*) or מָרִאי (*my Lord*). Compare the text with the Hebrew (which uses many cognate words): יִתֶּן־לְךָ כִלְבָבֶךָ *May he give to you according to your heart.* (Cf. van der Toorn 2018, 165–7.)

Reading

Translate the following passage from Ezra 4 using the glossary and the notes that follow the text.

EZRA 4:11

a דְּנָה פַּרְשֶׁגֶן אִגַּרְתָּא דִּי שְׁלַחוּ עֲלוֹהִי עַל־אַרְתַּחְשַׁשְׂתְּא מַלְכָּא
b עַבְדָיךְ אֱנָשׁ עֲבַר־נַהֲרָה וּכְעֶנֶת

EZRA 4:12

a יְדִיעַ לֶהֱוֵא לְמַלְכָּא דִּי יְהוּדָיֵא דִּי סְלִקוּ מִן־לְוָתָךְ עֲלֶינָא
b אֲתוֹ לִירוּשְׁלֶם
c קִרְיְתָא מָרָדְתָּא וּבִאישְׁתָּא בָּנַיִן
d וְשׁוּרַיָּא שַׁכְלִלוּ וְאֻשַּׁיָּא יַחִיטוּ

EZRA 4:13

a כְּעַן יְדִיעַ לֶהֱוֵא לְמַלְכָּא דִּי הֵן קִרְיְתָא דָךְ תִּתְבְּנֵא וְשׁוּרַיָּא יִשְׁתַּכְלְלוּן
b מִנְדָּה־בְלוֹ וַהֲלָךְ לָא יִנְתְּנוּן וְאַפְּתֹם מַלְכִין תְּהַנְזִק

EZRA 4:14

a כְּעַן כָּל־קֳבֵל דִּי־מְלַח הֵיכְלָא מְלַחְנָא
b וְעַרְוַת מַלְכָּא לָא אֲרִיךְ לַנָא לְמֶחֱזֵא
c עַל־דְּנָה שְׁלַחְנָא וְהוֹדַעְנָא לְמַלְכָּא

Ezra 4:11

a

דְּנָה – *This (is) . . .*

שְׁלַחוּ – Either *they sent* or as an impersonal construction with a passive translation *was sent*.

עֲלוֹהִי עַל־אַרְתַּחְשַׁשְׂתְּא מַלְכָּא – to him: To Artaxerxes, the king

b

אֱנָשׁ – *the people of* This is the construct singular form, though the singular absolute would look identical. The singular is used as a collective noun.

וּכְעֶ֫נֶת – This marks the beginning of the letter proper and really should go with the following verse.

Ezra 4:12

a

לֶהֱוֵא – *let it be* This is the pə ʿal 3ms jussive or prefix conjugation of הוי *to be.*

b

אֲתוֹ – *they have come* This is the pə ʿal 3ms suffix conjugation of אתי to come.

c

מָרָדְתָּא – This is the f.s. determined form of the adjective מָרָד *rebellious.*

בָּנַ֫יִן – *they are building* This is the pə ʿal m.p. participle of בני *to build.* The preceding words of this line are the grammatical object of the verb.

d

שַׁכְלִ֫לוּ – *they have completed* This is the 3mp suffix conjugation of the verb שׁכלל, which (like שׁיזב) reflects the morpheme of another stem associated with causation (the shaphʿel), familiar from other Semitic languages.

יַחִיטוּ – This seems to be a jussive form of the root חוט *to examine*, but we expect instead a suffix conjugation. In fact, it is more likely that this should be understood as a paʿʿel suffix conjugation of a root יחט spelled with a mater, though we would expect instead no mater: יַחִ֫טוּ.

Ezra 4:13 תִּתְבְּנֵא (it) will be rebuilt -- The peʿal 3ms prefix conjugation of בני.

יִשְׁתַּכְלְלִין (they) will be completed -- The hitpəʿel 3mp prefix conjugation of שׁכלל.

Ezra 4:14

a

מְלַח הֵיכְלָא מְלַ֫חְנָא – *we salt with the salt of the palace* The expression presumably expresses the loyalty of the speakers to the Persian emperor. More idiomatically, it might be translated *we use the salt of the palace*. The *CAL* gloss this usage as *to share someone's salt*, i.e. *to dine together.*

Test yourself

1 Vocalize the vowel-less verb forms (all of which are either I-aleph, I-yod, or I-nun). Then, match each verse with its translation, using the glossary where necessary.

a	מַן־דִּי־לָא יפל וְיִסְגֻּד	1	*the vessels of gold that they had removed (from the temple)*
b	כִּדְנָה תאמרון לְהוֹם	2	*Then, Arioch made the matter known*
c	אֱדַ֫יִן מִלְּתָא הודע אַרְיוֹךְ	3	*The interpretation he will make known to the king.*
d	מָאנֵי דַהֲבָא דִּי הנפקו	4	*he will be able to deliver like this . . .*
e	מהודעין אֲנַ֫חְנָא לְמַלְכָּא	5	*to destroy the sages of Babel*
f	לָא יהובדון חַבְּרֹ֫והִי	6	*who will not fall and worship . . .*

g יכל לְהצלה כִּדְנָה **7** *like this you will say to them*

h פִּשְׁרָא לְמַלְכָּא יהודע **8** *I will know that its interpretation you are able to tell me*

i לְהובדה לְחַכִּימֵי בָבֶל **9** *We are informing the king.*

j אנדע דִּי פִּשְׁרֵהּ תְּהַחֲוֻנַּנִי **10** *they will not destroy his companions*

2 Identify the root of these irregular forms and then complete the translations.

a תַּחֵת בְּבֵית אֱלָהָא ______________________ *(them) in the temple of God*

b הֵיבֵל הִמּוֹ לְהֵיכְלָא ______________________ *them to the temple*

c הוּבַד גִּשְׁמַהּ *its body* ______________________

d הָנְחַת מִן־כָּרְסֵא מַלְכוּתֵהּ ______________________ *from the throne of his kingdom*

e הֵימַן בֵּאלָהֵהּ ______________________ *in his God*

f אֱזֶל־אֲחֵת הִמּוֹ בְּהֵיכְלָא ______________________, ______________________ *them in the temple!*

g לְהֵיבָלָה כְּסַף וּדְהַב דִּי מַלְכָּא *to* ______________________ *silver and gold of the king*

h הַסִּקוּ לְשַׁדְרַךְ מֵישַׁךְ וַעֲבֵד נְגוֹ ______________________ *Shadrach, Meshach, and Abed-Nego*

i מַצִּל וְעָבֵד אָתִין וְתִמְהִין *he* ______________________ *and does signs and miracles*

j הֻסַּק דָּנִיֵּאל מִן־גֻּבָּא *Daniel* ______________________ *from the den*

Suggestions for further study

Make flashcards for the most basic forms of the weak roots listed in this unit (e.g. the 3ms and 3mp suffix/prefix conjugations, the m.s. imperatives, and the infinitives). Shuffle these flashcards among your vocabulary flashcards.

SELF-CHECK

I CAN...
form I-nun verbs
form I-aleph verbs
form I-waw/yod verbs

17 *II-waw/yod verbs*

In this unit you will learn how to:

- **form II-waw/yod verbs in the pəʿal**
- **form II-waw/yod verbs in the haphʿel**

In this unit you will read:

- **Ezra 4:17–21**

Grammar

SUFFIX AND PREFIX CONJUGATIONS OF II-WAW/YOD VERBS

Originally, yod and waw functioned as discrepant root consonants, independent of each other. However, as Aramaic developed, the distinctions between roots containing a historical waw or a historical yod diminished, as mentioned in Unit 16. As a result, it is often difficult to discern whether a root had a waw as its original second consonant, or a yod. In general, the pəʿal suffix conjugation of these roots has a long ā in the first syllable (קָם from the root קום *to arise* and שָׂם from שׂים *to set*). In the pəʿal prefix conjugation, the prefix has a murmured vowel followed by a long ū in the second syllable (יְקוּם) with II-waw roots or a long ī (יְשִׂים) with II-yod roots. It is a consistent feature of verbs of this type to carry a murmured vowel or half-vowel as part of any prefixed element.

The paʿʿel stem often has a yod as the second consonant, which never disappears (קַיֵּם paʿʿel 3ms suffix conj. / יְקַיֵּם paʿʿel 3ms prefix conj.), though the waw is retained with roots that are also III-aleph/waw/yod (אֲחַוֵּא *I will declare*). The form of these verbs in the paʿʿel is identical to that of the strong verb.

The prefix of the haphʿel on the suffix conjugation is הֲ. The vowel of the second syllable is either ī or ē (ֵ) (as in הֲקִים or הֲקֵים). For the haphʿel prefix conjugation, the prefix usually carries just a murmured vowel (יְקִים), though sometimes it exhibits a qamets (יְהָקֵים / יָקֵים / יָקִים /). Unlike in other verb types, for these roots the aphʿel is more common than the haphʿel. In slightly later periods of Aramaic the aphʿel forms totally eclipse haphʿel forms, and II-waw/yod verbs can appear with the following three vowel sequences: יְקִים, יָקִים, or יָקֵים.

Because the verbal forms of this type of root are characterized by long vowels that do not reduce, the inflection shows limited changes in the base of the verbal form.

	pəʿal suffix conj.	pəʿal prefix conj.	haphʿel suffix conj.	haphʿel prefix conj.
3ms	קָם	יְקוּם	הֲקִים or הֲקֵים	יְקִים (most common) or יְהָקֵים or יְקֵים or יָקִים
3fs	קָ֫מַת	תְּקוּם	הֲקִ֫ימַת or הֲקֵ֫ימַת	תְּקִים / etc.
2ms	קָ֫מְתָּ qāmtā	תְּקוּם	הֲקֵ֫ימְתָּ	תְּקִים / etc.
2fs	קָ֫מְתִּי qāmtī^{y}	תְּקוּמִין	הֲקֵ֫ימְתִּי	תְּקִימִין / etc.
1cs	קָ֫מֶת	אֲקוּם	הֲקֵ֫ימֶת	אֲקִים / etc.
3mp	קָ֫מוּ	יְקוּמוּן	הֲקִ֫ימוּ or הֲקֵ֫ימוּ	יְקִימוּן / etc.
3fp	קָ֫מָה	יְקוּמָן	הֲקִ֫ימָה or הֲקֵ֫ימָה	יְקִימָן / etc.
2mp	קָמְתּוּן qāmtū^{w}n	תְּקוּמוּן	הֲקֵימְתּוּן	תְּקִימוּן / etc.
2fp	קָמְתֵּן qāmtēn	תְּקוּמָן	הֲקֵימְתֵּן	תְּקִימָן / etc.
1cp	קָ֫מְנָא	נְקוּם	הֲקֵ֫ימְנָא	נְקִים / etc.

As can be seen from the table, all the forms contain a long vowel between the two root consonants. The long ā is characteristic of the pəʿal suffix conjugation, while long ē and ī are typical of the haphʿel. As for the prefix conjugation, the pəʿal exhibits ū and the haphʿel ē or ī between the root consonants. The vowel ā also appears in the pəʿal prefix conjugation with the root **הוך** *to go*, a variation of the root **הלך** *to go* that only occurs in the pəʿal prefix conjugation: **יְהָךְ** *he will go* and infinitive **מְהָךְ** *to go*.

An exceptional form is **רִם**, the pəʿal 3ms suffix conjugation *it was high*.

PRACTICE

Translate the following phrases using the vocabulary provided: אֲרַע (det. אַרְעָא) *land*, בְּ *in*, דור *to dwell*, הֵיכַל *palace*, כֹּל *all*, מִלָּה *word*, מֶ֫לֶךְ (det. מַלְכָּא) *king*, מַלְכוּ *kingdom*, מַנְדַּע *understanding*, סוף pəʿal *to be fulfilled*, haphʿel *to bring to an end*, עַל *to*, צְלֵם *image*, קום haphʿel *to erect*, שְׁלָם *peace*, תוב pəʿal *to return* (intrans.), haphʿel *to return (something)*.

- **a** *His word was fulfilled* (pəʿal 3fs suff. conj.).
- **b** *They returned* (haphʿel 3mp suff. conj.) *the word of the king.*
- **c** *My understanding will return* (pəʿal 3ms pref. conj.) *to me.*
- **d** *I have erected* (haphʿel 1cs suff. conj.) *the image of the king.*
- **e** *You will dwell* (pəʿal 2ms pref. conj.) *in peace.*
- **f** *It will bring to an end* (haphʿel 3fs pref. conj.) *all the kingdoms.*
- **g** *The king dwelled* (pəʿal 3ms suff. conj.) *in the palace.*
- **h** *I will bring to an end* (haphʿel 1cs pref. conj.) *the kingdom.*
- **i** *We dwelled* (pəʿal 1cp suff. conj) *in the palace.*
- **j** *A word of peace will return* (pəʿal 3fs pref. conj.).

IMPERATIVES, PARTICIPLES, AND INFINITIVES OF II-WAW/YOD VERBS

The imperatives, based on the prefix conjugation forms, and the infinitives are presented here.

	pəʿal	haphʿel
masc. sing.	קוּם	הֲקֵים or הֲקִים
fem. sing.	קֻוּמִי	הֲקִ֫ימִי
masc. pl.	קֻוּמוּ	הֲקִ֫ימוּ
fem. pl.	קֻוּמָה	הֲקִ֫ימָה
infinitive	מְקָם	הֲקָמָה

CULTURAL INSIGHT

In Mark 5:41, as mentioned, Jesus is quoted in Aramaic, through Greek transliteration, ταλιθα κουμ = talitha koum *Little girl, get up!* The transliteration of the second word presumes the Aramaic pəʿal m.s. imperative **קוּם**, though the subject is feminine. Some New Testament manuscripts, however, attest an alternative transliteration that represents the feminine singular imperative: koumi = קֻוּמִי. The absence of the final vowel in most manuscripts may reflect an ancient mistake or may reflect the actual pronunciation in the colloquial variety of Aramaic used by Jesus.

Pəʿal participles have aleph as the middle root consonant (קָאְמִין *ones standing*). This spelling is unusual since we would have expected a hateph vowel under the aleph. This inconsistency reflects something about the Aramaic language and the transmission of the biblical text. The consonants of the biblical text preserve one pronunciation tradition and the vowels reflect a separate tradition. In the case of middle-weak participles, the vowels reflect an earlier pronunciation with a middle yod: qāyəmīn (= קָיְמִין). That is, even though the scribes wrote the word with an aleph, they pronounced it with a yod, as reflected by the simple shewa under the aleph. The pronunciation with yod seems early because it preserves a consonant that is closer to the original waw than aleph and because it is consistent with the purely consonantal spelling of the same form in Aramaic texts from the fifth century BCE, קימן. The consonants of the biblical form, קָאְמִין, on the other hand, reflect a later pronunciation with aleph instead of yod: qāʾămīn (= קָאֲמִין), as reflected in the consonantal spelling קאמין from the Dead Sea Scrolls, dating to the first century BCE. This pronunciation reflects the same phonetic development found in inflected forms of ordinal numerals and gentilic nouns, that is, -āy- becoming -āʾ- before word-final morphemes like the masculine plural -īn (i.e. קַדְמָיִן becoming קַדְמָאִין).

	pəʿal	pəʿal passive	haphʿel
masc. sing.	קָאֵם	קִים	מְקִים / מְהָקִים / מָקִים

fem. sing.	קָאְמָה (vow. קָיְמָה / cons. קָאֲמָה)	קִימָה	מְקִימָה
masc. pl.	קָאְמִין (vow. קָיְמִין / cons. קָאֲמִין)	קִימִין	מְקִימִין
fem. pl.	קָאְמָן (vow. קָיְמָן / cons. קָאֲמָן)	קִימָן	מְקִימָן

OTHER FORMS AND IDIOSYNCRACIES

The pəʿal prefix conjugation of **שׂים** is **יְשִׂים**. The haphʿel prefix conjugation might look identical for this root if it occurred, though it does not. In addition, the pəʿal 3ms passive suffix conjugation would look identical to the pəʿal m.s. passive participle: **שִׂים**.

The hitpəʿel forms of these roots typically have a doubled t-prefix. Thus, in the hitpəʿel 3ms prefix conjugation we have **יִתְּשָׂם** (yittəśām) *it will be made* (from **שׂים**) and **יִתְּזִין** *it will be fed* (from **זון**). In both cases, there is a long vowel between the two root consonants. The suffix conjugation is not well attested, but, based on other dialects, it would have shown a similar variation in long vowels: **הִתְּשָׂם*** and **הִתְּזִין***. Hitpaʿʿal forms are easily identified due to doubling of the middle waw or yod: **יִשְׁתַּוֵּה** *it will be made like* (3ms pref. conj. of **שׁוי**).

The huphʿal/hophʿal stem appears with only one verb (**קום**) in the 3fs suffix conjugation: **הֳקִימַת** *it was reestablished*.

A rare polel and hitpolal stem are found with the root **רום** *to rise*: **מְרוֹמֵם** *(I) am exalting* and **הִתְרוֹמַמְתָּ** *you exalted yourself*.

Although most verbs are listed under the pəʿal 3ms suffix-conjugation form, verbs that are from a middle weak root are listed by root; so to look up the meaning of **קָם**, look under **קום**.

Reading

Translate the following passage from Ezra 4 using the glossary and the notes that follow the text.

EZRA 4:17

a פִּתְגָמָא שְׁלַח מַלְכָּא עַל־רְחוּם בְּעֵל־טְעֵם
b וְשִׁמְשַׁי סָפְרָא וּשְׁאָר כְּנָוָתְהוֹן דִּי יָתְבִין בְּשָׁמְרָיִן
c וּשְׁאָר עֲבַר־נַהֲרָה
d שְׁלָם וּכְעֶת

EZRA 4:18

a נִשְׁתְּוָנָא דִּי שְׁלַחְתּוּן עֲלֶינָא
b מְפָרַשׁ קֱרִי קָדָמָי

EZRA 4:19

a וּמִנִּי שִׂים טְעֵם וּבַקַּרוּ וְהַשְׁכַּחוּ דִּי קִרְיְתָא דָךְ
b מִן־יוֹמָת עָלְמָא עַל־מַלְכִין מִתְנַשְּׂאָה
c וּמְרַד וְאֶשְׁתַּדּוּר מִתְעֲבֶד־בַּהּ

EZRA 4:20

a וּמַלְכִין תַּקִּיפִין הֲווֹ עַל־יְרוּשְׁלֶם
b וְשַׁלִּיטִין בְּכֹל עֲבַר נַהֲרָה
c וּמִדָּה בְלוֹ וַהֲלָךְ מִתְיְהֵב לְהוֹן

EZRA 4:21

a כְּעַן שִׂימוּ טְעֵם לְבַטָּלָה גֻּבְרַיָּא אִלֵּךְ
b וְקִרְיְתָא דָךְ לָא תִתְבְּנֵא עַד־מִנִּי טַעְמָא יִתְּשָׂם

Ezra 4:17

a

רְחוּם בְּעֵל־טְעֵם – *Rehum, commander* The title translates more literally as *master of decree*.

b

שִׁמְשַׁי – *Shimshai*

d

שְׁלָם וּכְעֶת – This appears to be the beginning of the letter: *Greetings* (lit. *peace*). *And now, . . .* The last word introduces a transition in a letter or document (here, from the greeting to the main subject of the correspondence).

Ezra 4:18

a

נִשְׁתְּוָנָא – *letter* This is a loanword from Persian.

b

מְפָרַשׁ קֱרִי קָדָמָי – *it was read (with) explanation before me* The line might more literally be rendered as *an explained thing it was read before me*. The first word is a pa''el m.s. passive participle of the root **פרש**. It functions as an adverb in this case. The second word is the pəʿīl 3ms suffix conjugation of **קרי** *to be read*. The third word would ordinarily be vocalized with a hateph-qamets beneath the first letter and a patach under the mem (**קֳדָמַי**); the first qamets is simply an alternative pronunciation and the qamets under the mem is due to the word's location at the end of the verse, where sometimes a patach is lengthened to qamets.

Ezra 4:19

a

מִנִּי שִׂים – *by me was set* or just *I set* The min preposition occurs with the 1cs pronominal suffix followed by the pəʿal passive / pəʿīl m.s. participle of **שׂים**.

בַקַּ֫רוּ – *a search was made* Here, the plural verb form (literally *they searched*) is used in an impersonal way and translated into English in the passive voice.

הַשְׁכַּחוּ – *there was found* The plural verb form is used again in an impersonal construction.

b

מִתְנַשְּׂאָה *has risen up* This is the hitpa. f.s. part. of **נשׂי**.

c

אֶשְׁתַּדּוּר – *insurrection* This is a noun from the root **שדר**.

Ezra 4:20

a

הֲוֹו – *were* This is the pəʿal 3mp suffix conjugation of הוי *to be.*

b

עֲבַר נַהֲרָה – *Abar-Nahara* or *Across the River* or *Trans-Euphrates*, the region of Syria and the Levant west (or across, from a Persian perspective) the Euphrates river. We would expect the final letter to be aleph since the word *river* is in the determined state: עֲבַר נַהֲרָא.

Ezra 4:21

a

שִׂימוּ – This is the pəʿal m.s. imperative of שׂים *to set.*

b

תִתְבְּנֵא – *it will (not) be rebuilt* This is the hitpəʿel 3fs prefix conjugation of בני *to build.*

יִתְּשָׂם – This is the hitpəʿel 3ms prefix conjugation of שׂים *to set, make.*

Test yourself

Write out the paradigms for קום in the pəʿal and haphʿel until they are familiar. In the following list of word pairs, one word is a noun/adjective and the other is a II-waw/yod verb form. For each pair identify the II-waw/yod verb. Then, translate both words, looking up unfamiliar items in the glossary.

- **a** גַּב   תּוּב
- **b** זָעוֹ   גְּלוֹ
- **c** דָּת   נָח
- **d** מְשַׁח   מְהָךְ
- **e** דַּיָּנִין   דָּאְרִין

Suggestions for further study

Make flashcards for the third person forms of the weak roots listed in this unit (the 3m/fs and 3m/fp suffix/prefix conjugations) as well as the infinitives. Shuffle these flashcards among your vocabulary flashcards.

SELF-CHECK

	I CAN...
●	form II-waw/yod verbs in the pəʿal
●	form II-waw/yod verbs in the haphʿel

18 III-aleph/waw/yod verbs

In this unit you will learn how to:

- **produce the forms of III-aleph/waw/yod verbs**
- **produce the forms of some doubly weak verbs like אתי and הוי**

In this unit you will read:

- **Ezra 5:1–5**

Grammar

III-ALEPH/WAW/YOD VERBS

Roots that originally ended with aleph, waw, or yod have similar forms in Biblical Aramaic. Typically, you cannot distinguish them. In the pəʿal 3ms suffix conjugation, the verb forms from roots with an original waw or yod often end in a mater he in Biblical Aramaic (e.g. בְּעָה *he requested*), though sometimes they end in an aleph mater (e.g. בְּעָא *he requested*). Conversely, roots originally ending with aleph often appear in the pəʿal 3ms suffix conjugation with a final aleph mater (e.g. מְטָא *he reached*), though sometimes *he is found* (e.g. מְטָה *he reached*). In the prefix conjugation, however, verbs from III-aleph/waw/yod roots all end in a similar manner (with final aleph mater): יִבְנֵא *he will build* and יִמְטֵא *he will reach* (though in later dialects they end in a yod: יִבְנֵי). In any case, the final consonant of all these forms is merely a mater, not a true root consonant.

Since verbs are often listed in dictionaries according to their form in the pəʿal 3ms suffix conjugation, sometimes verbs from historical III-waw/yod roots are listed with he as a third root consonant (e.g. בעה). Those with a historical III-aleph are sometimes listed as III-aleph (e.g. מטא). Nevertheless, this only makes sense if the language consistently distinguishes them. Since Biblical Aramaic and later dialects do not distinguish them, many dictionaries (like the glossary in this course) list all III-aleph/waw/yod roots as III-yod (e.g. בעי and מטי).

PəʿAL (AND PəʿĪL) OF III-ALEPH/WAW/YOD VERBS

The typical root used to illustrate this paradigm is the one indicating building: בני. The pəʿal suffix and prefix conjugations, imperative, and the pə ʿīl suffix conjugation have the following forms. Many verb forms are unattested and it is unclear how they were realized.

	pə ʿal suffix conj.	pə ʿal prefix conj.	pə ʿal imperative	pə ʿīl passive suffix conj.
3ms	בְּנָה	יִבְנֵא		בְּנִי
3fs	בְּנָת	תִּבְנֵא		-
2ms	בְּנַ֫יְתָ bə naytā and בְּנַיְת benayt	תִּבְנֵא	בְּנִי	-
2fs	בְּנַ֫יְתִי bə naytīʸ	-	בְּנַי*	-
1cs	בְּנֵית	אֶבְנֵא		-
3mp	בְּנוֹ	יִבְנוֹן		בְּנִיו
3fp	בְּנָה*	יִבְנְיָן		-
2mp	בְּנֵיתוֹן	תִּבְנוֹן	בְּנוֹ	-
2fp	בְּנֵיתֵן	תִּבְנְיָן	-	-
1cp	בְּנֵ֫ינָא	נִבְנֵא		-

This table illustrates some of the peculiarities of this type of verb. The aleph/waw/yod that has disappeared in the pə ʿal 3ms suffix conjugation appears as a yod in the pəʿal 2ms, 2fs suffix conjugation, as well as in the pə ʿal 3fp, 2fp prefix conjugation forms.

There are also certain inconsistencies in the paradigm, likely reflecting inconsistent pronunciations in antiquity. We would expect for the 1cp suffix conjugation בְּנַ֫יְנָא* based on the preserved a vowel in the second person forms (e.g. בְּנַ֫יְתָ). Instead, בְּנֵ֫ינָא attests the resolution of the diphthong (i.e. ay became ē). In later vocalized versions of Aramaic from the targums, there is greater consistency; all the second person forms have an ē vowel, even the second person forms (i.e. בְּנֵ֫יתָ) and such may also have been the pronunciation in some earlier varieties of Aramaic too.

Rarely, a verb will exhibit an ī in the pə ʿal suffix conjugation, as with צְבִית *I wish*.

The masculine plural forms in the suffix and prefix conjugations and imperative are all characterized by the final -ōʷ (or, -ōʷn) ending. This will help to distinguish III-aleph/waw/yod roots from II-waw/yod roots; compare the final long ū in קָמוּ (pəʿal 3mp suffix conj.), יְקוּמוּן (pə ʿal 3mp prefix conj.), קוּמוּ (pə ʿal m.s. imperative).

For the pə ʿīl suffix conjugation, note that there are only two forms attested. The 3ms form is identical to the pə ʿal m.s. imperative. As will be seen in the following table, the ending of this form, -ī, bears a similarity to the ending of the paʿʿel 3ms suffix conjugation and the paʿʿel m.s. imperative. The pə ʿīl 3mp suffix conjugation bears an ending, -īʸw, that is also similar to the ending on the paʿʿel and haphʿel 3mp suffix conjugations.

PRACTICE 1

Copy out the paradigms for the pə ʿal of בני. Then, vocalize the vowel-less pə ʿal forms based on the translation.

a *They reached the bottom of the den.* מטו לְאַרְעִית גֻּבָּא
b *It* (f.s.) *struck the image.* מחת לְצַלְמָא
c *May your well-being be abundant.* שְׁלָמְכוֹן ישׂגא
d *I will read the writing to the king.* כְּתָבָא אקרא לְמַלְכָּא
e *I was at rest in my house.* שְׁלֵה הוית בְּבֵיתִי
f *The tree that you saw which grew.* אִילָנָא דִּי חזית דִּי רבה
g *Anyone who will make a request.* כָּל־אֱנָשׁ דִּי יבעה
h *I saw a dream.* חֵלֶם חזית
i *They sought Daniel and his companions.* וּבעו דָּנִיֵּאל וְחַבְרוֹהִי
j *Then, this Sheshbazzar came.* אֱדַיִן שֵׁשְׁבַּצַּר דֵּךְ אתא

CULTURAL INSIGHT

Ostraca are pieces of broken pottery that were used as writing surfaces for letters and other documents when papyrus was deemed too expensive. In the cities of Syene-Elephantine, ostraca reveal some of the common, everyday concerns of the residents. In one (*TAD* D7.6), the writer addresses a man, Hoshiyahu, regarding the care of children and the time of the Passover celebration. The ostracon lacks all vowel marks and does not differentiate between final and non-final letter shapes, but according to Biblical Aramaic pronunciation, it would read in part:

שְׁלָמָכְ כְּעַנ חֱזִי עַל יָנְקַיָּא עַד תֵּאתֵה אַחִטָב . . . הֵן גְּרֵס לַחְמְהֹמ לֻשׁו [read לוּשׁ] לְחֶמ קַב 1 [חַד] עַד תֵּאתֵה אִמְּהֹמ שְׁלַח לִי אִמַּת תַּעַבְדֻן פִּסְחָא

Your well-being (i.e. *(may the gods seek) your well-being*)*! Now, look after the children until Aḥitab comes . . . If he has ground their bread, knead 1 qab of bread* (lit. *knead bread, 1 qab*) *before their mother comes. Send to me (word) when you will observe* (lit. *make*) *Passover.*

PA‘‘EL AND HAPH‘EL OF III-ALEPH/WAW/YOD VERBS

	pa‘‘el suffix conj.	pa‘‘el prefix conj.	pa‘‘el imperative
3ms	בַּנִּי	יְבַנֵּא	
3fs	בַּנִּיַּת*	תְּבַנֵּא	
2ms	בַּנִּיתָ	תְּבַנֵּא	בַּנִּי
2fs	בַּנִּיתִי	-	בַּנִּי*
1cs	בַּנִּית	אֲבַנֵּא	
3mp	בַּנִּיו	יְבַנּוֹן	
3fp	בַּנִּיָה*	יְבַנְיָן	
2mp	בַּנִּיתוּן	תְּבַנּוֹן	בַּנּוֹ
2fp	בַּנִּיתֵן	תְּבַנְיָן	-
1cp	בַּנִּינָא	נְבַנֵּא	

Notice that although the pa‘‘el 3mp suffix conjugation ends in -īʸw, the pa‘‘el m.p. imperative ends in -ōʷ, and the pa‘‘el 3mp, 2mp prefix conjugation end in -ōʷn.

	haph‘el suffix conj.	haph‘el prefix conj.	haph‘el imperative	haph‘el suffix conj. of the root אתי	huph‘al/hoph‘al suffix conj. of the root אתי
3ms	הַבְנִי	יַבְנֵא or יְהַבְנֵא		הַיְתִי	-
3fs	הַבְנִיַת*	תַּבְנֵא or תְּהַבְנֵא		-	הֵיתָיִת
2ms	הַבְנִ֫יתָ	תַּבְנֵא or תְּהַבְנֵא	הַבְנִי	-	-
2fs	הַבְנִ֫יתִי	תַּבְנַיִן* or תְּהַבְנַיִן*	הַבְנַי*	-	-
1cs	הַבְנִית	אַבְנֵא or אֲהַבְנֵא		-	-
3mp	הַבְנִיו	יַבְנוֹן or יְהַבְנוֹן		הַיְתִיו	הֵי֫תָיו
3fp	הַבְנִיָה*	יַבְנְיָן or יְהַבְנְיָן		-	-
2mp	הַבְנִיתוּן	תַּבְנוֹן or תְּהַבְנוֹן	הַבְנוֹ	-	-
2fp	הַבְנִיתֵן	תַּבְנְיָן or תְּהַבְנְיָן	-	-	-
1cp	הַבְנִ֫ינָא	נַבְנֵא or נְהַבְנֵא		-	-

The haph‘el has many of the same endings as the pa‘‘el. The anomalous forms **הֵי֫תָיִת** and **הֵי֫תָיו** are explained later in this unit.

PRACTICE 2

Copy the pa‘‘el and haph‘el suffix conjugations for בני then translate the following sentences using the vocabulary provided:

אבד haph‘el *to destroy*, **בָּבֶל** *Babel*, **גְּבַר** *man*, **חוי** pa‘‘el and haph‘el *to tell, declare*, **חַכִּים** *sage*, **יְהוּדָי** *Judean*, **לְ** *to* (direct object marker), **מִלָּה** *word*, **מֶ֫לֶךְ** *king*, **מני** pa‘‘el *to appoint*, **מַתְּנָה** *gift*, **פְּשַׁר** *interpretation*, **קבל** pa‘‘el *to receive*, **שׁני** haph‘el *to alter*.

- **a** *We will tell* (pa‘‘el 1cp pref.) *the interpretation of the word.*
- **b** *You appointed* (pa‘‘el 2ms suff.) *a Judean man.*
- **c** *The king appointed* (pa‘‘el 3ms suff.) *me to destroy* (haph‘el infinitive) *the sages of* (use cstr. form) *Babel.*
- **d** *You will declare* (haph‘el 2mp pref.) *an interpretation and you will receive* (pa‘‘el 2mp pref.) *gifts.*
- **e** *The sages did not alter* (haph‘el 3mp suff.) *the word of the king.*

PARTICIPLES AND INFINITIVES OF III-ALEPH/WAW/YOD VERBS

The participles, especially for the pəʿal, also exhibit idiosyncracies.

	pəʿal participle	pəʿal passive participle	pa‘‘el part./pass. part.	haph‘el part./ pass. part.
m.s.	בָּנֵה	בְּנֵה	מְבַנֵּי / מְבַנֵּא	מְהַבְנֵי / מְהַבְנֵא
f.s.	בָּנְיָה	בַּנְיָה	מְבַנְּיָה	מְהַבְנְיָה
m.p.	בָּנַ֫יִן	בְּנַ֫יִן	מְבַנַּ֫יִן	מְהַבְנַ֫יִן
f.p.	בָּנְיָן	בַּנְיָן	מְבַנְּיָן	מְהַבְנְיָן

The only distinction between pəʿal f.s., f.p. participles and the pəʿal f.s., f.p. passive participles appears in the first vowel, qamets (ā) versus patach (a). Note the anomalous form of the pəʿal m.s. passive participle אֱזֵה *heated* (from the root אזי).

The only distinction between the paʿʿel participle and the paʿʿel passive participle would appear in the m.s. form, though the paʿʿel m.s. passive participle is not attested. As in the paradigm for the regular root כתב, the other forms of the paʿʿel participle are identical. The same holds true for the distinction between the haphʿel participles and the haphʿel passive participles. The haphʿel participles may also appear without the he prefix, i.e. as aphʿel participles: מַבְנֵא, etc.

The infinitives are somewhat more predictable.

pəʿal infinitive	paʿʿel infinitive	haphʿel infinitive
מִבְנֵא	בַּנָּיָה	הַבְנָיָה

CULTURAL INSIGHT

What modern people today associate with the Aramaic language is at least partially reflected in the way that Aramaic appears in popular culture. Consider recent movies where Aramaic is spoken. In Mel Gibson's *The Passion of the Christ*, all the actors speak either Latin or Aramaic, mimicking what the ancients might have sounded like. Nevertheless, many of the soldiers likely would have spoken Greek not Latin and Jesus would have spoken a different variety of Aramaic. By contrast, other movies like *Fallen* (starring Denzel Washington), *Stigmata* (starring Patricia Arquette), and *The Exorcism of Emily Rose* (starring Laura Linney) often reserve Aramaic speech for demons or humans who are possessed. While an association of Jesus with Aramaic is clearly derived from evidence like the New Testament passages cited in previous notes, the association between Aramaic and demonic possession seems likely to be part of a long-standing cultural bias. For instance, St Jerome (ca. 400 CE) records two instances of an Aramaic-speaking demon possessing someone in Roman Palestine: a Frankish soldier and a camel. That the camel was possessed was easy to recognize since it was speaking, but that the Frankish soldier suffered similarly only became clear when it was discovered that the soldier knew only Frankish and Latin.

OTHER STEMS, DOUBLY WEAK ROOTS, AND OTHER PECULIARITIES

Roots that have an aleph, waw, or yod as a third root consonant also occur in other stems like the hitpəʿel and hitpaʿʿal. But, these are entirely predictable based on the earlier paradigms:

הִתְמְלִי (hitpəʿel 3ms suff. of מלי) *he was filled*
יִתְמְחֵא (hitpəʿel 3ms pref. of מחי) *he will be impaled*
תִּתְבְּנֵא (hitpəʿel 3ms pref. of בני) *it will be built*
תִּתְרְמוֹן (hitpəʿel 2mp pref. of רמי) *you will be thrown*
הִתְנַבִּי (hitpaʿʿal 3ms suff. of נבי) *he prophesied*
יִשְׁתַּנֵּא (hitpaʿʿal 3ms pref. of שׁני) *it will be changed*

Some verbs exhibit not only an aleph, waw, or yod as third root consonant, but also one of these same weak letters as a first root consonant. So, for example, the root **ידי** in the haph'el means *to praise, give thanks*. In its participial form it appears in the m.s. as **מְהוֹדֵא** and in the aph'el as **מוֹדֵא**.

The most common of these verbs is **אתי**, which has the sense *to come* in the pə'al (e.g. **אֲתוֹ** *they came*), and *to bring* in the haph'el. In the latter stem, the verb exhibits an initial ay: **הַיְתִי** *he brought*, **הַיְתִיו** *they brought*, **לְהַיְתָיָה** *to bring*. (The prefix conjugation is not attested, but would presumably reflect this same vowel pattern: **יְהַיְתֵא** *he will bring*.) In the huph'al/hoph'al, the vowel pattern is unusually ē-ā: **הֵיתָיִת** *it* (fem.) *was brought* and **הֵיתָיו** *they were brought*. Compare the more conventional huph'al 3ms suffix conjugation **הוּבַד** *it was destroyed* (from **אבד**).

Note also that the root **שׁרי** *to loosen, solve, begin* occurs in the pa''el with ā after the shin due to compensatory lengthening (since the resh cannot double): **שָׁרִיו** *they solved*. For the same reason, ā appears after the taw (after metathesis) in the hitpa''al: **מִשְׁתָּרַיִן** *they were loosened*.

Another common root, **שׁתי** *to drink*, occurs in the pə'al suffix conjugation with a prefixed aleph so that it at first appears to be in the aph'el (though it lacks the characteristic a vowel): **אִשְׁתִּיו** *they drank*. The other verbal forms are regular: **יִשְׁתּוֹן** (pə'al 3mp prefix conj.) *they might drink*, **שָׁתֵה** (pə'al m.s. participle) *he was drinking* and **שָׁתַיִן** (pə'al m.p. participle) *they were drinking*.

The common verb **הוי** *to be* exhibits the expected inflection in the suffix conjugation, the initial guttural letter precipitating a hateph patach instead of a shewa: **הֲווֹ** *they were*. However, in the prefix conjugation instead of a yod to mark the third masculine forms, we find a lamed. The relevant forms are isolated in the following table.

	pə'al suffix conj.	**pə'al prefix conj.**	**pə'al imperative**
3ms	הֲוָה	לֶהֱוֵא	
3fs	הֲוָת	תֶּהֱוֵא	
2ms	הֲוַיְתָ	-	-
2fs	-	-	-
1cs	הֲוֵית	-	
3mp	הֲווֹ	לֶהֱוֺן	
3fp	-	לֶהֶוְיָן	
2mp	-	-	הֱווֹ
2fp	-	-	-
1cp	-	-	

A suffix or prefix conjugation of **הוי** often is used with a following participle to specify a temporal nuance (e.g. **הֲווֹ זָאְעִין** *they were trembling* Dan 5:19 and **כָּל־דִּי־לָא לֶהֱוֵא עָבֵד** *anyone who will not do* Ezra 7:26).

Based on these attested forms, it is often possible to make an educated guess as to the pronunciation of other forms that lack vowels, like those in the Dead Sea Scrolls. For instance, the itpa‘‘al m.s. imv. of **שעי** *to tell, narrate* appears as **אשתעי** *tell!* Since it is an itpa‘‘al, it should have the same final vowel as the pa‘‘el imperative, -ī, and the rest of the form likely has the same vocalization as other (h)itpa‘‘al verbs. Therefore, its pronunciation in Biblical Aramaic symbols would be rendered: **אִשְׁתַּעִי**.

CULTURAL INSIGHT

The association between Aramaic and esoteric knowledge and magic is also a long-standing preconception. Chaldean, as a noun, refers in its most basic sense to a group of Aramaic-speaking people from southern Mesopotamia, whose leaders were prominent in Babylon in the first millennium BCE. However, because the Babylonians (both those who were Chaldean and those that preceded them) were interested in observing and documenting the constellations and inferring future events from these, the word *Chaldean* came to mean a diviner or magician. In Daniel 4:4 (Engl. 4:7), for instance, Chaldeans are mentioned after magicians and diviners.

Reading

Translate the following passage from Ezra 5 using the glossary and the notes that follow the text.

EZRA 5:1

a וְהִתְנַבִּי חַגַּי נְבִיָּאה וּזְכַרְיָה בַר־עִדּוֹא נְבִיַּאיָּא עַל־יְהוּדָיֵא דִּי בִיהוּד וּבִירוּשְׁלֶם

b בְּשֻׁם אֱלָהּ יִשְׂרָאֵל עֲלֵיהוֹן

EZRA 5:2

a בֵּאדַ֫יִן קָמוּ זְרֻבָּבֶל בַּר־שְׁאַלְתִּיאֵל וְיֵשׁוּעַ בַּר־יוֹצָדָק

b וְשָׁרִיו לְמִבְנֵא בֵּית אֱלָהָא דִּי בִירוּשְׁלֶם

c וְעִמְּהוֹן נְבִיַּאיָּא דִי־אֱלָהָא מְסָעֲדִין לְהוֹן

EZRA 5:3

a בֵּהּ־זִמְנָא אֲתָה עֲלֵיהוֹן תַּתְּנַי פַּחַת עֲבַר־נַהֲרָה וּשְׁתַר בּוֹזְנַי וּכְנָוָתְהוֹן

b וְכֵן אָמְרִין לְהֹם מַן־שָׂם לְכֹם טְעֵם בַּיְתָא דְנָה לְמִבְנֵא

c וְאֻשַּׁרְנָא דְנָה לְשַׁכְלָלָה

EZRA 5:4

a אֱדַ֫יִן כְּנֵמָא אֲמַ֫רוּ לְהֹם מַן־אִנּוּן שְׁמָהָת גֻּבְרַיָּא דִּי־דְנָה בִנְיָנָא בָּנַ֫יִן

EZRA 5:5

a וְעֵין אֱלָהֲהֹם הֲוָת עַל־שָׂבֵי יְהוּדָיֵא וְלָא־בַטִּ֫לוּ הִמּוֹ עַד־טַעְמָא לְדָרְיָוֶשׁ יְהָךְ

b וֶאֱדַ֫יִן יְתִיבוּן נִשְׁתְּוָנָא עַל־דְּנָה

Ezra 5:1

a

חַגַּי נְבִיָּאה וּזְכַרְיָה בַר־עִדּוֹא נְבִיַּאיָּא – *Haggai, the prophet, and Zechariah Bar-'Iddo, the prophets* The phrase *the prophet* is obviously redundant. It is easiest to assume that it is a mistake and not translate it. Formally, the consonants and vowels of this word (נְבִיָּאה) do not match up. The consonants reflect the pronunciation nəbīʾā that is, the determined form of the noun nəbī *prophet*, which we would expect to be written נְבִיאָא. Because the noun was spelled according to its historical form with an aleph as a final root consonant, a scribe used a heh mater to mark the final ā of the determined form and thus diminish the chances a future reader might think the two alephs to be a mistake (i.e. נביאה simply reflects nəbīʾā). The vowels of נְבִיָּאה, on the other hand, reflect a phonological shift of -īʾā to -iyyā (i.e. nəbīʾā נְבִיאָא becoming nəbiyyā נְבִיָּא). The same phonological shift is reflected in the vocalization of נְבִיַּאיָּא.

Ezra 5:2

a

זְרֻבָּבֶל בַּר־שְׁאַלְתִּיאֵל וְיֵשׁוּעַ בַּר־יוֹצָדָק – *Zerubbabel Bar-Shealtiʾel and Jeshua Bar-Yotsadaq*

Ezra 5:3

a

תַּתְּנַי פַּחַת עֲבַר־נַהֲרָה וּשְׁתַר בּוֹזְנַי – *Tattenay, governor of Abar-Naharah and Shetar Boznai*

c

שַׁכְלָלָה – *to complete* This is the infinitive of the irregular verb שכלל.

Ezra 5:4

a

אֲמַ֫רוּ – *they said* In the Leningrad Codex, the word is actually the 1cp *we said*, though this does not fit the context. Alternatively, you could assume the participle אָמְרִין and retain the translation *they said*.

מַן – Usually this interrogative pronoun is translated *who* (as in the preceding verse), but here English 'what' seems more appropriate.

אִנּוּן – *are* This pronoun functions as the verb *to be*.

Ezra 5:5

a

יְהָךְ – *it could go* This is the prefix conjugation form of the verb הוך *to go*. Here it has a modal nuance.

יְתִיבוּן – *they could return*

Test yourself

Vocalize the following vowel-less III-aleph/waw/yod verbs and then translate them. Then, using these same verbs, fill in the appropriate blanks in the phrases that follow. This will require you to translate the Aramaic and infer the most appropriate verb for each phrase.

- **a** **הוית** (pəʿal 1cs suff. conj. of **הוי**)
- **b** **יבנון** (pəʿal 3mp pref. conj. of **בני**)
- **c** **שׂרא** (pəʿal 3ms suff. conj. of **שׂרי**)
- **d** **מהודא** (haphʿel m.s. part. of **ידי**)
- **e** **היתיו** (haphʿel 3mp suff. conj. of **אתי**)
- **f** **להוא** (pəʿal 3ms pref. conj. /juss. of **הוי**)
- **g** **החויה** (haphʿel inf. of **חוי**)
- **h** **אחוא** (paʿʿel 1cs pref. conj. of **חוי**)
- **i** **חזית** (pəʿal 1cs suff. conj. of **חזי**)
- **j** **שׂריו** (paʿʿel 3mp suff. conj. of **שׂרי**)

- **a** פִּשְׁרָא לְמַלְכָּא ______________
- **b** בֵּאדַ֫יִן ______________ מָאנֵי דַהֲבָא
- **c** ______________ שְׁמֵהּ דִּי־אֱלָהָא מְבָרַךְ
- **d** ______________ יִשְׂרָאֵל בְּאַרְעָא הַהִיא
- **e** חָזֵא ______________ בְּחֶזְוֵי רֵאשִׁי
- **f** לָךְ אֱלָהּ אֲבָהָתִי ______________ וּמְשַׁבַּח אֲנָה
- **g** אִיתַי אֱנָשׁ . . . דִּי מִלַּת מַלְכָּא יוּכַל (= יִכֻּל) לְ ______________
- **h** בֵּית אֱלָהָא דֵךְ ______________ עַל־אַתְרֵהּ
- **i** ______________ לְמִבְנֵא בֵּית אֱלָהָא
- **j** דְּנָה חֶלְמָא ______________ אֲנָה

Suggestions for further study

Make flashcards for the third person forms of the weak roots listed in this unit (e.g. the 3m/fs and 3m/fp suffix/prefix conjugations) as well as the infinitives. Shuffle these flashcards among your vocabulary flashcards. Then, go back to Daniel 4 in the appendix and attempt to read the first five verses.

SELF-CHECK

	I CAN...
○	produce the forms of III-aleph/waw/yod verbs
○	produce the forms of some doubly weak verbs like **אתי** and **הוי**

19 Geminate verbs

In this unit you will learn how to:

- **produce the forms of the geminate verbs in the pəʿal and haphʿel**

In this unit you will read:

- **Ezra 5:6–10**

Grammar

SUFFIX AND PREFIX CONJUGATIONS OF GEMINATE VERBS

Some roots, like עלל (*to enter*), have the same letter for their second and third consonants. This produces unexpected verbal forms, especially for the pəʿal and haphʿel. (The paʿʿel for these types of roots is regular: מְמַלִּל *one who speaks.*)

	pəʿal suffix conj.	pəʿal prefix conj.	haphʿel suffix conj.	haphʿel prefix conj.
3ms	עַל	יֵעֹל (yeʿʿol)	הַעֵל or הַנְעֵל	יְהַעֵל or יַעֵל
3fs	עַלַּת	תֵּעֹל	הַעֶלֶת or הַנְעֶלֶת	תְּהַעֵל or תַּעֵל
2ms	עֲלַלְתָּ	תֵּעֹל	הַעֶלְתָּ / etc.	תְּהַעֵל / etc.
2fs	עֲלַלְתִּי	תֵּעֲלִין	הַעֶלְתִּי	תְּהַעֲלִין
1cs	עַלֵּת	אֵעֹל	הַעֶלֶת	אֲהַעֵל
3mp	עַלּוּ	יֵעֲלוּן	הַעִלּוּ	יְהַעֲלוּן
3fp	עַלָּה	יֵעֲלָן	הַעִלָּה	יְהַעֲלָן
2mp	עֲלַלְתּוּן	תֵּעֲלוּן	הַעֶלְתּוּן	תְּהַעֲלוּן
2fp	עֲלַלְתֵּן	תֵּעֲלָן	הַעֶלְתֵּן	תְּהַעֲלָן
1cp	עֲלַלְנָא	נֵעֹל	הַעֵלְנָא	נְהַעֵל

Many of the forms are not attested in the Bible, but can be reconstructed based on analogy. Note that there is a disparity between the consonantal text and vowels in the form עַלַּלַת *she entered*. The consonants presuppose עַלְּלַת but the vowels imply the spelling עַלַּת.

The characteristic feature of this type of root is that when a prefix is added, the second root consonant assimilates backwards into the first. In other words, in the case of עלל, the first lamed is assimilated into the preceding ʿayin; we could represent the pəʿal 3ms prefix conjugation in transliteration: yeʿʿol. This form is derived from an earlier form *yiʿlol or יִעְלֹל*. Similarly, the haphʿel 3ms suffix conjugation could be represented haʿʿel and the haphʿel 3ms prefix conjugation yəhaʿʿel, though in an earlier stage of Aramaic they would have been, respectively, *haʿlel and *yəhaʿlel (הַעְלֵל* and יְהַעְלֵל*).

Sometimes, the gemination or doubling of a consonant, as in the double ʻayin of haʻʻel, is replaced by the sequence nun + consonant, so that we may find hanʻel, instead of haʻʻel. Nasalization is something we have seen before in discussing I-nun and I-waw/yod roots.

PRACTICE 1

Copy out the paradigms for the pəʻal and haphʻel suffix/prefix conjugations of עלל. Then, translate the following sentences into Aramaic, using the vocabulary provided:

אכל *eat*, דקק haphʻel *to crush*, וְ *and, but*, חֵיוָה *beast*, חַכִּים *sage*, כהל *to be able*, כֹּל *all*, כַּשְׂדָּי *Chaldean*, כְּתָב *a writing*, לְ *to*, לָא *not*, מַלְכָּה *queen*, עלל pəʻal *to enter*, haphʻel *bring*, קרי *to read*, שְׁאָר *remainder*, תַּקִּיף *strong*.

- **a** *The queen brought* (haphʻel 3fs suff. conj.) *the Chaldeans to him.*
- **b** *All the sages of the queen entered* (pəʻal 3mp suff. conj.) *but were not able* (pəʻal 3mp suff. conj.) *to read* (pəʻal infinitive) *the writing.*
- **c** *The Chaldean will bring* (haphʻel 3ms pref. conj.) *the writing of his queen.*
- **d** *A strong beast ate* (pəʻal 3fs suff. conj.) *and crushed* (haphʻel 3fs suff. conj.) *the remainder.*
- **e** *The strong queen will bring* (haphʻel 3fs pref. conj) *the Chaldeans to her sage.*

CULTURAL INSIGHT

In later Eastern Aramaic dialects (from the first millennium CE, both Christian and Jewish), the word *Aramean* is pronounced in two slightly different ways. The pronunciation ʼărammāʼāh (or ʼrāmāyâ) is the more neutral term implying only the ethnic identification *Aramean*, while the pronunciation ʼarmāʼāh / ʼarmāyâ means *pagan* implying non-Christian and non-Jewish beliefs.

IMPERATIVES, PARTICIPLES, AND INFINITIVES OF GEMINATE VERBS

Based on the given inflections, the imperatives, participles, and infinitives are not difficult to understand.

Imperatives	pəʻal		haphʻel	
m.s.	עֹל		הַעֵל	
f.s.	עֹלִּי		הַעֵלִּי	
m.p.	עֹלּוּ		הַעֵלּוּ	
f.p.	עֹלָּה		הַעֵלָּה	
Participles	**pəʻal**	**pəʻal passive / pəʻīl**	**haphʻel**	**haphʻel passive**
m.s.	עָלֵל	עֲלִיל	מְהַעֵל	מְהַעַל
f.s.	עָלְּה	עֲלִילָה	מְהַעֲלָה	מְהַעֲלָה
m.p.	עָלִּין	עֲלִילִין	מְהַעֲלִין	מְהַעֲלִין
f.p.	עָלָּן*	עֲלִילָן	מְהַעֲלָן	מְהַעֲלָן
Infinitives	**pəʻal**		**haphʻel**	
	מֵעַל		הַנְעָלָה or הֶעָלָה	

The presence of a long vowel in a closed, non-stressed syllable in עָלִּין is unusual. Notice that in the Bible this form is spelled with two lameds: עָלִּלִין, implying that an alternative pronunciation was עָלְלִין* in which case the long vowel would not be in a closed syllable.

Note also the huph'al/hoph'al forms that appear: הֻעַל *he was brought* and הֻעַ֫לוּ *they were brought*.

In addition to these stems, the geminate roots sometimes appear in stems that involve reduplication. These appear more frequently in other dialects of Aramaic (i.e. not in Biblical Aramaic). For instance, the root בלל *to mix*, *confuse* occurs in the 1cp prefix conjugation in the palpel stem in Targum Onqelos נְבַלְבֵּיל (equivalent to the pronunciation נְבַלְבֵּל) *let us confuse*. Usually the stems involving reduplication (note too itpalpel) are used in place of the pa''el and related stems.

PRACTICE 2

Identify the following words with their possible roots and stems. Double check the answers in the glossary and then translate the verbs.

a גֹּ֫דּוּ
b תֵּעֹל
c נַדַּת
d מְרָעַע
e הַנְעָלָה
f מְהַדֵּק
g הַעֵל
h מִחַן
i תֵּרֹעַ
j תַּדִּק or תַּדֵּק

Reading

Translate the following passage from Ezra 5 using the glossary and the notes that follow the text.

EZRA 5:6

a פַּרְשֶׁ֫גֶן אִגַּרְתָּא דִּי־שְׁלַח תַּתְּנַי פַּחַת עֲבַר־נַהֲרָה וּשְׁתַר בּוֹזְנַי וּכְנָוָתֵהּ אֲפַרְסְכָיֵא דִּי בַּעֲבַר נַהֲרָה
b עַל־דָּרְיָוֶשׁ מַלְכָּא

EZRA 5:7

a פִּתְגָמָא שְׁלַ֫חוּ עֲלוֹהִי וְכִדְנָה כְּתִיב בְּגַוֵּהּ
b לְדָרְיָוֶשׁ מַלְכָּא שְׁלָמָא כֹ֫לָּא

EZRA 5:8

a יְדִיעַ לֶהֱוֵא לְמַלְכָּא דִּי־אֲזַ֫לְנָא לִיהוּד מְדִינְתָּא לְבֵית אֱלָהָא רַבָּא
b וְהוּא מִתְבְּנֵא אֶ֫בֶן גְּלָל וְאָע מִתְּשָׂם בְּכֻתְלַיָּא
c וַעֲבִידְתָּא דָךְ אָסְפַּרְנָא מִתְעַבְדָא וּמַצְלַח בְּיֶדְהֹם

EZRA 5:9

a אֱדַיִן שְׁאֵלְנָא לְשָׂבַיָּא אִלֵּךְ כְּנֵמָא אֲמַרְנָא לְהֹם
b מַן־שָׂם לְכֹם טְעֵם בַּיְתָא דְנָה לְמִבְנְיָה
c וְאֻשַּׁרְנָא דְנָה לְשַׁכְלָלָה

EZRA 5:10

a וְאַף שְׁמָהָתְהֹם שְׁאֵלְנָא לְהֹם לְהוֹדָעוּתָךְ דִּי נִכְתֻּב שֻׁם־גֻּבְרַיָּא דִּי בְרָאשֵׁיהֹם

Ezra 5:6

a

דִּי בַּעֲבַר נַהֲרָה – *who (were) in Aber-Naharah* There is no verb *to be* or any other marker of the predication.

Ezra 5:7

b

שְׁלָמָא כֹלָּא – *May all be well* There is no verb, simply the juxtaposition of the determined nouns שְׁלָם and כֹּל.

Ezra 5:8

a

לֶהֱוֵא – The form of this verb is ambiguous; it could be either a prefix conjugation with an indicative sense *it will be* or a jussive. Context suggests a jussive sense *let it be*. The verb has an impersonal subject, *it*, referring to the information that follows.

b

אֶבֶן גְּלָל – *with hewn stone* The phrase is an adverbial accusative (see Unit 21) and indicates the material with which the temple is being built. Such adverbial accusative words and phrases are usually translated with a preposition in English though they lack a preposition in Aramaic.

מִתְּשָׂם – *is set* The hitpəʿel m.s. participle of שׂים.

Test yourself

1 Being able to distinguish a given verb type is often dependent on recognizing a few basic vowel patterns quickly. In order to internalize these patterns, it is helpful to take one attested verbal form and try to imagine what the same form would be with another verb type. Since geminate verbs often resemble II-waw/yod verbs, you can take a form like עַל (the pəʿal 3ms suffix conj. of the geminate verb עלל) and imagine what the same verb form would be if the root were instead II-waw/yod root עול* (which does not occur in Biblical Aramaic): it would be עָל*. Take the following geminate verb forms and indicate what the corresponding forms would be if these verbs were not from geminate roots but from II-waw/yod roots instead.

a גֹּדּוּ → II-waw/yod גוד* would be ______________________

b תֵּעֹל → II-waw/yod עול* would be ______________________

c נַדֵּת → II-waw/yod **נוד** (in aph'el *to disturb*) would be ______________________________

d מְרָעַע → II-waw/yod **רוע*** would be ______________________________

e הַנְעָלָה → II-waw/yod **עול*** would be ______________________________

f מְהַדֵּק → II-waw/yod **דוק** (in haph'el *to look at*) would be ______________________________

g הַעֵל → II-waw/yod **עול*** would be ______________________________

h מִחַן → II-waw/yod **חון*** would be ______________________________

i תֵּרֹעַ → II-waw/yod **רוע*** would be ______________________________

j תַּדִּק or תַּדֵּק → II-waw/yod **דוק** (in aph'el *to look at*) would be

____

2 Translate the following phrases that all contain a geminate verb.

a אֱדַ֫יִן אַרְיוֹךְ הַנְעֵל לְדָנִיֵּאל קֳדָם מַלְכָּא

b אֱדַ֫יִן דָּנִיֵּאל עִם־מַלְכָּא מַלִּל

c שְׁלִ֫טוּ בְהוֹן אַרְיָוָתָא וְכָל־גַּרְמֵיהוֹן הַדִּ֫קוּ

d דָּנִיֵּאל עַל וּבְעָה מִן־מַלְכָּא דִּי זְמָן יִנְתֵּן לֵהּ

e מִנִּי שִׂים טְעֵם לְהַנְעָלָה קֳדָמַי לְכֹל חַכִּימֵי בָבֶל

SELF-CHECK

I CAN...
produce the forms of the geminate verbs in the pə'al and haph'el

20 Verbs with suffixes

In this unit you will learn how to:
- **recognize how verb forms inflect with object suffixes**
- **recognize object suffixes on suffix and prefix conjugation verb forms**
- **recognize object suffixes on infinitives**

In this unit you will read:
- **Ezra 5:11–15**

Grammar

SUFFIX CONJUGATION WITH PRONOMINAL SUFFIXES

In Aramaic, it is not uncommon for verbal forms to bear pronominal suffixes, just like nouns. In these cases, the suffix is the grammatical object of the verb. Note, however, that a reflexive object (in English *myself*, *yourself*, etc.) is usually not represented by a suffixed pronoun.

Because of the nature of vowel reduction in Biblical Aramaic, you can often predict what the form of a given verb + suffix will be. In the pəʿal, we find חַתְמַהּ *he sealed it* (3ms suffix conj. + 3fs pronominal object suffix) and סַתְרֵהּ *he hid it* (3ms suffix conj. + 3ms pronominal object suffix). Although the actual historical development is more complicated, you can imagine these forms beginning as ḥatamah and satareh. When short vowels in the syllable before the stressed syllable reduced, the words became ḥatmah and satreh. Where the vowel of the verb is long, as in שָׂם *he set*, there is no reduction: שָׂמֵהּ *he set him*. Similarly, with בְּנָה *he built*, the long vowel is retained: בְּנָ֫הִי *he built it*. As in this last example, although most suffixes are identical to those that follow the singular noun, where a vowel appears just before the suffix, the suffix can have a slightly different form, like the suffixes on nouns like אַב *father* (e.g. אֲבֽ֫וּהִי *his father*). Note similarly שַׁנּ֫וֹהִי *they changed him* (without suffix שְׁנוֹ). The 1cs pronominal object suffix is נִי- but does not occur in the pəʿal; see the following paragraph for an example. In the 1cs of III-aleph/waw/yod verbs (e.g. בְּנֵית *I built*), the verb form exhibits a diphthong -ay-: בֱּנַיְתַהּ *I built it*.

In the paʿʿel, we find חַבְּל֫וּנִי *they harmed me*. The form without suffix would be חַבִּלוּ. The short i reduces to shewa when it is no longer in the stressed syllable.

In the haphʿel, we find more examples. Without object suffix, the 3ms of שׁלט is הַשְׁלֵט *he caused to rule*, but with suffix it becomes הַשְׁלְטֵהּ *he caused him to rule*. The short e reduces in the syllable that precedes the stress. Similarly, we find הַשְׁלְטָךְ *he caused you to rule*, הַשְׁלְמַהּ *he has brought it to completion*, הַקְרְב֫וּהִי *they brought him near*, הוֹדְעָךְ *he caused you to know*. Where the verbal form has a long vowel, no reduction takes place: הֲקִימֵהּ *he established him*, אֲקִימֵהּ *he established it* (note the 3ms aphʿel form), הֲתִיב֫וּנָא *they returned us*. Similarly, where the short vowels of the verb remain in closed syllables, there is no reduction as with the second vowel of *hawdaʿtánīʸ, which became hōʷdaʿtánīʸ = הוֹדַעְתַּ֫נִי *you made me know*. (Here, the accent sign (i.e. á) marks the stressed syllable.) Note too the form שַׁכְלְלֵהּ *he finished it* from the root שׁכלל.

CULTURAL INSIGHT

In the New Testament (at Mark 15:34), Jesus famously quotes Psalm 22 in Aramaic: elōi elōi lema sabachthani *my God, my God, why have you forsaken me?* The same phrase would be rendered in Biblical Aramaic (with the medieval vowel points): אֱלָהִי אֱלָהִי לְמָה שְׁבַקְתַּ֫נִי. The last word is the pəʿal 2ms suffix conjugation of שׁבק with the 1cs suffix. Jesus's pronunciation of *my God* differs in some ways from what we would expect from Biblical Aramaic, and may, at least in part, reflect his colloquial pronunciation of Aramaic.

Knowing something of the historical development of the verb + suffix helps illustrate again the phenomenon of vowel reduction, which in turn helps to demonstrate the inflection of Biblical Aramaic words and prepares students to read Aramaic texts that lack vowels. The following table, based on the attested words in Biblical Aramaic, illustrates the development of certain verbal forms attested in Biblical Aramaic and those that can be reconstructed based on analogy to these forms. Verbal forms for which there is less evidence are not included. Recall that a short vowel in a pre-stress open syllable reduces, as in the second a of the etymological form *qaṭaleh *he killed him* that became qaṭleh = קַטְלֵהּ. In the case of the pəʿal 3fs suffix conjugation (e.g. the etymological form *qaṭalateh *she killed him*), not only does the a in the pre-stress open syllable reduce, *qaṭalteh, but the initial a also reduces to a muttered vowel since it is in an open non-stressed syllable. Therefore, *qaṭalateh became qəṭalteh = קְטַלְתֵּהּ.

Suffix		3ms suff. conj. קְטַל(from *qaṭal-)	3fs suff. conj. קִטְלַת(from *qaṭalat-)
3ms	־ֵהּ	*qaṭaleh → qaṭleh = קַטְלֵהּ	*qaṭalatēh → qəṭaltēh = קְטַלְתֵּהּ
3fs	־ַהּ	*qaṭalah → qaṭlah = קַטְלַהּ	*qaṭalatah → qəṭaltah = קְטַלְתַּהּ
2ms	־ָךְ	*qaṭalāk → qaṭlāk = קַטְלָךְ	*qaṭalatāk → qəṭaltāk = קְטַלְתָּךְ
2fs	־ֵכִי	-	-
1cs	־ַנִי	*qaṭalánī → qaṭlánī = קַטְלַ֫נִי	*qaṭalatánī → qəṭaltánī = קְטַלְתַּ֫נִי
3mp	-	-	-
3fp	-	-	-
2mp	־כוֹן	-	-
2fp	־כֵן	-	-
1cp	־ַנָא	*qaṭalánā → qaṭlánā = קַטְלַ֫נָא	-

Most other suffix-conjugation verbal forms follow the same vowel reduction patterns as seen in these forms. The 1cs has almost the same form as the 3fs, the only distinction being in the dagesh in the taw: *qaṭalteh → qəṭalteh = קְטַלְתֵּהּ *I killed him*. The 2ms suffix conjugation

(קְטַ֫לְתָּ) with 3ms suffix would be *qaṭaltáhīʸ → qəṭaltáhīʸ = קְטַלְתַּ֫הִי you killed him and the 3mp verb (קְטַ֫לוּ) with 3ms suffix would be *qaṭalūʷhīʸ → qaṭlūʷhīʸ = קַטְל֫וּהִי they killed him.

For the pa‘‘el and the haph‘el, the same rules apply, but the initial closed syllable prevents the reduction of the first vowel. In the pa‘‘el, the 3fs suff. conj. (קַטְּלַת) with 3ms object suffix develops like this: *qaṭṭilateh → qaṭṭilteh = קַטִּלְתֵּהּ she slayed him. In the haph‘el, the same form (הַקְטְלַת) with 3ms suffix reflects the development *haqṭilateh → haqṭilteh = הַקְטִלְתֵּהּ she caused him to kill.

PRACTICE 1

1 Indicate the verbal form as it would occur in Biblical Aramaic, based on the following (simplified) historical forms. Write the word in transliteration and then in Aramaic letters. In the following, non-final syllables that are stressed are marked with an accent sign (e.g. á).

Remember: Vowel reduction affects short vowels in open syllables. The first short vowel to reduce is the one closest to the syllable that bears the stress. A vowel will entirely disappear as long as this does not result in an irregular type of syllable (like a closed non-stressed syllable with a long vowel or a syllable with a final cluster of consonants). In these cases, reduction results in a muttered vowel. Resulting short vowels in closed syllables are preserved; but short vowels in other open syllables are reduced to a muttered vowel.

Example: *zaqapah → zaqpah זַקְפַהּ *he raised it* (3fs)

- **a** *paraseh — *he spread it* (3ms)
- **b** *haškaḥah — *he found it* (3fs)
- **c** *šabaqeh — *he left him* (3ms)
- **d** *palaḥtah — *I served her*
- **e** *haškaḥatánâ — *she found us*
- **f** *hassiqtánâ — *you brought us up* (סלק)
- **g** *’akalánīʸ — *it* (m.s.) *consumed me*
- **h** *šalaḥtánīʸ — *you* (m.s.) *sent me*
- **i** *yahabtāk — *I gave you* (m.s.)
- **j** *’akalateh — *it* (f.s.) *consumed him*

2 Match the Aramaic construction to the correct translation, looking up verbs you are unfamiliar with in the glossary.

- **a** שַׁבְקֵהּ — *he informed me* (lit. *caused me to know*)
- **b** הוֹדְעַ֫נִי — *he caused you to rule*
- **c** הַקְרְבֻהִ — *they established him*
- **d** הֲקִימ֫וּהִי — *he left him alone*
- **e** הַתִיבָךְ — *I built it*
- **f** בְּנַיְתַהּ — *he set you*

g	הַשְׁלְטָךְ	*he destroyed me*
h	חַבְּלַנִי	*they established us*
i	הֲקִימֹוּנָא	*he returned you*
j	שָׂמָךְ	*he brought her near*

PREFIX CONJUGATION WITH PRONOMINAL SUFFIXES

In the prefix conjugation, a supplementary syllable (-inn-) comes between the verbal form and the suffix. Therefore, the verbal form **יִנְתְּנִנַּהּ** *he will give it* (from **נתן**) is composed of a verbal stem **יִנְתְּן** (*he will give*) + the suffix **נ ִ** + the pronominal suffix **ה ַ** (*it*). We would expect the same verb without object suffix to be **יִנְתֵּן** *he will give*. The e vowel is reduced when it is no longer in the stressed syllable. Before the 2mp object suffix, the -inn- becomes -ɛn- (**יְשְׁאֲלֶנְכוֹן** *he will ask you*) or -in- (**יְשֵׁיזְבִנְכוֹן** *he will save you*). When the verb form has a long vowel, there is no reduction: **תְּדוּשִׁנַּהּ** *it* (*the beast*) *will trample it* (*the kingdom*).

In the pa‘‘el prefix conjugation (as in the suffix conjugation) the short theme vowel (e or i) reduces before the object suffix: **יְדַחֲלִנַּנִי** *it was frightening me*. Most of the pa‘‘el prefix forms are 3mp forms and would exhibit vowel reduction even without the object suffix: **יְבַהֲלֻנַּנִי** *they were terrifying me*, **יְבַהֲלֻנֵּהּ** and **יְבַהֲלוּנֵּהּ** *they were terrifying him*, **יְטַעֲמוּנֵּהּ** *they will feed him*, **יְשַׁמְּשׁוּנֵּהּ** *they will serve him*. In these forms, the shuruq symbol (**וּ**) likely represents a short u; if not, the long ū would be in a closed unstressed syllable and this is very rare in Aramaic. With III-aleph/waw/yod roots, only two forms occur: **יְחַוִּנַּהּ** *he will tell it* and **יְחַוִּנַּנִי** *he will tell me*.

Where the prefix conjugation occurs without the supplementary syllable -inn-, -in-, or -ɛn-, the form is assumed to be a jussive, as is made more explicit in the two examples in the pa‘‘el where the verbs are negated by **אַל** *not* which only occurs with jussive verbs: **אַל־יְבַהֲלָךְ** *may it not terrify you* and **אַל־יְבַהֲלוּךְ** *may they not terrify you*.

The same patterns pertain to the haph‘el prefix conjugation plus object suffix: **יְהוֹדְעִנַּנִי** *he will cause me to know*, **יְהוֹדְעֻנַּנִי** *they will cause me to know*, **אֲהוֹדְעִנֵּהּ** *I will cause him to know*, **תְּהוֹדְעֻנַּנִי** and **תְּהוֹדְעוּנַּנִי** *you will cause me to know*, **תְּהַחֲוֻנַּנִי** *you will tell me*, **תַּדִּקִנַּהּ** *it* (*the beast*) *will crush it* (*the kingdom*).

The verb **שׁיזב** *to deliver* also appears with object suffixes: **יְשֵׁיזְבִנָּךְ** *he will deliver you*, **יְשֵׁיזְבִנְכוֹן** *he will deliver you*.

The following table illustrates the non-jussive prefix conjugation with suffixes. Here, there is no need to illustrate the historical forms since the process of vowel reduction is clearer (i.e. the theme vowel – the short u in *yiqṭul- – reduces to a muttered vowel ə).

Suffix		3ms pref. conj. יִקְטֻל (from *yiqṭul-)		3mp pref. conj. יִקְטְלוּן (from *yiqṭulūn-)
3ms	־ִנֵּהּ	יִקְטְלִנֵּהּ	נֵּהּ	יִקְטְלוּנֵּהּ
3fs	־ִנַּהּ	יִקְטְלִנַּהּ	נַּהּ	יִקְטְלוּנַּהּ
2ms	־ִנָּךְ	יִקְטְלִנָּךְ	נָּךְ	יִקְטְלוּנָּךְ

2fs	־ֵ נְּכִי	-	־נְּכִי	-
1cs	־ֵ נַּנִי	יִקְטְלִנַּנִי	־נַּנִי	יִקְטְלוּנַּנִי
3mp	-	-	-	-
3fp	-	-	-	-
2mp	־ִ נְכוֹן	יִקְטְלִנְכוֹן	־כוֹן	יִקְטְלוּנְכוֹן
2fp	־ִ נְכֵן	יִקְטְלִנְכֵן	־כֵן	יִקְטְלוּנְכֵן
1cp	־ִ נַּנָא	יִקְטְלִנַּנָא	־נַּנָא	יִקְטְלוּנַּנָא

OTHER VERBAL FORMS WITH PRONOMINAL SUFFIXES

As for the imperative with object suffix, only three such forms are found in Biblical Aramaic, one pa‘‘el (חַבְּלוּהִי *destroy it*) and two haph‘el (הַחֲוֺנִי *tell me* and הַעֵלְנִי *bring me*).

The infinitive with object suffix in the pə‘al exhibits the typical vowel reduction of Aramaic: מִקְרֵב *approach* with 3ms suffix is מִקְרְבֵהּ *its approach*, with the short e vowel reducing. In III-aleph/waw/yod roots, the final consonant is represented by a yod: מִצְבְּיֵהּ *his wishing* and מֵזְיֵהּ *its heating* (infinitive to **אזה**).

There are no examples of the pa‘‘el infinitive with pronominal suffixes, but in the haph‘el infinitive the final -$\bar{a}^h$ is replaced by -ūt or -$\bar{u}^w$t. Therefore, the haph‘el infinitive of **ידע** without suffix is הוֹדָעָה *to make known*, but the same infinitive with suffix is הוֹדָעֻתַנִי *to make me know*, and הוֹדָעוּתָךְ *to make you know*. Note too the examples of infinitives from a I-nun root (הַצָּלוּתֵהּ *to deliver him*); from II-waw/yod roots (הֲתָבוּתָךְ *to return you* and הֲקָמוּתֵהּ *to establish him*); and from the root **שיזב** *to deliver*: שֵׁיזָבוּתָךְ *to deliver you*.

Participles take suffixes just like other nouns, though these can be interpreted either as possessive suffixes or as object suffixes. We find שָׂנְאָיךְ *your haters* or *those hating you*, יָעֲטוֹהִי *his counsellors* or *those counseling him*.

PRACTICE 2

For the following items, identify the verbal form and suffix and then give a translation. (The words are drawn from the targums, but spelled and vocalized according to Biblical Aramaic norms).

a מִפְלְחַהּ
b קַטְלֵהּ
c יִקְטְלִנַּנִי
d יַשְׁכְּחִנֵּהּ
e מְבָרְכָךְ
f אֲבָרְכִנָּךְ
g אִתְּנְנֵהּ or אִנְתְּנִנֵּהּ
h חַבָּלוּתַהּ
i נִקְטְלִנֵּהּ
j הַשְׁכְּחַהּ

Reading

Translate the following passage from Ezra 5 using the glossary and the notes that follow the text.

EZRA 5:11

a כְּנֵמָא פִּתְגָמָא הֲתִיבוּנָא לְמֵמַר
b אֲנַחְנָא הִמּוֹ עַבְדוֹהִי דִּי־אֱלָהּ שְׁמַיָּא וְאַרְעָא
c וּבָנַיִן בַּיְתָא דִּי־הֲוָה בְנֵה מִקַּדְמַת דְּנָה שְׁנִין שַׂגִּיאָן
d וּמֶלֶךְ לְיִשְׂרָאֵל רַב בְּנָהִי וְשַׁכְלְלֵהּ

EZRA 5:12

a לָהֵן מִן־דִּי הַרְגִּזוּ אֲבָהָתַנָא לֶאֱלָהּ שְׁמַיָּא יְהַב הִמּוֹ בְּיַד נְבוּכַדְנֶצַּר מֶלֶךְ־בָּבֶל כַּסְדָּיאָ
b וּבַיְתָא דְנָה סַתְרֵהּ וְעַמָּה הַגְלִי לְבָבֶל

EZRA 5:13

a בְּרַם בִּשְׁנַת חֲדָה לְכוֹרֶשׁ מַלְכָּא דִּי בָבֶל
b כּוֹרֶשׁ מַלְכָּא שָׂם טְעֵם בֵּית־אֱלָהָא דְנָה לְמִבְנֵא

EZRA 5:14

a וְאַף מָאנַיָּא דִי־בֵית־אֱלָהָא דִּי דַהֲבָא וְכַסְפָּא
b דִּי נְבוּכַדְנֶצַּר הַנְפֵּק מִן־הֵיכְלָא דִּי בִירוּשְׁלֶם
c וְהֵיבֵל הִמּוֹ לְהֵיכְלָא דִּי בָבֶל
d הַנְפֵּק הִמּוֹ כּוֹרֶשׁ מַלְכָּא מִן־הֵיכְלָא דִּי בָבֶל
e וִיהִיבוּ לְשֵׁשְׁבַּצַּר שְׁמֵהּ דִּי פֶחָה שָׂמֵהּ

EZRA 5:15

a a וַאֲמַר־לֵהּ אֵל מָאנַיָּא שֵׂא אֵזֶל־אֲחֵת הִמּוֹ בְּהֵיכְלָא דִּי בִירוּשְׁלֶם
b b וּבֵית אֱלָהָא יִתְבְּנֵא עַל־אַתְרֵהּ

Ezra 5:11

a

הֲתִיבוּנָא לְמֵמַר – *they returned to us, saying* (lit. *they returned us a letter saying*) The first word is the haph'el 3mp suffix conj. with a 1cp object suffix. The second word is the lamed preposition followed by the infinitive of **אמר** *to say*, but functioning as an indication of a following quotation.

b

אֲנַחְנָא הִמּוֹ – The two words would seem to say *we they*, though the second pronoun is really functioning like the verb **הוי** *to be*.

c

וּבָנַיִן – The grammatical subject of the participle is **אֲנַחְנָא** of line b.

מִקַּדְמַת – *before* (**מִן** + **קַדְמַת**)

שְׁנִין שַׂגִּיאָן – *many years (ago)* The first Aramaic word is the word for *year* (**שְׁנָה**) and the second is the adjective *many*. English idiom requires the additional word *ago*, though this is not required in Aramaic.

Ezra 5:12

a

מִן־דִּי – *because* The combination of the preposition and relative pronoun often has this sense.

אֲבָהָתַנָא – This is the plural form of **אַב** with the 1cp pronominal suffix.

כַּסְדָּיאָ – We would have expected the spelling **כַּשְׂדָּיָא**. This modifies the word **מֶלֶךְ**.

b

עַמָּה – We would have expected the spelling **עַמָּא**; this is the determined form of the masculine singular noun **עַם**.

Ezra 5:14

e וִיהִיבוּ – The sequence of wə+yə becomes wī. See the glossary under **וְ**.

לְשֵׁשְׁבַּצַּר שְׁמֵהּ – *to someone named Sheshbatsar* More literally, the phrase reads *to Sheshbatsar, his name.*

Ezra 5:15

a

שֵׂא אֱזֶל־אֲחֵת – These are three m.s. imperatives from the roots respectively of **נשׂא** *to lift, take*, **אזל** *to go*, and **נחת** *to go down*, here in the aph'el: *to deposit, though we would expect* **אַחֵת***).

b

יִתְבְּנֵא – This has a jussive or modal sense *let . . .*

Test yourself

It is often easy to identify when a verbal form has a pronominal suffix. You must consider more carefully, however, the verb form and its possible roots. Parse the following verbal forms that have pronominal suffixes and translate the phrases, using the glossary when needed.

a פִּשְׁרֵהּ הַחֲוֺנִי
b כָּל־דִּי יִשְׁאֲלֶנְכוֹן
c חֱלֶם חֲזֵית וִידַחֲלִנַּנִי
d הֵן־חֶלְמָא לָא תְהוֹדְעֻנַּנִי
e תֵּאכֻל כָּל־אַרְעָא וּתְדוּשִׁנַּהּ
f הֲקִימֵהּ אֲבוּךְ מַלְכָּא
g קֳדָמוֹהִי הַקְרְבוּהִי
h יְחַוִּנַּהּ קֳדָם מַלְכָּא
i לַהֲקָמוּתֵהּ עַל־כָּל־מַלְכוּתָא
j כָּל־אַרְעָא . . . תַּדְקִנַּהּ

SELF-CHECK

	I CAN...
○	recognize how verb forms inflect with object suffixes
○	recognize object suffixes on suffix and prefix conjugation verb forms
○	recognize object suffixes on infinitives

21 *Syntax of clauses and numerals*

In this unit you will learn how to:

- **identify the usual word order in sentences**
- **recognize how numerals agree with nouns**
- **identify adverbial accusatives**
- **perceive when infinitives are used as finite verbs**

In this unit you will read:

- **Ezra 5:16–6:7**

Grammar

WORD ORDER

The order of words in Aramaic sentences varies quite a bit. In many cases, it is hard to know exactly why a particular sequence of elements has been chosen by an author. But, some general tendencies should be kept in mind (remembering that there are many exceptions).

In Biblical Aramaic, it is not uncommon that in independent clauses the subject precedes the verb (e.g. בֵּאדַיִן מַלְכָּא הַצְלַח לְשַׁדְרַךְ *then the king promoted Shadrach*; כָּל־קֳבֵל דְּנָה מַלְכָּא בְּנַס *Because of this, the king grew angry*). In those cases where there is no specific subject (i.e. it is implied by the verb form) then the verb often comes first (e.g. בֵּאדַיִן הַיְתִיו מָאנֵי דַהֲבָא *Then they brought the vessels of gold*). In these cases, the word order will not present problems to English speakers. However, in some instances the order of words will be different than that found commonly in English. Numerous examples of this have been read in preceding exercises and passages. It is helpful to recognize that the grammatical subject of a verb sometimes follows the verb. In other cases, the verb appears at the end of its clause.

Often where speech is reported or quoted, the verb for speaking and/or answering appears first in the clause, followed by its grammatical subject (e.g. עֲנוֹ כַשְׂדָּיֵא *the Chaldeans answered . . .*; עָנֵה מַלְכָּא *the king answered*), followed in turn by the speech itself.

In clauses that begin with דִּי, the verb often comes just after the particle with the subject following the verb (e.g. צְלֵם דַּהֲבָא דִּי הֲקֵים נְבוּכַדְנֶצַּר *the image of gold that Nebuchadnezzar had erected*; כְּדִי שָׁמְעִין כָּל־עַמְמַיָּא קָל קַרְנָא *when all the peoples heard the sound of the horn*; and בְּנֵי גָלוּתָא דִּי יְהוּד דִּי הַיְתִי מַלְכָּא אַבִי מִן־יְהוּד *. . . the children of the exile of Judah whom the king, my father, brought from Judah*). In some cases the sequence of words will not follow this order and ambiguity will arise. Note this passage in Aramaic from the book of Jeremiah (which is otherwise in Hebrew): כִּדְנָה תֵּאמְרוּן לְהֹם אֱלָהַיָּא דִּי שְׁמַיָּא וְאַרְקָא לָא עֲבַדוּ יֵאבַדוּ מֵאַרְעָא וּמִן־תְּחוֹת שְׁמַיָּא אֵלֶּה *like this you will say to them: 'The gods, who did not make the heaven or earth, will* *disappear from the earth and from under these heavens*'. That the verb לָא עֲבַדוּ is part of the דִּי clause may not at first be apparent.

In other cases where the subject follows the verb, the sentence otherwise resembles others where the subject precedes the verb. Compare the following phrases with those that are listed in the previous paragraph: בֵּאדַיִן קְרֵב נְבוּכַדְנֶצַּר *Then Nebuchadnezzar approached* . . . and כָּל־קֳבֵל דְּנָה בֵּהּ זִמְנָא קְרִבוּ גֻּבְרִין כַּשְׂדָּאִין *on account of this, at that time, the Chaldean men approached* . . . Notice that although the word order in the Aramaic might vary, the order of words in the English should follow English idiom.

Sometimes a sentence begins with a word that is neither the subject, verb, nor object of the verb, but instead draws the reader's attention to a particular focus of the sentence. For example, in the following sentence, the reader's attention is pointed toward the object of the prepositions בְּ and לְ which occur later in the sentence: וַאֲנָה לָא־בְחָכְמָה דִּי־אִיתַי בִּי מִן־כָּל־חַיַּיָּא רָזָא דְנָה גֱּלִי לִי *As for me, this secret was revealed to me not due to wisdom which (is) in me more than in all other living things* . . . In the following case, the reader's attention is drawn to the king, whose face and thoughts are the grammatical subjects of the following verbs: אֱדַיִן מַלְכָּא זִיוֺהִי שְׁנוֺהִי וְרַעְיֹנֹהִי יְבַהֲלוּנֵּהּ *Then, as for the king, his face changed him* (i.e. his appearance changed) *and his thoughts were terrifying him.*

CULTURAL INSIGHT

In the region of Kandahar, in what is today Afghanistan, the Buddhist emperor Ashoka (ca. 250 BCE) inscribed an edict declaring his adoption of the principle of truth (i.e. Buddha's teachings, dharma) which, among other things, meant restraint and an abstention from meat. The inscription is written in standard Official Aramaic orthography, which lacks final forms of letters. After a dating formula, the inscription reads (vocalized according to the model of Biblical Aramaic) מָרַאנָ פרידרש מַלְכָּא קַשִׁיטָא מְהַקְשֵׁט *Our lord, Prydrš (Priyadarshi* (?), i.e. *Ashoka*), *the king, promotes the truth* (lit. *justifies the truth*). The inscription continues, incorporating some Iranian words: זְעֵיר מַרְעָא לְכָלְהֹמ אֱנָשׁנ וְכָלְהֹמ אדושיא הוֹבֵד וּבְכֹל אַרְקָא ראמ שתי . . . *sickness (was) little for all people* (lit. *for all of them, people*) *and all afflictions* (?) *he abolished and in all the earth (is) joy and happiness* (?). Then, it says: וְאַף זִי זְנָה בְּמֵאכְלָא לְמָרַאנָ זְעֵיר קָטְלִנ *Also, because of this* (?), *for the food of our lord, the king, few (animals) are killed* (lit. *they kill few*). (See Mukherjee, Dupont-Sommer, and Skjærvø 1995).

THE SYNTAX OF NUMERALS

Many of the features of numerals have already been described in Unit 14, including that the cardinal numerals from three to ten are masculine in form when modifying feminine nouns and are feminine in form when modifying masculine nouns (e.g. מַלְכִין שִׁבְעָה *seven kings* and מַלְכָן שְׁבַע *seven queens*). Nevertheless, some further points should be mentioned in relation to the syntax of these words.

First, the mismatch between gendered morphemes (masc. form with fem. noun, etc.) is also seen among the larger numerals themselves. Note the phrase אִמְּרִין אַרְבַּע מְאָה *four hundred lambs*, where the numeral אַרְבַּע *four* has a masculine form since it is technically modifying the feminine word מְאָה *hundred*, not the thing counted, the lambs, which is masculine in gender. (There is only one word for *hundred*, and it is always marked as feminine, even when the word it modifies is feminine too.)

The construct state of the cardinal numerals is rarely found before nouns. Instead, the cardinal numeral appears in the absolute state either before or after the noun it modifies, where the noun is often in the absolute plural. For example, note גֻּבְרִין תְּלָתָה *three men*; זִמְנִין תְּלָתָה *three times*; תְּלָת עִלְעִין *three ribs*; אַרְבַּע חֵיוָן *four beasts*. Where the noun is in construct with a following numeral, the words usually express a date: שְׁנַת־שֵׁת לְמַלְכוּת דָּרְיָוֶשׁ *year six to the reign of Darius*.

Sometimes a pronominal suffix appears on a numeral, as in תְּלָתֵהוֹן *the three of them*.

ADVERBIAL ACCUSATIVES

In Aramaic, as in other Semitic languages, a noun in the absolute or determined state can modify another noun or verb though the word or phrase is not preceded by a preposition. Such nouns are called adverbial accusatives since they often function as adverbs and in some Semitic languages are in the accusative case. For example, in the following clause (read in Unit 19) the phrase אֶבֶן גְּלָל indicates the material with which the temple in Jerusalem is being built: וְהוּא מִתְבְּנֵא אֶבֶן גְּלָל *and it* (i.e. the temple) *is being built with hewn stone*. As in this example, the adverbial accusative does not make good sense as the subject of the verb or as the object of the verb. Such adverbial accusative nouns or phrases are often translated with an English preposition, though the Aramaic lacks one.

INFINITIVES AS REGULAR VERBS

Sometimes infinitives function as regular verbs (suffix and prefix conjugations). They can be used in a temporal construction, as with וּכְמִקְרְבֵהּ לְגֻבָּא *as he approached the den* (Dan 6:21). Infinitives can also indicate possibility or obligation, often where the infinitive is active, but can be translated into the English passive voice. Note, for example, the following phrase: כְּעַן מַלְכָּא תְּקִים אֱסָרָא וְתִרְשֻׁם כְּתָבָא דִּי לָא לְהַשְׁנָיָה *Now, O king, may you establish the prohibition and sign the order so that it cannot be changed* (Dan 6:9). The final phrase דִּי לָא לְהַשְׁנָיָה is composed of the particle דִּי *so that* followed by the negative particle לָא *not*, the preposition lamed, and the haph'el infinitive of שׁני. More literally it might be translated *which not to change* or even *which (one) cannot change*. Nevertheless, in the context of the passage, the establishment of the prohibition and its signing are for the purpose of making it impossible for anyone to change. So, the translation *so that* . . . really makes better sense. Another example is from Ezra 6:8: נִפְקְתָא תֶּהֱוֵא מִתְיַהֲבָה לְגֻבְרַיָּא אִלֵּךְ דִּי לָא לְבַטָּלָא *let the expenses be given to these men who must not be stopped*. Again, the infinitive is an active verbal form (in this case a pa''el from בטל) and might be translated more literally *whom (one) must not stop*, though the passive construction seems more idiomatic in English.

Reading

Translate the following passage from Ezra 5–6 using the glossary and the notes that follow the text.

EZRA 5:16

a אֱדַיִן שֵׁשְׁבַּצַּר דֵּךְ אֲתָה יְהַב אֻשַּׁיָּא דִּי־בֵית אֱלָהָא דִּי בִירוּשְׁלֶם
b וּמִן־אֱדַיִן וְעַד־כְּעַן מִתְבְּנֵא וְלָא שְׁלִם

EZRA 5:17

a וּכְעַן הֵן עַל־מַלְכָּא טָב יִתְבַּקַּר בְּבֵית גִּנְזַיָּא דִּי־מַלְכָּא תַמָּה דִּי בְּבָבֶל
b הֵן אִיתַי דִּי־מִן־כּוֹרֶשׁ מַלְכָּא שִׂים טְעֵם לְמִבְנֵא בֵּית־אֱלָהָא דֵךְ בִּירוּשְׁלֶם
c וּרְעוּת מַלְכָּא עַל־דְּנָה יִשְׁלַח עֲלֶינָא

EZRA 6:1

a בֵּאדַיִן דָּרְיָוֶשׁ מַלְכָּא שָׂם טְעֵם
b וּבַקַּרוּ בְּבֵית סִפְרַיָּא דִּי גִנְזַיָּא מְהַחֲתִין תַּמָּה בְּבָבֶל

EZRA 6:2

a וְהִשְׁתְּכַח בְּאַחְמְתָא בְּבִירְתָא דִּי בְּמָדַי מְדִינְתָּא מְגִלָּה חֲדָה
b וְכֵן־כְּתִיב בְּגַוַּהּ דִּכְרוֹנָה

EZRA 6:3

a בִּשְׁנַת חֲדָה לְכוֹרֶשׁ מַלְכָּא כּוֹרֶשׁ מַלְכָּא שָׂם טְעֵם
b בֵּית־אֱלָהָא בִירוּשְׁלֶם בַּיְתָא יִתְבְּנֵא
c אֲתַר דִּי דָבְחִין דִּבְחִין וְאֻשּׁוֹהִי מְסוֹבְלִין
d רוּמֵהּ אַמִּין שִׁתִּין פְּתָיֵהּ אַמִּין שִׁתִּין

EZRA 6:4

a נִדְבָּכִין דִּי־אֶבֶן גְּלָל תְּלָתָא וְנִדְבָּךְ דִּי־אָע חֲדַת
b וְנִפְקְתָא מִן־בֵּית מַלְכָּא תִּתְיְהִב

EZRA 6:5

a וְאַף מָאנֵי בֵית־אֱלָהָא דִּי דַהֲבָה וְכַסְפָּא
b דִּי נְבוּכַדְנֶצַּר הַנְפֵּק מִן־הֵיכְלָא דִּי־יְרוּשְׁלֶם וְהֵיבֵל לְבָבֶל
c יַהֲתִיבוּן וִיהָךְ לְהֵיכְלָא דִּי־בִירוּשְׁלֶם לְאַתְרֵהּ
d וְתַחֵת בְּבֵית אֱלָהָא

EZRA 6:6

a כְּעַן תַּתְּנַי פַּחַת עֲבַר־נַהֲרָה שְׁתַר בּוֹזְנַי וּכְנָוָתְהוֹן אֲפַרְסְכָיֵא דִּי בַּעֲבַר נַהֲרָה רַחִיקִין הֲווֹ מִן־תַּמָּה

EZRA 6:7

a שְׁבֻקוּ לַעֲבִידַת בֵּית־אֱלָהָא דֵךְ
b פַּחַת יְהוּדָיֵא וּשָׂבֵי יְהוּדָיֵא
c בֵּית־אֱלָהָא דֵךְ יִבְנוֹן עַל־אַתְרֵהּ

Ezra 5:17

a

יִתְבַּקַּר – This has a jussive nuance *let a search be made.*

בֵּית גִּנְזַיָּא – The singular for the second word is גְּנַז and usually means *treasury*, though in this context (together with the preceding words *house of*) it means *archives*.

b

הֵן אִיתַי דִּי – A comprehensible English translation can be made by translating each word in its standard manner *if it is that . . .*, though a better idiomatic English might be *If it is true that . . .*

Ezra 6:1

a

וּבַקַּרוּ – This is an active form, but the plural verb without a clear subject is best construed as an impersonal expression that should be translated into the English passive voice.

b

מְהַחֲתִין – This is a haph'el passive participle from the root נחת.

Ezra 6:2

a

וְהִשְׁתְּכַח – This is the hitpəʻel 3ms suffix conjugation of the root שׁכח *to find*. Remember that where a root with an initial sibilant occurs in the hitpəʻel or hitpaʻʻal stems the sibilant often metathesizes or switches places with the taw of the t-stem. The subject of the verb is the phrase from the end of the line: מְגִלָּה חֲדָה. In this case, the verb does not agree in gender with its subject.

בְּאַחְמְתָא – *In Ecbatana*

b

דִּכְרוֹנָה – This would have probably been the first word of the document and thus more logically should be grouped with the following verse.

Ezra 6:3

c

This line is in apposition to the preceding line. דָבְחִין דִּבְחִין (where) *sacrifices were made* (lit. (where) *they made sacrifices*). Again, a plural verbal form is used in an impersonal expression.

מְסוֹבְלִין – *let (subject) be laid down* This is the m.p. participle of סבל in the rare polel stem. Literally it might mean *they laid down*, though this is another impersonal construction to be rendered in English with the passive voice.

d

This line forms its own sentence. We may infer a verb: *let its height be* or *its height will be.*

Ezra 6:4

a

The line is also its own sentence. We may infer a verb: *let there be three courses . . .*

Ezra 6:5

a

דִּי דַהֲבָה וְכַסְפָּא – This is a genitive construction (i.e. *of*…), but the nouns are best translated as English adjectives in front of *vessels*.

b

הֵיבֵל – *he brought* This is the haph'el 3ms suffix conjugation of the root יבל *to bring*.

c

יַהֲתִיבוּן וִיהָךְ – *Let them be returned and let them go* The first verb is a haph'el 3mp prefix conjugation of תוב *to return* and the second is the pəʻal 3ms prefix conjugation of הוך *to go*. The first verb is again a plural verb used in an impersonal construction and translated by the English passive voice. The waw conjunction may indicate a break between two sentences here. The subject of הוך is the vessels, despite the fact יְהָךְ is singular. Note that the 3ms pronominal suffix at the end of the line also refers to the vessels.

d

תַּחֵת – The haph'el 2ms prefix conjugation of נחת.

Ezra 6:6

a

הֱווֹ – This is the pəʻal m.p. imperative of הוי *to be*.

Test yourself

Fill in the blanks to the translation of Ezra 7:25–6.

a וְאַנְתְּ עֶזְרָא כְּחָכְמַת אֱלָהָךְ דִּי־בִידָךְ
b מֶנִּי (= מַנִּי) שָׁפְטִין וְדַיָּנִין
c דִּי־לֶהֱוֺן דָּאְנִין (= דָּיְנִין) לְכָל־עַמָּה (= עַמָּא) דִּי בַּעֲבַר נַהֲרָה
d לְכָל־יָדְעֵי דָּתֵי אֱלָהָךְ
e וְדִי לָא יָדַע תְּהוֹדְעוּן
f וְכָל־דִּי־לָא לֶהֱוֵא עָבֵד דָּתָא דִי־אֱלָהָךְ וְדָתָא דִּי מַלְכָּא אָסְפַּרְנָא
g דִּינָה (= דִּינָא) לֶהֱוֵא מִתְעֲבֵד מִנֵּהּ
h הֵן לְמוֹת הֵן לִשְׁרֹשׁוּ (= לִשְׁרֹשִׁי) הֵן־לַעֲנָשׁ נִכְסִין וְלֶאֱסוּרִין

a *And you, Ezra,* ____________________ *the* ____________________ *of your* ____________________ *which you possess* (lit. *which is in* ____________________ ____________________),

b *appoint* ____________________ *and* ____________________

c *so they can* ____________________ *all the* ____________________ *who are in Abar-Naharah,*

d *all who* ____________________ *the laws of* ____________________ ____________________,

e *and you will* ______________________ *(those) who do not* ______________________ *(these laws).*

f ______________________ ______________________ *will not observe* (lit. *do*) *the* ______________________ *of your God and the* ______________________ *of the* ______________________ *precisely*

g ______________________ *will be done because of him,*

h *whether for death, or corporal punishment, or fine of* ______________________, *or imprisonment.*

SELF-CHECK

	I CAN...
○	identify the usual word order in sentences
○	recognize how numerals agree with nouns
○	identify adverbial accusatives
○	perceive when infinitives are used as finite verbs

22 Readings in the targums

In this unit you will learn how to:

- **recognize the genre of targums**
- **read the Aramaic dialect of Targum Onqelos**
- **read the Aramaic dialect of Targum Neofiti**

In this unit you will read:

- **Gen 1:1–13 in Targum Onqelos**
- **Gen 11:1–9 in Targum Onqelos**
- **Gen 11:1–9 in Targum Neofiti**

Grammar 1

TARGUMS

A targum is an Aramaic translation of scripture. There are various Aramaic translations of what we now think of as the Bible, one of the earliest being that of Job found among the Dead Sea Scrolls. From at least a few centuries later is Targum Onqelos, a translation of the first five books of the Bible (Genesis–Deuteronomy). The origin of this targum is unclear, though it is often assumed to have emerged first in Palestine and then to have been copied and transmitted in Babylonia for centuries before becoming more widely disseminated. It is the most frequently cited Aramaic translation of the Torah or Pentateuch and is evidenced in numerous different manuscripts and editions. Due to its relatively early age, its language bears numerous similarities with the language of Biblical Aramaic. Some variations of the grammar have been noted.

Targum Neofiti was discovered comparatively recently, in the library of the Vatican (Ms Neofiti.1). In contrast to Onqelos, Neofiti demonstrates many more characteristics typical of Palestinian Aramaic, and generally many more characteristics typical of later Aramaic. It is particularly interesting given the numerous additions to the biblical text it attests.

CULTURAL INSIGHT

The targums in general reflect the theological perspectives of the translators and scribes who transmitted the text through the generations. One peculiarity found in most, if not all, targums is the reticence towards depicting or even talking about God in human or anthropomorphic terms. Instead of referring to God as *my Lord*, as is done in the Hebrew text where the name יהוה (i.e. Yahweh) is pronounced ʾădōnāy or *my Lord*, the targums translate יהוה with the noun מֵאמְרָא memrâ *the word*. Genesis 11:7 in Targum Neofiti reveals another theologically motivated translation. While the Hebrew has *let us go down* and Targum Onqelos has *let us appear*, Neofiti has the same verb in the singular *let me appear*, thus reducing the impression that there were multiple divinities involved in communicating with humanity.

THE GRAMMAR OF TARGUM ONQELOS

The first thing you will notice is that vowels are often marked differently. In many of the actual manuscripts, the vowels are actually above the letters and have forms distinct from those found in Biblical Aramaic. These are referred to as Babylonian vowel symbols. In this system, there are fewer symbols. There is no symbol equivalent to a seghol (representing ε). The symbol corresponding to the shewa marks only a muttered vowel (including after gutturals – there are no hateph-vowels like the hateph-patach). There is no symbol to mark the absence of a vowel. Where no vowel is present, there is no symbol. There is also no mark corresponding to the dagesh (dot) to distinguish the hard from the soft begadkephat letters or to indicate doubled consonants. This does not mean that no distinction was made between begadkephat consonants or that consonants were never doubled, only that this was not recorded in the writing. There is also no dot above the שׂ or שׁ; where ש is found, it usually represents שׁ. Etymological שׂ is usually represented with ס. In the rare cases where ש represents שׂ a small swoosh appears above the letter.

LANGUAGE INSIGHT

The spelling אַפֵּי *face of*, the plural construct form of אַף *nose*, implies doubling of the peh due to the preservation of the short a under the aleph. If the peh were not doubled, we would expect the a of the singular to reduce to a muttered vowel, represented by a shewa.

While there are generally fewer vowel and reading marks, there are more maters within words (e.g. the yod to mark e in עָבֵיד *makes, bears*, the pəʿal m.s. participle of עבד; and אַפְרֵיש *he separated*, the aphʿel 3ms suffix conjugation of פרשׁ; also with the 3ms pronominal suffix: זְנֵיה *its kind*). A word-final long ā is regularly marked by an aleph mater, not a he (e.g. קְרָא *he called* (pə. 3ms suff. conj. of קרי) and עֲקַרְתָּא... צַדְיָא *barren* (pə. f.s. part. of צדי)). A word final ē is marked by yod instead of aleph or he (e.g. נִבְנֵי *let us build*). Within a word, a short i can be represented with a yod (e.g. לִישָּׁן = liššān *tongue*).

The pronouns in Targum Onqelos (and in later dialects of Aramaic) are sometimes slightly different than in Biblical Aramaic. Note, for example, דֵּין *this* (instead of Biblical Aramaic דְּנָה *this*). Also, whereas in Biblical Aramaic the relative particle is דִּי, in Targum Onqelos it is simply דְ and attaches directly to the following word, just like the prepositions בְּ *in, with*, כְּ *as, like*, and לְ *to, for*.

In Targum Onqelos, the normal, basic form for many nouns is no longer the absolute state, but instead the determined state. That is, where in Biblical Aramaic we would expect a noun in the absolute, we find in Targum Onqelos (and in later varieties of Aramaic too) a noun in the determined state. This means that many nouns are in the determined state. Far fewer are in the absolute. The ending for masculine plural determined nouns is still -ayyā, though sometimes it is represented as simply -ē (יַמְמֵי *(the) seas*), a pronunciation more common in Eastern Aramaic.

Among peculiarities of the verb, note that the haphʿel has been entirely replaced by the aphʿel. Similarly, the hitpəʿel and hitpaʿʿal have been replaced by the itpəʿel and itpaʿʿal. In addition to these stems, there also exists a t-stem version of the aphʿel, that is, the ittaphʿal, as in אִתַּחְזִי *it appeared* and יִתַּחְזֵי *it might appear*.

In contrast to Biblical Aramaic, where the 3fs and 1cs suffix-conjugation verb forms exhibit an initial closed syllable (i.e. in the pəʿal **כִּתְבַת** *she wrote* and **כִּתְבֵת** *I wrote*), which is unlike the other forms of the paradigm (e.g. **כְּתַב** *he wrote*), in the Aramaic of Onqelos, the 3fs and 1cs exhibit the same initial syllabic and vocalic pattern as the other forms of the paradigm. So, the pattern of the 3ms is **כְּתַב** and the 3fs and 1cs exhibit the same ə-a pattern: **כְּתַבַת** *she wrote* and **כְּתַבִית** *I wrote*. Unlike in Biblical Aramaic, the verb can combine with the 3mp pronoun **אִנּוּן** (= Biblical Aramaic **אִנּוּן**) to form a single word, as in **נִשְׂרוֹפִנּוּן** *let us bake them.*

The word order in targumic texts often reflects the word order of the original Hebrew. Therefore, often the verb comes first in a clause in targumic texts, as fits the expectations of Hebrew syntax.

Reading 1

1 Translate the following passage from Genesis 1 (based on the British Library Ms OR 2228), using the glossary and the notes that follow the text.

GENESIS 1:1

a בְּקַדמִין בְּרָא יוָי יָת שְׁמַיָא וְיָת אַרעָא

GENESIS 1:2

a וְאַרעָא הְוָת צָדיָא וְרוֹקָניָא
b וַחְשׁוֹכָא עַל אַפֵּי תְהוֹמָא
c וְרוּחָא מִן קֳדָם יוָי מְנַשְׁבָא עַל אַפֵּי מַיָא

GENESIS 1:3

a וְאְמַר יוָי יְהֵי נְהוֹרָא וַהְוָה נְהוֹרָא

GENESIS 1:4

a וַחְזָא יוָי יָת נְהוֹרָא אְרֵי טָב
b וְאַפרֵישׁ יוָי בֵּין נְהוֹרָא וּבֵין חְשׁוֹכָא

GENESIS 1:5

a וּקרָא יוָי לִנהוֹרָא יְמָמָא
b וְלַחְשׁוֹכָא קְרָא לֵילְיָא
c וַהְוָה רְמַשׁ וְהְוָה צְפַר יוֹם חַד

GENESIS 1:6

a וַאְמַר יוָי יְהֵי רְקִיעָא בִמצִיעוּת מַיָא
b וִיהֵי מַפרֵישׁ בֵּין מַיָא לְמַיָא

GENESIS 1:7

a וַעְבַד יוָי יָת רְקִיעָא
b וְאַפרֵישׁ בֵּין מַיָא דְמִלְרַע לִרקִיעָא
c וּבֵין מַיָא דְמֵיעַל לִרקִיעָא וַהְוָה כֵין

GENESIS 1:8

a וּקְרָא יְיָ לִרקִיעָא שְׁמַיָא
b וַהְוָה רְמַשׁ וַהְוָה צְפַר יוֹם תִנְיָן

GENESIS 1:9

a וַאְמַר יְיָ יִתכַּנשׁוּן מַיָא מִתְחוֹת שְׁמַיָא לְאַתרָא חַד
b וְתִתַחזֵי יַבֶּשׁתָא וַהְוָא כֵין

GENESIS 1:10

a וּקְרָא יְיָ לְיַבַּשׁתָא אַרעָא
b וּלבֵית כְּנֵישַׁת מַיָא קְרָא יַמְמֵי
c וַחְזָא יְיָ אְרֵי טָב

GENESIS 1:11

a וַאְמַר יְיָ תַדְאֵית אַרעָא דִתאָה עִסבָא
b דְבַר זַרעֵיה מִזדְרַע
c אִילָן פֵירִין עָבֵיד פֵירִין לִזנֵיה
d דְבַר־זַרעֵיה בֵיה עַל אַרעָא
e וַהְוָה כֵין

GENESIS 1:12

a וְאַפֵיקַת אַרעָא דִתאָה עִסבָה
b דְבַר־זַרעֵיה מִזדְרַע לִזנוֹהִי
c וְאִילָן עָבֵיד פֵירִין
d דְבַר־זַרעֵיה בֵיה לִזנוֹהִי
e וַהְזָא יְיָ אֲרֵי טָב

GENESIS 1:13

a וַהְוָה רְמַשׁ וַהְוָה צְפַר יוֹם תְלִיתָי

NOTES

Genesis 1:1

a

בְקַדמִין – This is the preposition **בְ** followed by the adverb **קַדמִין**.

בְרָא – This is the pə. 3ms suff. conj. of **ברי**. Note the aleph mater for what we would expect to be a he mater in Biblical Aramaic.

שְׁמַיָא – There is no dagesh to mark the doubling of the yod, but the doubling is implied by the preservation of the short a vowel just before it. A short vowel in an open, pre-stress syllable would otherwise reduce.

Genesis 1:2

a

הְוָת – This is the pə. 3fs suff. conj. of **הוי**.

צָדְיָא – This is the pə. f.s. part. of **צדי**.

b

חֲשׁוֹכָא – Although the context and the Hebrew text both suggest this should be in the absolute state it appears in the determined. This reflects the tendency (in later Aramaic) for nouns not to appear in the absolute, even where they would be found in the absolute in earlier dialects, like Biblical Aramaic. See also, e.g. **רוּחָא** in **c** and **נְהוֹרָא** in 1:3, etc.

c

מְנַשְּׁבָא – This is the pa. f.s. part. of **נשׁב**.

Genesis 1:3

a

יְהֵי – This is the jussive form of **הוי**, though similar forms (of III-waw/yod roots) do not occur elsewhere; this form is likely derived from the Hebrew text (where similar jussive forms of III-waw/yod roots are more common).

Genesis 1:4

a

חֲזָא – This is the pə. 3ms suff. conj. of **חזי**. What is usually marked with a he mater in Biblical Aramaic is often marked with an aleph mater in Onqelos and later Aramaic.

b

אַפְרֵישׁ – This is the aph. 3ms suff. conj. of **פרשׁ**.

בֵּין . . . וּבֵין – The preposition **בֵּין** *between* repeats in Aramaic, but should be represented only once in an English translation, though here it is unnecessary in the English translation.

Genesis 1:5

c

יוֹם חַד – The use of the cardinal numeral *one* instead of the ordinal *first* reflects the Hebrew text. While in Hebrew the cardinal for *one* can be used in place of the ordinal *first*, this is not typical in Aramaic.

Genesis 1:6

a

יְהֵי – See 1:3.

בִּמְצִיעוּת – This is the preposition **בְּ** followed by **מְצִיעוּ** in the construct state.

b

וִיהֵי – This is the waw conjunction plus **יְהֵי** (see 1:3 above and the glossary under **וְ** for the lack of shewa.).

מַפְרֵישׁ – This is the aph. m.s. part. of **פרשׁ**.

בֵּין מַיָא לְמַיָא – The sequence of **בֵּין . . . לְ** has the same sense and translation as that of **בֵּין . . . וּבֵין** in 1:4.

Genesis 1:7

b

דְמִלְרַע – This is the relative particle, דְ, followed by a compound preposition (listed under מִלְּרַע) made up of the preposition מִן and the adverb לְרַע.

דְמֵיעַל – This is the relative particle, דְ, followed by a compound preposition (listed under מֵיעַל) made up of the prepositions מִן and עַל.

Genesis 1:9

a

יִתְכַּנְשׁוּן – This is the itpa. 3mp pref. conj. of כנשׁ.

מִתְּחוֹת – This is a compound preposition (listed under מִתְּחוֹת) made up of the prepositions מִן and תְּחוֹת.

b

תִּתַחֲזֵי – This is the ittaph'al 3fs pref. conj. of חזי.

Genesis 1:10

b

יַמְּמֵי – Note the alternative masc. pl. determined ending (-ē^{y}) that resembles the plural construct. This form of the determined ending is typical of Babylonian Aramaic. The presence of this feature in Targum Onqelos presumably reflects the text's transmission in the east.

Genesis 1:11

a

תַּדְאֵית – This is the aph. 3fs of דאת.

b

דְבַר־זַרְעֵיה מִזְדְּרַע – This expression is made up of the particle דְּ followed by the construct phrase בַּר־זַרְעֵה, literally *son of its seed*, though the phrase בַּר זְרַע simply means *seed*.

מִזְדְּרַע – This is the itpə. m.s. part. of זרע. The original -ת- of the stem has metathesized with -ז- of the root and shifted to -ד- due to influence of the -ז- root consonant.

Genesis 1:12

a

אַפֵּיקַת – This is the aph. 3fs suff. conj. of נפק.

2 Translate the following passage from Genesis 11 (based on the British Library Ms OR 2228), using the glossary and the notes that follow the text.

GENESIS 11:1

a וַהֲוָת כָּל אַרעָא לִישָׁן חַד וּמַמלַל חַד

GENESIS 11:2

a וַהֲוָה בְמִיטַלהוֹן בְקַדמֵיתָא
b וְאַשׁכַחוּ בִקעְתָא בְאַרעָא דְבָבַל
c וִיתִיבוּ תַמָן

GENESIS 11:3

a וַאְמַרוּ גְבַר לְחַברֵיה
b הַבוּ נִרמֵי לִבנִין
c וְנִשׂרוֹפִנוּן בְנוּרָא
d וַהוָת לְהוֹן לְבֵינְתָא לְאַבנָא
e וְחֵימָרָא הְוָה לְהוֹן לִשיָע

GENESIS 11:4

a וַאְמַרוּ הַבוּ נִבנֵי לַנָא קַרתָא וּמַגדְלָא
b וְרֵישֵׁיה מָטֵי עַד צֵית שְׁמַיָא
c וְנַעְבֵיד לַנָא שֵׁם
d דִלמָא נִתבַדַר עַל אַפֵי כָל אַרעָא

GENESIS 11:5

a וְאִתגְלִי יְוָי לְאִתפְרָעָה
b עַל עוֹבָד קַרתָא וּמִגדְלָא דִבנוֹ בְנֵי אֲנָשָׁא

GENESIS 11:6

a וַאְמַר יְוָי הָא עַמָא חַד וְלִשָׁן חַד לְכוּלְהוֹן
b וְדֵין דְשָׁרְיָן (דְשָׁרִיוּ read) לְמַעֲבַד
c וּכעַן לָא יִתמְנַע מִנְהוֹן כֹל דְחַשִׁיבוּ לְמַעְבַד

GENESIS 11:7

a הַבוּ נִתגְלֵי וּנבַלבֵיל תַמָן לִישָׁנְהוֹן
b דְלָא יִשׁמְעוּן אְנָשׁ לִישָׁן חַברֵיה

GENESIS 11:8

a וּבַדַר יְוָי יָתְהוֹן מִתַמָן עַל אַפֵי כָל אַרעָא
b וְאִתמְנַעוּ מִלְמִבנֵי קַרתָא

GENESIS 11:9

a עַל כֵין קְרָא שְׁמַה בָבַל
b אְרֵי תַמָן בַלבֵל יְוָי לִישָׁן כָל אַרעָא
c וּמִיתַמָן בַדרִינוּן יְוָי עַל אַפֵי כָל אַרעָא

NOTES

Genesis 11:2

a

וַהֲוָה בְמִיטַלהוֹן בְקַדמֵיתָא – *When they first travelled*... This expression, reflecting the grammar of the Hebrew original, could more literally be rendered *and it was in their travelling at first*...

בְּמִיטַּלְהוֹן – The expression is made up of the bet preposition followed by the pə. inf. of **נטל** and then the 3mp pronominal suffix.

בְּקַדְמֵיתָא – This adverb (listed under **בְּקַדְמֵיתָא**) is made up of the bet preposition and the word **קדמית**. The final -ā is an adverbial suffix.

c

יתִיבוּ – This is the pə. 3mp suff. conj. of **יתב**. In Biblical Aramaic it would be written **יְתִ֫בוּ**.

Genesis 11:3

a

וַאְמַרוּ גְּבַר לְחַבְרֵיה – The literal translation of the clause is *and they said, a person to his companion*, though from context it might be rendered more idiomatically in English *they said to each other*.

b

הַבוּ נִרְמֵי – This is the imperative of **יהב** (used as an interjection) followed by the pə. 1cp pref. conj. of **רמי**. Preceded by the imperative, the pref. conj. **נִרְמֵי** should be interpreted as expressing a jussive nuance *let us* . . . Note that the yod mater comes at the end of pref. conj. verbs in this and other varieties of Aramaic; this is in contrast to Biblical Aramaic where the same vowel is often marked by the aleph mater in (e.g. **תֶּעְדֵּא** *it will pass away*) and less often by the he mater (**יֶעְדֵּה** *it will pass away*).

c

נִשְׂרוֹפִנּוּן – The pə. 1cp pref. conj. of **שׂרף** has again a jussive nuance based on context. The verb form also bears the suffixed 3mp pronoun -innūn (an abbreviation of the independent pronoun **אִנּוּן** *they*).

d

הֲוָת – This is the pə. 3fs suff. conj. of **הוי** taking **לְבֵנְתָא** as subject.

לְאַבנָא – *as stone* The preposition **לְ** implies how **לְבֵנְתָא** was put to use.

Genesis 11:4

a

הַבוּ נִבנֵי – See the notes to 11:3a.

קַרתָא – This is the fem. det. form of **קְרַת**, which is an alternative form for the more common noun **קִרְיָה** *city*.

b

וְרֵישֵׁיה מָטֵי עַד צֵית שְׁמַיָא – The clause indicates circumstantial information and can be translated into English as a subordinate clause *with* . . .

c

נַעְבֵיד – This is the pə. 1cp pref. conj. of **עבד**. Although the haph‘el would look identical, the sense here is that of the pə‘al (cf. ha. *to produce*). A jussive nuance is again implied from context *let us* . . .

d

דִלְמָא – *lest* This is another compound particle (listed under דִּלְמָא), made up of the relative particle דְ followed by the preposition לְ and the interrogative מָא *what?*

Genesis 11:5

a

אִתגְלִי – This is the itpə. 3ms suff. conj. of גלי.

אִתפְּרָעָה – This is the itpə. infin. of פרע.

Genesis 11:6

b

שָׁרְיָן – Ms OR 2228 has a pə. f.p. part. of שרי, though the context suggests the 3mp suff. conj. of the same root.

c

חַשִׁיבוּ – This is the pa. 3mp suff. conj. of חשב. Note the mater for what is a short i vowel.

Genesis 11:7

a

הַבוּ נִתגְלֵי וּנבַלבֵּיל – See the notes to 11:3a.

נבַלבֵּיל – This is the palpel 1cp pref. conj. of בלל.

Genesis 11:8

b

מִלְמִבנֵי – This is the preposition מִן followed by the preposition לְ followed by the pə. infin. of בני.

Genesis 11:9

c

בַדרִינוּן – This is the pa. 3ms suff. conj. of בדר followed by the 3mp pronominal suffix *them.*

Grammar 2

THE GRAMMAR OF TARGUM NEOFITI

The first distinction a student will notice is the absence of any vowel marks, like those seen above and below letters in Biblical Aramaic and in Targum Onqelos. This makes reading the text more challenging. It also makes knowing the exact pronunciation of the language more difficult. Although scholars have inferred some details of the dialect from rare vocalized forms and parallels to other contemporaneous texts (e.g. that there was no distinction between short a and long ā; see Fassberg 52), it is easier (and pedagogically more useful) for the beginning student to follow a well-attested vocalic system. As a pedagogical guide, therefore, the text has been vocalized in the appendix according to the vowel inventory reflected in Targum Onqelos, but using the same symbols found in Biblical Aramaic (i.e. the Tiberian, non-Babylonian system). With only few exceptions (noted here), the morphology of Biblical Aramaic is followed.

You will also notice that there are not quite as many maters as in Targum Onqelos. But, where a waw or yod is doubled and/or used as a true consonant, it will often be written twice (e.g. **דיירי** (pronounced **דַּיָּרֵי**) *dwellers of*).

Often a word that would have ended in a long vowel in Biblical Aramaic or in Targum Onqelos is, in Targum Neofiti, accompanied by a final mem or nun (e.g. **הוון** (pron. **הְווֹן**) *they were* vs. **הֲווֹ** in Bib. Aram., Onq. and **ארום** (pron. **אְרוּם**) *because* vs. **אֲרוּ** *behold* in Bib. Aram. and cf. **אֲרֵי** *because, that* in Bib. Aram., Onq.).

Unlike in Onqelos, but like in Biblical Aramaic, the most basic form of the noun is the absolute state. Targum Neofiti attests not only the particle **דִּי** (as in Biblical Aramaic), but also the shorter **דְּ** (as in Targum Onqelos).

In relation to the morphology, note that the 1cp suffix on prepositions sometimes lacks a final mater. This implies perhaps a varying pronunciation, perhaps -an (e.g. **לן** lan (**לַן**) *to us*) and -anā (**לנא** lanā (**לַנָא**)).

Two other peculiarities relate to verbs. The 3fp suffix conjugation of III-aleph/waw/yod roots was likely vocalized with a final e: **הְוֵין** *they were*. Also, the 1cs prefix conjugation of all roots could be articulated with a prefixed aleph (as in Biblical Aramaic **אֶכְתֻּב**) or with a prefixed nun (making the 1cs and 1cp identical in sound and appearance **נִכְתֻּב**). With a nun the 1cs prefix conjugation often indicates a nuance like that implied by English *would, should, could,* or *let me* (see Fassberg 166–7).

Reading 2

Translate the following passage from Genesis 11 (based on the main text of Neofiti.1 (i.e. not the marginal alternatives)), using the glossary and the notes that follow the text. While translating, add the vowels, following the model of Biblical Aramaic. The vocalized text is offered in the answers appendix.

LANGUAGE INSIGHT

In order to vocalize a word, that is to supply the vowels, first identify what the word is, then look it up in the glossary or in a dictionary. If the word in the text is a noun in the absolute, then the lexical or dictionary form of the word will be listed in the entry for the word. Simply copy the vowels from the entry. If the word is an inflected noun or a verbal form, begin with the basic, dictionary form of the word. Next, determine the form of the word in the text being read (based on the spelling and the context, e.g. 3fs, 2ms, etc. for verbs; construct or determined for nouns/adjectives) and then, based on the paradigms, add the correct vowels. The glossary of this course as well as dictionaries will often list the singular determined form of the noun (after the initial entry) if the vowels shift in the noun's inflection; the vowels in the singular determined form are also those that will usually appear when the noun takes suffixes. When there is some ambiguity as to the correct analysis of a word, for example with a form that could be either a itpə. or itpa. participle (e.g. משתעין), the reader must rely on the glossary or dictionary (which are, in turn, based on information from other dialects of Aramaic that include vowels). Although the precise articulation of some vowel sounds is unknown, the relationship between vowels is likely similar to that found in Biblical Aramaic or Targum Onqelos. The purpose of vocalizing is, first, to encourage the student to internalize the vowel patterns that characterize the language's morphology. Second, vocalizing a text forces the reader to consider the exact relationship between words, which is important since the precise meaning of a phrase may hinge on very subtle differences in the vowels.

GENESIS 11:1

a והוון כל דיירי דארעא לשן חד וממלל חד
b ובלשן בית קדשה הוון משתעין
c דבה אתברי עלמא מן שרויה

GENESIS 11:2

a והווה כד אסעו לבבהון
b ואשכחו בקעה בארעא דבבל
c ושרון תמן

GENESIS 11:3

a ואמרו גבר לחבריה
b אתון ונלבן לבנין
c ונזי יתהון באתונ׳ (באתונא read)
d והוין להון לבניה (לבניא read) לאבנין
e וחמרא הווה להון לשיע

GENESIS 11:4

a ואמרון אתון ונבנה לן קריה ומגדל
b וראשה מטי עד צית שמיא
c ונעבד לן בראשיה סגדה
d ונתן חרבא בידיה
e ותיהווי עבד׳ (עבדה read) לקבליה סדרי קרבא
f קדם עד לא נדרי על אפי כל ארעא

GENESIS 11:5

a ואתגלית איקר שכינתיה דייי
b למחמי ית קרתא וית מגדלא דבנו בני אנשה

GENESIS 11:6

a ואמר ייי הא אומה חדה ולשון חד לכולהון
b והא כדון שרון למעבד
c וכדון לא יתמנע מנהון כל מה די חשבו למעבד

GENESIS 11:7

a אתון כען ואתגלי ונערבב תמן לשניהון
b דלא ישמעון גבר לשנה דחבריה

GENESIS 11:8

a ודרי ייי יתהון מן תמן על אפי כל ארעא
b ואתמנעו מן למבני קרתא

GENESIS 11:9

a בגין כדן (כן read) קרא שמה בבל
b ארו׳ (ארום read) כדן ערבב ייי לשני כל דאירי ארעא
c ומן תמן דרי יתהון ייי על אפי כל ארעא

CULTURAL INSIGHT

The depiction of humans crafting an idol or god in order to wage war against God is reminiscent of the battle between fallen angels and God described in various post-biblical apocalyptic works. In as much as it implies a conflict between wicked humans and divine forces it resembles works from the Dead Sea Scrolls, like the War Scroll (written in Hebrew).

NOTES

N.B. Comments for words that are identical in the corresponding passage from Onqelos are not reduplicated.

Genesis 11:1

a

הוון – This is the pə. 3ms suff. conj. of הוי. There are two waws in this word, the first is consonantal and the second is a mater for the preceding long ō vowel. The final nun following a long vowel (ā, ō, ū) is typical for this targum.

דיירי – The first two yods in this word represent the doubled consonantal yod, what would be written in Biblical Aramaic as דָּיָּרֵי. The word is in construct with the following phrase דארעא *of the earth*, which means that the earth is marked twice as a genitive expression (once with the construct form of the preceding word and once with the particle דְּ). This type of construction is rather uncommon, but occurs in other phrases in targumic Aramaic.

b

קדשה – As in Biblical Aramaic and in Onqelos, the final -ā of the determined state is sometimes marked with a he mater instead of the more common aleph mater.

משתעין – This is the itpa. m.p. part. of שׂעי.

c

דבה – The letters are a combination of the particle דְּ followed by the bet preposition followed by the 3ms pronominal suffix.

אתברי – This is the itpə. 3ms suff. conj. of ברי.

שרויה –This is the sing. determined form of שֵׁרוּי.

Genesis 11:2

a

והווה – *It was* or more literally *And, it was*... The syntax attempts to mimic the syntax of the Hebrew original.

אסעו – This is the aph. 3mp suff. conj. of נסע.

c

שרון – This is the pə. 3mp suff. conj. of שׁרי. For the final nun, see comments to 11:1 a.

Genesis 11:3

b

אתון – This is the pə. m.p. imper. of אתי. For the final nun, see comments to 11:1 a.

נלבן – This is the pə. 1cp pref. conj. of לבן. Preceded by an imperative, the form should be understood as expressing a jussive nuance.

c

נזי – This is the pə. 1cp pref. conj. of אזי, expressing a jussive nuance *let us* . . . The final yod represents the sere vowel, just as it does in similar forms in Targum Onqelos.

אתונ׳ – The scribe has abbreviated the spelling of the word to accommodate the spacing in the manuscript.

d

הוין – This is the pə. 3fp suff. conj. of הוי, vocalized most likely הֲוְיָן. For the final nun, see comments to 11:1 a.

Genesis 11:4

a

אמרון – This is the pə. 3mp suff. conj. of אמר. For the final nun, see comments to 11:1 a.

לן – The pronominal suffix lacks a final aleph mater (cf. Biblical Aramaic לַנָא) and so presumably was pronounced lan = לַן.

c

סגדה – Although this word elsewhere implies a sense like *worship* or *worshipping place*, here the context would seem to demand a sense like *object of worship* or even *idol*.

e

תיהווי עבד׳ – This is the pə. 3fs pref. conj. of הוי followed by the pə. f.p. part. of עבד. The first yod mater in תיהווי represents the i vowel of the prefix. The two waws represent a single consonantal waw. The final yod mater represents the final e vowel.

סדרי קרבא – This would seem to be the noun סְדַר (det. סִדְרָא) *order, battle line* in construct with the word *war* in the determined state. This construction is also found elsewhere among the targums. Together with the preceding verbs, the text would seem to reflect the sense *it* (i.e. the object of worship, the idol, and by extension the deity represented by the idol) *will ready* (lit. make) *against him* (i.e. Yahweh) *battle lines of war.*

f

קדם עד לא – This combination of particles implies the sense *before.*

נדרי – This is the itpa. 1cp pref. conj. of דרי, vocalized according to Biblical Aramaic symbols: נִדָּרֵי. In this case, the taw of the itpa. stem has assimilated into the dalet of the root; the short a vowel that we would have expected under the dalet has lengthened into a long ā due to compensatory lengthening (i.e. because the following resh, which should double, cannot double).

Genesis 11:5

a

אתגלית – This is the itpə. 3fs suff. conj. of **גלי**.

איקר שכינתיה דייי – This is an elaborate way of referring to God. Direct reference to God, especially in anthropomorphic language, is often avoided in this targum.

b

מחמי – This is the pə. infin. of **חמי**.

Genesis 11:6

c

מה די – The interrogative pronoun is used together with the relative pronoun **דִּי** for the sense *that*.

Genesis 11:7

a

אתגלי – This is the itpə. 1cs pref. conj. of **גלי**.

נערבב – This is an irregular verb stem, the pa'lel of the root **ערב** and would be vocalized **נְעַרְבֵּב**. In addition, although this appears to be the 1cp pref. conj. it is actually better to construe it in this context as the 1cs pref. conj.

b

לשנה – This is either the determined form of the noun (in which case we might expect **לשנא**) or it is the noun with the 3ms suffix.

Genesis 11:8

a

דרי – This is the pa. 3ms suff. conj. of **דרי**.

b

מן למבני – The combination of these two prepositions (**מִן** and **לְ**) is best translated simply *from*.

Genesis 11:9

a

בגין כדן – This seems to be a misspelling of **בגין כן** (see the glossary under **בגין כן**).

b

ארו' – The scribe once again abbreviated his spelling to accommodate spacing in the manuscript.

דאירי – This is an alternative spelling and pronunciation to the word **דיירי**; see 11:1a. Here, the word can be vocalized **דַּאָירֵי**. The shift of -ayyā- to -a'ā- is seen in other dialects too.

Test yourself

In the Hebrew book of Jeremiah, there is one verse that is in Aramaic: Jer 10:11 (see the introduction to Unit 20). The same verse is found in the Targum to Jeremiah in an expanded form, rendered in Targumic Aramaic (in a dialect close to that of Onqelos). Translate both versions of Jer 10:11. How does the targumic version differ in its grammar from the biblical version?

In the Hebrew Bible:

a כִּדְנָה תֵּאמְרוּן לְהֹם
b אֱלָהַיָּא דִּי שְׁמַיָּא וְאַרְקָא לָא עֲבַ֫דוּ
c יֵאבַ֫דוּ מֵאַרְעָא וּמִן־תְּחוֹת שְׁמַיָּא אֵ֫לֶּה

In the Targum to Jeremiah:

d דְּנָא פַּרְשֶׁגֶן אִגַּרְתָּא דִּי שְׁלַח יִרְמְיָה נְבִיָּא
e לְוָת שְׁאָר סָבֵי גָלוּתָא דִּבְבָבַל
f דִּי אִם יֵימְרוּן לְכוֹן עַמְמַיָּא דְּאַתּוּן בֵּינֵיהוֹן
g פְּלַ֫חוּ לְטָעֲוָתָא בֵּית יִשְׂרָאֵל
h כְּדֵין תְּתִיבוּן וּכְדֵין תֵּימְרוּן לְהוֹן
i טָעֲוָן דִּי אַתּוּן פָּלְחִין לְהוֹן
j טָעֲוָן דְּלֵית בְּהוֹן צְרוֹךְ
k אִנִּין מִן שְׁמַיָּא לָא יָכְלָן לְאַחָתָא (= לְאַחָתָה) מִטְרָא
l וּמִן אַרְעָא לָא יָכְלָן לְצַמָּחָא (= לְצַמָּחָה) פֵּירִין
m אִנִּין וּפָלְחֵיהוֹן יֵיבַ֫דוּ מֵאַרְעָא וְיִשְׁתֵּיצוֹן מִן תְּחוֹת שְׁמַיָּא אִלֵּין

Suggestions for further study

Find the full text to Daniel 4–5 in the appendix and translate this using just the glossary and the notes.

SELF-CHECK

	I CAN...
○	recognize the genre of targums
○	read the Aramaic dialect of Targum Onqelos
○	read the Aramaic dialect of Targum Neofiti

23 Readings in the Dead Sea Scrolls

In this unit you will learn how to:

- **recognize some grammatical features of Aramaic from the Dead Sea Scrolls**
- **read unvocalized Dead Sea Scrolls texts**

In this unit you will read:

- **a portion of the Genesis Apocryphon (1Q20 col. 19, line 14 through col. 20, line 18)**
- **a portion of the Apocryphon of Levi (4Q541 frag. 9, col. i, lines 2–7)**

Grammar

THE DEAD SEA SCROLLS

The Dead Sea Scrolls are a corpus of hundreds of ancient manuscripts (most dating to the first century BCE) which were discovered in caves along the coast of the Dead Sea in the middle of the twentieth century. The manuscripts are written in three languages: Hebrew, Aramaic, and Greek. Of the Aramaic manuscripts, some of them (like the Book of Tobit and the Book of Enoch) are known from other sources and in other languages, but many of the Aramaic texts from the Dead Sea are otherwise unknown.

GRAMMAR OF THE ARAMAIC OF THE DEAD SEA SCROLLS

Recall that although the writing of the Dead Sea Scrolls does not include vowel marks, it does include more maters than Biblical Aramaic. As in the Aramaic of the targums, sometimes even what must be a short vowel is marked with a mater (e.g. יכתוב yiktub *he will write* corresponding to Biblical Aramaic יִכְתֻּב). In other cases, a long ā is marked with an aleph within a word (e.g. כלאן kallân *brides*, what would be vocalized with Biblical Aramaic vowels כַּלָּאן).

Much of the grammar of the Aramaic found in the scrolls is similar, if not identical to, that of Biblical Aramaic. Nevertheless, some minor differences might be mentioned.

Most important to notice is that there is hardly ever a uniform spelling of a word or verbal form and this likely reflects alternative pronunciations among the scribes in the first century BCE (due to the scribes' different social positions, places of origin, etc.). In addition, it may reflect changes in the language over time. For, although the scrolls were made in the first century BCE, some texts were composed one hundred or more years before their being written in the scrolls.

As for inconsistencies, note that the 3fs pronominal suffix on some prepositions and nouns is spelled with a final aleph (-הא) or he mater (-הה). On analogy with other pronouns from Biblical Aramaic (e.g. 1cp on singular nouns -ָנָא) and the 3fs suffix on masculine plural nouns in Targum Onqelos (בְּנַהָא *her children*), we can tentatively suggest the pronunciation -ahā (e.g. להא lahā (לַהָא) *to her* and בעלהא baʿlahā (בַּעְלַהָא) *her husband*). At the same time, the 3fs suffix also appears on the lamed preposition and singular nouns in the scrolls as simply ה-, presupposing the same articulation as in Biblical Aramaic, -ah (e.g. לה lah (לַהּ) and בעלה baʿlah (בַּעְלַהּ) *her husband*). This implies that the same suffix on singular nouns was pronounced in two ways among the people who wrote the scrolls.

The same (3fs) suffix on dual and masculine plural nouns (as well as related prepositions) may also have exhibited two pronunciations, reflected in two distinct spellings, again one with mater (יהא-), and one without (יה-). In this case the form with mater might have been pronounced -ayhā (e.g. עליהא ʿălayhā (עֲלַיְהָא) *over her* and ידיהא yədayhā (יְדַיְהָא) *her two hands*), while the spelling without mater might reflect a pronunciation like that in Biblical Aramaic, where the yod is not pronounced, עֲלַיַהּ ʿălah *over her* (also found in Targum Onqelos).

A two-fold pronunciation also is evident with the 2ms independent pronoun. In Biblical Aramaic, the 2ms pronoun is spelled אַנְתְּה, preserving evidence of two different pronunciations, one reflecting the consonants, ʾantā, and the other reflecting the vowels, ʾant. In the scrolls, the pronoun is usually spelled אנתה, reflecting ʾantā, though אנת (reflecting ʾant) is also found.

Nouns like קְשֹׁט *truth* that derive from an earlier form with a single u vowel (e.g. qušṭ) sometimes have a waw mater (representing o or u) between the first and second root consonants (e.g. קושט), sometimes between second and third consonants (e.g. קשוט), very rarely between both (e.g. קושוט). It is hard to know the articulation of such words, but this alternation might again imply a varying pronunciation (i.e. qŏšuṭ/qŏšoṭ or qəšuṭ/qəšoṭ). In the exercises that follow, the nouns with a mater will be vocalized according to the Biblical Aramaic model קְשׁוֹט or will be vocalized like קוֹשֶׁט. In both cases, although the vowel is marked with a mater, it is most likely short. For nouns of this type, the singular determined, plural forms, and forms with suffix all exhibit a short o or u vowel in the first syllable (sometimes marked by a waw mater).

Some verbal forms also suggest two different pronunciations. The spelling of 3fs suffix-conjugation verbs from III-aleph/waw/yod roots in the non-pəʿal stems (e.g. itpəʿel and aphel) presupposes either the ending -iyyat (e.g. אתמלית ʾitməliyyat (אִתְמְלִיַּת) *she was filled*) or -īʾat (e.g. אכליאת ʾaklīʾat (אַכְלִיאַת) *she screamed*). The same dichotomy may pertain to analogous 1cs endings -iyyet vs. -īʾet (e.g. aphel אודית ʾōdiyyet (אוֹדִיֵּת) *I gave thanks* vs. itpəʿel אתחזיאת ʾitḥăzīʾet (אִתְחֲזִיאֵת) *I appeared*). However, it is also possible that spellings of 1cs forms like אודית may reflect instead ʾōdīt (אוֹדִית), on analogy to other dialects like that of Targum Onqelos. It is rarely possible to know exactly the pronunciation of the words.

CULTURAL INSIGHT

The figurative pairing of cedar and palm trees is also found in the Bible, in Psalm 92, and in the Song of Songs, where the female is associated with the palm (7:7–8) and the male with the cedar (5:15).

Reading 1

Translate the following passage from the Genesis Apocryphon (1Q20), which parallels events described in the book of Genesis, using the glossary and the notes that follow the text. While translating, add the vowels, following the model of Biblical Aramaic (modifying this pronunciation where appropriate, as with להא *to her*). The vocalized text is offered in the answers appendix.

Note that I have broken the text up into clauses; these do not match the actual line numbers in the scroll. Some reconstructions are based on the work of previous scholars (see most recently Daniel A. Machiela, *Dead Sea Genesis Apocryphon* (Leiden: Brill, 2009)), other readings are my own based on the photographs.

COL. 19

14 וחלמת אנה אברם חלם בלילה מעלי לארע מצרין
וחזית בחלמי והא ארז חד ותמרא **15** חדא כחדא צמח[ו] מן שר[ש חד]
ובני אנוש אתו ובעין למקץ ולמעקר ל[א]רזא
ולמשבק תמרתא בלחודיהה
16 ואכליאת תמרתא ואמרת
אל תקוצו לארזא
ארי תרינא מן שרש [ח]ד צ[מח]נא
ושביק ארזא בטלל תמרתא
17 לא קצוה[י]
ואתעירת בליליא מן שנתי
ואמרת לשרי אנתתי חלם **18** חלמת
מן [ד]אנה דחל מ[ן] חלמא דן
ואמרת לי אשתעי לי חלמך ואנדע
ושרית לאשתעיא לה חלמא דן
19 ואמרת . . . די יבעון למקטלני ולכי למשבק
ברם דא כול טבותא **20** [ד]י תעבדין עמי
בכול עקת די יא[ת]ה אמרי עלי די אחי הוא
ואחה בטליכי ותפלט נפשי בדיליכי
21 . . . יבעון לאעדיותכי מני ולמקטלני
ובכת שרי על מלי בליליא דן

NOTES

Line 14

חלמת – This is the pə. 1cs suff. conj., vocalized **חַלְמֵת** due to the first guttural. **לילה** – This word is in construct with the following word. **מעלי** – This is the pə. infinitive of the root **עלל** plus the 1cs suff. The infinitive without suffix would be vocalized **מֵעַל**. Knowing the historical development of the form helps to explain the vocalization. The earliest form would be *miʿlal; the first lamed assimilated backwards into the ʿayin resulting in two ʿayins: *miʿʿal; then, the i vowel shifted to e: meʿʿal. With suffix, the e vowel did not reduce, but the following short vowel in an open pre-stress syllable did **מֵעֲלִי** meʿʿălī. **חזית** – This is the pə. 1cs suff. conj. תמרא – This is a fem. sing. abs. noun; in Biblical Aramaic we might expect a final he mater instead of aleph.

Line 15

כחדא – This is an adverb, listed in the glossary under כַּחְדָה as *one, together*. אנוש – This is a Hebrew spelling, presumably reflecting אֱנוֹשׁ, though the Aramaic word is אֱנָשׁ (or אֲנָשׁ) and appears frequently in the scrolls. אתו ובעין – This is the pə. 3mp suff. conj. of אתי followed by the pə. m.p. part. of בעי. A similar syntax is found in Dan 2:10. מקץ and מעקר – These are the pə. infinitives of קצץ and עקר, respectively. משבק – This is a pə. infinitive. בלחודיהה – This is a compound particle followed by the 3fs suff.; it is listed in the glossary under בלחודי.

Line 16

אכליאת – This is the aph. 3fs suff. conj. of כלי; the subject is the palm tree. תקוצו – This is a pə. 2mp jussive of קצץ; the jussive is presupposed by the negator אל and the absence of final nun. תרינא – This is the numeral *two* (in its construct form תְּרֵי) plus נָא-, the 1cp pronominal suff. שרש – The vocalization among the Dead Sea Scrolls is unknown; in the exercises, it is שְׁרֹשׁ and שָׁרְשָׁא in the det. state. שביק – This is the pəʿīl 3ms suff. conj. בטלל – This is a compound particle, listed in this way in the glossary.

Line 17

קצוה[י] – This is the pəʿal 3mp suff. conj. of קצץ with a 3ms suff. Assuming a pronunciation like that of Biblical Aramaic, the form would be pronounced קַצּוּהִי. The 3ms suff. is like that found on nouns like אַב *father*. אתעירת – This is the itpəʿel 1cs suff. conj. of עור, pronounced אִתְּעִירֶת ʾittəʿīrɛt. שנתי – This is the word שְׁנָה with a 1cs suff. אמרת – This is the pə. 1cs suff. conj. אנתתי – This is the noun אִנְתָּה with 1cs suff.

Line 18

דחל – This is the pə. m.s. part. אמרת – Although the same letters were 1cs in the preceding line, here they represent the pə. 3fs suff. conj. אשתעי – This is the itpaʿʿal m.s. impv. of שעי. The taw of the prefix and the shin of the root have metathesized. אנדע – This is the pə. 1cs pref. conj. of a I-yod root. שרית – This is the pa. 1cs suff. conj. אשתעיא – This is the itpa. infinitive.

Line 19

יבעון – This is the pə. 3mp pref. conj. of בעי. מקטלני– This is the pə. infinitive plus 1cs suff.

Line 20

תעבדין – This is the pə. 2fs pref. conj. עקת – This is the noun עָקָה in construct with the following relative clause. יא[ת]ה – This is the pə. 3ms pref. conj. of אתי, though we might have expected the 3fs. This and the preceding word are educated guesses based on traces of letters (cf. 4Q537, line 4). אמרי – This is the pə. f.s. impv. אחה – This is an abbreviated form of the pə. 1cs pref. conj. of חיי, vocalized אֶחֱה. The next word, בטליכי, is a compound particle, בטל, followed by the 2fs suff. בדיליכי – This is another compound particle, made up of the prep. בְּ, the relative דִּי, and the prep. לְ and here followed by the 2fs suff.

Line 21

אעדיותכי – This is the aph. inf. plus the 2fs suff. Ordinarily, the aph. inf. would be **אַעֲדָיָה**, but with the suffix, as here, the final -āyā^h becomes -āyū^wt. **בכת** – This is the pə. 3fs suff. conj. of **בכי**.

Reading 2

Add the vowels to the following passage and translate it. The text continues the same story, picking up after some fragmentary lines that mention, among other things, that Abram read aloud the books of the words of Enoch. Here, the Pharaoh's messengers describe to Pharaoh Sarai's beauty.

COL. 20

2 כמה נציח ושפיר לה צלם אנפיהא . . .

3 . . . וכמא רקיק לה שער ראישה

כמא יאין להין לה עיניהא

ומא רגג הוא לה אנפהא וכול נץ 4 אנפיהא . . .

כמא יאא לה חדיה וכמא שפיר לה כול לבנהא

דרעיהא מא שפירן וידיהא כמא 5 כלילן

וחמיד כול מחזה ידיהא כמא יאין כפיהא

ומא אריכן וקטינן כול אצבעת ידיהא

רגליהא 6 כמא שפירן וכמא שלמא להן לה שקיהא

וכל בתולן וכלאן די יעלן לגנון לא ישפרן מנהא

ועל כול 7 נשין שופר שפרת ועליא שפרהא לעלא מן כולהן

ועם כול שפרא דן חכמא שגיא עמהא

ודלידיהא יאא

Following this description, the pharaoh determines to take Sarai as a consort, though she does not go willingly. As in Abram's dream, the pharaoh attempts to kill Abram, but Sarai deters this by claiming that Abram is her brother. Subsequently, Abram weeps and then prays. The following is still from column 20.

12 בליליא דן צלית ובעית ואתחננת

ואמרת באתעצבא ודמעי נחתן

בריך אנתה אל עליון מרי לכול 13 עלמים

די אנתה מרה ושליט על כולא

ובכול מלכי ארעא אנתה שליט למעבד בכולהון דין

וכען 14 קבלתך מרי על פרעו צען מלך מצרין

די דברת אנתתי מני בתוקף

עבד לי דין מנה ואחזי ידך רבתא 15 בה ובכול ביתה

ואל ישלט בליליא דן לטמיא אנתתי מני

וינדעוך מרי די אנתה מרה לכול מלכי 16 ארעא
ובכית וחשית בליליא דן
שלח לה אל עליון רוח מכדש למכתשה ולכול אנש ביתה רוח 17 באישא
והואת כתשא לה ולכול אנש ביתה
ולא יכל למקרב בהא ואף לא ידעהא והוא עמה 18 תרתין שנין

NOTES

Line 2

כמה – This is the combination of the preposition **כְּ** *like* and the interrogative **מָא** *what* (listed in the glossary under **כְּמָה**) to form an exclamation. **נציח ושפיר לה צלם אנפיהא** – The syntax of this and the following clauses is difficult to discern, especially as relates to the prepositional phrase **לה**. The pronoun likely refers to Sarai herself *for her* (and not her body part). The construction is perhaps meant to emphasize that Sarai's beauty is for her own benefit, not for that of an observer. Her beauty is not for the purpose of pleasing others. The word **אנפיהא** is the plural of **אַף** with the 3fs pronoun; the nun is due to nasalization of the originally doubled pe.

Line 3

יאין – This is the f.p. adj. **יאה** *fitting, perfect*. **להין לה** – The pronouns on the lamed preposition presumably refer respectively to Sarai's eyes and then to Sarai herself. The perfection of her eyes are beneficial to the eyes themselves and to Sarai, not to those observing them.

Line 4

חדיה – This is the noun **חֲדֵה** with 3fs suff.

Line 5

רגלהא – The historical base of the word in Biblical Aramaic is ragl-, though in most other dialects of Aramaic it is rigl-. Here, we vocalize **רַגְלַיִן** following Biblical Aramaic.

Line 6

שלמא – This is the pə. 3fp of **שׁלם** with **שקיהא** as subject. **כלאן** – This is the absolute pl. form of **כַּלָּה**; the aleph in the plural is a mater for a long ā. **יעלן** – This is the pə. 3fp. pref. conj. of **עלל**.

Line 7

שופר שפרת – The phrase can be translated literally: *(as regards) beauty, she was beautiful* or *(her) beauty is beautiful*. That is, the subject of the pə. 3fs suff. conj. verb **שפרת** is either Sarai or the noun **שופר** *beauty*, which is apparently a feminine noun (at least in this text). The feminine gender of the noun is unexpected, but seems to be reflected in the following expression. Although the pronunciation of the word is unknown, it is vocalized in the exercises as **שׁוּפַר** and **שָׁפְרָא** in the determined state. **עליא** – This is the f.s. absolute form of the adjective **עִלָּי** *highest, unsurpassed*. **שפרהא** and **שפרא** – These are both the noun **שופר** spelled without the waw mater, the first having the 3fs suff. and the second in the determined state. **לעלא מן** – This is the lamed preposition plus the adverb **עֵלָּא** followed by the min preposition. Together, they can be translated *above*. **כולהן** – This is the noun **כֹּל** with the 3fp suffix. In Biblical Aramaic, it would appear with a short o vowel and it is presumed that this is what the waw represents here and might be represented כֻּולְּהֶן kolləhen. שגיא – This is presumably the f.s. adjective pronounced saggiyyā (שַׂגִּיָּא), exhibiting a phonetic assimilation of an expected -īʾā (שַׂגִּיאָה) to -iyyā. דלידיהא – This is the relative particle דְּ followed by the lamed preposition, the word יַד *hand* in the dual, and the 3fs suff. Together, they can be translated *what is of her hands* or *what belongs to her*.

Line 12

צלית ובעית ואתחננת – These are three 1cs suff. conj. verbs, the first pa. (צלי), the second pə. (בעי), the third itpa. (חנן), each with Abram as subject. אתעצבא – This is the ithpə. inf. דמעי – This is the pl. form of the noun דְּמַע with the 1cs suff. The noun is feminine though it lacks the feminine morpheme. נחתן – This is the pə. f.p. part. בריך אנתה – This is the pə. m.s. pass. part. followed by the 2ms independent pronoun.

Line 13

עלמים – The final mem, likely due to Hebrew influence, should be a nun. מעבד – This is the pə. inf. דין – This is the noun דִּין *judgment*.

Line 14

קבלתך – This is the pə. 1cs suff. conj. of קבל with the 2ms suff. The verb has the sense *to complain to* and takes a direct object in Aramaic. פרעו צען – *Pharaoh of Zoan* or *Pharaoh, Zoan*. Either Zoan is used as a place name (also known as Tanis) or it is used as an imaginary name of Pharaoh. דברת – This is the pəʿīl 3fs suff. conj. תוקף – This is another word like שופר and is vocalized in the exercises תֹּוקֶף and תָּקְפָּא in the determined state. עבד – This is the pə. m.s. impv. אחזי – This is the aph. m.s. impv. of חזי.

Line 15

ישלט – This is a jussive, though would be pronounced just like a regular pref. conj. טמיא – This is the pa. inf. of טמי *to defile*. מני – *(who is far) from me* The prepositional phrase indicates Sarai's distance and separation from Abram. ינדעוך – This is the pə. 3mp jussive of ידע with a 2ms suff. Here, following the jussive ישלט, the jussive has a purpose/result nuance: *so that they . . .*

Line 16

בכית וחשית – These are two pə. 1cs suff. conj. verbs (from בכי and חשי, respectively). שלח – This is a pə. 3ms suff. conj. Notice that the subject, אל עליון, follows the verb. רוח מכדש – In this phrase, the first noun is in construct with the second noun. מכתשה – This is the pə. inf. of כתש followed by the 3ms suff. רוח / באישא – In this phrase, the second word is an adjective that modifies the preceding feminine noun. The entire phrase is a second object to שלח, the initial verb of the line.

Line 17

הואת כתשא – The first word is the pə. 3fs suff. conj. of the verb הוי, with an aleph mater to mark the preceding long ā vowel. The second is the pə. f.s. part. The two verbs together function as one predication, where the antecedent is the רוח / באישא from the preceding sentence.

יכל – This is the pə. 3ms suff. conj. of יכל *to be able*. מקרב – This is the pə. inf. ידעהא – This is the pə. 3ms suff. conj. of ידע followed by the 3fs suff. הוא – This is either the pə. 3ms suff. conj. of הוי or the 3ms pronoun הוא.

CULTURAL INSIGHT

Zoan is the Hebrew name for one of the ancient capitals of Egypt, Tanis (called Avaris by the Hyksos), but in the Genesis Apocryphon perhaps functions as the personal name of Pharaoh. Zoan most likely appears in this story since the city was thought to be contemporaneous with the city from which Abram and Sarai travel, Hebron. (See Fitzmyer 2004.)

Reading 3

Add the vowels and translate the following passage from the 4Q541, often labelled the Apocryphon of Levi, a text with messianic images that includes many allusions to the servant songs of the book of Isaiah (e.g. Isaiah 53). Use the glossary and the notes that follow the text. The scroll is preserved in many fragments. The following is from the first column of fragment 9.

4Q541 FRAG. 9, COL. I

2 . . . ויכפר על כול בני דרה וישתלח לכול בני 3 [עמ]ה
מאמרה כמאמר שמין ואלפונה כרעות אל
שמש עלמה תניר 4 ויתזה נורהא בכול קצוי ארעא
ועל חשוכא תניר
אדין יעדה חשוכא 5 מן ארעא וערפלא מן יבישתא
שגיאן מלין יאמרון ושגה 6 [כדב]ין
ובדיאן עלוהי יבדון וכול גנואין עלוהי ימללון
דרה באיש ואפיך 7 . . .ודי שקר וחמס מקמה
[ו]יטעה עמא ביומוהי וישתבשון

NOTES

Line 2

יכפר – This is the pa. 3ms pref. conj. On the loss of shewa after the prefix, see the glossary under ְ. דרה – This is the noun דָּר followed by the 3ms suff. ישתלח – This is the itpə. 3ms pref. conj. of שׁלח. Note the metathesis of taw and shin.

Line 3

[עמ]ה – This is the noun עַם with the 3ms suff. עלמה – This can be interpreted as the determined form of the noun עָלַם *eternity, world*. תניר – This is the aph. 3fs pref. conj. of נור, and takes שמש as subject. The latter word is here feminine, though elsewhere it appears as masculine.

Line 4

יתזה – This is the itpə. 3ms pref. conj. of אזי with the following word, נור, as subject. The verb was perhaps vocalized יִתֵּזֵה or יִתְזֵה from an earlier יִתְאֲזֵה* before the aleph quiesced. קצוי – This is the construct plural form of קְצֵה, a noun from the root קצי. When an ending appears, the weak root consonant is preserved, as with חַדְיָא *the breast* and the f.s. part. בָּנְיָה *one who builds*. יעדה – This is the aph. 3ms pref. conj. of עדי.

Line 5

יאמרון – This is the pə. 3mp pref. conj. likely used in an impersonal construction and translated into the English passive voice. שגה – This is presumably the noun שְׂגֵא *multitude* in construct with the following word. The final he is simply a mater, an alternative to the yod.

Line 6

בדיאן – This is the fem. pl. abs. noun בְּדְיָה. The aleph is a mater for the preceding long ā of the fem. pl. morpheme. גנואין –This is the pl. abs. form of גְּנוּי, vocalized גְּנוּאִין, reflecting the phonetic shift of -ūyīn (גְּנוּיִין) to -ū'īn.

Line 7

מקמה – This is the noun מקם with the 3ms suff., the antecedent being דרה *his generation*. ישתבשון – This is the itpa. 3mp pref. conj. of שׁבשׁ, exhibiting metathesis of the taw and shin.

Test yourself

1 Match the Aramaic phrases to the English translations. The text is part of a wisdom poem from the Aramaic Levi Document (as attested in the medieval manuscript T-S 16.94), though the same larger work, of which the poem is a part, is also found among the Dead Sea Scrolls. The Aramaic is unvocalized in the manuscript and uses extra maters to mark vowels, some of which would be considered short in Biblical Aramaic. For example, חוכמה corresponds to חָכְמָה in Biblical Aramaic and אליף (c) corresponds to what would be אַלֵּף (the pa''el m.s. imperative) while אליף (f) corresponds to what would be אָלֵף (the pə'al m.s. participle). Next, vocalize the words with Biblical Aramaic vowel symbols and double-check your work in the Answer key.

a	וכען בני (read ברי)	**1**	*so that wisdom* (literally, *the wisdom*) *will be with you*
b	ספר מוסר חוכמה	**2**	*who despise wisdom* (literally, *the wisdom*)
c	אליף לבניכון	**3**	*it is an honour in him*
d	ותהוי חוכמתא עמכון	**4**	*And, now, my child* (or, *my son*)
e	ליקר עלם	**5**	*will be made a disgrace*
f	די אליף חוכמתא	**6**	*for an eternal glory* (literally, *a glory of eternity*)
g	ויקר היא בה	**7**	*writing, instruction, wisdom*
h	די שאיט חוכמתא	**8**	*For, he who learns wisdom* (lit. *the wisdom*)
i	לבשרון מתיהב	**9**	*teach to your children*

2 The expansive version of Targum Esther includes much material that does not correspond to the original biblical text. In Chapter 1, Verse 2, for instance, we find a description of an interaction between Solomon and the Queen of Sheba, in which the queen asks Solomon three riddles. Translate the following text (based on the manuscript BL Or 2375), that describes part of the encounter and the second riddle.

From Targum Esther 1:2

1 וְכַד שְׁמַע מַלְכָּא שְׁלֹמֹה דַאֲתָת מַלְכַּת שְׁבָא לְוָתֵיה
2 קָם וַאֲזַל וִיתִיב בְּבֵית זוֹגִיתָא
3 וְכַד חֲזָת מַלְכַּת שְׁבָא יָת מַלְכָּא שְׁלֹמֹה
4 דַאֲזַל וִיתִיב בְּבֵית זוֹגִיתָא
5 מְתִיבָה וּמַחַשְׁבָה בְּלִיבַּהּ וְאָמְרָה
6 דְמַלְכָּא שְׁלֹמֹה בְמַיָּא יָתֵיב
7 וַחְלֵיזַת חֲלוּזַהּ דְתִיעֲבַר
8 וַחֲזָא לַהּ מַלְכָּא שְׁלֹמֹה שְׂעַר בְּרַגְלַהּ
9 מְתִיב וְאָמַר לַהּ שׁוּפְרִיךְ שׁוּפְרָא דִנְשֵׁי
10 וְשַׂעְרִיךְ שְׂעַר גֻּבְרָא
11 שְׂעַר לְגֻבְרָא שַׁפִּיר וּלְאִיתְּתָא גְּנָאי
12 מְתִיבָא מַלְכַּת שְׁבָא וְאָמְרָה לֵיה
13 מָרִי מַלְכָּא שְׁלֹמֹה אַמְתֵּל לָךְ מַתְלִין תְּלָת (read תְּלָתָא)
14 וְאִין תִּפַשַּׁר יָתְהוֹן לִי יָדַעְנָא (= יָדְעָה אֲנָה) דְּגֻבְרָא חַכִּים אַתְּ
15 וְאִילָא אַתְּ כִּשְׁאָר בְּנֵי אֱנָשָׁא

. . .

16 מְתִיבָה וְאָמְרָה לֵהּ
17 מַה הוּא עֲפַר מִן אֲדַמְתָא נְפַק
18 וּמַאכְלֵיה מִן עַפְרָא דְאַרְעָא
19 נִשְׁפַּךְ כַּמַּיִם וּמַבִּיט לַבָּרוּת

(Line 19 is spelled as if it is Hebrew, *it is poured like water and looks to the exterior*)

(But, it can still be read as Aramaic with a few slight changes:)

*וּשְׁפִּךְ *כְּמַיִן *וּנָבֵיט *לְבָרָה

20 מְתִיב וַאֲמַר לַהּ נִפְטָא

Suggestions for further study

Work through another short section of the Genesis Apocryphon or another Dead Sea scroll, using either online tools or printed books.

SELF-CHECK

I CAN...
recognize some grammatical features of Aramaic from the Dead Sea Scrolls
read unvocalized Dead Sea Scrolls texts

24 Readings in the Egyptian Aramaic texts

In this unit you will learn how to:
- **recognize some grammatical features of Official Aramaic texts from Egypt**
- **read and understand unvocalized Aramaic texts**

In this unit you will read:
- **portions of The Words of Aḥiqar (= *TAD* C1.1)**
- **Hermopolis letter 1 (= *TAD* A2.3)**

Grammar

EGYPTIAN ARAMAIC TEXTS

At the first cataracts in the Nile river (when travelling south) lie two ancient towns, referred to in the mid-fifth century BCE as Yeb and Syene (Aramaic יב and סון). Yeb was also called Elephantine and Syene is now known as Aswan. Yeb/Elephantine is located on an island in the middle of the river and Syene/Aswan on the eastern shore. In the mid-fifth century BCE the Persian Empire stretched from Egypt to the subcontinent of Asia. Its borders were garrisoned with troops from various backgrounds. In the twin cities of Syene-Elephantine lived Judeans, Egyptians, and other peoples, many of whom spoke and wrote in Aramaic since Aramaic was like English today, a language used for communication among people who speak different languages at home. The variety of Aramaic they used is very close to that of Biblical Aramaic.

In addition to the texts found in Syene-Elephantine, other Aramaic letters and documents have been recovered from other parts of Egypt. One intriguing set of letters are dead letters, that is, letters that never reached their destination. Written in Memphis, near today's Cairo, the letters were addressed to individuals in Syene, but discovered about halfway between Memphis and Syene, near the city of Hermopolis. They are of a personal nature and reveal aspects of everyday life among the ex-patriot community of Arameans.

From Syene-Elephantine we have many ancient documents (letters, contracts, etc.) from the fifth century BCE, including a text titled *The Words of Aḥiqar*. The text is written on a large papyrus scroll, but this was not the first time this particular manuscript was used. In fact, its first use was to record the items coming off of ships, essentially a long inventory. This text is still visible – or portions of it are – erased under the Aḥiqar text. The Words of Aḥiqar is interesting, in part, because it is a court tale of the eponymous sage and his adventures at court (in his case in the court of the Assyrian kings, Sennacherib and Esarhaddon) and, therefore, parallels in some aspects the stories about Daniel from the Bible. In addition, it contains many proverbs that have parallels to biblical and later Hebrew proverbs.

CULTURAL INSIGHT

The stories and proverbs of Aḥiqar were apparently quite popular in the ancient world. The story and proverbs were translated into Syriac, Armenian, Arabic, and numerous other languages. Aḥiqar also appears in another court tale, that of Tobit (found among the Aramaic Dead Sea Scrolls (4Q196)), where he is also described as the advisor to Sennacherib and Esarhaddon. Aḥiqar is also mentioned by some Greek authors and Aḥiqar's storyline is borrowed by the author of the Greek Life of Aesop, dating to around the first century CE.

GRAMMAR OF EGYPTIAN ARAMAIC

As a pedagogical guide, in the Answer key the text has been vocalized according to the vowel inventory, symbols, and morphology of Biblical Aramaic.

The way that the letters are formed is distinct from the way they are formed in later times, including just 300 years later in the time of the Dead Sea Scrolls, as well as in the time of the medieval manuscripts. Most obviously, there are no final forms of the kaph, mem, nun, peh, and sadeh letters. These letters have the same form within a word as at its end. The shapes of the letters look more like what their final forms would look like in later times. But, for the sake of consistency, in the transliteration of texts all these letters are represented with their word-initial/medial form: kaph כ, mem מ, nun נ, peh פ, and sadeh צ.

The orthography (or spelling) of the words from Elephantine texts is different from that of Biblical Aramaic in several ways. The 3ms independent pronoun (הו) is spelled without a final aleph unlike in Biblical Aramaic (הוּא). The III-aleph/waw/yod verbs in the prefix conjugation often have the mater he instead of aleph (e.g. תבעה *you will seek out)*. Also, the demonstrative pronouns and relative pronoun/particle which appear in Biblical and later Aramaic dialects with a dalet (e.g. דֵּךְ *this*, דִּי *who, of*) appear in Elephantine and earlier dialects with a zayin (i.e. זך *this*, זי *who, of*).

LANGUAGE INSIGHT

The distinction in spelling of various words between Elephantine and later dialects of Aramaic (e.g. זך vs. דֵּךְ *this* and זי vs. דִּי *who, of*) reflects an underlying shift in the inventory of sounds peculiar to Aramaic. In earlier Aramaic, the ז represented two sounds, z and ḏ, a soft d sound like the soft (i.e. spirantized) dalet in Biblical Aramaic (= the th in *this*). Unlike the different pronunciations of dalet in Biblical Aramaic, the differences between z and ḏ were significant for meaning so that two words otherwise identical would have been distinguished based solely on the different pronunciation of the same ז symbol. At some point slightly before the Elephantine texts were written (ca. 500s BCE) the ḏ sound merged with the hard d sound represented by dalet. So, a word like זך was originally pronounced like ḏek, but by the time of the Elephantine texts it had shifted to dek. Despite this shift in pronunciation, the word was still written with a zayin out of convention. The spelling of other words, however, like the verb for *to hold, seize*, was already changing by the time of the Elephantine documents; sometimes the verb is written in the older way, אחז, but often it is represented with the newer spelling אחד. In both cases, however, it would have been pronounced in the newer way; for instance, in the pəʿal 3ms suffix conjugation ʾăḥad.

In other respects, the grammar of the Aramaic in the Elephantine texts is largely similar to that in Biblical Aramaic. Note, however, some small distinctions. The jussive form of singular verbs often has a nun (e.g. אל תלקחנ *do not take (Aḥiqar TAD* C1.1, 167)). The pronunciation of some forms is unknown, but may be conjectured. The 3ms suffix on a prefix conjugation verb may have been -innahī^{y} as in תְּהַנְצְלִנַּהִ[י] *you will save hi(m)*.

Reading 1

Translate the following passage from The Words of Aḥiqar, using the glossary and the notes that follow the text. While you do this, vocalize the text according to the vowels and symbols of Biblical Aramaic. Some parts must be reconstructed due to the poorly preserved quality of the manuscript. Reconstructions are based on A. E. Cowley's edition (*Aramaic Papyri of the Fifth Century B.C.* (Oxford: Clarendon, 1923)) and the edition in *TAD* (C1.1). The line numbers follow those in *TAD*. The better preserved portions start in column 2 of the manuscript, line 17.

Note that I have broken the text up into clauses; these do not match the actual line numbers. The text with vowels is presented in the answers appendix. These reflect only one possible realization of the vowels.

17. שב אנה לא אכהל למפלח בבב היכלא []
18. [הא] נדנ שמה ברי רבא והו יחלפ לי ספר []
[הו] 19. [צבי]ת עזקה יהוה לכ
אפ חכמתי וע[טתי חכמתה]
[ענה אסרחאדנ] 20. [מל]כ אתור אמר כותא . . .
21. עבידתכ הו יעבד . . .

Some partially preserved lines follow that seem to describe how Nadin, Aḥiqar's nephew, actually plots against his uncle. Then, in column 3, the text is less damaged and we find Esarhaddon appointing Nabusumiskun, a court official, to hunt down Aḥiqar and kill him. (Line numbers continue from the preceding column.)

32. באדינ התמלי חמא אס[רחאדנ מלכ אתור]
ואמר 33. [יאתה לי נבוסמסכנ ח]ד מנ רבי אבי זי לחמ אבי 34. [אכל]
[אמר מלכא אחיקר] תבעה
אתר זי אנת תהשכח 35. [ותקטלנהי]
הנ לו [אח]יק[ר] זכ שבא ספר 36. חכימ [ויעט כל אתו]ר למה הו יחבל מתא עלינ . . .

Esarhaddon then appoints other people to accompany Nabusumiskun in his hunt for Aḥiqar. Not soon after, Nabusumiskun and the henchmen run into Aḥiqar in a vineyard.

40. אנה מהלכ בינ כרמיא [41. כזי חזני נב]וסמסכנ רביא [זכ]
[קרב]תא בזע כתונה . . .

Nabusumiskun seems upset to have actually found Aḥiqar, but Aḥiqar then reminds him that one good deed deserves another.

46. אנה הו אחיקר
זי קדמנ שזבכ מנ קטל זכי 47. [כזי סנחאריב] אבוהי זי אסרחאדנ זנה מלכא חמר עליכ 48. [למקטלכ]
[קרב]תא יבלתכ לביתא זילי

תמה הוית מסבל לכ. 49 כאיש עמ אחוהי
והצפנתכ אמרת קטלתה
עד זי לעד[נ א]חרנ וליומנ אחרננ. 50 שגיאנ קרבתכ קדמ סנחאריב מלכא
והעדית חטאיכ קדמוהי ובאיש[תא] 51 לא עבד לכ
אפ שגיא סנחאריב מלכא רחמני על זי החיתכ ולא קטלתכ
כענ אנת 52 לקבל זי אנה עבדת לכ כנ אפו עבד לי
אל תקטלני . . .

Nabusumiskun does save him, though unfortunately it is at the price of a young slave's life. Aḥiqar gives the slave to Esarhaddon's henchmen to kill so that it looks like they have really killed Aḥiqar. What follows are just a few of the proverbs that are included after this part of the story.

82 מנ כל מנטרה טר פמכ ו[על] זי ש[מעת] הוקר לבב כי צנפר הי מלה ומשלחה גבר לא לב[ב] . . .
89 אנה זעררתא [טעמת אנזעררתא read] מררתא ו[טעמ]א חסינ ולא איתי זי [מ]ריר מנ ענוה
רכיב לשנ מ[לכ] **90** ועלעי תנינ יתבר כמותא זי [ל]א מתחזה
בשגיא בננ לבבכ אל יחדה ובזעריהמ . . .

176 אל תהחשכ ברכ מנ חטר הנ לו לא תכהל תהנצלנה[י מנ באישתא]
177 הנ אמחאנכ ברי לא תמות והנ אשבקנ על לבבכ [לא תחיה] . . .

CULTURAL INSIGHT

The proverbs in the passage of Aḥiqar in Reading 2 have strong parallels with proverbs from the Hebrew Bible, some of which incorporate etymologically related vocabulary. In particular, note *With patience a leader may be persuaded – a soft tongue* (Heb לְשׁוֹן רַכָּה) *can break bones* (Prov 25:15) and *Do not withhold instruction from the young, for you may strike him with a rod and he will not die* (לֹא יָמוּת). *You may with the rod strike him and deliver* (תַּצִּיל from נצל) *his life from Sheol* (Prov 23:13–14). In addition to these, note the similarities to the Hebrew proverbs of Ben Sira (from ca. 180 BCE): *Do not rejoice in wicked children! If they are fruitful, do not rejoice in them . . . to die childless is better than one having many wicked children* (Sir 16:1–3).

NOTES

Line 17

מפלח – This is the pə. inf. of **פלח**.

Line 19

יהוה – The context, of Aḥiqar speaking to the king, suggests the verb should be translated as a jussive though in its form it is identical to the pref. conj. **חכמתה** – This is the pa. 1cs suff. conj. +3ms suff. [**ענה אסרחאדנ**] – It is assumed that the verbs of speaking are in the suff. conj. here and in what follows, though in Biblical Aramaic they would likely be participial forms.

Line 33

[**יאתה**] – The context suggests this should be translated as a jussive though in its form it is identical to the pref. conj. **רבי** – This is an alternative form of the m.p. adj. in the const. state (i.e. **רַבֵּי**) instead of the expected **רַבְרְבֵי** *nobles of.*

Lines 33–4

[אכל] זי לחמ אבי – *who ate the bread of my father* This is an idiomatic way of expressing dependence on the king.

Line 34

אתר זי – *where* This is a combination of the noun *place* followed by the relative pronoun.

Line 46

אנה הו אחיקר – The 3ms independent pronoun (הו) is not spelled with a final aleph and is used in place of the verb *to be*. **שזבכ** – This is the 3ms suff. conj. of the verb **שׁזב** that is more commonly spelled in later Aramaic with a yod mater **שׁיזב**; it is followed by the 2ms object suffix.

Line 48

מקטלכ – This is the pə. inf. of **קטל** with the 2ms suffix. **יבלתכ** – This is the pə. 1cs suff. conj. of **יבל** followed by a 2ms object pronoun. **זילי** – This is a compound particle, made up of the particle **זִי** (later **דִּי**) followed by the lamed preposition and the 1cs suff.; the compound particle **זִיל** (later **דִּיל**) has the same function and meaning as a possessive suffix directly affixed to the noun. Here, with the preceding noun, it would be translated *my house*. **מסבל** – This is the pa. m.s. part.

Line 49

הצפנתכ – This is the ha. 1cs suff. conj. of **צפן** followed by the 2ms object suffix. **קטלתה** – This is the pə. 1cs suff. conj. of **קטל** followed by the 3ms object suffix.

Line 50

קרבתכ – This is the pa. 1cs suff. conj. of **קרב** followed by the 2ms object suffix.

Line 51

רחמני – This is the pə. 3ms suff. conj. of **רחם** followed by the 1cs object suffix. **החיתכ** – This is the ha. 1cs suff. conj. of **חיי** followed by the 2ms object suffix, possibly to be vocalized **הַחְיִתָכְ** haḥyītāk. **קטלתכ** – This is the pə. 1cs suff. conj. of **קטל** followed by the 2ms object suffix.

Line 52

עבד – This is the pə. m.s. imper. **תקטלני** – This is the pə. 2ms jussive of **קטל** followed by the 1cs object suffix. Since the jussive forms also carried a final nun in this variety of Aramaic, we may conjecture the pronunciation **תִּקְטְלַנִּי**.

Line 82

טר – This is the pə. m.s. imper. of **נטר**. The vowel that appears in the imperative is the same vowel that appears in the prefix conjugation. **ש[מעת]** – This is the pə. 2ms suff. conj. **הוקר** – This is the ha. m.s. imper. of **יקר**. The vowel between the qoph and resh is a. **צנפר** – This is the word **צִפַּר**, which usually exhibits a doubled pe. Here, the doubling has been replaced by the insertion of a nun: ṣinpar. **משלחה** – This is likely the pa. m.s. participle with 3fs suff. **גבר לא לב[ב]** – This expression lacks the particle **זִי** (or **דִּי**) between the noun and the words that modify it. Such abbreviated syntax is common in poetry. Comparable expressions with the relative are **יוֹם בְּיוֹם דִּי־לָא שָׁלוּ** *day by day without fail* (Ezra 6:9) and **מְלַח דִּי־לָא כְתָב** *salt without limit* (lit. *writing*) (Ezra 7:22).

Line 90

מותא – This is the masculine noun **מות** in the determined state. **בשגיא בננ** – *with many children* The word *many* appears before the word it modifies, which is unusual for attributive adjectives; presumably it is used on analogy to numerals which can appear before or after the words they modify. The consonants of the word **בננ** would appear as **בנין** in Biblical Aramaic. **יחדה** – This is the pə. 3ms jussive of **חדי**, as implied by the negative particle **אל** *not*. **זעריהמ** – This likely means *their few (number)*, though the exact vocalization is unknown, perhaps **זְעֵרֵיהֹמ** (i.e. **זְעֵירֵיהֹמ**). Alternatively, we can emend to **זרעיהמ**.

Line 176

ברכ – This is the noun **בר** with the 2ms suff. **הנ לו** – The combination of particles is translated *lest*. **תכהל תהנצלנה[י]** – The two pref. conj. verbs are a single expression, the first (pə. 2ms pref. conj. of **כהל**) indicating ability/possibility *(lest) you are (not) able*. The second verb (ha. 2ms pref. conj. of **נצל** plus 3ms suff.) would be translated on its own *you will rescue him*; but here, with the preceding **הנ לו לא תכהל**, it is translated by an infinitive in English *to rescue him*. Notice that a nun breaks up the earlier doubled sadeh (i.e. **תְּהַצְּלְנַּהִי***), which was, in turn, due to the nun of the root **נצל** assimilating təhanṣil- → təhaṣṣil- (assimilation) → təhanṣil- (nasalization).

Line 177

אמחאנכ – This is the pə. 1cs pref. conj. of **מחי** followed by a 2ms suff. The aleph is a mater or part of a historical spelling. **אשבקנ** – This is a rare verbal form, called the energic; it is marked by an -an (or -anna) suffix: **אֶשְׁבְּקַנ**. The 2ms object (*you*) is understood from context. **לבבכ** – The noun **לבב** followed by the 2ms suff.

Reading 2

Translate and vocalize the following letter found in the remains of the Egyptian city of Hermopolis (Hermopolis letter 1 = *TAD* A2.3), using the glossary and the notes that follow the text. The letter was actually sent from Memphis to Syene, but never reached its destination.

VERSO

1 שלמ בית נבו
אל אחתי רעיה מן אחכי מכבנת
2 ברכתכי לפתח זי יחזני אפיכ בשלמ
שלמ בנתסרל וארג 3 ואסרשת ושרדר
חרוצ שאל שלמהנ
וכעת שלמ 4 לחרוצ תנה
אל תצפי לה
כדי תכלנ תעבדנ לה עבד אנה 5 לה
ותפמת ואחתסנ מסבלנ לה
וכעת ארה ספר לה [לא read] שלחתי 6. בשמה

וכעת זי מלתי לבתי לאמר לה [לא read לא] שאל על חרוצ
כעת 7. הלו כזי עבד אנה לחרוצ כות תעבד בנת עלי

RECTO

8. ארה לא אחי הו חרוצ
וכעת הלו יהב להנ פרס 9. תנה
ויתלקח קדמתהנ בסונ
וכעת הנ את ערב עליכי 10. אתיה לתפמת
וכעת מדעמ אל תזבני בכסת ותשרי לה
11. שלמ יקיה הוי שלחת לה
וכעת הוי חזית על תשי ועל 12. ברה
ושלחי כל טעמ זי הוה בביתי
לשלמכי שלחת ספר 13. ה [ספרא read] זנה
14. אל אבי פסמי בר נבונתנ מנ מכבנת
סונ יבל

NOTES

Line 1

שלמ – The construct form שְׁלָם (the same form as the abs.) is part of a formulaic greeting. Here it forms the expression *Greetings to the Temple of Nabu*. **נבו** – This is the Mesopotamian god of wisdom and writing, pronounced נְבוּ in Aramaic, and Nabu in English. **אל** – This is the preposition אֶל which is used like the preposition lamed. **אחתי** – This is the word *sister* with a 1cs suffix. **רעיה** – The personal name, vocalized רֶעְיָה Reiah. **מכבנת** – The personal name, vocalized מַכִּבָנִת Makkibanit. The last component of the name is the divine name of a Mesopotamian goddess, Banit, associated with birth.

Line 2

ברכתכי – This is the pa. 1cs suff. conj. of **ברך** with 2fs suff. **פתח** – The Egyptian god (פְּתַח Ptaḥ). **זי** – This marks a quotation or direct speech. **יחזני** – This is the aph. 3ms jussive of **חזי** with 1cs suff. **אפיכ** – This is the plural form of אַף with the 2fs suff. The word would more commonly be spelled **אפיכי**; the final yod is sometimes left off in the 2fs suff. due perhaps to a shifting pronunciation. **בנתסרל** and **ארג** – These are personal names, the exact pronunciation of which is not known.

Line 3

אסרשת and **שרדר** – These are personal names, the exact pronunciation of which is not known. **חורצ** – This seems likely to be an Egyptian personal name, pronounced something like חֹֽרוּצ ḥŏrūdj, the sadeh here representing the Egyptian sound dj. **שאל** – This may be the pə. 3ms suff. conj. or the pə. 3ms part. **שלמהנ** – This is the noun שְׁלָם with the 3mp suff.

Line 4

לחרוצ – The lamed preposition marks possession. **תצפי** – This is the pə. 2fs jussive of **יצף**. The jussive is implied not only by the negative adverb **אַל** but also by the lack of a final nun. **תכלנ תעבדנ** – This is a sequence of two verbs used together to express one idea. The first verb is the pə. 2fs pref. conj. of **יכל** and the second is the pə. 2fs pref. conj. of **עבד**. The first verb qualifies the idea of the second and in English can be expressed by the subjunctive *would be able*, while the second verb can be expressed by the English infinitive *to do* such that the entire phrase can be translated: *just as you would be able* (**יכל**) *to do* (**עבד**) . . . A similar syntax (that is, two pre. conj. verbs used together) is not found in Biblical Aramaic but is known from Aḥiqar line 176 and in the Dead Sea Scrolls. **עבד** – This is the pə. m.s. part.

Line 5

תפמת and **אחתסנ** – These are personal names. The first, **תפמת**, is Egyptian in origin. The second is Aramaic and would be pronounced **אֲחָתְסִנ** ʾăḥātsin (ʾAḥatsin) and could be translated *daughter of Sin*. Sin is the Assyrian name of the moon god known from Syria and Mesopotamia. **מסבלנ** – This is the pa. f.p. part of **סבל** *to support*. **לה** – From context, it is assumed that this is a spelling mistake for the negative adverb **לָא** *not*. **שלחתי** – This is the pə. 2fs suff. conj.

Line 6

בשמה – This is the bet preposition followed by the word **שֻׁם** *name* and the 3ms suff. **וכעת זי** – The first expression, **וכעת** *and now* initiates a new topic in the letter. The second word, **זי**, is understood as a conjunction and can be translated *because*. **מלתי לבתי** – The expression is composed of the pə. 2fs suff. conj. of **מלי** and the noun **לְבָּת** *rage* with the 1cs suff. Together it might be translated literally *you are filled with my rage*, though more idiomatically it would be *you are filled with rage against me*. **לאמר** – This is the lamed preposition and an abbreviated form of the pə. inf. of **אמר**, pronounced **לֵאמַר** lēmar *saying*.

Line 7

עבד – This is the pə. m.s. part. **תעבד** – This is the pə. 3fs pref. conj.

Line 8

ארה לא אחי הו חרוצ – Based on context this is best understood as a question. Often questions are only recognizable as such based on context. **הו** – This is the 3ms independent pronoun. Here it functions like the verb *to be*. **יהב** – This is the pəʿīl 3ms suff. conj. and takes **פרס** as subject. **להנ** – This is the lamed preposition followed by the 3fp suff. (with Tpmt and ʾAḥatsin as antecedent) or it is the 3mp suff.

Line 9

קדמתהנ – This is the preposition **קדמת** with again either the 3fp or 3mp suff. as in **להנ** in line 8. The preposition has either a spatial or temporal sense *before*. **סונ** – This is the Aramaic spelling of Syene. **את** – This is the particle of existence, usually spelled **איתי** (in Biblical Aramaic **אִיתַי**). The pronunciation here is unknown, but likely was ʾīt. **ערב** – This is likely the noun **עֲרַב** *guarantor, surety*. **עליכי** – This is the **עַל** preposition followed by the 2fs suff. In this context, it seems to mark possession, just as the lamed preposition usually functions.

Line 10

אתיה – This is the aph. f.s. impv. of **אתי** with a 3ms suff. (the antecedent to which is **עֲרָב**). The vocalization **אֵתַיֵּהּ** 'ētayyeh is very hypothetical. **תזבני** – This is the pə. 2fs jussive of **זבן**, as implied by the lack of final nun and the preceding **אַל** negative adverb. **בכסת** – This is the bet preposition with the noun **כְּסֶת**, together translated *for clothing*. **תשרי** – This is the aph. 2fs jussive of **ישר**. The adverb **אַל** also implicitly negates this verb. The interpretation outlined presupposes that the two women, Tpmt and 'Aḥatsin, are looking after Makkibanit's brother, Ḥorudj, all of whom are together in Memphis (500 miles north of Syene). Tpmt is soon to return and Reiah is to give Tpmt some surety presumably in exchange for a loan.

Line 11

הוי שלחת – This is the pə. f.s. impv. of **הוי** followed by a peculiar form of the pə. f.s. participle, presumably **שָׁלְחַת** šāləḥat. The entire expression would seem to mean *please send greetings to Yqyh* (lit. *greetings of Yqyh*). **הוי חזית** – This is the same construction, the pə. f.s. impv. of **הוי** followed by a peculiar form of the pə. f.s. participle, **חָזְיַת** ḥāzəyat *please watch!*

Line 12

שלחי – This is the pə. f.s. impv. From the context, it likely means *send (a message concerning)!* **הוה** – This is either the pə. 3ms suff. conj. or the pə. m.s. part. **שלחת** – This is the pə. 1cs suff. conj.

Line 13

ספר ה – Notice how the determined ending is separated from the word **ספר** by a line break.

Line 14

This is the address, appearing on the outside of the letter when it was folded. **נבונתנ** – The name Nebunatan is made up of the divine name **נְבוּ** and the pə. 3ms suff. conj. of **נתן** which might be translated *Nabu has given*. **יבל** – This is the oph./uph. 3ms juss. of **יבל**. Although scholars debate the existence of this stem with the sense *to be brought*, note the form **אובלת** *I was brought* among the Dead Sea Scrolls.

CULTURAL INSIGHT

The Hermopolis letters reveal the cosmopolitan nature of the Syene-Elephantine military colony. The letter presented here mentions Nabu, the Mesopotamian god associated with writing and wisdom, the Egyptian god Ptaḥ, who was associated with the city of Memphis in particular. The personal names of the individuals addressed also reveal a cosmopolitan cultural environment with Semitic names (like **רעיה** and **מכבנת**) and Egyptian names like **חרוצ**.

Test yourself

As described before, the Egyptian Aramaic texts shown precede the texts of the Dead Sea Scrolls, which, in turn, precede Targumic Aramaic. Biblical Aramaic falls somewhere between Egyptian Aramaic and the dialect of the scrolls, though it is largely attested in medieval manuscripts. Considering only these text corpora, what general trends can be detected in the development of Aramaic? Think of the way words were spelled, the way they were pronounced, and their forms.

Suggestions for further study

Work through another short Egyptian text in Official Aramaic, using either online tools or printed books.

SELF-CHECK

	I CAN...
○	recognize some grammatical features of Official Aramaic texts from Egypt
○	read and understand unvocalized Aramaic texts

Text of Daniel 4–5

For additional reading practice, this is a reproduction of the text of Daniel 4–5 from Leningrad Codex B19a. The text is found in various resources, including in online images. The standard scholarly edition is *Biblia Hebraica Stuttgartensia* (Stuttgart: Deutsche Bibelgesellschaft, 1967–77, edited by W. Baumgartner), though this version does not represent all the mistakes and infelicities found in the actual Leningrad Codex (at least based on the facsimiles and online representations). A facsimile edition is *The Leningrad Codex: A Facsimile Edition* (ed. Astrid B. Beck, David Noel Freedman, and James A. Sanders; Leiden: Brill, 1998).

The text is accompanied by brackets that annotate features that might be confusing. Within brackets, the form following = represents the pronunciation of the word in the oral tradition, as reflected in the vowel symbols. The parenthetical symbol (K) beside a word represents the pronunciation of the word in the consonantal tradition (Aramaic kətīb). The Leningrad Codex contains numerous small errors in the vowel pointings and I have offered suggestions for how words with such errors should be read in brackets, accompanied by the English word **read**.

In the translation that follows, the Aramaic is rendered into idiomatic English, with more literal renderings in parentheses (accompanied by the abbreviation **lit.**). Nevertheless, as much as possible, the word order of the Aramaic text is mimicked to make clearer the correspondences between the Aramaic and English words. Words implicit in the Aramaic but necessary for English idiom are also presented in parentheses.

DANIEL CHAPTER 4

1. אֲנָה נְבוּכַדְנֶצַּר [נְבוּכַדְנֶצַּר read] שְׁלֵה הֲוֵית בְּבֵיתִי וְרַעְנַן בְּהֵיכְלִי׃

2 חֵלֶם חֲזֵית וִידַחֲלִנַּנִי וְהַרְהֹרִין עַל־מִשְׁכְּבִי וְחֶזְוֵי רֵאשִׁי יְבַהֲלֻנַּנִי׃

3 וּמִנִּי שִׂים טְעֵם לְהַנְעָלָה קָדָמַי לְכֹל חַכִּימֵי בָבֶל דִּי־פְשַׁר חֶלְמָא יְהוֹדְעֻנַּנִי׃

4. בֵּאדַיִן עָלִּלִין [= עָלִּין / עָלְלִין (K)] חַרְטֻמַיָּא אָשְׁפַיָּא כַּשְׂדָּיֵא [= כַּשְׂדָּאֵא / כַּשְׂדָּיֵא (K)] וְגָזְרַיָּא וְחֶלְמָא
אָמַר אֲנָה קֳדָמֵיהוֹן וּפִשְׁרֵהּ לָא־מְהוֹדְעִין לִי׃

5. וְעַד אָחֳרֵין עַל קָדָמַי דָּנִיֵּאל דִּי־שְׁמֵהּ בֵּלְטְשַׁאצַּר [בֵּלְטְשַׁאצַּר read] כְּשֻׁם אֱלָהִי וְדִי רוּחַ־
אֱלָהִין קַדִּישִׁין בֵּהּ וְחֶלְמָא קָדָמוֹהִי אַמְרֵת

6 בֵּלְטְשַׁאצַּר רַב חַרְטֻמַיָּא דִּי אֲנָה יִדְעֵת דִּי רוּחַ אֱלָהִין קַדִּישִׁין בָּךְ וְכָל־רָז לָא־אָנֵס לָךְ חֶזְוֵי חֶלְמִי דִי־חֲזֵית
וּפִשְׁרֵהּ אֱמַר׃

7 וְחֶזְוֵי רֵאשִׁי עַל־מִשְׁכְּבִי חָזֵה הֲוֵית וַאֲלוּ אִילָן בְּגוֹא אַרְעָא וְרוּמֵהּ שַׂגִּיא׃

8. רְבָה אִילָנָא וּתְקִף וְרוּמֵהּ יִמְטֵא לִשְׁמַיָּא וַחֲזוֹתֵהּ [וַחֲזוּתֵהּ read] לְסוֹף כָּל־אַרְעָא׃

9. עָפְיֵהּ שַׁפִּיר וְאִנְבֵּהּ שַׂגִּיא וּמָזוֹן לְכֹלָּא־בֵהּ תְּחֹתוֹהִי תַּטְלֵל חֵיוַת בָּרָא וּבְעַנְפּוֹהִי יְדֻרָן [יְדוּרָן /
יְדֻרוּן (K)] צִפֲּרֵי שְׁמַיָּא וּמִנֵּהּ יִתְּזִין כָּל־בִּשְׂרָא׃

10 חָזֵה הֲוֵית בְּחֶזְוֵי רֵאשִׁי עַל־מִשְׁכְּבִי וַאֲלוּ עִיר וְקַדִּישׁ מִן־שְׁמַיָּא נָחִת׃

11 קֳרֵא בְחַ֫יִל וְכֵן אָמַר גֹּ֫דּוּ אִילָנָא וְקַצִּ֫צוּ עַנְפ֫וֹהִי אַתַּ֫רוּ עָפְיֵהּ וּבַדַּ֫רוּ אִנְבֵּהּ תְּנֻד חֵיוְתָא מִן־תַּחְתּ֫וֹהִי וְצִפְּרַיָּא
מִן־עַנְפ֫וֹהִי: 12 בְּרַם עִקַּר שָׁרְשׁוֹהִי בְּאַרְעָא שְׁבֻ֫קוּ וּבֶאֱסוּר דִּי־פַרְזֶל וּנְחָשׁ בְּדִתְאָא דִּי בָרָא וּבְטַל שְׁמַיָּא
יִצְטַבַּע וְעִם־חֵיוְתָא חֲלָקֵהּ בַּעֲשַׂב אַרְעָא:

13. לִבְבֵהּ מִן־אֲנָשָׁא [= אֲנָשָׁא/ אֱנוֹשָׁא (K)] יְשַׁנּוֹן וּלְבַב חֵיוָה יִתְיְהִב לֵהּ וְשִׁבְעָה עִדָּנִין יַחְלְפוּן עֲל֫וֹהִי:

14. בִּגְזֵרַת עִירִין פִּתְגָמָא וּמֵאמַר קַדִּישִׁין שְׁאֵלְתָא עַד־דִּבְרַת דִּי יִנְדְּעוּן חַיַּיָּא דִּי־שַׁלִּיט עִלָּיָא [=
עִלָּאָא / עִלָּיָא (K)] בְּמַלְכוּת אֲנָשָׁא [= אֲנָשָׁא / אֱנוֹשָׁא (K)] וּלְמַן־דִּי יִצְבֵּא יִתְּנִנַּהּ וּשְׁפַל אֲנָשִׁים יְקִים עֲלַיהּ:

15. דְּנָה חֶלְמָא חֲזֵית אֲנָה מַלְכָּא נְבוּכַדְנֶצַּר וְאַנְתְּה בֵּלְטְשַׁאצַּר [read בֵּלְטְשַׁאצַּר] פִּשְׁרֵא [= פִּשְׁרֵהּ
/ פִּשְׁרָא (K)] אֱמַר כָּל־קֳבֵל דִּי כָּל־חַכִּימֵי מַלְכוּתִי לָא־יָכְלִין פִּשְׁרָא לְהוֹדָעֻתַ֫נִי וְאַנְתְּה כָּהֵל דִּי רוּחַ־
אֱלָהִין קַדִּישִׁין בָּךְ:

16. אֱדַ֫יִן דָּנִיֵּאל דִּי־שְׁמֵהּ בֵּלְטְשַׁאצַּר [read בֵּלְטְשַׁאצַּר] אֶשְׁתּוֹמַם כְּשָׁעָה חֲדָה וְרַעְיֹנֹ֫הִי יְבַהֲלֻנֵּהּ עָנֵה מַלְכָּא
וְאָמַר בֵּלְטְשַׁאצַּר [read בֵּלְטְשַׁאצַּר] חֶלְמָא וּפִשְׁרֵא [= פִּשְׁרֵהּ / פִּשְׁרָא (K)] אַל־ יְבַהֲלָךְ עָנֵה בֵלְטְשַׁאצַּר
וְאָמַר מָרְאִי חֶלְמָא לְשָׂנְאָיךְ וּפִשְׁרֵהּ לְעָרָיךְ:

17. אִילָנָא דִּי חֲזַיְתָ דִּי רְבָה וּתְקִף וְרוּמֵהּ יִמְטֵא לִשְׁמַיָּא וַחֲזוֹתֵהּ [read וַחֲזוֹתֵהּ] לְכָל־אַרְעָא:

18 וְעָפְיֵהּ שַׁפִּיר וְאִנְבֵּהּ שַׂגִּיא וּמָזוֹן לְכֹלָּא־בֵהּ תְּחֹת֫וֹהִי תְּדוּר חֵיוַת בָּרָא וּבְעַנְפ֫וֹהִי יִשְׁכְּנָן צִפֲּרֵי שְׁמַיָּא:

19 אַנְתְּה־הוּא מַלְכָּא דִּי רְבַית וּתְקֵפְתְּ וּרְבוּתָךְ רְבָת וּמְטָת לִשְׁמַיָּא וְשָׁלְטָנָךְ לְסוֹף אַרְעָא:

20 וְדִי חֲזָה מַלְכָּא עִיר וְקַדִּישׁ נָחִת מִן־שְׁמַיָּא וְאָמַר גֹּ֫דּוּ אִילָנָא וְחַבְּלוּהִי בְּרַם עִקַּר שָׁרְשׁ֫וֹהִי בְּאַרְעָא שְׁבֻ֫קוּ
וּבֶאֱסוּר דִּי־פַרְזֶל וּנְחָשׁ בְּדִתְאָא דִּי בָרָא וּבְטַל שְׁמַיָּא יִצְטַבַּע וְעִם־חֵיוַת בָּרָא חֲלָקֵהּ עַד דִּי־שִׁבְעָה עִדָּנִין
יַחְלְפוּן עֲל֫וֹהִי:

21 דְּנָה פִשְׁרָא מַלְכָּא וּגְזֵרַת עִלָּיָא הִיא דִּי מְטָת עַל־מָרְאִי מַלְכָּא:

22 וְלָךְ טָרְדִין מִן־אֲנָשָׁא וְעִם־חֵיוַת בָּרָא לֶהֱוֵה מְדֹרָךְ וְעִשְׂבָּא כְתוֹרִין לָךְ יְטַעֲמוּן וּמִטַּל שְׁמַיָּא לָךְ מְצַבְּעִין
וְשִׁבְעָה עִדָּנִין יַחְלְפוּן עֲלָיךְ עַד דִּי־תִנְדַּע דִּי־שַׁלִּיט עִלָּיָא בְּמַלְכוּת אֲנָשָׁא וּלְמַן־דִּי יִצְבֵּא יִתְּנִנַּהּ:

23 וְדִי אֲמַ֫רוּ לְמִשְׁבַּק עִקַּר שָׁרְשׁ֫וֹהִי דִּי אִילָנָא מַלְכוּתָךְ לָךְ קַיָּמָה מִן־דִּי תִנְדַּע דִּי שַׁלִּטִן שְׁמַיָּא

24 לָהֵן מַלְכָּא מִלְכִּי יִשְׁפַּר עֲלָיךְ וַחֲטָיָךְ בְּצִדְקָה פְרֻק וַעֲוָיָתָךְ בְּמִחַן עֲנָיִן הֵן תֶּהֱוֵא אַרְכָה לִשְׁלֵוְתָךְ:

25 כֹּלָּא מְטָא עַל־נְבוּכַדְנֶצַּר מַלְכָּא

26 לִקְצָת יַרְחִין תְּרֵי־עֲשַׂר עַל־הֵיכַל מַלְכוּתָא דִּי בָבֶל מְהַלֵּךְ הֲוָה:

27 עָנֵה מַלְכָּא וְאָמַר הֲלָא דָא־הִיא בָּבֶל רַבְּתָא דִּי־אֲנָה בֱנַיְתַהּ לְבֵית מַלְכוּ בִּתְקַף חִסְנִי וְלִיקָר הַדְרִי:

28. עוֹד מִלְּתָא בְּפֻם מַלְכָּא קָל מִן־שְׁמַיָּא נְפַל לָךְ אָמְרִין נְבוּכַדְנֶצַּר מַלְכָּא מַלְכוּתָה
[read מַלְכוּתָא] עֲדָת מִנָּךְ:

29. וּמִן־אֲנָשָׁא לָךְ טָרְדִין וְעִם־ חֵיוַת בָּרָא מְדֹרָךְ עִשְׂבָּא כְתוֹרִין לָךְ יְטַעֲמוּן וְשִׁבְעָה עִדָּנִין יַחְלְפוּן עֲלָיךְ
עַד דִּי־תִנְדַּע דִּי־שַׁלִּיט עִלָּיָא [= עִלָּאָא / עִלָּיָא (K)] בְּמַלְכוּת אֲנָשָׁא וּלְמַן־דִּי יִצְבֵּא יִתְּנִנַּהּ:

30 בַּהּ־שַׁעֲתָא מִלְּתָא סָפַת עַל־נְבוּכַדְנֶצַּר וּמִן־ אֲנָשָׁא טְרִיד וְעִשְׂבָּא כְתוֹרִין יֵאכֻל וּמִטַּל שְׁמַיָּא גִּשְׁמֵהּ יִצְטַבַּע
עַד דִּי שַׂעְרֵהּ כְּנִשְׁרִין רְבָה וְטִפְר֫וֹהִי כְצִפְּרִין:

31. וְלִקְצָת יוֹמַיָּה [read יוֹמַיָּא] אֲנָה נְבוּכַדְנֶצַּר עַיְנַי לִשְׁמַיָּא נִטְלֵת וּמַנְדְּעִי עֲלַי יְתוּב וּלְעִלָּיָא [=
עִלָּאָא / עִלָּיָא (K)] בָּרְכֵת וּלְחַי עָלְמָא שַׁבְּחֵת וְהַדְּרֵת דִּי שָׁלְטָנֵהּ שָׁלְטָן עָלַם וּמַלְכוּתֵהּ עִם־דָּר וְדָר:

32. וְכָל־דָּאְרֵי אַרְעָה כְּלָה [read כְּלָא] חֲשִׁיבִין וּכְמִצְבְּיֵהּ עָבֵד בְּחֵיל שְׁמַיָּא וְלָא אִיתַי דִּי־
יְמַחֵא בִידֵהּ [read בִּידֵהּ] וְיֵאמַר לֵהּ מָה עֲבַדְתְּ:

בֵּהּ־זִמְנָא מַנְדְּעִי יְתוּב עֲלַי וְלִיקַר [וְלִיקָר read] מַלְכוּתִי הַדְרִי וְזִוִי יְתוּב עֲלַי וְלִי הַדָּבְרַי וְרַבְרְבָנַי יְבַעוֹן .33
וְעַל־מַלְכוּתִי הָתְקְנֵת [הָתְקְנַת read] וּרְבוּ יַתִּירָה הוּסְפַת לִי׃

כְּעַן אֲנָה נְבוּכַדְנֶצַּר מְשַׁבַּח וּמְרוֹמֵם וּמְהַדַּר לְמֶלֶךְ שְׁמַיָּא דִּי כָל־ .34
מַעֲבָדוֹהִי קְשֹׁט וְאֹרְחָתֵהּ דִּין וְדִי מְהַלְכִין [מַהְלְכִין read] בְּגֵוָה יָכִל לְהַשְׁפָּלָה׃

DANIEL CHAPTER 5

בֵּלְשַׁאצַּר מַלְכָּא עֲבַד לְחֶם רַב לְרַבְרְבָנוֹהִי אֲלַף וְלָקֳבֵל אַלְפָּא חַמְרָא שָׁתֵה׃ 1

בֵּלְשַׁאצַּר אֲמַר בִּטְעֵם חַמְרָא לְהַיְתָיָה לְמָאנֵי דַּהֲבָא וְכַסְפָּא דִּי הַנְפֵּק נְבוּכַדְנֶצַּר אֲבוּהִי מִן־הֵיכְלָא דִּי 2
בִירוּשְׁלֶם וְיִשְׁתּוֹן בְּהוֹן מַלְכָּא וְרַבְרְבָנוֹהִי שֵׁגְלָתֵהּ וּלְחֵנָתֵהּ׃

בֵּאדַיִן הַיְתִיו מָאנֵי דַהֲבָא דִּי הַנְפִּקוּ מִן־הֵיכְלָא דִּי־בֵית אֱלָהָא דִּי בִירוּשְׁלֶם וְאִשְׁתִּיו בְּהוֹן מַלְכָּא וְרַבְרְבָנוֹהִי 3
שֵׁגְלָתֵהּ וּלְחֵנָתֵהּ

אִשְׁתִּיו חַמְרָא וְשַׁבַּחוּ לֵאלָהֵי דַּהֲבָא וְכַסְפָּא נְחָשָׁא פַרְזְלָא אָעָא וְאַבְנָא׃ 4

בַּהּ־שַׁעֲתָה [־שַׁעֲתָא read] נְפַקוּ [= נְפַקָה / נְפַקוּ (K)] אֶצְבְּעָן דִּי יַד־אֱנָשׁ וְכָתְבָן לָקֳבֵל נֶבְרַשְׁתָּא עַל־ .5
גִּירָא דִּי־ כְתַל הֵיכְלָא דִּי מַלְכָּא וּמַלְכָּא חָזֵה פַּס יְדָה [יְדָא read] דִּי כָתְבָה׃

אֱדַיִן מַלְכָּא זִיוֹהִי שְׁנוֹהִי [שְׁנוֹ עֲלוֹהִי read] וְרַעְיֹנֹהִי [וְרַעְיֹנֹהִי read] יְבַהֲלוּנֵּהּ וְקִטְרֵי חַרְצֵהּ .6
מִשְׁתָּרַיִן וְאַרְכֻבָּתֵהּ דָּא לְדָא נָקְשָׁן׃

קָרֵא מַלְכָּא בְּחַיִל לְהֶעָלָה לְאָשְׁפַיָּא כַּשְׂדָיאָ [=כַּשְׂדָּאֵא / כַּשְׂדָּיֵא (K)] .7
וְגָזְרַיָּא עָנֵה מַלְכָּא וְאָמַר לְחַכִּימֵי בָבֶל דִּי כָל־אֱנָשׁ דִּי־יִקְרֵה [יִקְרֵא read] כְּתָבָה [כְּתָבָא
read] דְנָה וּפִשְׁרֵהּ יְחַוִּנַּנִי אַרְגְּוָנָא יִלְבַּשׁ וְהַמְונְכָא [= וְהַמְנִכָא / וְהַמּוּנְכָא (K)] דִּי־דַהֲבָא
עַל־צַוְּארֵהּ וְתַלְתִּי בְמַלְכוּתָא יִשְׁלַט׃

אֱדַיִן עָלְלִין [= עָלִּין / עָלְלִין (K)] כֹּל חַכִּימֵי מַלְכָּא וְלָא־כָהֲלִין כְּתָבָא לְמִקְרֵא וּפִשְׁרֵא [= וּפִשְׁרֵהּ / .8
וּפִשְׁרָא (K)] לְהוֹדָעָה לְמַלְכָּא׃

אֱדַיִן מַלְכָּא בֵלְשַׁאצַּר שַׂגִּיא מִתְבָּהַל וְזִיוֹהִי שָׁנַיִן עֲלוֹהִי וְרַבְרְבָנוֹהִי מִשְׁתַּבְּשִׁין׃ 9

מַלְכְּתָא לָקֳבֵל מִלֵּי מַלְכָּא וְרַבְרְבָנֹהִי לְבֵית מִשְׁתְּיָא עַלַּלת [= עַלַּת / עַלְלַת (K)] .10
עֲנָת מַלְכְּתָא וַאֲמֶרֶת מַלְכָּא לְעָלְמִין חֱיִי אַל־יְבַהֲלוּךְ רַעְיוֹנָךְ וְזִיוָיךְ אַל־יִשְׁתַּנּוֹ׃

אִיתַי גְּבַר בְּמַלְכוּתָךְ דִּי רוּחַ אֱלָהִין קַדִּישִׁין בֵּהּ וּבְיוֹמֵי אֲבוּךְ נַהִירוּ וְשָׂכְלְתָנוּ וְחָכְמָה כְּחָכְמַת־ 11
אֱלָהִין הִשְׁתְּכַחַת בֵּהּ וּמַלְכָּא נְבֻכַדְנֶצַּר אֲבוּךְ רַב חַרְטֻמִּין אָשְׁפִין כַּשְׂדָּאִין גָּזְרִין הֲקִימֵהּ אֲבוּךְ מַלְכָּא׃

כָּל־קֳבֵל דִּי רוּחַ יַתִּירָה וּמַנְדַּע וְשָׂכְלְתָנוּ מְפַשַּׁר חֶלְמִין וַאַחֲוָיַת אֲחִידָן וּמְשָׁרֵא קִטְרִין הִשְׁתְּכַחַת בֵּהּ .12
בְּדָנִיֵּאל דִּי־מַלְכָּא שָׂם־ שְׁמֵהּ בֵּלְטְשַׁאצַּר כְּעַן דָּנִיֵּאל יִתְקְרֵי [יִתְקְרֵא read] וּפִשְׁרָה [וּפִשְׁרָא read] יְהַחֲוֵה
[יְהַחֲוֵא read]׃

בֵּאדַיִן דָּנִיֵּאל הֻעַל קֳדָם מַלְכָּא עָנֵה מַלְכָּא וְאָמַר לְדָנִיֵּאל אַנְתְּה־הוּא דָנִיֵּאל דִּי־מִן־בְּנֵי גָלוּתָא דִּי יְהוּד דִּי 13
הַיְתִי מַלְכָּא אַבִי מִן־יְהוּד׃

וְשִׁמְעֵת עֲלָיךְ דִּי רוּחַ אֱלָהִין בָּךְ וְנַהִירוּ וְשָׂכְלְתָנוּ וְחָכְמָה יַתִּירָה הִשְׁתְּכַחַת בָּךְ׃ 14

וּכְעַן הֻעַלּוּ קֳדָמַי חַכִּימַיָּא אָשְׁפַיָּא דִּי־כְתָבָה דְנָה יִקְרוֹן וּפִשְׁרֵהּ לְהוֹדָעֻתַנִי וְלָא־כָהֲלִין פְּשַׁר־מִלְּתָא לְהַחֲוָיָה׃ 15

16. וַאֲנָה שִׁמְעֵת עֲלָיךְ דִּי־תוּכֻל [= תִּכֻּל / תּוּכַל (K)] פִּשְׁרִין לְמִפְשַׁר וְקִטְרִין לְמִשְׁרֵא כְּעַן הֵן תּוּכֻל [=תִּכֻּל
/ תּוּכַל (K)] כְּתָבָא לְמִקְרֵא וּפִשְׁרֵהּ לְהוֹדָעֻתַנִי אַרְגְּוָנָא תִלְבַּשׁ וְהַמְונכָא [= הַמְנִכָא / הַמּוּנְכָא (K)] דִּי־
דַהֲבָא עַל־צַוְּארָךְ וְתַלְתָּא בְמַלְכוּתָא תִּשְׁלַט׃

17 בֵּאדַיִן עָנֵה דָנִיֵּאל וְאָמַר קֳדָם מַלְכָּא מַתְּנָתָךְ לָךְ לֶהֶוְיָן וּנְבָזְבְּיָתָךְ לְאָחֳרָן הַב בְּרַם כְּתָבָא אֶקְרֵא לְמַלְכָּא
וּפִשְׁרָא אֲהוֹדְעִנֵּהּ׃

18. אַנְתְּה מַלְכָּא אֱלָהָא עִלָּיָא מַלְכוּתָא וּרְבוּתָא וִיקָרָא וְהַדְרָה [read וְהַדְרָא] יְהַב לִנְבֻכַדְנֶצַּר אֲבוּךְ׃

19. וּמִן־רְבוּתָא דִּי יְהַב־לֵהּ כֹּל עַמְמַיָּא אֻמַיָּא [read אֻמַּיָּא] וְלִשָּׁנַיָּא הֲווֹ זָאְעִין [= זָיְעִין / זָאֲעִין (K)]
וְדָחֲלִין מִן־קֳדָמוֹהִי דִּי־הֲוָה צָבֵא הֲוָא קָטֵל וְדִי־הֲוָה צָבֵא הֲוָה מַחֵא וְדִי־הֲוָה צָבֵא הֲוָה מָרִים וְדִי־
הֲוָה צָבֵא הֲוָה מַשְׁפִּיל [read מַשְׁפִּל]׃

20. וּכְדִי רִם לִבְבֵהּ וְרוּחֵהּ תִּקְפַת לַהֲזָדָה הָנְחַת מִן־כָּרְסֵא מַלְכוּתֵהּ וִיקָרָה [read וִיקָרָא] הֶעְדִּיו מִנֵּהּ׃

21. וּמִן־בְּנֵי אֲנָשָׁא טְרִיד וְלִבְבֵהּ עִם־חֵיוְתָא שַׁוִּי [= שַׁוִּיו / שַׁוִּי (K)] וְעִם־עֲרָדַיָּא מְדוֹרֵהּ עִשְׂבָּא כְתוֹרִין
יְטַעֲמוּנֵּהּ וּמִטַּל שְׁמַיָּא גִּשְׁמֵהּ יִצְטַבַּע עַד דִּי־יְדַע דִּי־ שַׁלִּיט אֱלָהָא עִלָּיָא בְּמַלְכוּת אֲנָשָׁא וּלְמַן־דִּי
יִצְבֵּא יְהָקֵים עֲלַהּ׃

22 וְאַנְתְּה בְּרֵהּ בֵּלְשַׁאצַּר לָא הַשְׁפֵּלְתְּ לִבְבָךְ כָּל־קֳבֵל דִּי כָל־דְּנָה יְדַעְתְּ׃

23 וְעַל מָרֵא־שְׁמַיָּא הִתְרוֹמַמְתְּ וּלְמָאנַיָּא דִּי־בַיְתֵהּ הַיְתִיו קָדָמָיךְ וְאַנְתְּה וְרַבְרְבָנָיךְ שֵׁגְלָתָךְ וּלְחֵנָתָךְ חַמְרָא
שָׁתַיִן בְּהוֹן וְלֵאלָהֵי כַסְפָּא־וְדַהֲבָא נְחָשָׁא פַרְזְלָא אָעָא וְאַבְנָא דִּי לָא־חָזַיִן וְלָא־שָׁמְעִין וְלָא
יָדְעִין שַׁבַּחְתָּ וְלֵאלָהָא דִּי־נִשְׁמְתָךְ בִּידֵהּ וְכָל־אֹרְחָתָךְ לֵהּ לָא הַדַּרְתָּ׃

24. בֵּאדַיִן מִן־קֳדָמוֹהִי שְׁלִיַח [read שְׁלִיחַ] פַּסָּא דִי־יְדָא וּכְתָבָא דְנָה רְשִׁים׃

25 וּדְנָה כְתָבָא דִּי רְשִׁים מְנֵא מְנֵא תְּקֵל וּפַרְסִין׃

26 דְּנָה פְּשַׁר־מִלְּתָא מְנֵא מְנָה־אֱלָהָא מַלְכוּתָךְ וְהַשְׁלְמַהּ׃

27. תְּקֵל תְּקִילְתָּה [read תְּקִילְתָּ] בְמֹאזַנְיָא וְהִשְׁתְּכַחַתְּ חַסִּיר׃

28 פְּרֵס פְּרִיסַת מַלְכוּתָךְ וִיהִיבַת לְמָדַי וּפָרָס׃

29. בֵּאדַיִן אֲמַר בֵּלְשַׁאצַּר וְהַלְבִּישׁוּ [read וְהַלְבִּשׁוּ] לְדָנִיֵּאל אַרְגְּוָנָא וְהַמְונכָא [= הַמְנִיכָא
/ הַמּוֹנְכָא (K)] דַהֲבָא עַל־צַוְּארֵהּ וְהַכְרִזוּ עֲלוֹהִי דִּי־לֶהֱוֵא שַׁלִּיט תַּלְתָּא בְּמַלְכוּתָא׃

30. בֵּהּ בְּלֵילְיָא קְטִיל בֵּלְאשַׁצַּר מַלְכָּא כַשְׂדָּיָא [= כַּשְׂדָּאָא / כַּשְׂדָּיָא (K)]׃

TRANSLATION

Daniel 4

1 *I, Nebuchadnezzar, was at ease in my house, and serene in my palace.* **2** *I saw a dream and it frightened me* (lit. *was frightening me*); *thoughts over my bed and the visions of my head terrified me* (lit. *were terrifying me*). **3** *So, I made a decree* (lit. *and by me was made a decree*) *to bring before me all the sages of Babel so that an interpretation of the dream they might make known to me* (lit. *make me know*). **4** *Then, the magicians, the exorcists, the Chaldeans, and the diviners each came* (lit. *were coming*). *The dream I spoke before them but its interpretation they did not make known to me* (lit. *were not making me know*). **5** *At last, Daniel, whose name (is) Belteshazzar, according to the name of my god, and in whom was the spirit of the holy gods, came before me and the dream I spoke before him.* **6** *'O Belteshazzar, captain of the magicians, what I know (is) that the spirit of the holy gods is in you and no secret troubles you. As for the visions of my dream* *that I saw, their interpretation* (lit. *its interpretation*), *speak to me!* **7** *As for the visions of my head, over my bed I saw: Lo, a tree in the midst of the earth and its height was great.* **8** *The tree grew and became strong until* (lit. *and*) *its height reached* (lit. *was reaching*) *the heavens and the sight of it* (lit. *its sight*) *to the end of all the earth.* **9** *Its foliage (was) beautiful and its fruit abundant, and in it (was) food for all* (lit. *the all*). *Beneath* (lit. *beneath it*), *it would shade the beasts of the field and in its branches were dwelling the birds of the heavens and from it were fed* (lit. *were being fed*) *all flesh.* **10** *I was watching in the visions of my head over my bed and lo, a watcher, that is* (lit. *and*) *a holy one, from heaven was coming down.* **11** *He called* (lit. *was calling*) *loudly and thus said: 'Cut down the tree and chop off its branches! Strip off its foliage and scatter its fruit! Let the beasts flee from under it and the birds from its branches!* **12** *Nevertheless, the stump of its root leave in the earth, in a fetter of iron and bronze, in the grass of the field! Let it be drenched in the dew of the heavens and (let) its share (be) with the beasts, with the grass of the earth!* **13** *His heart will be changed* (lit. *they will change*) *from a human (one) and a heart of a beast will be given to it. Seven time periods will pass over it.* **14** *By decree of watchers (comes) the verdict, a word of holy ones (is) the response – so that the living might know that the Most High (is) sovereign over the human realm* (lit. *the realm of the human*) *and to whomever he wishes he gives it. One who is low among humans he will lift over it.'* **15** *This was the dream that I, king Nebuchadnezzar, saw. Now* (lit. *and*) *you, Belteshazzar, the interpretation speak because all the sages of my kingdom are not able to make known to me* (lit. *to make me know*) *the interpretation but you are able to because the spirit of the holy gods (is) in you.'* **16** *Then Daniel, whose name (was) Belteshazzar, was dumb-founded for one moment, his thoughts terrifying him. The king spoke up and said, 'Belteshazzar, the dream and its interpretation, do not let it terrify you.' Belteshazzar answered and said, 'My lord, the dream (is) for those who hate you; its interpretation (is) for your enemies.'* **17** *The tree that you saw, that grew and became strong, and whose height reached* (lit. *was reaching*) *to the heavens and the sight of it to all the land*, **18** *whose foliage (was) beautiful and its fruit abundant, and in which (was) food for all* (lit. *the all*), *under which dwelled the beasts of the field and in whose branches sat the birds of the heavens –* **19** *it is you, O king, who has grown* (lit. *you have grown*) *and become strong* (lit. *you have become strong*) *and your greatness has grown and reached the heavens and your power to the end of the earth.* **20** *And, what the king saw – a watcher, that is* (lit. *and*) *a holy one, who was coming down from the heavens and said 'Cut down the tree and destroy it! Nevertheless, the stump of its root leave in the earth, in a fetter of iron and bronze, in the grass of the field! Let it be drenched in the dew of the heavens and (let) its share (be) with the beasts of the field until seven time periods will pass over it.'* **21** *This is the interpretation, O king: it is a decree of the Most High that reaches to my lord, the king.* **22** *You will be chased away* (lit. *they will be chasing you away*) *from humanity and with the beasts of the field will be your dwelling. You will be fed grass* (lit. *they will be feeding you*) *like oxen and from the dew of heaven you will be drenched* (lit. *they will be drenching you*) *until* (lit. *and*) *seven time periods will pass over you, until you know that the Most High is sovereign in the human realms* (lit. *the realm of the human*) *and to whom he wishes he gives it.* **23** *That it was said* (lit. *they said*) *to leave the stump of the root of the tree, (it concerns) the (re)establishment of your kingdom for you after you know that the heavens are sovereign.* **24** *Therefore, O king, may my counsel be pleasing to you! Redeem your sin through righteousness and your iniquities through*

showing mercy to the poor, if (you wish) your prosperity to be long (lit. *if length will belong to*
your prosperity)!' **25** *All of it* (lit. *the all*) *happened to Nebuchadnezzar, the king.* **26** *At the end of*
twelve months, at the palace of the kingdom, which (is) in Babel, he was walking about. **27** *The*
king spoke up and said: 'Is this not great Babel, which I built (lit. *I built it*) *for a royal residence* (lit.
house of kingship) *with my powerful strength* (lit. *strength of my power*) *and for the glory of my*
honour?' **28** *The statement (was) still in the mouth of the king (when) a voice from heaven fell: 'To*
you it is said (lit. *they said*), *Nebuchadnezzar, O king, 'The kingdom has passed away from you.*
29 *From humanity you are (hereby) chased away* (lit. *they will be chasing you away*) *and with*
the beasts of the field (is) your dwelling. Grass (lit. *the grass*) *like oxen you will be fed* (lit. *they will*
feed you). *Seven time periods will pass over you, until you know that the Most High is sovereign*
in the kingdom of humans and to whom he wishes he gives it.'' **30** *In that moment the verdict*
was fulfilled against Nebuchadnezzar and from humans he was chased and grass (lit. *the grass*)
like oxen he ate (lit. *he would eat*) *and from the dew of the heavens his body was drenched* (lit.
would be drenched) *until his hair grew like (the feathers of) eagles and his nails like (the talons of)*
birds. **31** *At the end of these days* (lit. *the days*), *I, Nebuchadnezzar, lifted my eyes to the heavens*
and my intelligence returned (lit. *was returning*) *to me. I blessed the Most High and I praised and*
honoured the one eternally alive (lit. *the one alive* (cstr.) *for the eternity*), *whose power is an eternal*
power (lit. *a power of eternity*) *and whose kingdom is with every generation* (lit. *generation after*
generation). **32** *All the dwellers of the earth are considered as nothing* (כְּ *as* + לָא *nothing*). *As he*
wishes, he does with the host of the heavens and the dwellers of the earth. There is not one who
can prevent his hand and say to him 'What have you done?' **33** *In that time, my knowledge*
returning to me, and my honour to the glory of my kingdom, and my appearance returning to me,
and my counsellors and my nobles seeking me out, I was (re)established over my kingdom and a
surpassing greatness was added to me. **34** *Now, I, Nebuchadnezzar, am praising and exalting and*
honouring the king of the heavens whose deeds are true and whose ways are just and who is able
to bring low those who walk about in pride.

Daniel 5

1 *Belshazzar, the king, made a great feast for his thousand nobles and before the thousand he was*
drinking wine. **2** *Belshazzar commanded, under influence of the wine, to bring out the vessels of*
gold and silver which Nebuchadnezzar, his father, had removed from the temple which (was) in
Jerusalem so that (lit. *and*) *the king and his nobles, his consorts and his concubines might drink*
with them. **3** *Then, the vessels of gold were brought in* (lit. *they brought in*), *(the vessels) which had*
been removed (lit. *which they removed*) *from the temple which (was) the house of the God which*
(was) in Jerusalem and the king and his nobles, his consorts and his concubines drank with them.
4 *They drank the wine and praised the gods of gold and silver, bronze and iron, wood and stone.*
5 *In that moment fingers of a human hand* (lit. . . . *of a hand of a human*) *emerged and wrote* (lit.
were writing) *before the lamp, upon the plaster of the wall of the king's palace* (lit. *the palace of*
the king), *so that* (lit. *and*) *the king saw* (lit. *was seeing*) *the palm of the hand that wrote* (lit. *was*
writing). **6** *Then, as for the king, his appearance changed upon him, his thoughts frightening him*
and the joints of his hips (lit. *hip*) *coming loose and his knees knocking against each other* (lit. *this*
against that). **7** *The king cried* (lit. *was crying*) *loudly* (lit. *in strength*) *to bring in the exorcists, the*
Chaldeans, and the diviners. The king spoke up and said to the sages of Babel: 'Any person who

can read this writing and its interpretation tell me will wear purple (robes) (lit. *the purple) and the*
golden necklace (will be) over his neck and as the third (ruler), the kingdom he will rule.' **8** *Then*
all the royal sages (lit. *sages of the king) came but* (lit. *and) were not able to read the writing*
nor (lit. *and) its interpretation to make known to the king* (lit. *to make the king know*). **9** *Then,*
the king, Belshazzar, became very alarmed, his appearance changing upon him and his nobles
confused. **10** *The queen, because of the words of the king and his nobles, entered the banquet*
hall (lit. *the house of the drinking). The queen responded and said: 'O king, live forever! Do not let*
your thoughts disturb you and may your appearance not be changed! **11** *There is a man in your*
kingdom in whom is (the) spirit of (the) holy gods. In the days of your father, illumination, insight
and wisdom were found in him, like (the) wisdom of (the) gods. As for the king, Nebuchadnezzar,
your father – captain of magicians, of exorcists, of Chaldeans, of diviners – your father, the king
made him – **12** *because a great spirit, knowledge, and insight of one interpreting dreams and*
(insight) to declare riddles, (insight) of one solving difficult problems were (all) found in him, in
Daniel, whom the king named Belteshazzar (lit. *whose name the king set as B.). Now, let Daniel*
be called so (lit. *and) the interpretation he might declare.*' **13** *Then, Daniel was brought before*
the king. The king spoke up and said to Daniel: 'You are Daniel, who is from among the exiles (lit.
children of the exile) of Judah, whom the king, my father, brought from Judah. **14** *I have heard*
about you that (the) spirit of (the) gods (is) in you and (that) illumination, insight, and great
wisdom is found in you. **15** *And now, the sages, the exorcists were brought before me so that they*
might read this writing and (that) its interpretation they should make known to me (lit. *make me*
know), but (lit. *and) they were not able to declare the interpretation of the thing.* **16** *I have heard*
about you that you are able to give interpretations and to solve difficult problems. Now, if you
are able to read the writing and to make known to me (lit. *make me know) its interpretation, you*
will wear purple (robes) (lit. *the purple) and the gold necklace (will be) around your neck and as*
the third (ruler), the kingdom you will rule.' **17** *Then, Daniel answered and said before the king:*
'*Let your gifts remain* (lit. *be) yours and your rewards give to another! Nevertheless, I will read the*
writing to the king and the interpretation I will make known to you (lit. *make you know*). **18** *(As*
for) you, O king, the God, Most High, gave the kingdom, greatness (lit. *the greatness), glory* (lit. *the*
glory), and honour (lit. *the honour) to Nebuchadnezzar, your father.* **19** *And due to the greatness*
that he had given to him all the peoples, the nations, and the tongues were trembling and afraid
before him. Whomever he wished (lit. *was wishing) he would kill and whomever he wished* (lit.
was wishing) he would keep alive; whomever he wished (lit. *was wishing) he would exalt and*
whomever he wished (lit. *was wishing) he would bring low.* **20** *And when his heart was lifted up*
and his spirit grew strong to act arrogantly, he was deposed from the throne of his kingship and
glory (lit. *the glory) was removed from him* (lit. *they removed from him*). **21** *And, from humanity*
(lit. *the children of the man) he was chased and his heart was transformed* (lit. *they transformed*
(oral)) *into the (heart of a) beast; his dwelling (was) with the wild donkeys; grass like oxen he was*
fed (lit. *they were feeding him) and from the dew of the heavens his body was drenched* (lit. *he*
was being drenched) until he knew that the God, Most High, was ruler in the human realm (lit.
the realm of the human) and whomever he wishes he will establish over it. **22** *You, Belshazzar, his*
son, you have not humbled (lit. *lowered) your heart despite knowing all this* (lit. *as a consequence*
of the fact that you have known all this). **23** *You have exalted yourself against the Lord of the*

heavens. The vessels of his temple were brought (lit. *they brought*) *before you and (then) you, your nobles, your consorts, and your concubines drank* (lit. *were drinking*) *wine with them and you praised the gods of silver and gold, of bronze, iron, wood, and stone, which do not see and do not hear and do not know. But* (lit. *and*), *the God in whose power* (lit. *hand*) *(is) your breath and belonging to whom (are) all your ways you did not honour.* **24** *Then, from before him* (i.e. *God*) *the palm of the hand was sent and this writing inscribed.* **25** *And, (as for) this writing, which is inscribed* 'mene, mene, tqel, *and* pharsin,' **26** *this (is) the interpretation of the word* 'mene': *God has assessed your rule (or kingdom) and has brought it to completion.* **27** *(As for)* tqel, *you have been weighed in the scales and been found wanting.* **28** *(As for)* pres, *your kingdom is divided and is (hereby) given to the Medes and Persians.* **29** *Then Belshazzar commanded and Daniel was clothed* (lit. *they clothed Daniel*) *with purple (robes)* (lit. *the purple*) *and the gold necklace (was set) around his neck. And it was proclaimed* (lit. *they proclaimed*) *about him that he would be the third ruler in the kingdom.* **30** *In that (same) night, Belshazzar, the Chaldean king, was killed.*

NOTES

4:2 The pa. pref. conj. forms **וִידַחֲלִנַּנִי** and **יְבַהֲלֻנַּנִי** indicate a continuous feeling of fear in the past.

4:3 The verb **שִׂים** is either a pəʿīl 3ms suff. conj. or pəʿal passive/pəʿīl m.s. part. (of **שׂים**). The ha. pref. conj. **יְהוֹדְעֻנַּנִי** (from **ידע**) indicates possibility: *might make known . . .*

4:4 The pə. part. **עָלְלִין** indicates repeated action in the past, that is, each of the groups of soothsayers came separately. The same applies to the ha. part. **מְהוֹדְעִין** (from **ידע**).

4:8 The verbs **רְבָה** and **תְקִף** are both pə. 3ms suff. conj. (from **רבי** and **תקף** respectively). The pə. pref. conj. **יִמְטֵא** (from **מטי**) indicates the continuous nature of the tree's height and visibility.

4:9 The pref. conj.s **תַּטְלֵל** (aph.), **יְדֻרוּן** (pə. **דור**) and **יִתְּזִין** (hitpə. **זון**) indicate the repeated/continuous nature of the shading, dwelling, and feeding.

4:11 The verse contains a series of m.p. imperatives: pə. **גדד**; pa. **קצץ**; aph. **נתר**; pa. **בדר**. The verb **תְּנֻד** is pə. 3fs of **נוד**.

4:12 The hitpa. pref. conj. **יִצְטַבַּע** (from **צבע**) indicates repeated drenchings. Note the metathesis of the sadeh and original taw as well as the shift of taw to tet, due to the preceding sadeh.

4:13 The pa. pref. conj. **יְשַׁנּוֹן** (from **שׁני**) indicates a future event. It is active and plural, but with no clear antecedent it must be interpreted as an impersonal construction and translated into the English passive voice.

4:14 The pə. pref. conj. **יִנְדְּעוּן** (from **ידע**) indicates either possibility (*might*) or a future event. The two pə. pref. conj.s **יִצְבֵּא** (from **צבי**) and **יִתְּנִנַּהּ** (from **נתן**) imply repeated actions of wishing and giving, reflecting a general truth that is timeless and so are translated by the English present tense. The ha. pref. conj. **יְקִים** (from **קום**) likely indicates a future action.

4:15 The pə. part.s **יָכְלִין** and **כָּהֵל** indicate a continuous action (*being able*) in the present tense. The form **הוֹדָעֻתַנִי** is the ha. inf. of **ידע** followed by the 1cs object suff.

4:16 The verb אֶשְׁתּוֹמַם is an itpoʿal 3ms suff. conj. from the root שׁמם. On יְבַהֲלֻנָּהּ, see notes to 4:2. The verb יְבַהֲלָךְ is a pa. 3ms juss. with a 2ms object suff. The form שָׂנְאָיךְ is the pə. m.p. part. of שׂני with the 2ms poss. suff. The form with aleph reflects a historical spelling, the root originally being שׂנא.

4:19 In the phrase דִּי רְבַית וּתְקֵפְתְּ the relative refers to *you* (2ms) and so the following pə. suff. conj. verbs are both 2ms. By contrast, the following two pə. suff. conj. verbs רְבָת וּמְטָת take רְבוּתָךְ *your greatness* as subject and are, therefore, 3fs.

4:22 The pə. m.p. part. טָרְדִין has no clear subject and so it should be interpreted as an impersonal construction and translated in the passive voice. The part. implies a continuous or repeated act of ostracization. The expression לָךְ יְטַעֲמוּן (made up of the prep. lamed marking the direct object and the pa. 3mp pref. conj.) similarly indicates repeated feeding.

4:23 The pə. 3mp suff. conj. אֲמַרוּ is an active form, but without a clear subject, it is interpreted as another impersonal construction and translated into the English passive. The verb קַיָּמָה is the pa. inf. of קום; the pa. usually has the sense of *establish* but the context suggests the nuance *reestablish*. Here the inf. is used as a noun. The phrase stands in apposition to the preceding clause and given the context suggests it represents the interpretation of that portion of the dream.

4:24 From context, the pə. 3ms verb יִשְׁפַּר is a juss.

4:28 The pə. m.p. part. אָמְרִין has no clear subject and should be interpreted as another impersonal construction and translated with the passive voice.

4:30 The pə. 3ms pref. conj. יֵאכֻל and pa. 3ms pref. conj. יִצְטַבַּע both imply repeated action.

4:31 The pə. 3ms pref. conj. יְתוּב implies a gradual return of Nebuchadnezzar's intelligence.

4:32 The word חֲשִׁיבִין is the pə. m.p. pass./pəʿīl m.p. part. The word מִצְבְּיֵהּ is the pə. inf. of צבי with the 3ms poss. suff. The pref. conj. forms יְמַחֵא and יֵאמַר imply possibility.

4:33 For יְתוּב, see comments to 4:31. The pə. 3mp pref. conj יְבַעוֹן indicates a repeated petition for help on the part of the counsellors. The form הָתְקְנַת is the hu./ho. 3fs of תקן though we expect the 1cs (הָתְקְנֵת).

5:2 The pə. 3ms pref. conj. יִשְׁתּוֹן (of שׁתי) expresses possibility.

5:3 The 3mp suff. conj.s הַיְתִיו (ha. אתי) and הַנְפִּקוּ (ha. נפק) have no clear subject, so they should be interpreted as impersonal constructions and be translated by the English passive. The word אִשְׁתִּיו is the irregular pə. 3ms suff. conj. of שׁתי.

5:5 The pə. part.s כָּתְבָן (f.p.), חָזֵה (m.s.), and כָּתְבָה (f.s.) imply continuous action.

5:6 The pref. conj. (יְבַהֲלוּנֵּהּ pə. 3mp בהל + 3ms obj. suff.) and part.s (מִשְׁתָּרַיִן hitpa. m.p. שׁרי and נָקְשָׁן pə. f.p. נקשׁ) imply continuous action.

5:7 The word הֶעָלָה is the ha. inf. of עלל.

5:8 The irregular pə. m.p. part. עָלְלִין of עלל implies repeated action.

5:9 The word מִשְׁתַּבְּשִׁין is the hitpa. m.p. of שׁבשׁ. Note the metathesis of the shin and taw.

5:10 The pə. 3fs suff. conj. אֲמַ֫רֶת *she said* is likely a later alteration of an earlier אַמְרַת, since the vowel pattern of אֲמַ֫רֶת is unlike that of other pə. 3fs suff. conj. verbs in Biblical Aramaic but matches the vowel pattern of pə. 3fs suff. conj. verbs in later Targum Onqelos. That the verbs יְבַהֲלוּךְ and יִשְׁתַּנּוֹ are jussives is implied not only by the negative adverb אַל, but also by the lack of a nun after the long ū and ō, respectively.

5:11 The word הִשְׁתְּכַ֫חַת is the hitpə. 3fs suff. conj. of שׁכח. Note the metathesis of the shin and taw.

5:12 The pa. part.s מְפַשַּׁר and וּמְשָׁרֵא are used as nouns, *one who* . . . The word וַאַחֲוָיַת is the aph. infinitive (אַחֲוָיָה) from the root חוי in construct with the following noun. Given their context, the two verbs יִתְקְרֵי and יְהַחֲוֵה are juss.s (hitpə. 3ms pref. conj. and ha. 3ms pref. conj., respectively).

5:13 The verb הֻעַל is the hu./ho. 3ms suff. conj. of עלל. The word הַיְתִי is the ha. 3ms suff. conj. of אתי.

5:14 On הִשְׁתְּכַחַת, see 5:11.

5:15 The verb הֻעַ֫לּוּ is 3mp, though otherwise identical to הֻעַל from 5:13. The pə. 3mp pref. conj. יִקְרוֹן implies possibility. On הוֹדָעֻתַ֫נִי, see 4:15. The word הַחֲוָיָה is the ha. inf. of חוי.

5:16 The verse contains three pə. inf.s: מִפְשַׁר and מִשְׁרֵא and מִקְרֵא. On הוֹדָעֻתַ֫נִי, see 4:15.

5:17 The form הַב is the pə. m.s. imv. of יהב.

5:19 The pə. m.p. part. זָאְעִין is from the root זוע; the aleph consonant reflects the shift from an earlier זָיְעִין to a later זָאֲעִין. The part. reflects a continuous action.

5:20 The verb רִם is the pə. 3ms suff. conj. of רום. The word הֲזָדָה is the ha. inf. from זוד. The verb הָנְחַת is the hu./ho. 3ms suff. conj. of נחת. The verb הֶעְדִּיו is the ha. 3mp suff. conj. of עדי.

5:21 The form שַׁוִּי should be read with the oral tradition (i.e. שַׁוִּיו); it is an active form and lacks an obvious subject so should be understood as an impersonal construction and translated with the English passive.

5:23 The word הִתְרוֹמַ֫מְתָּ is the hitpoʿal 2ms suff. conj. of רום. On הַיְתִיו, see 5:3.

5:24 Both שְׁלִיחַ and רְשִׁים are pəʿīl 3ms suff. conj. verbs.

5:26 The verb הַשְׁלְמַהּ is the ha. 3ms suff. conj. of שלם with a 3fs obj. suff.

5:27 The verb תְּקִילְתָּה is a pəʿīl 2ms suff. conj. verb with an unusual final mater. On הִשְׁתְּכַ֫חַתְּ, see 5:11.

5:28 Both פְּרִ֫יסַת and יְהִיבַת are pəʿīl 3fs suff. conj. verbs.

5:29 Both הַלְבִּ֫ישׁוּ and הַכְרִ֫זוּ are ha. 3mp suff. conj. verbs that lack an obvious subject and should be interpreted as impersonal constructions and translated with the English passive.

5:30 The verb קְטִיל is a pəʿīl 3ms suff. conj. verb.

Answer key

UNIT 1

Practice 1

1 ה and ח

2 ק

3 ר

4 כ

Practice 2

1 The sequence of letters in the practice is the same as that in the preceding chart.

2

left col.: ע ʻ ayin, ק q qoph, ו w waw, ל l lamedh, שׁ š šin, ר r resh, ח ḥ ḥet, ב b bet, ט ṭ ṭet, צ ṣ ṣadeh, נ n nun

right col.: ד d dalet, מ m mem, כ k kaph, ס s samekh, א ʼ aleph, ת t taw, י y yod, ז z zayin, ג g gimmal, ה h he, פ p peh

4

א ʼ(aleph) and ע ʻ (ʻayin); ב b and כ k; ג g and נ n; ד d and ר r; ה h and ח ḥ; ח ḥ and ת t; כ k and פ p; ע ʻ and צ ṣ

Practice 3

1 Dalet. The vertical mark of the final kaph descends lower than the vertical mark of the dalet (e.g. דך).

2 Samekh. The final mem looks more like a square (ם) and the samekh more like a circle (ס).

3 Waw. The vertical mark of the final nun descends lower than the vertical mark of the waw (e.g. ון).

Daniel 5:1

a mlkʼ, **b** ʻbd, **c** lḥm, **d** rb, **e** lrbrbnwhy, **f** ʼlp, **g** wlqbl, **h** ʼlpʼ, **i** ḥmrʼ, **j** šth

Daniel 5:2

a 3, **b** 9, **c** 7, **d** 2, **e** 10, **f** 8, **g** 1, **h** 5, **i** 4, **j** 6

Daniel 5:3

a bʼdyn hytyw mʼny dhbʼ; **b** dy hnpqw mn hyklʼ; **c** dy byt ʼlhʼ dy byrwšlm; **d** wʼštyw bhwn mlkʼ; **e** wrbrbnwhy šglth wlḥnth

Daniel 5:4

a ʼštyw ḥmrʼ wšbḥw lʼlhy dhbʼ; **b** wkspʼ nḥšʼ przlʼ ʻʼ wʼbnʼ

Daniel 5:5

a bh š‘th npqw ’ṣb‘n dy yd ’nš; **b** wktbn lqbl nbršt’; **c** ‘l gyr’ dy ktl hykl dy mlk’; **d** wmlk’ ḥzh ps ydh dy ktbh

Daniel 5:6

a אדין; **b** מלכא; **c** זיוהי; **d** שׂנוהי; **e** ורעינהי; **f** יבהלונה; **g** וקטרי חרצה; **h** משׂתרין; **i** וארכבתה; **j** דא לדא נקשׁן

Daniel 5:7

a 5, **b** 8, **c** 9, **d** 6, **e** 4, **f** 1, **g** 10, **h** 2, **i** 7, **j** 3

Daniel 5:8

a אדין עללין כל חכימי מלכא; **b** ולא כהלין כתבא למקרא; **c** ופשׂרא להודעה למלכא

Daniel 5:9

a אדין מלכא בלשׁאצר שׂגיא מתבהל; **b** וזיוהי שׁנין עלוהי; **c** ורברבנוהי משׁתבשׁין

Test yourself

a wṣly’t ḥnh brwḥ nbw’h

b w’mrt kbr šmw’l bry

c ‘tyd lmhwy nby’ ‘l yśr’l

d bywmwhy ytprqwn myd’ dplšt’y

e w‘l ydwhy yt‘bdn nsyn wgbwrn

f bkyn tqyp lby

g bḥwlq’ dyhb ly yyy

For future reference, the version of the text with targumic spelling is the following (see Unit 22):

a וְצַלִיאַת חַנָה בְרוּחַ נְבוּאָה

b וַאֲמַ֫רַת כְבָר שְמוּאֵל בְרִי

c עֲתִיד לְמִהוֵי נְבִיָא עַל יִשְׂרָאֵל

d בְיוֹמוֹהִי יִתְפַרְקוּן מִיְדָא דִפלִשְתָאֵי

e וְעַל יְדוֹהִי יִתעַבדָן נִסִין וּגבוּרָן

f בְכֵין תְקֵיף לִבִי

g בְחוּלָקָא דִיהַב לִי יְיָ

Unit 2

Practice 1

The symbols for a vowels have horizontal lines (ַ a, ָ ā). The symbols for i vowels are all composed of dots (ִ i, ֵ e and ē, ֶ ε).

Practice 2

1 a חַכִימֵי; **b** וְלָא כָהֲלִין; **c** כְתָבָא; **d** לְמִקרֵא; **e** לְהוֹדָעָה; **f** שַׂגִיא; **g** עֲלוֹהִי; **h** מִלֵי; **i** וַאֲמֶ֫רֶת; **j** לְעָלְמִין; **k** חֱיִי; **l** יְבַהֲלוּךְ; **m** וּבְיוֹמֵי; **n** נַהִירוּ; **o** אָשְׁפִין; **p** יַתִירָה; **q** וּמְשָׁרֵא; **r** יְהַחֲוֵה; **s** עָנֵה; **t** גָלוּתָא

2 a ḥakī^{y}mē^{y}; **b** wəlâ kāhălī^{y}n; **c** kətābâ; **d** ləmiqrê; **e** ləhō^{w}dā‘ā^{h} **f** śagī^{y}’; **g** ‘ălō^{w}hī^{y}; **h** milē^{y}; **i** wa’ămɛrɛt; **j** lə‘āləmī^{y}n; **k** ḥĕyī^{y}; **l** yəbahălū^{w}k; **m** ū^{w}bəyō^{w}mē^{y}; **n** nahī^{y}rū^{w}; **o** ’āšəpī^{y}n; **p** yatī^{y}rā^{h}; **q** ū^{w}məšārê; **r** yəhaḥăwē^{h}; **s** ‘ānē^{h}; **t** gālū^{w}tâ

Daniel 5:10, second part

a ‘ănāt malkətâ wa’ămɛrɛt; **b** malkâ lə‘āləmī^{y}n ḥĕyī^{y}; **c** ’al yəbahălū^{w}k ra‘yō^{w}nāk; **d** wəzī^{y}zāk ’al yištanō^{w}

Daniel 5:11

a ’ī^{y}tay gəbar bəmalkū^{w}tāk dī^{y} rū^{w}ḥ ’ĕlāhī^{y}n qadī^{y}šī^{y}n beh; **b** ū^{w}bəyō^{w}mē^{y} ’ăbū^{w}k nahī^{y}rū^{w} wəśoklətānū^{w} wəḥokmā^{h}; **c** kəḥokmat ’ĕlāhī^{y}n hištəkaḥat bēh; **d** ū^{w}malkâ nəbūkadnɛṣar ’ăbū^{w}k; **e** rab ’āšəpī^{y}n kaśdā’ī^{y}n gāzərī^{y}n; **f** hăqī^{y}mēh ’ăbū^{w}k malkâ

Daniel 5:12

a kol qŏbel dī^{y} rū^{w}ḥ yatī^{y}rā^{h} ū^{w}manda‘ wəśoklətānū^{w}; **b** məpašer ḥelmī^{y}n wa’aḥăwāyat ’ăḥī^{y}dān; **c** ū^{w}məšārê qiṭrī^{y}n hištəkaḥat beh; **d** bədāniyēl dī^{y} malkâ śām šəmeh bēlṭəša’ṣar; **e** kə‘an dāniyēl yitqərē^{y} ū^{w}pišrâ yəhaḥăwē^{h}

Daniel 5:13

a bêdayin dāniyēl hu‘al qŏdām malkâ; **b** ‘ānē^{h} malkâ wə’āmar lədāniyēl; **c** ’ant hū^{w}’ dāniyēl dī^{y} min bənē^{y} gālū^{w}tâ dī^{y} yəhū^{w}d; **d** dī^{y} haytī^{y} malkâ ’abī^{y} min yəhū^{w}d.

Daniel 5:14

a וְנַהִירוּ וְשָׂכְלְתָנוּ; **b** וְחָכְמָה יַתִּירָה הִשְׁתְּכַ֫חַת בָּךְ

Daniel 5:15

a וּכְעַן הֻעַ֫לּוּ קֳדָמַי חַכִּימַיָּא אָשְׁפַיָּא; **b** דִּי כְתָבָה דְנָה יִקְרוֹן; **c** וּפִשְׁרֵהּ לְהוֹדָעֻתַנִי; **d** וְלָא כָהֲלִין פְּשַׁר מִלְּתָא לְהַחֲוָיָה

Daniel 5:16

a וַאֲנָה שִׁמְעֵת עֲלָךְ דִּי תִכּוּל; **b** פִּשְׁרִין לְמִפְשַׁר וְקִטְרִין לְמִשְׁרֵא; **c** כְּעַן הֵן תִּכּוּל כְּתָבָה לְמִקְרֵא; **d** וּפִשְׁרֵהּ לְהוֹדָעֻתַנִי; **e** אַרְגְּוָנָא תִלְבַּשׁ וְהַמְנִיכָא דִי דַהֲבָא עַל צַוְּרָךְ; **f** וְתַלְתָּא בְמַלְכוּתָא תִּשְׁלַט

Test yourself

a בַּר בְּרִי *son of my son*

b בְּנוֹהִי *his sons*

c אָמְרִין *they say*

d בְּבֵית מַקְדְּשָׁא *in the holy temple*

e קַרְנִי *my horn*

f וְאַף עַל *And also over*

g אֲרוֹנָא *the ark*

h אֲשָׁמָא *the guilt offering*

i דְּיִשְׂרָאֵל *of Israel*

j בַּעֲלֵי דְבָבַי *my enemies*

For future reference, the version of the text with targumic spelling is the following (see Unit 22):

a וְאַף הֵימָן בַר יוֹאֵל בַר בְרִי שְׁמוּאֵל

b דַעֲתִיד דִיקוּם הוּא וְאַרבְעַת עֲסַר בְנוֹהִי

c לְמִהוֵי אָמְרִין בְשִׁירָא [= שִׁירָה] עַל יְדֵי נִבלִין וְכִנָרִין

d עִם אֲחֵיהוֹן לֵיוָאֵי לְשַבָחָא בְבֵית מַקדְשָׁא

e בְכֵין רֵימַת קַרְנִי בְמַתַנתָא דְמַנִי לִי יְיָ

f וְאַף עַל פּוּרעָנוּת נִסָא דַעֲתִיד לְמִהוֵי בִפלִשתָאֵי

g דַעֲתִידִין דְיַיתוֹן [= יְהֵיתוֹן < אתי] יָת אֲרוֹנָא

h בַעֲגַלתָא חֲדַתָא וְעִמֵיה קֵרבַן [read קֻרבָן] אֲשָׁמָא

i בְכֵין תֵימַר כְנִשתָא דְיִשׂרָאֵל אִתפְתַח פוּמִי לְמַלָלָא [= מַלָלָה]

j רַברְבָן עַל בַעֲלֵי דְבָבַי אֲרֵי חֲדִיתִי בְפֻרקָנָך

UNIT 3

Practice 1

a bayteh; **b** haytī^{y}w; **c** rabrəbānāk; **d** šēgəlātāk (note ē without mater); **e** ḥamrâ; **f** kaspâ; **g** parzəlâ; **h** lâ šāmə‘ī^{y}n; **i** lâ yādə‘ī^{y}n; **j** nišmətāk; **k** ’ōrəḥātāk (note ō without mater); **l** ū^{w}kətābâ dənā^{h}; **m** dənā^{h} kətābâ; **n** malkū^{w}tāk; **o** bəmôzanyâ (note how the aleph seems to function as a mater for ō); **p** pərī^{y}sat; **q** wī^{y}hī^{y}bat

Practice 2

a bay-teh; **b** hay-tī^{y}w; **c** rab-rə-bā-nāk; **d** šē-gə-lā-tāk; **e** ḥam-râ; **f** kas-pâ; **g** par-zə-lâ; **h** lâ šā-mə-‘ī^{y}n; **i** lâ yâ-də-‘ī^{y}n; **j** niš-mə-tāk; **k** ’ō-rə-ḥā-tāk; **l** ū^{w}-kə-tā-bâ də-nā^{h}; **m** də-nā^{h} kə-tā-bâ; **n** mal-kū^{w}-tāk; **o** bə-mô-zan-yâ; **p** pə-rī^{y}-sat; **q** wī^{y}-hī^{y}-bat

Practice 3

a šabbaḥtā; **b** lâ haddartā; **c** passâ; **d** millətâ; **e** təqī^{y}ltā^{h}; **f** wəhištəkaḥat; **g** ḥassī^{y}r; **h** šallī^{y}ṭ; **i** qabbel; **j** šittī^{y}n

Daniel 5:23, second part

a ū^{w}ləmānayyâ dī^{y}-bayteh haytī^{y}w qŏdāmāk; **b** wə’ant wərabrəbānāk wəšēgəlātāk ū^{w}ləḥēnātāk; **c** ḥamrâ šātayin bəhō^{w}n; **d** wəlēlāhē^{y} kaspâ-wədahăbâ nəḥāšâ parzəlâ ’ā‘â wə’abnâ; **e** dī^{y} lâ-ḥāzayin wəlâ-šāmə‘ī^{y}n wəlâ-yādə‘ī^{y}n šabbaḥtā; **f** wəlēlāhâ dī^{y}-nišmətāk bī^{y}deh wəkol-’ōrəḥātāk leh lâ haddartā

a ‘*The vessels of his temple (they) were brought before you,*

b *and you and your nobles, your wives and your concubines*

c *drank the wine in them.*

d *The gods of (the) silver and gold, bronze, (the) iron, wood and stone*

e *that do not see, (they) do not listen, and (they) do not know you praised.*

f *But, the god in whose hand is your breath and belonging to whom (are) all your ways you did not honour.*

Daniel 5:24

a bêdayin min-qŏdāmō^{w}hī^{y}; **b** šəlī^{y}ḥ passâ dī^{y} yədâ; **c** ū^{w}kətābâ dənā^{h} rəšī^{y}m

a *Then, from before him* (i.e., *before God*),

b *the palm of the hand was sent*

c *and this writing was inscribed.*'

Daniel 5:25

a ū^{w}dənā^{h} kətābâ dī^{y} rəšī^{y}m; **b** mənê mənê təqel ū^{w}parsī^{y}n

a '*and this was the writing that was inscribed,*

b *mene, mene, tqel, and pharsin.*'

Daniel 5:26

a dənā^{h} pəšar-millətâ mənê; **b** mənā^{h} 'ĕlāhâ malkū^{w}tāk wəhašləmah

a '*This is the interpretation of the word mina (məne)*

b *God has determined your reign and has brought it to completion.*'

Daniel 5:27

a təqel təqī^{y}ltā^{h} bəmōzanyâ; **b** wəhištəkaḥat ḥassī^{y}r

a '*(As for) shekel (təqel), you have been weighed in the scales*

b *and you have been found lacking.*'

Daniel 5:28

a pəres pərī^{y}sat malkū^{w}tāk; **b** wī^{y}hī^{y}bat ləmāday ū^{w}pārās

a '*(As for) half-mina (pə res), your kingdom is divided,*

b *and it is (hereby) given to the Medes and Persians.*'

Daniel 5:29

a וְהַלְבִּ֫שׁוּ לְדָנִיֵּאל אַרְגְּוָנָא

b וְהַמְנִיכָא דִי דַהֲבָא עַל־צַוְּארֵהּ

c וְהַכְרִ֫זוּ עֲלוֹהִי דִּי־לֶהֱוֵא שַׁלִּיט תַּלְתָּא בְּמַלְכוּתָא

Daniel 5:30

בֵּהּ בְּלֵילְיָא קְטִיל בֵּלְאשַׁצַּר מַלְכָּא כַשְׂדָּיָא

Daniel 6:1

a וְדָרְיָוֶשׁ מָדָיָא קַבֵּל מַלְכוּתָא

b כְּבַר שְׁנִין שִׁתִּין וְתַרְתֵּין

Test yourself

a məqī^{y}m mē'aprâ (note the long ē without mater) miskē^{y}nâ (**מִסְכֵּינָא**) miqqilqiltâ (**מִקִּלְקְלְתָּא**)

b mərī^{y}m ḥaśśī^{y}kâ lə'ātābū^{w}təhō^{w}n 'im ṣaddī^{y}qayyâ rabrəbē^{y} (**רַבְרְבֵי**) 'āləmâ.

c wəkursē^{y} (**וְכָרְסֵי**) yəqārâ maḥsē^{y}n ləhō^{w}n.

d 'ărē^{y} qədām yəyāy gəlan 'ō^{w}bādē^{y} bənē^{y} 'ănāšâ

e millǝra‘ ’atqēʸn (אַתְקֵין) gēʸhinnām lǝraššīʸ‘ayyâ.

f wǝṣaddīʸqayyâ ‘ābǝdēʸ rǝ‘ūʷtēʸh (note the dot in the he indicating this is a true consonant, not a mater) šaklēʸl (שַׁכְלֵיל) lǝhōʷn tēbel (note the long ē without mater).

For future reference, the version of the text with targumic spelling is the following (see Unit 22):

a מְקִים מֵעַפְרָא מְסכֵינָא מְקַלְקְלְתָא

b מְרִים חַשִׁיכָא לְאָתָבוּתְהוֹן עִם צַדִיקַיָא רַבְרְבֵי עָלְמָא

c וְכֻרסֵי יְקָרָא מַחסֵין לְהוֹן

d אֲרֵי קֳדָם יְיָ גְלַן עוֹבָדֵי בְנֵי אֱנָשָׁא

e מִלְרַע אַתקֵין גֵיהִנָם לְרַשִׁיעַיָא

f וְצַדִיקַיָא עָבְדֵי רְעוּתֵיה שַׁכלֵיל לְהוֹן תֵבֵל

UNIT 4

Practice 1

2 a הוּא אֱלָהָא חַיָא; **b** מְהֵימַן הוּא; **c** הוּא מִתְבְּנֵא; **d** הִיא תְּקוּם לְעָלְמַיָּא; **e** הִיא בָּבֶל; **f** אַנְתְּ עֶזְרָא; **g** עִדָּנָא אֲנָה יָדְעֵת **j** ;אֲנָה נְבוּכַדְנֶצַּר **i** ;אִנּוּן בְּנֵיהוֹן וּנְשֵׁיהוֹן **h** ;אַנְתּוּן זָבְנִין

Practice 2

a קבל; **b** שפר; **c** נשם; **d** קדם; **e** נזק; **f** מנח; **g** שפר; **h** קים/קום; **i** אלה; **j** עבד; **k** אנש; **l** יתר; **m** עשׁת; **n** מלך; **o** קדשׁ

Practice 3

a יום; **b** טין; **c** רוח; **d** קול; **e** סוף; **f** אות; **g** שׂים; **h** טור

Practice 4

a 6, **b** 5, **c** 1, **d** 9, **e** 10, **f** 4, **g** 8, **h** 3, **i** 2, **j** 7

Practice 5

a 9 + כ; **b** 5; **c** 8 + ב; **d** 10; **e** 1 + ב; **f** 11 + ב; **g** 2; **h** 4 + ב; **i** 7 + ב; **j** 6 + ל; **k** 12; **l** 3

Test yourself

a 2 or 10, **b** 4, **c** 9, **d** 6, **e** 8, **f** 5, **g** 1, **h** 2 or 10, **i** 3, **j** 7

UNIT 5

Practice 1

a אֱלָהִין; **b** קַרְנַיִן; **c** חַכִּימִין; **d** רַגְלַיִן; **e** חֵיוָן; **f** יוֹמִין; **g** פִּתְיחָן; **h** עָלְמִין; **i** שִׁנַּיִן; **j** רַבְרְבָן

Practice 2

a תַּקִּיף; **b** זַמָּר; **c** מַחְלְקָה; **d** סוֹף; **e** שַׂגִּיאָה

Practice 3

1 a 4 (-ēʸ); **b** 2 (-â); **c** 5 (-āt); **d** 1 (-ān); **e** 6 (-ayyâ); **f** 3 (no ending)

2

a סָרְכַיָּא; **b** כְּתָבָא; **c** אֶצְבְּעָן; **d** לְחֵנָתָא; **e** לִשָּׁנַיָּא; **f** תַּקִּיפָה; **g** גַּבָּא; **h** גֻּבְרַיָּא; **i** חַיָּא; **j** שַׂגִּיאָן

3

a חָכְמַת; b אֱלָהֵי; c סָרְכֵי; d יְקֵדַת; e שְׁמָהָת; f נִכְסֵי; g עֲבִידַת; h חֲנֻכַּת; i בְּנֵי; j זְנֵי

4

Noun/adj.abs./cstr. sing.	det. sing.	plural abs.	pl. cstr.	pl. det.
עַתִּיק (*old*)	עַתִּיקָא	עַתִּיקִין	עַתִּיקֵי	עַתִּיקַיָּא
טָב (*good*, root: טוב)	טָבָא	טָבִין	טָבֵי	טָבַיָּא
זְעֵיר zə ʿēʸr (*little*)	זְעֵירָא	זְעֵירִין	זְעֵירֵי	זְעֵירַיָּא
דִּין (*judgment*, root: דין)	דִּינָא	דִּינִין	דִּינֵי	דִּינַיָּא
טוּר (*mountain*)	טוּרָא	טוּרִין	טוּרֵי	טוּרַיָּא
חַכִּים (*wise*)	חַכִּימָא	חַכִּימִין	חַכִּימֵי	חַכִּימַיָּא
לִשָּׁן (*tongue*)	לִשָּׁנָא	לִשָּׁנִין	לִשָּׁנֵי	לִשָּׁנַיָּא
קָל (*voice*, root: קול)	קָלָא	קָלִין	קָלֵי	קָלַיָּא
שְׁאָר (*remnant*)	שְׁאָרָא	שְׁאָרִין	שְׁאָרֵי	שְׁאָרַיָּא

5

Noun/adj.abs. sing.	cstr. sing.	det. sing.	plural abs.	pl. cstr.	pl. det.
עַתִּיקָה (*old*)	עַתִּיקַת	עַתִּיקְתָּא	עַתִּיקָן	עַתִּיקָת	עַתִּיקָתָא
טָבָה (*good*, root: טוב)	טָבַת	טָבְתָּא	טָבָן	טָבָת	טָבָתָא
זְעֵירָה zə ʿēʸrāʰ (*little*)	זְעֵירַת	זְעֵירְתָּא	זְעֵירָן	זְעֵירָת	זְעֵירָתָא
חֲבוּלָה (*crime*)	חֲבוּלַת	חֲבוּלְתָּא	חֲבוּלָן	חֲבוּלָת	חֲבוּלָתָא
חֵיוָה (*animal*, root: חיי)	חֵיוַת	חֵיוְתָא	חֵיוָן	חֵיוָת	חֵיוָתָא
חַכִּימָה (*wise*)	חַכִּימַת	חַכִּימְתָּא	חַכִּימָן	חַכִּימָת	חַכִּימָתָא
תַּקִּיפָה (*strong*)	תַּקִּיפַת	תַּקִּיפְתָּא	תַּקִּיפָן	תַּקִּיפָת	תַּקִּיפָתָא
חָכְמָה ḥokmāʰ (*wisdom*)	חָכְמַת	חָכְמְתָא	חָכְמָן	חָכְמָת	חָכְמָתָא

Practice 4

a חֵיוְתָא תַּקִּיפְתָּא; b מַלְכְּתָא חַכִּימְתָּא; c בְּרָא חַכִּים; d חֵיוָתָא תַּקִּיפָן; e בְּנַיָּא חַכִּימִין; f קַדִּישֵׁי אֱלָהָא; g חַכִּימֵי מַלְכָּא; h מַלְכִין תַּקִּיפִין; i מַלְכָתָא חַכִּימָתָא; j מִלַּת סָרְכַיָּא

Daniel 6:2

b ־ִין - masc. pl. abs. on עֲשַׂר

c ־ַיָּא - masc. pl. det. on אֲחַשְׁדַּרְפַּן

Daniel 6:3

a ־ִין - masc. pl. abs. on סָרֵךְ

b ־ָא - masc. sing. det. on טְעֵם

c ־ָא - masc. sing. det. on מֶלֶךְ

Daniel 6:4

a יָּא - masc. pl. det. on סָרֵךְ

b ה ָ - fem. sing. abs. on יַתִּיר

c א ָ - masc. sing. det. on - מֶלֶךְ; תָא- fem. sing. det. ending on מַלְכוּ

Test yourself

a נְבִיאֲתָא f.s. det. of נְבִיאָה *prophetess*

b עִדָּנָא m.s. det. of עִדָּן *time*

e דִּקְלִין m.p. abs. of דְּקֶל *date-palm*

f זֵיתִין m.p. abs. of זַיִת *olive tree*; בִּקְעֲתָא f.s. det. of בִּקְעָה *valley*

g מַלְכָּא m.s. det. of מֶלֶךְ *king*

h בְּנֵי m.p. cstr. of בַּר *son, child*; דִּינָא m.s. det. of דִּין *judgment*

UNIT 6

Practice 1

1

a שָׁאֵל; **b** יָהֲבִין; **c** יָכְלִין; **d** כָּתְבָה; **e** נָקְשָׁן; **f** סָלְקָן; **g** יָדְעֵי; **h** רָפְסָה; **i** יָהֵב; **j** יָקְדְתָּא

2

root	m.s. abs.	f.s. abs.	m. pl. abs.	f. pl. abs.
אבד (*to perish*)	אָבֵד	אָבְדָה	אָבְדִין	אָבְדָן
שׁאל (*to ask for or request*)	שָׁאֵל	שָׁאֲלָה	שָׁאֲלִין	שָׁאֲלָן
נפק (*to go out*)	נָפֵק	נָפְקָה	נָפְקִין	נָפְקָן
סלק (*to go up*)	סָלֵק	סָלְקָה	סָלְקִין	סָלְקָן
עבד (*to do, make*)	עָבֵד	עָבְדָה	עָבְדִין	עָבְדָן

Practice 2

1 a m.s. abs.; **b** m.s. abs.; **c** m.p. abs.; **d** m.s. abs.; **e** f.s. abs.; **f** m.p. cstr.; **g** m.p. abs.; **h** m. pl. abs.; **i** f. pl. abs.; **j** m. pl. cstr.

2 (Word order may vary.)

a חָכְמָה אָמְרָה; **b** שָׁמַע קַרְנָא; **c** עָבְדָה אָתִין וְתִמְהִין; **d** יָדְעִין דִּבְחִין; **e** פָּלְחָן אֱלָהָא

Practice 3

a בְּרִיךְ; **b** פְּלִיגָה; **c** זְקִיף; **d** חֲשִׁיבִין; **e** פְּתִיחָן

Daniel 6:5

b עִלָּה (with ה ָ - fem. sing. abs. עִלָּה)

מַלְכוּתָא (with תָא- fem. sing. det. ending on מַלְכוּ)

c יָכְלִין m.p. abs. part. of יכל

שְׁחִיתָה f.s. abs. pass. part. of שׁחת

Daniel 6:6

a גֻּבְרַיָּא (with יָּא- - masc. pl. det. גְּבַר)

אָמְרִין m.p. part. of אמר

Test yourself

a אַנְתְּי אָזְלָה

b אֲנַחְנָא סָלְקָן וְנָחֲתָן or אֲנַחְנָא סָלְקִין וְנָחֲתִין

c אִנּוּן יָדְעִין

d יָדְעַת בִּינָה

e אַנְתְּ יָתֵב

f הוּא פָּלַח

g אִנּוּן פָּלְחֵי בֵּית אֱלָהָא

h אֲנַחְנָא אָזְלָן or אֲנַחְנָא אָזְלִין

i יָדְעַת זְמָר

j יָתְבֵי אַרְעָא

UNIT 7

Practice 1

1

sing. abs./cstr.	sing. det.	pl. abs.	pl. cstr.	pl. det.
חֲמַר (*wine*)	חַמְרָא	חַמְרִין	חַמְרֵי	חַמְרַיָּא
תְּרַע (*gate*)	תַּרְעָא	תַּרְעִין	תַּרְעֵי	תַּרְעַיָּה

2

a פְּשַׁר; **b** אֲרַע; **c** סְגַן; **d** מְדִינָה; **e** חַכִּים; **f** אֲחִידָה; **g** קְטַר; **h** כְּתָב; **i** יְקָר; **j** הֲדַר

3

a אַנְתְּי אָמְרָה פִּשְׁרָא; **b** חַכִּימֵי בָבֶל שָׁמְעִין אֲחִידְתָא; **c** הִיא אָכְלָה אַרְעָא; **d** אֲנָה כָּתֵב לִסְגְנַיָּא or אֲנָה כָּתְבָה לִסְגְנַיָּא; **e** הוּא נָפֵק מִן מְדִינְתָא

4

sing. abs./cstr.	sing. det.	pl. abs.	pl. cstr.	pl. det.
בְּעֵל *master (of)*, like כְּסַף	בַּעֲלָא	בַּעֲלִין	בַּעֲלֵי	בַּעֲלַיָּא
צְלֵם *image (of)*, like כְּסַף	צַלְמָא	צַלְמִין	צַלְמֵי	צַלְמַיָּא
עֲבֵד *slave (of)*, like כְּסַף	עַבְדָא	עַבְדִין	עַבְדֵי	עַבְדַיָּא
תְּקֵל *shekel (of)*, like סְפַר	תִּקְלָא	תִּקְלִין	תִּקְלֵי	תִּקְלַיָּא

N.B. answer: If the shewa in **צַלְמָא** represented a murmured vowel, then the preceding patach (a short vowel) would be in an open, unaccented syllable. Short vowels are almost always in closed syllables (i.e. syllables beginning and ending with consonants), unless they are followed by a guttural and a hateph vowel (as in בַּעֲלָא).

5

a garmī^{y}n גַּרְמִין

b dayyānī^{y}n דַּיָּנִין

c nahărī^{y}n נַהֲרִין

d ḥabrī^{y}n חַבְרִין

e yarḥī^{y}n יַרְחִין

f dibḥī^{y}n דִּבְחִין

g zammārī^{y}n זַמָּרִין

h ḥadtī^{y}n חַדְתִּין

i signī^{y}n סִגְנִין

j liššānī^{y}n לִשָּׁנִין

6

a צַלְמָא; **b** טַעְמָא . . . יָהֲבִין; **c** עַבְדֵי; **d** מַלְכָּא וְאָמַר; **e** עַיְנִין כְּעַיְנֵי; **f** עֲבִידַת בֵּית אֱלָהָא; **g** חֶלְמָא וּפִשְׁרָא; **h** עָבְדֵי צִדְקְתָא; **i** אִגְּרָן; **j** מַלְכְּתָא לְבֵית

Practice 2

a *the kings*; **b** *ones arising* or *they were arising*; **c** *illumination of*; **d** *walls*; **e** *ones giving* or *they were giving*; **f** *haste of*; **g** *one writing* or *she was writing*; **h** *the slave*; **i** *gates of*; **j** *need of*; **k** *house of*; **l** *the greatness*; **m** *matter of*; **n** *the men*; **o** *the exile*

Practice 3

a מִלַּיָּא רַבְרְבָתָא; **b** אֻמְּתָא רַבְּתָא; **c** אֱלָהָא חַיָּא; **d** בַּאֲרַע חַיַּיָּא; **e** כָּל־עַמְמַיָּא וְאֻמַּיָּא וְלִשָּׁנַיָּא

Practice 4

a מַלְכַיָּא; **b** נָפְקָן; **c** נַהִירוּתָא; **d** עַיְנָא; **e** יָכְלִין; **f** טַעְמִין; **g** גָּלוּת; **h** בְּרִיכָה; **i** חָכְמְתָא; **j** פִּשְׁרַיָּא; **k** חַשְׁחוּת; **l** מִלֵּי; **m** בַּיְתָא; **n** עַמְמַיָּא; **o** כְּתָבָא; **p** עִדָּנִין; **q** מְדִינְתָא; **r** פְּתִיחָן; **s** רְעוּתָא; **t** כָּהֲנַיָּא

Daniel 6:7

a *Then the officials* (סָרְכַיָּא m.p. det. סָרֵךְ) *and the satraps gathered hectically around the king* (מַלְכָּא m.s. det. מֶלֶךְ)

b *and they said* (אָמְרִין m.p. abs. part. אֲמַר) *to him: 'O, Darius, O king* (מַלְכָּא m.s. det. מֶלֶךְ) (more literally, *the king*), *for ever* (עָלְמִין m.p. abs. עָלַם) *live!'*

Daniel 6:8

a *All the officials* (סָרְכֵי m.p. cstr. סָרֵךְ) *of the kingdom* (מַלְכוּתָא f.s. det. מַלְכוּ)

b – *the prefects* (סִגְנַיָּא m.p. det. סְגַן), *and the satraps, the counsellors, and the governors advised*

c *to establish the statute* (קְיָם m.s. cstr. קְיָם) *of the king* (מַלְכָּא m.s. det. מֶלֶךְ)

d *and to make severe a prohibition* (אֱסָר m.s. cstr. אֱסָר) *that anyone who prays a prayer* (lit. *who requests a request*)

e *to any god or person, within 30 days*

f *(except to you, O king), will be thrown to the den* (**גֹּב** m.s. cstr. **גֹּב**) *of the lions.*

Daniel 6:9

a *'Now, O king, you should establish the prohibition* (**אֱסָרָא** m.s. det. **אֱסָר**) *and you should sign the decree* (**כְּתָבָא** m.s. det. of **כְּתָב**)

b *so that no one will change (it),*

c *according to the law* (**דָּת** m.s. cstr. **דָּת**) *of the Medes and Persians, that it not be revoked.*

Test yourself

a חֵיוָן רַבְרְבָן סָלְקָן מִן־יַמָּא

b גַּפִּין

c חֵיוָה . . . דָּמְיָה

d עִלְעִין

e חֵיוְתָא

f חֵיוָה

g חֵיוָתָא

UNIT 8

Practice 1

a pəʿal; **b** paʿʿel; **c** pəʿal; **d** haphʿel; **e** pəʿal; **f** pəʿal; **g** paʿʿel; **h** haphʿel; **i** pəʿal; **j** haphʿel

Practice 2

a אֲזַל; **b** אֲכַלוּ; **c** נְפַלוּ; **d** נְטְלֵת; **e** עֲבַדְתְּ or עֲבַדְתָּ; **f** נְפַקָה; **g** שִׁמְעֵת; **h** תִּקְפַת; **i** שְׁלַחְנָא; **j** סִלְקַת

Practice 3

a עֲבַדוּ pəʿal 3mp *they made*; **b** הֲוַיְתָ pəʿal 2ms *you were*; **c** יְהַב pəʿal 3ms *he gave*; **d** אֲכַלוּ pəʿal 3mp *they ate*; **e** שַׁבְּחֵת paʿʿel 1cs *I praised*; **f** קַבֵּל paʿʿel 3ms *he received*; **g** הַנְפֵּק haphʿel 3ms *he brought out*; **h** הַשְׁפֵּלְתְּ haphʿel 2ms *you humbled*; **i** הַרְגִּזוּ haphʿel 3mp *they angered*; **j** הַכְרִזוּ haphʿel 3mp *they proclaimed*

Practice 4

a הַצְלַח; **b** שַׁבְּחֵת; **c** שַׁבְּחוּ; **d** הַשְׁכַּחְנָא; **e** הַשְׁכַּחוּ; **f** בַּקַּרוּ; **g** הַדַּרְתְּ or הַדַּרְתָּ; **h** הַשְׁפֵּלְתְּ or הַשְׁפֵּלְתָּ; **i** שַׁבַּחְתִּי; **j** הַדְּרֵת; **k** קַטִּלוּ; **l** הַנְפֵּק; **m** בַּטִּלוּ; **n** שַׁכֵּן; **o** הַשְׁפִּלוּ; **p** בַּקָּרָה; **q** הַכְרִזוּ; **r** שַׁבַּחְנָא; **s** הַרְגִּשׁוּ; **t** הַדְּרַת

Daniel 6:10

רְשַׁם; אֱסָרָא

Daniel 6:11

a יְדַע; **b** כְּתָבָא; **c** פְּתִיחָן; **d** יוֹמָא; **f** עָבֵד

Daniel 6:12

a הַרְגִּשׁוּ; **b** הַשְׁכַּחוּ

Daniel 6:13

a קְרֵבוּ or קְרִבוּ; אָמְרִין; **c** רְשַׁמְתָּ or רְשַׁמְתְּ; **e** יוֹמִין; **g** אָמַר; **h** מִלְּתָא

Test yourself

1 The pəʿal has the vowel pattern ə-a and no doubling of the middle root consonant, while the paʿʿel has a-e and a doubled middle root consonant.

2 The pəʿal indicates the basic idea of a verb. The paʿʿel represents either a transitivization of the pəʿal or an intensification of the basic verbal idea. The haphʿel often represents causation, where the subject causes something else to perform the verbal action.

3 אֲזַל אֲזַלַת or אַזְלַת, אֲזַלְתְּ, אֲזַלְתָּ, אֲזַלְתִּי, אַזְלֵת, אֲזַלוּ, אֲזַלָה, אֲזַלְתּוּן, אֲזַלְתֵּן, אֲזַלְנָא ; קְטַל, קַטְלַת, קְטַלְתְּ or קְטַלְתָּ, קַטֵּלְתְּ, קַטֵּלְתִּי,קַטְלֵת קַטִּלוּ, קַטִּלָה, קַטֵּלְתּוּן, קַטֵּלְתֵּן, קַטֵּלְנָא ; הַשְׁפֵּל, הַשְׁפְּלַת, הַשְׁפֵּלְתְּ or הַשְׁפֵּלְתָּ, הַשְׁפֵּלְתִּי, הַשְׁפְּלֵת, הַשְׁפִּלוּ, הַשְׁפִּלָה, הַשְׁפֵּלְתּוּן, הַשְׁפֵּלְתֵּן, הַשְׁפֵּלְנָא

UNIT 9

Practice 1

	לְ	בְּ	מִן	עִם	עַל	קֳדָם
1cs	לִי	בִּי	מִנִּי	עִמִּי	עֲלַי	קֳדָמַי
2ms	לָךְ	בָּךְ	מִנָּךְ	עִמָּךְ	עֲלָיךְ	קֳדָמָיךְ
2fs	לֵכִי	בֵּכִי	מִנֵּכִי	עִמֵּכִי	עֲלֵיכִי	קֳדָמֵיכִי
3ms	לֵהּ	בֵּהּ	מִנֵּהּ	עִמֵּהּ	עֲלוֹהִי	קֳדָמוֹהִי
3fs	לַהּ	בַּהּ	מִנַּהּ	עִמַּהּ	עֲלַיהּ	קֳדָמַיהּ
1cp	לַנָא	בַּנָא	מִנַּנָא	עִמַּנָא	עֲלֵינָא	קֳדָמֵינָא
2mp	לְכֹם	בְּכֹם	מִנְּכֹם	עִמְּכֹם	עֲלֵיכֹם	קֳדָמֵיכֹם
2fp	לְכֵן	בְּכֵן	מִנְּכֵן	עִמְּכֵן	עֲלֵיכֵן	קֳדָמֵיכֵן
3mp	לְהֹם	בְּהֹם	מִנְּהֹם	עִמְּהֹם	עֲלֵיהֹם	קֳדָמֵיהֹם
3fp	לְהֵן	בְּהֵן	מִנְּהֵן	עִמְּהֵן	עֲלֵיהֵן	קֳדָמֵיהֵן

Practice 2

a 4; **b** 7; **c** 1; **d** 5; **e** 10; **f** 8; **g** 2; **h** 3; **i** 6; **j** 9

Practice 3

a 4; **b** 5; **c** 2; **d** 1; **e** 3

Practice 5

a אֲמַר קֳדָמֵיהֹם; **b** שְׁמַעַת עֲלַיהּ; **c** אֲמַרְתְּ קֳדָמַי; **d** אֲמַרְנָא קֳדָמָיךְ; **e** שְׁמַעַת עֲלוֹהִי; **f** אֲמַרְתְּ קֳדָמוֹהִי; **g** אֲמַר קֳדָמַי; **h** שְׁמַעַת עֲלָיךְ; **i** שְׁמַעַת עֲלוֹהִי; **j** אֲמַרְתְּ קֳדָמַיהּ

Practice 6

a 6; **b** 1; **c** 11; **d** 7; **e** 12; **f** 4; **g** 2; **h** 15; **i** 13; **j** 8; **k** 3; **l** 5; **m** 10; **n** 9; **o** 14

Practice 7

a אִגְּרָתָךְ *your* (m.s.) *letters* אִגַּרְתָּךְ *your* (m.s.) *letter*

b מַלְכוּתַהּ *her kingdom* מַלְכְוָתַהּ *her kingdoms*

c אִגַּרְתִּי *my letter* — אִגְּרָתִי *my letters*

d מַלְכוּתְהֹם *their* (m.p.) *kingdom* — מַלְכְוָתְהֹם *their* (m.p.) *kingdoms*

e אִגְּרָתַ֫נָא *our letters* — אִגַּרְתַּ֫נָה *our letter*

Practice 8

1

a *his* 3ms // סָרְכֵהּ

b *their* 3mp // יוֹמְהֹם or יוֹמְהוֹן

c *my* 1cs // אֱלָהִי

d *his* 3ms // חַבְרֵהּ

e *their* 3mp // קַרְצְהֹם or קַרְצְהוֹן

f *your* 2ms // עֲרָךְ

g *your* 2ms // זִיוָךְ

h *my* 1cs // עַבְדִּי

i *his* 3ms // עַבְדֵּהּ

j *his* 3ms // בְּרֵהּ

2 (In the following, the sing. abs. form is listed first, followed by the pl. form.)

a בַּר // בְּנַיהּ; **b** מֶ֫לֶךְ // מַלְכַ֫יָּא; **c** חֲבַר // חַבְר֫וֹהִי; **d** מַלְכוּ // מַלְכְוָתְהֹם; **e** מִלָּה // מִלַּי; **f** מְדִינָה // מְדִינָתָךְ; **g** חֲבוּלָה // חֲבוּלָתְכֵן; **h** אָת // אָתוֹהִי; **i** אֱלָהּ // אֱלָהָיךְ; **j** זִיו // זִיוֹהִי

Daniel 6:17

a מַלְכָּא אֲמַר

c עָנֵה מַלְכָּא וְאָמַר

d אֱלָהָךְ... פָּלַח

Daniel 6:18

b מַלְכָּא בְּעִזְקְתֵהּ וּבְעִזְקָת רַבְרְבָנ֫וֹהִי

Daniel 6:19

a אֲזַל מַלְכָּא לְהֵיכְלֵהּ

b קֳדָמ֫וֹהִי

c עֲל֫וֹהִי

Daniel 6:20

a מַלְכָּא

b אֲזַל

Test yourself

1

a 3 מִן

b 8 בְּ and מַלְכוּ

c 10 כָּהֵן

d 9 עַם

e 2 מֶלֶךְ

f 5 יְעֵט

g 1 אֱלָהּ

h 4 בְּ and יַד

i 7 מִשְׁכַּן

j 6 אֱלָהּ

2

13 a *By me a decree was set* (or, *I set a decree*)

b *that anyone who volunteers in my kingdom from the people, Israel,*

c *and its priests, the Levites, to go to Jerusalem with you, may go.*

14 a *For, from before the king and his seven counsellors* (literally *seven of his counsellors*),

b *(a messenger) was sent to investigate about Judah and Jerusalem*

c *by the law of your God, which is in your hand,*

15 a *and to bring silver and gold*

b *that the king and his counsellors have donated*

c *to the God of Israel whose dwelling place is in Jerusalem (lit., who in Jerusalem is his dwelling place).*

UNIT 10

Practice 1

a 3; **b** 5; **c** 4; **d** 1; **e** 2

Practice 2

a. עַבְדֵהּ___ דִּי־אֱלָהָא; **b** שְׁמֵהּ___ דִּי־אֱלָהָא; **c** אֱלָהֲהֹם_// אֱלָהֲהוֹן__ דִּי־שַׁדְרַךְ מֵישַׁךְ וַעֲבֵד נְגוֹ;
d שָׁרְשֵׁהּ___ דִּי אִילָנָא; **e** אֱלָהֵהּ___ דִּי־דָנִיֵּאל

Practice 3

a בְּרַהּ דִּי־מַלְכְּתָא

b מִלְּתֵהּ דִּי־אֱלָהָא

c יוֹמֵיהֹם / יוֹמֵיהוֹן דִּי־מַלְכַיָּא

d אִגְּרַתְהֵן דִּי־מַלְכְּתָא

e עַבְדוֹהִי דִּי־אֱלָהָא

Practice 4

a *because*; **b** *who*; **c** *of, who*; **d** *so that, who*; **e** *whose*; **f** *which*; **g** *which*; **h** *who*; **i** *whose*; **j** *so that*

Daniel 6:21

a *And when he* (i.e. *the king*) *approached toward the den* (גב) *of Daniel*; **b** *with a despairing voice* (קָל) *he* (i.e. *the king*) *cried out*; **c** *the king* (מֶלֶךְ) *spoke up* (ענה) *and said* (אמר) *to Daniel* (דָנִיֵּאל);

d *'Daniel* (דָּנִיֵּאל), *servant* (עֲבֵד) *of the living God* (אֱלָהּ); **e** *your God* (אֱלָהּ) *whom you serve* (פלח) *continuously;* **f** *was he able to save you from* (מִן) *the lions* (אַרְיֵה)?

Daniel 6:22

a *Then* (אֱדַיִן), *Daniel* (דָּנִיֵּאל) *spoke with* (עִם) *the king* (מֶלֶךְ):

b *O king, for ever* (עָלַם) *live!*

Daniel 6:23

a *'My God* (אֱלָהּ) *sent* (שׁלח) *his angel* (מַלְאַךְ); **b** *and he closed* (סגר) *the mouth* (פֻּם) *of the lions* (אַרְיֵה); **c** *and they did not injure me;* **d** *since before* (קֳדָם) *him;* **e** *innocence* (זָכוּ) *was accredited to me* (lit. *was found to me*); **f** *and also before* (קֳדָם) *you, O king,;* **g** *a crime* (חֲבוּלָה) *I did not commit.'*

Test yourself

b דִּי עִדָּנָא

c מִלְּתָא

e דִּי הֵן חֶלְמָא

f כִּדְבָה וּשְׁחִיתָה The words are used as adjectives and match the noun in gender, number, and state

g עִדָּנָא

h חֶלְמָא

i דִּי פִשְׁרֵהּ The antecedent to *its* is *dream*, which is masculine

UNIT 11

Practice 1

(the word order is somewhat flexible and the verb can come before or after its subject and/or object):

a שְׁמַעוּ מִלְּתָא; **b** שִׁמְעֵת מִלַּת מַלְכְּתָא // שִׁמְעֵת מִלְּתַהּ דִּי מַלְכְּתָא; **c** מַלְכְּתָא אַמְרַת לְהֹם; **d** שְׁלַחְתְּ לַנָא מִלָּה; **e** אֲמַרְנָא לְהֵן מִלָּה; **f** שְׁלַחַת מִלָּה לְמַלְכְּתָא; **g** אֲמַרְתּוּן לְמַלְכְּתָא מִלָּה; **h** אֲמַרַת לַהּ; **i** שְׁלַחְתִּי מִלָּה לֵהּ; **j** שְׁמַעְנָא מִלְּתָא

Practice 2

a 2fp שׁלח *to send;* **b** 3ms סגד *to worship;* **c** 3mp פלח *to serve;* **d** 1cs סבר *to think;* **e** 2fs שׁפר *to be beautiful;* **f** 1cp סגד *to worship;* **g** 2mp סגד *to worship;* **h** 1cp שׁפר *to be beautiful;* **i** 3mp קטל *to kill;* **j** 2mp לבשׁ *to wear*

Practice 3

a אַל תִּקְטֻל; **b** לָא תִסְגְּדוּן; **c** אַל תִּשְׁמַעִי; **d** לָא יִשְׁלְחוּן פִּתְגָם לְמַלְכָּא; **e** אֶפְלַח בְּהֵיכְלָא

Practice 4

a כְּתֻבוּ; **b** אֲכֻל; **c** סְגֻדָה; **d** אֲכֻלִי; **e** שְׁבֻקוּ

Practice 5

a *The king sent (messengers) to gather* (מִכְנַשׁ from כנשׁ) *the prefects;* **b** *You are able to reveal* (מִגְלֵא from גלי) *this secret;* **c** *What is good to do* (מֶעְבַּד from עבד), *you will do;* **d** *They were not* *able to read* (**מִקְרֵא** from **קרי**) *the writing* (lit. . . . *the writing to read*); **e** *As he wishes* (**מִצְבְּיֵהּ** from **צבי**) (or, according to his wishing) *he does in the host of the heavens.* NB: In the phrase **כְּמִצְבְּיֵהּ**, the yod of the root **צבי** is preserved with the 3ms pronominal suffix.

Practice 6

a 3; **b** 1; **c** 5; **d** 2; **e** 4

Daniel 3:8

In that time Chaldean men approached and slandered the Judeans (lit. *they ate the Judeans' morsels*).

Daniel 3:9

They spoke up and said to Nebuchadnezzar, the king, O king, live forever!

Daniel 3:10

a *You, king, made a decree that every person who hears the sound of the horn,* **b** *the pipe, the lute, the lyre, harps, or a trumpet* **c** *and all the types of music will fall and bow down to the image of gold*

Daniel 3:11

and anyone who does not fall and bow down will be thrown to the middle of the furnace of burning fire.

Daniel 3:12

a *There are Judean men whom you appointed over the work of the province of Babylon – Shadrach, Meshach, and Abed-Nego.* **b** *These men do not pay heed to your decree, O king;* **c** *your God they do not serve and to the image of gold that you erected they are not bowing down.*

Test yourself

a בְּעִדָּנָא דִּי תִשְׁמְעוּן

b תִּסְגְּדוּן לְצֶ֫לֶם דַּהֲבָא

c כֹּל שָׁלְטָנַיָּא יִפְלְחוּן לֵהּ

d שְׁלַח לְמִכְנַשׁ כֹּל שִׁלְטוֹנֵי מְדִינָתָא

e שְׁבֻ֫קוּ לַעֲבִידַת בֵּית אֱלָהָא

UNIT 12

Practice 1

(With the exception of words in the construct state, the order of words in Aramaic is flexible.)

a רַעְיוֹנֵי (רַעְיוֹנַיהּ דִּי or) מַלְכְּתָא יְבַהֲלוּן הִמּוֹ

b מַלְכְּתָא תְּבַקַּר עַל־קִרְיְתָא

c חַבֵּל לְקִרְיְתָא אַל־תְּחַבֵּל הִמּוֹ

d אֱבַקַּר עַל־רַעְיוֹנָךְ

e לָא תְּבַהֲלִין הִמּוֹ

Practice 2

1a pa‘‘el 3mp pref. conj. טעם *you will feed*; **b** pa‘‘el infinitive קטל *to slay*; **c** pa‘‘el m.s. pass. part. ערב *mixed*; **d** pa‘‘el m.s. part. הלך *walking*; **e** pa‘‘el 2ms suff. conj. הדר *you honoured*; **f** pa‘‘el infinitive נסך *to pour out*; **g** pa‘‘el 3mp suff. conj. בטל *they caused to cease*; **h** pa‘‘el 3fs / 2ms pref. conj. קרב *she/you will offer sacrifice*; **i** pa‘‘el m.p. part. צבע *they will drench*; **j** pa‘‘el infinitive כפת *to bind*

2 a *I praise* (מְשַׁבַּח pa. m.s. act. part.) *you, God*; **b** *The name of God* (lit. *the God*) *is blessed* (מְבָרַךְ pa. m.s. pass. part. [cf. pa. m.s. act. part. מְבָרֵךְ or מְבָרֵךְ]) *for ever and ever* (lit. *from eternity to eternity*); **c** *Scatter* (בַּדַּרוּ pa. m.p. impv. [NB: the pa. 3mp suff. conj. would look and sound the same]) *its fruit!*; **d** *I praised* (שַׁבְּחֵת pa. 3ms suff. conj.) *the one alive forever* (lit. *the one alive of forever*); **e** *They praised* (שַׁבַּחוּ pa. 3mp suff. conj. [NB: the pa. m.s. impv. would look and sound the same]) *the gods of gold and silver*; **f** *Then, Daniel spoke* (מַלִּל pa. 3ms suff. conj.) *with the king*; **g** *Let him seek* (יְבַקַּר pa. 3ms juss. or pref. conj. [NB: both forms would look and sound the same]) *in the book of records*; **h** *He said to make these people cease* (בַּטָּלָה pa. inf.); **i** *And the God who established* (שַׁכִּן pa. 3ms suff. conj.) *his name there will overthrow* (יְמַגַּר pa. 3ms pref. conj.) *every king*.

Daniel 3:13

a *Then Nebuchadnezzar, in rage and anger, ordered* **b** *(his soldiers) to bring in Shadrach, Meshach, and Abed-Nego.* **c** *Then these men were brought before the king.*

Daniel 3:14

a *Nebuchadnezzar spoke up and said to them* **b** *Is it true, Shadrach, Meshach, and Abed-Nego* **c** *my gods you are not serving and to the image of gold that I have erected (you) are not bowing down?*

Daniel 3:15

a *Now, if you are ready,* (let it be the case) *that in the time that you hear the sound of the horn, the pipe, lute, the lyre, harps, or a trumpet,* **c** *and all the types of music you will fall and bow down to the image that I have made, (then all will be well).* **d** *If you do not bow down, immediately (or, in that moment) you will be thrown to the midst of the furnace of burning fire.* **e** *Who is (the) god who will deliver you from my hands?*

Daniel 3:16

a *Shadrach, Meshach, and Abed-Nego answered and said to the king* **b** *O Nebuchadnezzar, we do not need to return you an answer concerning this (matter).*

Test yourself

1. יְחַשֵּׁב pa‘‘el 3ms prefix-conj.; pə‘al: יַחְשֻׁב *he will consider*

2. יִתְקַף pə‘al 3ms prefix-conj.; pa‘‘el: יְתַקֵּף *he will strengthen*

3. יִקְרְבוּן pə‘al 3mp prefix-conj.; pa‘‘el: יְקָרְבוּן *they will bring near*

4. מְסָרֵיב pa‘‘el m.s. part.; pə‘al: סָרֵיב [= in Biblical Aramaic סָרֵב] *he will refuse;* שַׁלַּח pa‘‘el m.s. imperative.; pə‘al: שְׁלַח *send*

5. יַחְמְכוּן pə‘al 3mp prefix-conj.; pa‘‘el: יְחַמְּכוּן *they will instruct*

2.

וְכַסְפָּא זְנָה לָא מְקַבֵּל אֲנָה מִגַּבִּי

(If I, the seller [of this slave], say to you . . .) "*this silver I have not received from you . . .*"

The 2fs pronoun on the preposition מִן implies that the buyer and owner of the slave was a woman and, therefore, that women could own slaves and other property.

UNIT 13

Practice

a פָּלְחִין; **b** נִסְגֻּד; **c** יְהַשְׁפֵּל; **d** הַנְפֵּק; **e** יְבַהֵל; **f** הַרְגִּזוּ; **g** יַחְסְנוּן; **h** מִפְשַׁר; **i** כַּפָּתָה; **j** הַשְׁפֵּלְתְּ // הַשְׁפֵּלְתָּ; **k** מְהַחְצְפָה; **l** הַשְׁלֵט; **m** מְהַדַּר; **n** נְהַשְׁכַּח; **o** הַשְׁפָּלָה; **p** מַחְצְפָה; **q** הַשְׁמָדָה; **r** מְהַקְרְבִין; **s** יַצְּבָה; **t** הַשְׁכָּחָה

Daniel 3:17

a *If our God whom we serve is able* **b** *to deliver us from the furnace of burning fire and from your hand, O king, he will deliver (us).*

Daniel 3:18

a *But, if not, let it be known to you, O king, that we were not serving your god* **b** *and to the image of gold that you erected we did not bow down.*

Daniel 3:19

a *Then, Nebuchadnezzar was filled with rage . . . He responded and commanded to heat the furnace* **b** *seven times above (the temperature) to which it was normally heated.*

Daniel 3:20

a *and to (the) men, the valorous heroes who were in his army, he commanded (them) to bind Shadrach, Meshach, and Abed-Nego,* **b** *(then) to throw (them) into the furnace of burning fire.*

Test yourself

a יְהַנְפְּקוּן עֲלַיְכִי סְפַר

b אֲהַקְרֵב קֳדָמֹוהִי נִיחוֹחִין

c כֹּל סְפַר דִּי תְהַשְׁכְּחָן

d מָאנַיָּא הַשְׁלֵם קֳדָם אֱלָהּ

e תְהַשְׁכַּח דִּי קִרְיְתָא קִרְיָה מָרָדָה

UNIT 14

Practice

5:24 *Then, from before him the palm of the hand was sent* (שְׁלִיַח) *and this writing was inscribed* (רְשִׁים).

5:25 *This was the writing that was inscribed* (רְשִׁים)*: mina, mina, shekel, and half-minas.*

5:26 *This is the interpretation of the word mina* (məne)*: God has determined your reign and has brought it to completion;*

5:27 *(As for) shekel* (təqel)*: you have been weighed* (תְּקִילְתָּה) *in the scales and you have been found lacking;*

5:28 *(As for) half-mina* (pəres)*: your kingdom is divided* (פְּרִיסַת) *and (hereby) given* (יְהִיבַת) *to the Medes and Persians.*

Daniel 3:21

a *Then, these men were bound in their garments, their trousers, their hats, and their clothing* **b** *and were thrown to the midst of the furnace of burning fire.*

Daniel 3:22

a *Consequently, because the word of the king was urgent and (because) the furnace was heated exceedingly,* **b** *these men who had lifted Shadrach, Meshach, and Abed-Nego, the flame of the fire killed them.*

Daniel 3:23

a *These three (first) men – Shadrach, Meshach, and Abed-Nego fell* **b** *to the midst of the furnace of burning fire, bound.*

Daniel 3:24

a *Then, Nebuchadnezzar, the king, was amazed and rose in alarm.* **b** *He spoke up and said to his counsellors: Were not the three men we threw to the midst of the fire bound?* **c** *They answered and said Certainly, O king.*

Test yourself

1

5:24: **שְׁלַח** *he sent,* **רְשַׁם** *he inscribed*

5:25: **רְשַׁם** *he inscribed*

5:27: **תְּקַ֫לְתָּה** *you weighed*

5:28: **פְּרַס** *he divided,* **יְהַב** *he gave*

2

a אַרְבַּע

b קַדְמָיְתָא

c תִנְיָנָה

d אַרְבְּעָה

e רְבִיעָיָה

f **תְּלָת** and **קַדְמָיָתָא** (Note that the dual form **קַרְנַיָּא** is modified by a plural adj.)

g קַדְמָיֵא

h תְּלָתָה

UNIT 15

Practice

1a *A beast's heart was given to him.* **b** *Great wisdom was found in you.* **c** *Wood will be pulled from his house.* **d** *His kingdom (is one) which will not be destroyed.* **e** *The hair of their head(s) was not singed.*

2a כֹּל דִּי מִן טְעֵם אֱלָהּ שְׁמַיָּא יִתְעֲבֵד; **b** נִפְקְתָא מִתְיַהֲבָה לְגֻבְרַיָּא אִלֵּךְ; **c** אֱדַ֫יִן דָּנִיֵּאל מִתְנַצַּח עַל סָרְכַיָּא; **d** פַּרְזְלָא לָא מִתְעָרַב עִם חַסְפָּא; **e** בְּטַל שְׁמַיָּא יִצְטַבַּע

Daniel 3:25

a *(Nebuchadnezzar) answered and said: Lo, I see four men, unbound, walking in the midst of the fire* **b** *and there is no injury to them and the face of the fourth is similar to a divinity.*

Daniel 3:26

a *Then, Nebuchadnezzar approached the door of the furnace of burning fire.* **b** *He spoke up and said: Shadrach, Meshach, and Abed-Nego, servants of the most-high God, come out, come here!* **c** *Then, Shadrach, Meshach, and Abed-Nego came out from the midst of the fire.*

Daniel 3:27

a *The satraps, prefects, governors, and counsellors of the king gathered together,* **b** *watching these men, over whose body the fire had no power.* **c** *The hair of their head was not singed and their garments were not changed* **d** *and a smell of fire did not (even) touch them.*

Daniel 3:28

a *Nebuchadnezzar spoke up and said: Blessed is the God of Shadrach, Meshach, and Abed-Nego* **b** *who sent his angel and delivered his servants who trusted in him.*

Test yourself

1

a hitpəʿel 3ms suff. conj. of **כתב** and hitpəʿel m.s. imperat. of **כתב**

b haphʿel 3ms suff. conj. of **כתב** and haphʿel m.s. imperat. of **כתב**

c hitpaʿʿal 3mp suff. conj. of **כתב** and hitpaʿʿal m.p. imperat. of **כתב**

d paʿʿel 3mp suff. conj. of **כתב** and paʿʿel m.p. imperat. of **כתב**

e hitpaʿʿal 3ms suff. conj. of **כתב** and hitpaʿʿal m.s. imperat. of **כתב**

2

a מִתְיַהֲבָה; **b** מִתְעָרַב; **c** מִתְבָּהַל; **d** הַשְׁתְּכַ֫חַת; **e** יִתְיְהִב; **f** תִּתְחַבַּל; **g** הִתְקְטָלָה or הִתְקַטָּלָה; **h** יִצְטַבַּע; **i** מִתְנַצַּח; **j** מִשְׁתַּדַּר

UNIT 16

Practice 1

a יִפְּקוּן מִן־בַּיְתָא; **b** הַפְּקֵת כַּסְפָּא מִן־בַּיְתֵהּ; **c** דָּתָא נִפְקַת מִן־מַלְכָּא; **d** תִּטְלִין עַיְנֵ֫יכִי; **e** נְטֵל בַּיְתִי

Practice 2

a תְּהוֹדְעוּן haphʿel 2mp pref. conj. of **אדע** or **ידע** (it is **ידע**) *you will make known*

b תִּפְּלוּן pəʿal 2mp pref. conj. of **יפל** or **נפל** (it is **נפל**) *you will fall*

c תְּהַנְזִק haphʿel 3fs/2ms pref. conj. of **יזק** or **נזק** (it is **נזק**) *she/you will damage*

d מְהוֹדְעִין haphʿel m.p. part. (abs.) of **אדע** or **ידע** (it is **ידע**) *those who make known* or *they make known*

e הֵימִן haphʿel 3ms suff. conj. of **אמן** or **ימן** or (it is **אמן**) *he believes* or *he believed*

f אָמְרִין pəʿal m.p. part. (abs.) of **אמר** *those who say* or *they are saying*

g מְהַנְזְקָה haphʿel f.s. part. (abs.) of **יזק** or **נזק** (it is **נזק**) *it will damage* (or a haph. pass. part.)

h יָכְלִין pəʿal m.p. part. (abs.) of **יכל** *those who are able* or *they are able*

i הוֹתֵב haphʿel 3ms suff. conj. of **אתב** or **יתב** (it is **יתב**) *he settled*

j נָחִת pəʿal m.s. part. (abs.) of **נחת** *one who goes down* or *he is going down*

k הֵיבָלָה haphʿel infinitive of **אבל** or **יבל** (it is **יבל**) *to bring*

l תִּנְדַּע pəʿal 3fs/2ms pref. conj. of **ידע** or **נדע** (it is **ידע**) *she/you will know*

m נֵאמַר pəʿal 1cp pref. conj. of **אמר** *we will say*

n תַּחֵת aphʿel 3fs/2ms pref. conj. of **יחת** or **נחת** (it is **נחת**) *you will deposit* (The form could also be a paʿʿel 3ms suff. conj. of **תחת** but such a verb does not exist.)

o הַצָּלָה haphʿel infinitive of **יצל** or **נצל** (it is **נצל**) *to deliver*

p מְהַחֲתִין haphʿel m.p. part. (abs.) of **יחת** or **נחת** (it is **נחת**) *those depositing* or *they deposit* – Notice that the ḥet does not take a dagesh but the preceding patach does not lengthen. The ḥet is said to be virtually doubled.

q הֵיבֵל haphʿel 3ms suff. conj. of **אבל** or **יבל** (it is **יבל**) *he brought*

r יֵאבַד pəʿal 3ms pref. conj. of **אבד** *he will perish*

s יִתִּב pəʿal 3ms pref. conj. of **יתב** or **נתב** (it is **יתב**) *he will sit*

t נָפְלִין pəʿal m.p. part. (abs.) of **נפל** *those who fall* or *they fall*

Ezra 4:11

a *This is the copy of the letter that they* (i.e. Rehum, Shimshai, and their associates) *sent to him* (i.e. Artaxerxes)*: To Artaxerxes, the king,* **b** *(from) your servants, the people of the (region) Abar-Nahara. And now,*

Ezra 4:12

a *let it be known to the king that the Judeans who went up from you to us* **b** *have come to Jerusalem.* **c** *The rebellious, evil city they are (re)building. The walls they have completed and the foundations they have set in place.*

Ezra 4:13

a *Now, let it be known to the king that if this city is rebuilt and its walls completed* **b** *tribute, tax, and toll will not be given (lit. they will not give) and the royal revenue it* (i.e. Jerusalem) *will damage.*

Ezra 4:14

a *Now, because we salt with the salt of the palace* **b** *and the dishonour of the king is unfitting for us to see,* **c** *concerning this, we have sent and made known to the king.*

Test yourself

1

a (יִפֵּל) 6, **b** (תֵּאמְרוּן) 7, **c** (הוֹדַע) 2, **d** (הַנְפִּקוּ) 1, **e** (מְהוֹדְעִין) 9, **f** (יְהוֹבְדוּן) 10, **g** (יִכֻּל לְהַצָּלָה) 4, **h** (יְהוֹדַע) 3, **i** (הוֹבָדָה) 5, **j** (אִנְדַּע) 8

2

a aphʿel 3fs or 2ms pref. conj. of **נחת** *she/you will deposit*

b haphʿel 3ms suff. conj. of **יבל** *he brought*

c huph'el/hoph'al 3ms suff. conj. of **אבד** *was destroyed*

d huph'el/hoph'al 3ms suff. conj. of **נחת** *he was deposed*

e haph'el 3ms suff. conj. of **אמן** *he trusted.*

f pə'al m.s. imperat. of **אזל** *go* and aph'el m.s. imperat. of **נחת** *deposit*

g haph'el infinitive of **יבל** *to bring*

h haph'el 3mp suff. conj. of **סלק** *they lifted*

i aph'el m.s. part. of **נצל** *saves*

j huph'el/hoph'al 3ms suff. conj. of **סלק** *was lifted*

UNIT 17

Practice 1

a. מִלְּתֵהּ סָפַת; **b** הֲתִיבוּ מִלַּת מַלְכָּא; **c** מַנְדְּעִי יְתוּב לִי; **d** הֲקֵימֶת צַלְמֵהּ דִּי מַלְכָּא; **e** תְּדוּר בִּשְׁלָם; **f** תְּסִיף כָּל־מַלְכְוָתָא (or תְּהָסֵיף or תָּסֵיף or תָּסִיף); **g** מַלְכָּא דָּר בְּהֵיכְלָא; **h** אֲסִיף מַלְכוּתָא (or אֲהָסֵיף or אָסֵיף or אָסִיף); **i** דָּרְנָא בְּהֵיכְלָא; **j** מִלַּת שְׁלָם תְּתוּב

Ezra 4:17

a *The response the king sent: To Rehum, the commander* **b** *and Shimshai the scribe and the rest of their associates who dwell in Samaria* **c** *and the rest of the Abar-Nahara,* **d** *greetings* (lit. *peace*). *Now,*

Ezra 4:18

a *the letter that you sent to us* **b** *was read (with) explanation before me,*

Ezra 4:19

a *and a decree was made by me and it was searched and found that this city* **b** *from days of old has risen up against kings.* **c** *Rebellion and insurrection have been made in it.*

Ezra 4:20

a *Powerful kings were over Jerusalem* **b** *and rulers in all Abar-Nahara c and tribute, tax, and toll were given to them.*

Ezra 4:21

a *Now, set a decree to stop these people* **b** *so that this city will not be rebuilt until by me (another) decree will be made.*

Test yourself

a תּוּב pə'al m.s. imperat. of **תוב** *return!*; **גֹּב** *den*

b זָעוּ pə'al 3mp. suff. conj. of **זוע** *they trembled*; **גָּלוּ** *exile*

c נָח pə'al 3ms suff. conj. of **נוח** *he rested*; **דָּת** *law*

d מְהָךְ pə'al inf. of **הוך** *to go*; **מְשַׁח** *oil*

e דָּאְרִין pə'al m.p. part. of **דור** *those dwelling*; **דַּיָּנִין** *judges*

UNIT 18

Practice 1

a מְטוֹ; **b** מְחָת; **c** יִשְׂגֵּא; **d** אֶקְרֵא; **e** הֲוֵית; **f** חֲזַיְתָ and רְבָה; **g** יִבְעֵה; **h** חֲזֵית; **i** בְעוֹ; **j** אֲתָא

Practice 2

a נְחַוֵּא פְּשַׁר מִלְּתָא or נְחַוֵּא פִּשְׁרַהּ דִּי מִלְּתָא; **b** מַנִּיְתָ גְּבַר יְהוּדָי; **c** מַלְכָּא מַנִּי לִי לְהוֹבָדָה חַכִּימֵי בָבֶל; **d** תְּהַחֲווֹן פְּשַׁר וּתְקַבְּלוּן מַתְּנָן; **e** חַכִּימַיָּא לָא הַשְׁנִיו מִלְּתֵהּ דִּי מַלְכָּא **(**or מִלַּת מַלְכָּא **. . .)**

Ezra 5:1

a *Now, the prophets Haggay and Zekaryah Bar-Iddo made prophecies to the Judeans who were in Judah and in Jerusalem* **b** *in the name of the God of Israel (who was) over them.*

Ezra 5:2

a *Then, Zerubbabel Bar-Shealtiel and Jeshua Bar-Yotsadaq arose* **b** *and began to build the house of God which is in Jerusalem;* **c** *with them the prophets of God were helping them.*

Ezra 5:3

a *In that time Tattenay, governor of Abar-Nahara, and Shethar-Boznay and their associates came to them.* **b** *Thus, they said to them: Who made a proclamation for you to rebuild this house* **c** *and these furnishings to complete?*

Ezra 5:4

a *Then, accordingly they said to them: What are the names of the men who are building this construction?*

Ezra 5:5

a *But, the eye of their God was over the elders of the Judeans and they did not stop them until the decree could go to Darius* **b** *and then (after that) they could return a letter concerning this.*

Test yourself

a הֲוֵית (pəʻal 1cs suff. conj. of **הוי**) *I was*

b יִבְנוֹן (pəʻal 3mp pref. conj. of **בני**) *they will build/re-build*

c שְׁרָא (pəʻal 3ms suff. conj. of **שׁרי**) *he dwelled*

d מְהוֹדֵא (haphʻel m.s. part. of **ידי**) *one who gives thanks*

e הַיְתִיו (haphʻel 3mp suff. conj. of **אתי**) *they brought*

f לֶהֱוֵא (pəʻal 3ms pref. conj./juss. of **הוי**) *it will be/let it be*

g הַחֲוָיָה (haphʻel inf. of **חוי**) *to declare*

h אֲחַוֵּא (paʻʻel 1cs pref. conj. of **חוי**) *I will declare*

i חֲזֵית (pəʻal 1cs suff. conj. of **חזי**) *I saw*

j שָׁרִיו (paʻʻel 3mp suff. conj. of **שׁרי**) *they began*

a	פִּשְׁרָא לְמַלְכָּא אֲחַוֵּא	*its interpretation I will declare to the king*
b	בֵּאדַיִן הַיְתִיו מָאנֵי דַהֲבָא	*then, they brought the vessels of (the) gold*

c	לֶהֱוֵא שְׁמֵהּ דִּי־אֱלָהָא מְבָרַךְ	*let the name of (the) God be blessed*
d	שְׁרָא יִשְׂרָאֵל בְּאַרְעָא הַהִיא	*Israel dwelled in that land*
e	חָזֵא הֲוֵית בְּחֶזְוֵי רֵאשִׁי	*I was watching in the visions of my head*
f	לָךְ אֱלָהּ אֲבָהָתִי מְהוֹדֵא וּמְשַׁבַּח אֲנָה	*to you, God of my father, I give thanks and praise*
g	אִיתַי אֱנָשׁ . . . דִּי מִלַּת מַלְכָּא יוּכַל (= יִכֻל) לְהַחֲוָיָה	*there is a person who is able to declare the matter of the king*
h	בֵּית אֱלָהָא דֵךְ יִבְנוֹן עַל־אַתְרֵהּ	*this temple of (the) God they will (re)build over its place*
i	שָׁרִיו לְמִבְנֵא בֵּית אֱלָהָא	*they began to (re)build the temple of (the) God*
j	דְּנָה חֶלְמָא חֲזֵית אֲנָה	*this dream I saw*

UNIT 19

Practice 1

a מַלְכְּתָא הַעֲלֶת כַּשְׂדָּיֵא לֵהּ; **b** כָּל־חַכִּימֵי־מַלְכְּתָא עָלִּו וְלָא כָהֲלוּ לְמִקְרֵא כְּתָבָא; **c** כַּשְׂדָּיָא יְהַעֵל כְּתָב מַלְכְּתֵהּ; **d** חֵיוָה תַקִּיפָה אָכְלַת וְהַדֱּקֶת שְׁאָרָא; **e** מַלְכְּתָא תַּקִּיפְתָּא תְּהַעֵל כַּשְׂדָּיֵא לְחַכִּימַהּ

Practice 2

a **גדד** pəʿal *cut down!*

b **נעל** or **עלל** (it is **עלל**) pəʿal *she/you will enter*

c **נדד** pəʿal *she fled*

d **רעע** paʿʿel m.s. part. *one who crushes*

e **נעל** or **עלל** (it is **עלל**) hapʿel infinitive *to bring in* **הַנְעָלָה**

f **דקק** hapʿel m.s. participle *one who crushes* (Formally, it could also be paʿʿel m.s. part. of **הדק**, but this root does not occur in Bib. Aram.)

g **נעל** or **עלל** (it is **עלל**) hapʿel 3ms suff. conj. *he brought* or m.s. imperative *bring!*

h **חנן** pəʿal infinitive *to show favour*

i **רעע** pəʿal 3fs/2ms pref. conj. *she/you will crush*

j **דקק** hapʿel 3fs/2ms pref. conj. *she/you will crush*

Ezra 5:6

a *The copy of the letter that Tattenay, governor of Abar-Nahara, and Shetar-Boznay and his associates, the officials who were in Abar-Nahara, sent* **b** *to Darius, the king*

Ezra 5:7

a *the letter they sent to him – and thus was written in its midst:* **b** *To Darius, the king, may all be well.*

Ezra 5:8

a *Let it be known to the king that we have gone to Judah, the region, to the great house of the God* **b** *and it is being rebuilt with hewn stone and wood is being set in the walls* **c** *and this work is being done properly and is successful in their hand(s).*

Ezra 5:9

a *Then, we asked these elders. Thus, we said to them:* **b** *Who made for you a decree to rebuild this temple* **c** *and these furnishings to finish?*

Ezra 5:10

a *And, also their names we asked them for (the purpose of) informing you, so that we might write the name(s) of the men who were in charge (lit. at their heads).*

Test yourself

1

a גּוֹדוּ*

b תְּעוּל*

c נְדַת

d מְרַוַּע*

e הֲעָלָה*

f מְהָדִיק

g הֲעִיל or הַעֵיל

h מְחָן

i תְּרוּעַ

j תְּדִיק

2

a *Then, Arioch brought Daniel before the king.*

b *Then, Daniel spoke with the king.*

c *The lions took control of them and crushed all their bones.*

d *Daniel entered and requested from the king that he might give to him time.*

e *I made a decree* (lit. *a decree was made by me*) *to bring before me all the sages of Babel.*

UNIT 20

Practice 1

1

a	parseh	פַּרְסֵה
b	haškəḥah	הַשְׁכְּחַה
c	šabqeh	שַׁבְקֵה
d	pəlaḥtah	פְּלַחְתַּה
e	haškaḥtánâ	הַשְׁכַּחְתַּ֫נָא
f	hassiqtánâ	הַסִּקְתַּ֫נָא
g	ʼaklánīʸ	אַכְלַ֫נִי

h šəlaḥtánīy שְׁלַחְתַּ֫נִי

i yəhabtāk יְהַבְתָּךְ

j ʼăkalteh אֲכַלְתֵּהּ

2

a שַׁבְקֵהּ *he left him alone*

b הוֹדְעַ֫נִי *he informed me* (lit. *caused me to know*)

c הַקְרְבַהּ *he brought her near*

d הֲקִימ֫וּהִי *they established him*

e הֲתִיבָךְ *he returned you*

f בְּנַיְתֵהּ *I built it*

g הַשְׁלְטָךְ *he caused you to rule*

h חַבְּלַ֫נִי *he destroyed me*

i הֲקִימ֫וּנָא *they established us*

j שָׂמָךְ *he set you*

Practice 2

a pəʻal infinitive + 3fs suff. (**פלח**) *to serve her*

b pəʻal 3ms suff. conj. + 3ms suff. (**קטל**) *he killed him*

c pəʻal 3ms pref. conj. + 1cs suff. (**קטל**) *he will kill me*

d aphʻel 3ms pref. conj. + 3ms suff. (**שׁכח**) *he will find him*

e paʻʻel m.s. part. + 2ms suff. (**ברך**) *one blessing you*

f paʻʻel 1cs pref. conj. + 2ms suff. (**ברך**) *I will bless you*

g pəʻal 1cs pref. conj. + 3fs suff. (**נתן**) *I will give it*

h paʻʻel infinitive + 3fs suff. (**חבל**) *to destroy it*

i pəʻal 1cp pref. conj. + 3ms suff. (**קטל**) *we will kill him*

j haphʻel 3ms suff. conj. + 3fs suff. (**שׁכח**) *he found her*

Ezra 5:11

a *Accordingly, an answer they returned to us, saying:* **b** *We are the servants of the God of heaven and earth* **c** *and we are building the temple which was built before this many years (ago)* **d** *and (which) a great king of Israel built and completed (lit. which a great king of Israel built it and completed it).*

Ezra 5:12

a *However, because our fathers angered the God of heaven, he* (i.e. *the God*) *gave them into the hand of Nebuchadnezzar, the Chaldean king of Babylon* **b** *and as for this temple, he demolished it and the people he exiled to Babylon.*

Ezra 5:13

a *Nevertheless, in the first year of Koresh, the king of Babylon,* **b** *Koresh, the king, made a decree to rebuild this temple of the God.*

Ezra 5:14

a *Also, the vessels of the temple of the God, of gold and silver,* **b** *which Nebuchadnezzar took from the temple, which is in Jerusalem,* **c** *and brought to the temple which is in Babylon,* **d** *Koresh, the king, took them from the temple which is in Babylon* **e** *and gave (them) to someone named Sheshbazzar whom he made governor.*

Ezra 5:15

a *He said to him: 'These vessels, take, go, deposit them in the temple which is in Jerusalem* **b** *and let the temple of the God be rebuilt over its place.'*

Test yourself

a haph'el m.p. imv. of חוי with 1cs object suff. *declare its interpretation!* (cf. the haph'el 3mp suff. conj. without object suff. הַחֲוִיו; no form like this with object suff. is attested in Biblical Aramaic, but would be in Targ. Onq. הַחֲוִיאוּנִי*)

b pə'al 3ms pref. conj. of שׁאל with 2mp object suff. *all that he will ask you*

c pa''el 3ms pref. conj. of דחל with 1cs object suff. *a dream I saw and it frightened me* (cf. the pə'al form without suffix יִדְחַל and the aph'el יַדְחֵל*) . For the loss of shewa in the prefix, see the glossary under וְ.

d haph'el 2mp pref. conj. of ידע with 1cs object *if you do not make known to me the dream*

e pə'al 3fs (or 2ms) pref. conj. of דושׁ with 3fs object suff. *it* (or *you*) *will consume all the earth and trample it*

f haph'el 3ms suff. conj. (or m.s. imv.) of קום with 3ms object suff. *your father, the king, appointed him* (or less likely: *appoint him (as) your father, the king*)

g haph'el 3mp suff. conj. (or m.p. imv.) of קרב with 3ms object suff. *they brought him before him or bring him before him!*

h pa''el 3ms pref. conj. of חוי with 3fs object suff. *he can tell it before the king*

i haph'el inf. of קום with 3ms object suff. *to appoint him over all the kingdom*

j haph'el 3fs (or 2ms) pref. conj. of דקק with 3fs object suff. *all the earth . . . it* (or *you*) *will shatter*

UNIT 21

Ezra 5:16

a *Then, this Sheshbazzar came (and) set the foundations of the temple of the God which is in Jerusalem* **b** *and from then until now it has been under construction but not completed.*

Ezra 5:17

a *Now if it is good to the king, let a search be made in the archives of the king, there, in Babylon* **b** *(to see) if it was that a decree was made by Koresh, the king, to build this temple of the God in Jerusalem.* **c** *The decision of the king on this let him send to us.*

Ezra 6:1

a *Then, Darius, the king, made a decree* **b** *and a search was made in the archives where the documents were deposited, there in Babylon.*

Ezra 6:2

a *A scroll was found in Ecbatana, in the fortress which is in Media, the province,* **b** *and thus was written in its midst: Memorandum:*

Ezra 6:3

a *In year one of Koresh, the king, Koresh, the king, made a decree* **b** *'As for the temple of the God in Jerusalem, let the house be rebuilt,* **c** *(the place) where sacrifices were made. Let its foundations be laid down.* **d** *Let its height be 60 cubits, its width 60 cubits.*

Ezra 6:4

a *Let there be three courses of hewn stone and one course of wood.* **b** *Let expenses be given from the palace of the king.*

Ezra 6:5

a *Also, the golden and silver vessels of the temple of the God* **b** *that Nebuchadnezzar took from the temple of Jerusalem and brought to Babylon* **c** *let them be returned and let them go to the temple that is in Jerusalem, to their place.* **d** *You will deposit (them) in the temple of the God.'*

Ezra 6:6

a *Now, Tattenay, the governor of Abar-Nahara, Shethar-Boznai and their associates, the officials, who are in Abar-Nahara, be far from there!*

Ezra 6:7

a *Leave the work on that temple of the God.* **b** *The governor of the Judeans and the elders of the Judeans* **c** *will build that temple of the God over its place.*

Test yourself

a *according to, wisdom, your God; your hand*

b *magistrates, judges*

c *judge* (pəʿal 3ms pref. conj. of הוי; pəʿal m.s. part. of דין), *the people*

d *know, your God*

e *teach* (lit. *make known*, haphʿel 2mp pref. conj. of ידע), *know* (pəʿal m.s. part. of ידע)

f *all who, law, law, king*

g *judgment* (lit. *the judgment*)

h *property*

UNIT 22

Reading 1

1

Genesis 1:1

a *At first, the Lord created the heavens and the earth.*

Genesis 1:2

a *The earth was desolate and barren;* **b** *and darkness was over the face of the abyss.* **c** *A wind from before the Lord was blowing over the face of the water.*

Genesis 1:3

a *The Lord said Let there be light and there was light.*

Genesis 1:4

a *The Lord saw the light, that it was good.* **b** *The Lord separated (between) the light and the darkness.*

Genesis 1:5

a *The Lord called light day* **b** *and darkness he called night.* **c** *It was evening and it was morning, day one.*

Genesis 1:6

a *The Lord said Let there be a sky in the middle of the water* **b** *so that it might separate waters (lit. separate between water and water).*

Genesis 1:7

a *The Lord made the sky* **b** *and separated the water beneath the sky* **c** *from the water that is above the sky (lit. separated between the water . . . and the water . . .). And it was so.*

Genesis 1:8

a *The Lord called the sky heavens.* **b** *It was evening and it was morning, second day.*

Genesis 1:9

a *The Lord said Let the water under the heavens be gathered to one place* **b** *so (lit. and) dry ground might appear. And it was so.*

Genesis 1:10

a *The Lord called the dry ground earth* **b** *and the place of the gathering of the water he called seas.* **c** *The Lord saw that it was good.*

Genesis 1:11

a *The Lord said Let the earth sprout grass, plants (lit. plant)* **b** *whose seed is sown according to their kind (lit. its kinds),* **c** *and fruit trees (lit. tree of fruits) bearing fruit (lit. making fruits) according to their kind (lit. its kinds)* **d** *in which are seeds over the earth.* **e** *And it was so.*

Genesis 1:12

a *The earth brought forth grass, plants (lit. a plant)* **b** *whose seed is sown according to their kind (lit. its kinds)* **c** *and trees (lit. tree) bearing fruit (lit. making fruits)* **d** *in which are seeds according to their kind (lit. its kinds).* **e** *The Lord saw that it was good.*

Genesis 1:13

a *It was evening and it was morning, third day.*

2

Genesis 11:1

a *All the earth had (lit. was) one tongue and one speech.*

Genesis 11:2

a *When they (i.e., humans) first travelled (lit. and it was in their travelling at first),* **b** *they found a valley in the land of Babel* **c** *and they dwelled there.*

Genesis 11:3

a *Then, they said to each other (lit. and they said, a person to his companion),* **b** *Come! (lit. give!) Let us make (lit. throw) bricks* **c** *and let us bake them in the fire.* **d** *So (lit. and), the brick was for them as stone* **e** *and bitumen was for them as mortar.*

Genesis 11:4

a *They said: Come! (lit. give!) Let us build for ourselves a city and a tower* **b** *with (lit. and) its top reaching towards the heavens.* **c** *Let us make for ourselves a name* **d** *lest we be scattered over the face of all the earth.*

Genesis 11:5

a *Then (lit. and), the Lord appeared in order to take vengeance (lit. to be avenged)* **b** *on account of the work of the city and the tower which the humans built.*

Genesis 11:6

a *The Lord said Lo, all of them have one nation and one language (lit. one nation and one language there is to all of them).* **b** *and this (is) what they have begun to do.* **c** *Now, anything they ponder to do will not be beyond them (lit. will not be withheld from them).*

Genesis 11:7

a *Come! Let us appear and confuse their language there* **b** *so no one will understand the language of another (lit. and a person will not understand the language of his companion).*

Genesis 11:8

a *Then (lit. and), the Lord scattered them from there, over the face of all the earth* **b** *and they were prevented from building the city.*

Genesis 11:9

a *Therefore, he called its name Babel* **b** *because there the Lord confused the language of all the earth* **c** *and from there the Lord scattered them across the face of all the earth.*

Reading 2

Genesis 11:1

a) וַהֲווֹן כֹּל דַּיָּירֵי דְּאַרְעָא לִשָּׁן חַד וּמַמְלַל חַד
b) וּבְלִשָּׁן בֵּית קֻדְשָׁה [read קֻדְשָׁא] הֲווֹן מִשְׁתַּעַיִן
c) דְּבֵהּ אִתְבְּרִי עָלְמָא מִן שֵׁירוּיָה [read שֵׁירוּיָא]

Genesis 11:2

a) וַהֲוָוה כַּד אַסַּעוּ לְבַבְהוֹן
b) וְאַשְׁכַּחוּ בִּקְעָה בְּאַרְעָא דְּבָבַל
c) וּשְׁרוֹן תַּמָּן

Genesis 11:3

a) וַאֲמַרוּ גְּבַר לְחַבְרֵיהּ
b) אִתוֹן וְנִלְבַּן לִבְנִין
c) וְנֵזֵי יָתְהוֹן בְּאַתּוּנָ׳ [בְּאַתּוּנָא]
d) וַהֲוַין לְהוֹן לִבְנַיָּה [read לִבְנַיָּא] לְאַבְנִין
e) וְחֵמָרָא הֲוָוה לְהוֹן לִשְׁיָע

Genesis 11:4

a) וַאֲמַרוּן אֲתוֹן וְנִבְנֵה לַן קִרְיָה וּמַגְדַּל
b) וְרֵאשֵׁהּ מָטֵי עַד צֵית שְׁמַיָּא
c) וְנַעְבֵּד לַן בְּרֵאשֵׁיהּ סִגְדָּה
d) וְנִתֵּן חַרְבָּא בִּידֵיהּ
e) וְתִיהֲוֵי עָבְדָ׳ [read עָבְדָה] לְקָבְלֵיהּ סִדְרֵי קְרָבָא
f) קֳדָם עַד לָא נִדָּרֵי עַל אַפֵּי כֹּל אַרְעָא

Genesis 11:5

a) וְאִתְגְּלִיַּת אִיקָר שְׁכִינְתֵיהּ דַּייי
b) לְמַחְמֵי יָת קַרְתָּא וְיָת מַגְדְּלָא דִּבְנוֹ בְּנֵי אֱנָשָׁה

Genesis 11:6

a) וַאֲמַר ייי הָא אוּמָּה חֲדָה וְלִשׁוֹן חַד לְכוּלְהוֹן
b) וְהָא כַּדּוּן שָׁרוֹן לְמַעְבַּד
c) וְכַדּוּן לָא יִתְמְנַע מִנְהוֹן כֹּל מָה דִּי חַשִׁבוּ לְמַעְבַּד

Genesis 11:7

a) אִתוֹן כְּעַן וְאִתְגְּלֵי וּנְעַרְבֵּב תַּמָּן לִשָּׁנֵיהוֹן
b) דְּלָא יִשְׁמְעוּן גְּבַר לִשָּׁנֵהּ דְּחַבְרֵיהּ

Genesis 11:8

a) וְדָרִי ייי יָתְהוֹן מִן תַּמָּן עַל אַפֵּי כל אַרְעָא
b) וְאִתְמְנַעוּ מִן לְמִבְנֵי קַרְתָּא

Genesis 11:9

a) בְּגֵין כדן [read כֵּן] קְרָא שְׁמַהּ בָּבַל

b) אְרוּ׳ [read אְרוּם] כְּדֵין עַרְבֵּב ייי לִשָּׁנֵי כֹּל דַּאֲיֵרֵי [read דַּיָּרֵי] אַרְעָא

c) וּמִן תַּמָּן דָּרֵי יָתְהוֹן ייי עַל אַפֵּי כֹּל אַרְעָא

Genesis 11:1

a *All the dwellers of the earth had (lit. were) one tongue and one speech,* **b** *and were conversing in the language of the holy temple (lit. the temple of holiness)* **c** *in which the world was created at (lit. from) the beginning.*

Genesis 11:2

a *When they (i.e. the dwellers of earth) had taken their mind off (God) (lit. and it was when they removed their heart),* **b** *they found a valley in the land of Babel* **c** *and they dwelled there.*

Genesis 11:3

a *Then, they said to each other (lit. and they said, a person to his companion),* **b** *Come! Let us make bricks* **c** *and let us heat them in the oven.* **d** *So (lit. and), the bricks were for them as stones* **e** *and the bitumen was for them as mortar.*

Genesis 11:4

a *They said: Come! Let us build for ourselves a city and a tower* **b** *with (lit. and) its top reaching towards the heavens.* **c** *Let us make for ourselves at its top (lit. in its top) an object of worship* **d** *and let us place the sword in its hand* **e** *so (lit. and) it (the object of worship) will ready against him (i.e. God) the battle lines of war* **f** *before we are scattered over the face of all the earth.*

Genesis 11:5

a *Then (lit. and), the glory of the Shekinah of the Lord appeared* **b** *in order to see the city and the tower which the humans built.*

Genesis 11:6

a *The Lord said Lo, all of them have one nation and one language (lit, one nation and one language there is to all of them)* **b** *and lo, now, they have begun to work.* **c** *Now, anything they ponder to do will not be beyond them (lit. will not be withheld from them).*

Genesis 11:7

a *Come, now! Let me appear and let me confuse their languages there* **b** *so no one will understand the language of another (lit. and a person will not understand the language of his companion).*

Genesis 11:8

a *Then (lit. and) the Lord scattered them from there, over the face of all the earth* **b** *and they were prevented from building the city.*

Genesis 11:9

a *Therefore, he called its name Babel* **b** *because thus the Lord confused the languages of all the dwellers of the earth* **c** *and from there the Lord scattered them over all the face of all the earth.*

Test yourself

Hebrew Bible:

a *Like this you will say to them:*

b '*Let the gods, who did not make the heaven or earth,*

c *disappear* (a jussive) *from the earth and from under these heavens.*'

Targum to Jeremiah:

d *This is the copy of the letter that Jeremiah, the prophet, sent*

e *to the remainder of the elders of the exile who (were) in Babel:*

f *If the peoples, whom you (are) among, will say to you:*

g '*Serve the idols, O house of Israel!*'

h *Thus, you will answer and thus you will say to them:*

i *Idols (are) what you worship,*

j *idols in which there is no use.*

k *They from heaven are not able to bring down the rain,*

l *and from the earth are not able to make fruit grow.*

m *May they and their worshippers disappear* (a jussive) *from the earth and they will be wiped out from under these heavens.*

The targumic passage uses an aleph mater to mark final -ā^{h} (as in **דְּנָא** in line **a**) instead of a he (דְּנָה). The relative pronoun is often **דְּ** (as in **דִּבְבָבַל** *who (were) in Babel* in line **b**) instead of **דִּי**. I-aleph verbs in the prefix conjugation are marked with a yod mater, not an aleph: **תֵּימְרוּן** (vs. **תֵּאמְרוּן**). The 3mp pronominal suffix is **הוֹן-** (as in **בֵּינֵיהוֹן** in line **c**) instead of **הֹם-**.

UNIT 23

Col. 19

וְחַלְמֵת אֲנָה אַבְרָם חֵלֶם בְּלֵילְיָה מֵעֲלִי לַאֲרַע מִצְרַיִן **14**

וַחֲזֵית בְּחֶלְמִי וְהָא אֲרַז חַד וְתַמְרָא **15.** חֲדָא כַּחֲדָא צְמַח[וּ] מִן שְׁר[שׁ חַד]

וּבְנֵי אֱנוֹשׁ אֲתוֹ וּבָעַיִן לְמִקַּץ וּלְמֶעְקַר לְ[אַ]רְזָא

וּלְמִשְׁבַּק תְּמַרְתָּא בִּלְחוֹדַיְהָה

וְאַכְלִיאַת תְּמַרְתָּא וַאֲמֶרֶת **16**

אַל תִּקּוֹצוּ לְאַרְזָא

אֲרֵי תְּרֵינָא מִן שְׁרֹשׁ [חַ]ד צְ[מַחְ]נָא

וּשְׁבִיק אַרְזָא בִּטְלַל תְּמַרְתָּא

לָא קַצּוּהִ[י] **17**

וְאִתְעִירֶת בְּלֵילְיָא מִן שִׁנְתִּי

וַאֲמֶרֶת לְשָׂרַי אִנְתְּתִי חֵלֶם **18** חַלְמֵת

מִן [דַּ]אֲנָה דָּחֵל מִ[ן] חֶלְמָא דֵּן

וַאֲמֶ֫רֶת לִי אִשְׁתַּעִי לִי חֶלְמָךְ וְאִנְדַּע

וְשָׁרִית לְאִשְׁתַּעָיָא לַהּ חֶלְמָא דֵּן

וַאֲמְרֵת . . . דִּי יִבְעוֹן לְמִקְטְלַנִי וְלֵכִי לְמִשְׁבַּק 19

בְּרַם דָּא כּוֹל טָבוּתָא 20 [דִּ]י תַּעַבְדִין עִמִּי

בְּכוֹל עָקַת דִּי יֵא[תֵ]ה אֱמַ֫רִי עֲלַי דִּי אַחִי הוּא

וְאֶחֵה בְּטַלֵ֫יכִי וְתִפְלֵט נַפְשִׁי בְּדִילֵ֫יכִי

. . . יִבְעוֹן לְאַעְדָיוּתֵ֫כִי מִנִּי וּלְמִקְטְלַנִי 21

וּבְכָת שָׂרַי עַל מִלַּי בְּלֵילְיָא דֵּן

14 *Then I, Abram, dreamed a dream in the night of my entering the land of Egypt / and I saw in my dream and, lo, a cedar and a palm* **15** *(which) as one sprouted from a [single] root. / Then people came and were seeking to cut down and to uproot the cedar / but to leave the palm tree by itself. /* **16** *Then the palm tree screamed and said / Do not cut down the cedar! / for the two of us, we sprouted from one root. / And the cedar was left due to the help of the palm tree. /* **17** *They did not cut it down. / Then, I awoke in the night from my sleep / and I said to Sarai, my wife, I dreamed* **18** *a dream, / because I was afraid of this dream. / She said to me Tell me your dream so that I may know (it). / Then I began to tell her this dream. /* **19** *I said . . . they will seek to kill me and leave you alone. / Nevertheless, this is all the good* **20** *that you can do for me: / in every trouble that comes, speak about me, He is my brother. / Then, I will live because of you and my life will be spared because of you. /* **21** *. . . They will seek to remove you from me and to kill me. / Then Sarai wept over my words in that night.*

Col. 20

כְּמָה נַצִּיחַ וְשַׁפִּיר לַהּ צְלֵם אַנְפַּ֫יְהָא 2

וּכְמָא . . . רַקִּיק לַהּ שְׂעַר רֵאישַׁהּ 3

כְּמָא יָאיָן לְהֵין לַהּ עַיְנַ֫יְהָא

וּמָא רְגִג הוּא לַהּ אַנְפַּ֫הָא וְכוֹל נֵץ 4 אַנְפַּ֫יְהָא . . .

כְּמָא יָאֵא לַהּ חַדְיַהּ וּכְמָא שַׁפִּיר לַהּ כּוֹל לַבְנַ֫הָא

דְּרָעַ֫יְהָא מָא שַׁפִּירָן וִידַ֫יְהָא כְּמָא 5 כְּלִילָן

וַחֲמִיד כּוֹל מַחֲזֵה יְדַ֫יְהָא כְּמָא יָאיָן כַּפַּ֫יְהָא

וּמָא אֲרִיכָן וּקְטִינָן כּוֹל אֶצְבְּעָת יְדַ֫יְהָא

רַגְלַ֫יְהָא 6 כְּמָא שַׁפִּירָן וּכְמָא שְׁלַ֫מָא לְהֵן לַהּ שָׁקַ֫יְהָא

וּכֹל בְּתוּלָן וְכַלָּאן דִּי יֵעֲלָן לְגִנּוּן לָא יִשְׁפְּרָן מִנַּ֫הָא

וְעַל כּוֹל 7 נְשִׁין שׁ֫וֹפַר שִׁפְרַת וְעִלָּיָא שָׁפְרַ֫הָא לְעֵ֫לָּא מִן כָּולְּהֵן

וְעִם כּוֹל שָׁפְרָא דֵּן חָכְמָא שַׂגִּיָּא עִמַּ֫הָא

וּדְלִידַ֫יְהָא 8 יָאֵא

2 *How splendid and beautiful for her (is) the image of her face. /* **3** *. . . And how fine for her (is) the hair of her head. / How perfect for themselves, for her (are) her eyes. / And how precious for her (is) her nose and every blossom of* **4** *her face . . . / How perfect for her (is) her breast. And how beautiful for her (is) all her whiteness. / Her arms – how beautiful. And her hands, how* **5** *flawless. / And* *desirous (is) all the appearance of her hands how perfect her palms / and how long and thin all the fingers of her hands. / Her legs* **6** *how beautiful. And, how complete for themselves, for her (are) her thighs. / All young women and brides who enter the bridal chamber are not more beautiful than her / but above* **7** *all women, as to beauty, she is beautiful and unsurpassed (is) her beauty, above all of them. / And with all this beauty, great wisdom (is) with her. / What is hers is perfect.*

בְּלֵילְיָא דֵּן צַלִּית וּבְעֵית וְאֶתְחַנְּנֵת **12**

וַאֲמַרֵת בְּאִתְעֲצָבָא וְדִמְעַי נָחֲתָן

בְּרִיךְ אַנְתָּה אֵל עֶלְיוֹן מָרִי לְכוֹל **13** עָלְמִים

דִּי אַנְתָּה מָרֵה וְשַׁלִּיט עַל כּוֹלָּא

וּבְכוֹל מַלְכֵי אַרְעָא אַנְתָּה שַׁלִּיט לְמֶעְבַּד בְּכָוֹלְּהוֹן דִּין

וּכְעַן **14** קְבַלְתָּךְ מָרִי עַל פַּרְעוֹ צֹעַן מֶלֶךְ מִצְרַיִן

דִּי דְּבִרַת אִנְתְּתִי מִנִּי בְּתוֹקַף

עֲבֵד לִי דִּין מִנֵּהּ וְאַחְזִי יְדָךְ רַבְּתָא **15** בֵּהּ וּבְכוֹל בַּיְתֵהּ

וְאַל יִשְׁלַט בְּלֵילְיָא דֵּן לְטַמָּיָא אִנְתְּתִי מִנִּי

וְיִנְדְּעוּךְ מָרִי דִּי אַנְתָּה מָרֵה לְכוֹל מַלְכֵי **16** אַרְעָא

וּבְכֵית וַחֲשֵׁית בְּלֵילְיָא דֵּן

שְׁלַח לֵהּ אֵל עֶלְיוֹן רוּחַ מַכְדֵּשׁ לְמִכְתְּשֵׁהּ וּלְכוֹל אֱנָשׁ בַּיְתֵהּ רוּחַ **17** בְּאִישָׁא

וַהֲוָאת כָּתְשָׁא לֵהּ וּלְכוֹל אֱנָשׁ בַּיְתֵהּ

וְלָא יְכִל לְמִקְרַב בַּהָא וְאַף לָא יַדְעַהָא וַהֲוָא עִמַּהּ **18** תַּרְתֵּין שְׁנִין

12 *In that night, I prayed, sought, and asked for favour. / I said in sadness and with tears flowing / Blessed (are) you, God, Most High, my Lord, for all* **13** *eternities, / for you (are) Lord and ruler over all* (lit. *the all*). */ And, against all the kings of the earth you have power to bring* (lit. *to do*) *judgment – against all of them. / Now,* **14** *I complain to you, my Lord, over Pharaoh Zoan, king of Egypt / because my wife was taken from me through force: / Bring* (lit. *make*) *judgment for me against him* (i.e. *against Pharaoh*), *show your great hand* (or *power*) **15** *against him and against all his house. / Let him not have power in this night to defile my wife (who is far) from me, / so that they will know you, my Lord, that you are lord to all the kings* **16** *of the earth. / And, I wept and was silent in that night. / God, Most High sent to him* (i.e. *Pharaoh*) *a pestilent wind* (or *spirit*) (lit. *a wind/spirit of pestilence*) *to afflict him and an evil wind* (or *spirit*) *to all the people of his house.* **17** */ And, it was afflicting him and all the people of his house. / He was not able to approach her* (i.e. *Sarai*) *and also he did not know her, though he (was) with her* **18** *two years.*

4Q541 frag. 9, col. i

... וִיכַפֵּר עַל כּוֹל בְּנֵי דָרֵהּ וְיִשְׁתְּלַח לְכוֹל בְּנֵי **3** [עַמֵּ]הּ **2**

מֵאמְרֵהּ כְּמֵאמַר שְׁמַיִן וְאַלְפּוֹנֵהּ כִּרְעוּת אֵל

שְׁמַשׁ עָלְמָה תְּנִיר **4** וְיִתְזֵה נוּרַהָא בְּכוֹל קִצְוֵי אַרְעָא

וְעַל חֲשׁוֹכָא תְּנִיר

אֱדַיִן יַעֲדֵה חֲשׁוֹכָא **5** מִן אַרְעָא וַעֲרַפִּלָּא מִן יַבִּישְׁתָּא

שַׂגִּיאָן מִלִּין יֵאמְרוּן וּשְׂגֵה **6** [כַּדְבִ]ין

וּבְדְיָאן עֲלוֹהִי יִבְדוֹן וְכוֹל גִּנּוּאִין עֲלוֹהִי יְמַלְּלוּן

דָּרֵהּ בְּאִישׁ וַאֲפִיךְ **7** . . . וְדִי שְׁקַר וַחֲמַס מְקָמֵהּ

[וְ]יִטְעֵה עַמָּא בְּיוֹמוֹהִי וְיִשְׁתַּבְּשׁוּן

2 . . . *He will atone for all the children of his generation and will be sent to all the children of* **3** *his [people]. / His word is like the word of heaven and his teaching is according to the will of God. / The eternal sun will shine* **4** *and its fire will burn in all the ends of the earth. / And, over the darkness it will shine. / Then, he will remove the darkness* **5** *from the earth and shadow from the dry ground. / Many words will be spoken and* **6** *a multitude of lies. / And, falsehoods against him will be invented and all (sorts of) disgraceful things will be said about him. / His generation (is) evil and perverted* **7** *. . . and of conspiracy and violence (is) its position. / The people will wander in his days and will be confused.*

Test yourself

1

a (read בְּרִי) וּכְעַן בְּנִי **4**

b סְפַר מוּסַר חָוכְמָה **7**

c אֲלֵיף לִבְנֵיכוֹן **9**

d וְתִהְוֵי חָוכְמְתָא עִמְּכוֹן **1**

e לִיקָר עָלַם **6** (N.B. The shewa of the yod of יְקָר is lost before לְ in the same way that it is lost before וְ (see the glossary under וְ)).

f דִּי אָלֵיף חָוכְמְתָא **8**

g וִיקָר הִיא בַהּ **3**

h דִּי שָׁאֵיט חָוכְמְתָא **2**

i לְבִשְׂרוֹן מִתְיְהֵב **5**

2 (Although many of the nouns are formally in the determined state, they are translated with the English *a* or *an* since the determined state is often the basic state of the noun in this text.)

1 *Now, when the king, Solomon, heard that the Queen of Sheba came toward him,*

2 *he got up, went, and sat in the house of crystal* (i.e. = presumably a room with a crystal floor).

3 *When the Queen of Sheba saw the king, Solomon,*

4 *that he went and sat in the house of crystal,*

5 *she responded and thought in her mind and said (to herself)*

6 *that the king, Solomon, was sitting in water.*

7 *So, she pulled up her garment that wrapped around her* (lit. = *that crosses over*).

8 *Then, the king, Solomon, saw her, the hair on her leg.*

9 *He responded and said to her: Your beauty is the beauty of women,*

10 *but your hair is the hair of a man!*

11 *Hair for a man is attractive, but for a woman (is) disgraceful.*

12 *The Queen of Sheba answered and said to him:*

13 *My lord, king, Solomon, I will give you three riddles* (lit. = *I will riddle you three riddles*).

14 If *you are able to interpret them for me, then I will know you are a sage.*

15 *If not, (I will know) you are like the rest of humanity* (lit. = *like the remainder of the sons of man*).

. . .

16 *She responded and said to him:*

17 *What comes forth (as) mud from the ground,*

18 *but, its food (comes) from the dust of the earth;*

19 *it *pours like *water but *oozes *outward?*

20 *He responded and said to her Naphtha.*

Note: The passage contrasts the superficial evaluation of the queen's beauty by Solomon with the insightful evaluation of Solomon's wisdom by the queen. As for the riddle itself, in lines 17–18 it plays on the diverse range of meanings for **עֲפַר**. Naphtha refers to oil or petroleum that naturally seeps from the earth, either relatively clear or in a more sticky, tar-like form. In ancient times, it was processed by adding sand or other elements to it while it boiled (see Moorey, 334). Perhaps not surprisingly, the queen's words recall the most famous biblical riddle, that of Samson in Judg 14:14, which, in its Aramaic version, uses some of the same vocabulary: *from that which eats comes* (**נְפַק**) *the food* (**מֵיכְלָא**), *from the strong comes* (**נְפַק**) *the sweet.*

UNIT 24

Reading 1

17. שָׂב אֲנָה לָא אֶכְהַל לְמִפְלַח בִּבָב הֵיכְלָא [ ]

18. [הָא] נָדִן שְׁמֵהּ בְּרִי רְבָא

וְהוּ יַחְלֵפ לִי סָפַר [ ]

[הוּ] **19.** [צָבִי]ת עִזְקָה יֶהֱוֵה לָכְ

אַפ חָכְמְתִי וְעֵ[טְתִי חַכִּמְתֵּהּ]

[עֲנָה אֵסַרְחַאדֹּנ] **20.** [מֶלֶ]כְ אֲתוּר אֲמַר כוּתָא . . .

21. עֲבִידְתָכְ הוּ יַעְבֵד . . .

17 *I am old. I am unable to serve in the gate of the palace.* / **18** *[Lo,] my son, whose name is Nadin* (lit. *Nadin, his name, my son*) *has grown up. / Let him replace me (as) scribe. / [He]* **19** *will be [keep]er of the signet ring for you. / Also, my wisdom and [my] cou[nsel I have taught him]. / [Esarhaddon, kin]g of Assyria, answered (and) said: thus, . . /* **21** *your work he will do.*

32. [בֵּאדַיִנ הִתְמְלִי חֵמָא אֵסַ]רְחַאדֹּנ מֶלֶכְ אֲתוּר

וַאֲמַר **33.** [יֶאֱתֵה לִי נְבוּסֻמִּסְכֵּנ חַ]ד מִנ רַבֵּי אַבִי זִי לְחֶמ אַבִי **34.** [אֲכַל]

[אֲמַר מַלְכָּא אֲחִיקָר] תִּבְעֵה

אֲתַר זִי אַנְתְּ תְּהַשְׁכַּח **35.** [וְתִקְטְלִנֵּהִי]

הֵנ לוּ [אֲחִ]יקָ[ר] זֵכְ שָׂבָא סָפַר **36.** חַכִּימ [וְיָעֵט כֹּל אֲתוּ]ר לְמָה הוּ יְחַבֵּל מָתָא עֲלַינ . . .

32 *[Then, Es]arhaddon, king of Assyria, [was filled with rage] / and said:* **33** *[Let Nabusumiskun, o]ne of* (lit. *from*) *the nobles of my father, who* **34** *[serv]ed him* (lit. *[ate] the food of my father*), *[come to me. The king said:] You will seek out [Aḥiqar]* (lit. *Aḥiqar, you will seek out*). *Where you will find (him),*

35 *[you will kill him]. Even though this old [Aḥ]iqa[r] (may be) the scribe of –,* **36** *the sage of –, and the counsellor of all Assyria, why should he destroy the country in opposition to us* (lit. *against us*)*?. . .*

40. אֲנָה מְהַלֵּךְ בֵּין כַּרְמַיָּא [**41.** כְּזִי חֲזָנִי נְב]וּסֻמִּסְכֻּן רַבְיָא [זֵךְ]

[קְרֵבְ]תָא בְּזַע כִּתּוּנֵהּ . . .

40 *I was walking among the vineyards* **41** *[when this] official [Nab]usumiskun [saw me] / [Right] then, he tore his tunic . . .*

46. אֲנָה הוּ אֲחִיקָר זִי קֳדָמַן שֵׁזְבָךְ מִן קְטֵל זַכָּי

47. [כְּזִי סַנְחֵארִיב] אֲבוּהִי זִי אֵסַרְחַאדֹּן זְנָה מַלְכָּא חֲמַר עֲלָיךְ [**48.** לְמִקְטְלָךְ]

[קְרֵבְ]תָא יְבַלְתָּךְ לְבַיְתָא זִילִי

תַּמָּה הֲוֵית מְסַבֵּל לָךְ **49.** כְּאִישׁ עִם אֲחוּהִי

וְהַצְפִּנְתָּךְ אַמְרֵת קְטַלְתֵּהּ

עַד זִי לְעִדָּ[ן אָ]חֳרָן וּלְיוֹמִן אָחֳרָנִן **50.** שַׂגִּיאִן קָרִבְתָּךְ קֳדָם סַנְחֵארִיב מַלְכָּא

וְהֶעְדִּית חֲטָאָיךְ קֳדָמוֹהִי וּבְאִישְׁ[תָּא] **51.** לָא עֲבַד לָךְ

אַף שַׂגִּיא סַנְחֵארִיב מַלְכָּא רַחְמַנִי עַל זִי הַחְיִתָךְ וְלָא קְטַלְתָּךְ

כְּעַן אַנְתְּ **52.** לָקֳבֵל זִי אֲנָה עַבְדֵת לָךְ כֵּן אֱפוֹ עֲבֵד לִי

אַל תִּקְטְלַנִי . . .

46 *I am Aḥiqar / who, previously, saved you from a wrongful execution,* **47** *[when Sennacherib,] the father of this Esarhaddon, the king, grew angry at you* **48** *[(to the extent) of killing you] / [Right] after, I brought you to my house* (lit. *the house which is to me*)*./ There, I was taking care of you,* **49** *like a man (acts) with his brother. / I hid you. I said: I killed him. / When at another time, after many other days,* **50** *I brought you before Sennacherib, the king. / I removed your sins (from) before him. Harm* (lit. *the evil*) **51** *he did not do to you. / Indeed, greatly did Sennacherib, the king, loved me because I had preserved you* (lit. *caused you to live*) *and I had not killed you. / Now, you –* **52** *because I have done this for you, so, also do for me. / Do not kill me!*

82. . . . מִן כֹּל מַנְטְרָה טַר פֻּמָּךְ וְ[עַל] זִי שְׁ[מַעְתְּ] הוֹקַר לְבַב כִּי צִנְפַּר הִי מִלָּה וּמְשַׁלְּחַהּ גְּבַר לָא לְבַ[ב]

89. טְעִמֵת אנזעררתא [read אֲנָה זַעְרָרְתָא] מְרִרְתָּא וְ[טַעֲמָ]א חַסִּין וְלָא אִיתַי זִי [מָ]רִיר מִן עֲנָוָה

רַכִּיךְ לִשָּׁן מֶ[לֶךְ] **90.** וְעִלְעֵי תַנִּין יְתַבַּר כְּמוֹתָא זִי [לָ]א מִתְחֲזֵה

בְּשַׂגִּיא בָּנִן לִבְבָךְ אַל יֶחֱדֵה וּבִזְעֵירֵיהֹם . . . [or read וּבְזַרְעֵיהֹם]

176. אַל תְּהַחֲשֵׂךְ בְּרָךְ מִן חֻטַר הֵן לוּ לָא תִּכְהַל תְּהַנְצְלִנַּהְ[י מִן בְּאִישְׁתָּא]

177. . . . הֵן אֶמְחֵאנָךְ בְּרִי לָא תְמוּת וְהֵן אֶשְׁבְּקַן [אֶשְׁבְּקַנָּךְ or] עַל לִבְבָךְ [לָא תֶּחֱיֵה]

82 *More than all (other) concerns, guard your mouth and [concerning] that which [you h]ear, make your mind numb* (lit. *make your mind heavy*)*. For, a word is a bird and one who releases it (is) a senseless person* (lit. *a person (of) no min[d]*) *. . ./*

89 *I have tasted the bitter medlar fruit and the [tast]e is strong, but there is nothing more bitter than poverty* (or, perhaps *humiliation*)*. / Soft is a king's tongue* **90** *but a monster's ribs it will shatter like death* (lit. *the death*) *which is not seen. / In many children let your heart not rejoice and in their fewness . . .* (or, *in their seed . . .*)*/*

176 *Do not spare your child from the rod, lest you are not able to rescue hi[m from harm.]* **177** *If I beat you, my child, you will not die, but if I leave (you) to your heart, [you will not live] . . .*

Reading 2

Verso

1. שְׁלָם בֵּית נְבוּ

אֶל אֲחָתִי רֶעְיָה מִן אֲחֻכִי מַכִּבָנִת

2. בָּרְכְתֻּכִי לִפְתַח זִי יַחְזֵנִי אַפַּיִכִי בִּשְׁלָם

שְׁלָם בנתסרל וארג **3.** ואסרשת ושרדר

חֲרוּצ שְׁאֵל שְׁלָמְהֹן

וּכְעֶת שְׁלָם **4.** לַחֲרוּצ תְּנָה

אַל תְּצַפִּי לֵהּ

כְּדִי תִּכְלִן תַּעַבְדִן לֵהּ עָבֵד אֲנָה **5.** לֵהּ

ותפמת ואחתסן מְסַבְּלָן לֵהּ

וּכְעֶת אֲרֵה סֵפֶר לָה [read לָא] שְׁלַחְתִּי **6.** בִּשְׁמֵהּ

וּכְעֶת זִי מְלֵתִי לִבָּתִי לֵאמַר לָה [read לָא] שְׁאֵל עַל חֲרוּצ

כְּעֶת **7.** הֲלוּ כְּזִי עָבֵד אֲנָה לַחֲרוּצ כְּוָת תַּעֲבֵד בָּנִת עֲלַי

Recto

8. אֲרֵה לָא אַחִי הוּ חֲרוּצ

וּכְעֶת הֲלוּ יְהַב לְהֵן פְּרָס **9.** תְּנָה

וְיִתְלְקַח קַדְמַתְהֵן בִּסְוֵן

וּכְעֶת הֵן אִת עָרָב עֲלַיְכִי **10.** אֵתַיֵהּ לְתפמת

וּכְעֶת מַדְּעַם אַל תִּזְבְּנִי בִּכְסַת וְתִשְׁרִי לַהּ

11. שְׁלָם יקיה הֲוַי שָׁלְחַת לֵהּ

וּכְעֶת הֲוַי חָזְיַת עַל תשי וְעַל **12.** בְּרַהּ

וּשְׁלַחִי כֹּל טְעֵם זִי הָוֵה בְּבַיְתִי

לִשְׁלָמֵכִי שְׁלְחֵת סִפְרָ **13.** ה [read סִפְרָךְ] זְנָה

14. אֶל אַבִי פסמי בַּר נְבוּנְתַן מִן מַכִּבָנִת

סְוֵן יֵבַל

Verso

1 *Greetings to the Temple of Nabu. / To my sister, Reiah, from your brother, Makkibanit. /* **2** *I blessed you by Ptaḥ (requesting): May he show me your face in well-being. / Greetings to Bntsrl, ʾrg,* **3** *ʾsršt, and Šrdr. / Ḥorudj asks their well-being. / Now, Ḥorudj is well* **4** *here* (lit. *well-being belongs to Ḥorudj here*). */ Do not worry about him. / Just as you would be able to do for him, I am doing* **5** *for him. / And, Tpmt and ʾAḥatsin are supporting him. / And, now, lo, you have not sent a letter* **6** *in his name. / Now, because you are filled with rage against me* (lit. *you are filled with my rage*), *saying He has not looked after Ḥorudj – / Now,* **7** *lo, just as I do for Ḥorudj may Banit do for me.*

Recto

8 *Lo, is Ḥorudj not my brother? / Now, lo, (the) salary has been given to them* (i.e. the women Tpmt and ʼAḥatsin) / **9** *here but it can be taken ahead of them* (i.e. before they return) *in Syene. / Now, if there is something that can serve as surety for you,* **10** *bring it to Tpmt. / Now, do not buy anything* (i.e., any cloth, fabric) *for clothing and (do not) send (it) to him* (i.e. Ḥorudj?). / **11** *Please send greetings to Yqyh. Now, please look after Tšy and over* **12** *her son. Send (a message concerning) any matter that is (happening) in my house. / For your well-being I have sent this* **13** *letter. /* **14** *To my father, Psmy, son of Nabunetan, from Makkibanit. / Let it be brought (to) Syene.*

Test yourself

The following are just the most salient disctinctions as attested in the texts read in this grammar. Many more exist, including specific words that are attested only in earlier and not in later texts.

1 At first, no distinction was made between the final and non-final kaph, mem, nun, and sadeh. But, by at least the time of the Dead Sea Scrolls (i.e. the first century BCE), each of these letters had one form when they appeared at the beginning or in the middle of a word and another when they appeared at the end of a word.

2 The earlier Aramaic texts use fewer maters than later Aramaic texts. The later texts use waw and yod to mark what were at least historically short vowels. And, aleph is used within words (instead of just at the end of words) to indicate ā, while yod replaced aleph at the end of verbs to indicate the vowel corresponding to Biblical Aramaic sere.

3 Sometimes in later texts two waws or yods are used to indicate a single consonantal waw/yod (e.g. הֲווָה *it was*).

4 In the Egyptian Aramaic texts the letter zayin sometimes is used as a historical spelling for what would be represented in Biblical Aramaic and later dialects with a dalet. The letter śin (שׂ) is generally replaced by samekh (ס) in later dialects.

5 In Egyptian and Biblical Aramaic the relative pronoun/genitive marker/conjunction is spelled as an independent word, די (or זי), but in later dialects it is often spelled simply ד and attached to the following word.

6 In some later dialects the determined state becomes the default state, instead of the absolute.

7 In later dialects of Aramaic (as in the targums) the haphʻel is replaced consistently by the aphʻel (and the hitpəʻel/hitpaʻʻal by the itpəʻel/itpaʻʻal).

8 Masculine plural verb forms from III-aleph/waw/yod roots end in -ō in earlier Aramaic dialects, but in -ōn in later dialects (e.g. הֲוו vs. הֲוון *they were*).

9 In earlier dialects ל often marks the direct object of verbs, but in later Aramaic dialects יָת marks the direct object.

10 The suffixed pronouns change in various ways, such that the 3mp suffix **-הֹם** is realized as **-הוֹן** in later dialects and the 3ms suffix on masculine plural nouns, **-וֹהִי** in earlier dialects, is realized as **-וֹי** in later dialects.

Correspondences of verse numbers

Hebrew/Aramaic Bible		English-language Bibles
Dan	3:31	4:1
	3:32	4:2
	3:33	4:3
	4:1	4:4
	4:2	4:5
	4:3	4:6
	4:4	4:7
	4:5	4:8
	4:6	4:9
	4:7	4:10
	4:8	4:11
	4:9	4:12
	4:10	4:13
	4:11	4:14
	4:12	4:15
	4:13	4:16
	4:14	4:17
	4:15	4:18
	4:16	4:19
	4:17	4:20
	4:18	4:21
	4:19	4:22
	4:20	4:23
	4:21	4:24
	4:22	4:25
	4:23	4:26
	4:24	4:27
	4:25	4:28
	4:26	4:29
	4:27	4:30
	4:28	4:31

	4:29	4:32
	4:30	4:33
	4:31	4:34
	4:32	4:35
	4:33	4:36
	4:34	4:37
	6:1	5:31
	6:2	6:1
	6:3	6:2
	6:4	6:3
	6:5	6:4
	6:6	6:5
	6:7	6:6
	6:8	6:7
	6:9	6:8
	6:10	6:9
	6:11	6:10
	6:12	6:11
	6:13	6:12
	6:14	6:13
	6:15	6:14
	6:16	6:15
	6:17	6:16
	6:18	6:17
	6:19	6:18
	6:20	6:19
	6:21	6:20
	6:22	6:21
	6:23	6:22
	6:24	6:23
	6:25	6:24
	6:26	6:25
	6:27	6:26
	6:28	6:27
	6:29	6:28

Verb tables

Suffix conjugation of כתב and ברך

	כתב				ברך
	pə ʿal	pa ʿʿel	haph ʿel	aph ʿel	pa ʿʿel
3ms	כְּתַב	כַּתִּב or כַּתֵּב	הַכְתִּב or הַכְתֵּב	אַכְתִּב or אַכְתֵּב	בָּרִךְ or בָּרֵךְ
3fs	כִּתְבַת	כַּתְּבַת	הַכְתְּבַת	אַכְתְּבַת	בָּרְכַת
2ms	-תְּ or כְּתַ֫בְתָּ	-תְּ or כַּתֵּ֫בְתָּ	-תְּ or הַכְתֵּ֫בְתָּ	-תְּ or אַכְתֵּ֫בְתָּ	-תְּ or בָּרֵ֫כְתָּ
2fs	כְּתַ֫בְתִּי	כַּתֵּ֫בְתִּי	הַכְתֵּ֫בְתִּי	אַכְתֵּ֫בְתִּי	בָּרֵ֫כְתִּי
1cs	כִּתְבֵת	כַּתְּבֵת	הַכְתְּבֵת	אַכְתְּבֵת	בָּרְכֵת
3mp	כְּתַ֫בוּ	כַּתִּ֫בוּ	הַכְתִּ֫בוּ	אַכְתִּ֫בוּ	בָּרִ֫כוּ
3fp	כְּתַ֫בָה	כַּתִּ֫בָה	הַכְתִּ֫בָה	אַכְתִּ֫בָה	בָּרִ֫כָה
2mp	כְּתַבְתּוּן	כַּתֵּבְתּוּן	הַכְתֵּבְתּוּן	אַכְתֵּבְתּוּן	בָּרֵכְתּוּן
2fp	כְּתַבְתֵּן	כַּתֵּבְתֵּן	הַכְתֵּבְתֵּן	אַכְתֵּבְתֵּן	בָּרֵכְתֵּן
1cp	כְּתַ֫בְנָא	כַּתֵּ֫בְנָא	הַכְתֵּ֫בְנָא	אַכְתֵּ֫בְנָא	בָּרֵ֫כְנָא

The pə ʿīl, pu ʿʿal, and huph ʿal/hoph ʿal suffix conjugation of כתב

	כתב		
	pə ʿīl	pu ʿʿal	huph ʿal/hoph ʿal
3ms	כְּתִיב	כֻּתַּב*	הֻכְתַּב or הָכְתַּב
3fs	כְּתִיבַת	כֻּתְּבַת*	הֻכְתְּבַת
2ms	כְּתִיבְתְּ or כְּתִ֫יבְתָּ	כֻּתַּבְתְּ* or כֻּתַּ֫בְתָּ*	הֻכְתַּבְתְּ or הֻכְתַּ֫בְתָּ
2fs	כְּתִ֫יבְתִּי	כֻּתַּ֫בְתִּי*	הֻכְתַּ֫בְתִּי
1cs	כְּתִיבֵת	כֻּתְּבֵת*	הֻכְתְּבֵת
3mp	כְּתִ֫יבוּ	כֻּתַּ֫בוּ*	הֻכְתַּ֫בוּ
3fp	כְּתִ֫יבָה	כֻּתַּ֫בָה*	הֻכְתַּ֫בָה
2mp	כְּתִיבְתּוּן	כֻּתַּבְתּוּן*	הֻכְתַּבְתּוּן
2fp	כְּתִיבְתֵּן	כֻּתַּבְתֵּן*	הֻכְתַּבְתֵּן
1cp	כְּתִ֫יבְנָא	כֻּתַּ֫בְנָא*	הֻכְתַּ֫בְנָא

Prefix conjugation, jussive, imperative of כתב

	כתב								
	pəʿal			paʿʿel		hapʰʿel		apʰʿel	
	pref	juss	impv	pref	impv	pref	impv	pref	impv
3ms	יִכְתֻּב	יִכְתֻּב		יְכַתֵּב		יְהַכְתֵּב		יַכְתֵּב	
3fs	תִּכְתֻּב	תִּכְתֻּב		תְּכַתֵּב		תְּהַכְתֵּב		תַּכְתֵּב	
2ms	תִּכְתֻּב	תִּכְתֻּב	כְּתֻב	תְּכַתֵּב	כַּתֵּב	תְּהַכְתֵּב	הַכְתֵּב	תַּכְתֵּב	אַכְתֵּב
2fs	תִּכְתְּבִין	תִּכְתֻּבִי	כְּתֻבִי	תְּכַתְּבִין	כַּתִּבִי	תְּהַכְתְּבִין	הַכְתִּבִי	תַּכְתְּבִין	אַכְתִּבִי
1cs	אֶכְתֻּב			אֲכַתֵּב		אֲהַכְתֵּב		אַכְתֵּב	
3mp	יִכְתְּבוּן	יִכְתֻּבוּ		יְכַתְּבוּן		יְהַכְתְּבוּן		יַכְתְּבוּן	
3fp	יִכְתְּבָן	*יִכְתֻּבָה		יְכַתְּבָן		יְהַכְתְּבָן		יַכְתְּבָן	
2mp	תִּכְתְּבוּן	תִּכְתֻּבוּ	כְּתֻבוּ	תְּכַתְּבוּן	כַּתִּבוּ	תְּהַכְתְּבוּן	הַכְתִּבוּ	תַּכְתְּבוּן	אַכְתִּבוּ
2fp	תִּכְתְּבָן	*תִּכְתֻּבָה	כְּתֻבָה	תְּכַתְּבָן	כַּתִּבָה	תְּהַכְתְּבָן	הַכְתִּבָה	תַּכְתְּבָן	אַכְתִּבָה
1cp	נִכְתֻּב			נְכַתֵּב		נְהַכְתֵּב		נַכְתֵּב	
inf	מִכְתַּב			כַּתָּבָה		הַכְתָּבָה		אַכְתָּבָה	
part	כָּתֵב			מְכַתֵּב		מְהַכְתֵּב		מַכְתֵּב	
pass	כְּתִיב			מְכַתַּב		מְהַכְתַּב		מַכְתַּב	

The hitpəʿel and the hitpaʿʿal of כתב

	כתב					
	hitpəʿel			hitpaʿʿal		
	suff	pref	impv	suff	pref	impv
3ms	הִתְכְּתֵב	יִתְכְּתֵב		הִתְכַּתַּב	יִתְכַּתַּב	
3fs	הִתְכַּתְבַת	תִּתְכְּתֵב		הִתְכַּתְּבַת	תִּתְכַּתַּב	
2ms	הִתְכְּתֵבְתְּ	תִּתְכְּתֵב	הִתְכְּתֵב	הִתְכַּתַּבְתְּ	תִּתְכַּתַּב	הִתְכַּתַּב
2fs	הִתְכְּתֵבְתִּי	תִּתְכַּתְבִין	הִתְכְּתִבִי	הִתְכַּתַּבְתִּי	תִּתְכַּתְּבִין	הִתְכַּתַּבִי
1cs	הִתְכַּתְבֵת	אֶתְכְּתֵב		הִתְכַּתְּבֵת	אֶתְכַּתַּב	
3mp	הִתְכְּתִבוּ	יִתְכַּתְבוּן		הִתְכַּתַּבוּ	יִתְכַּתְּבוּן	
3fp	הִתְכְּתִבָה	יִתְכַּתְבָן		הִתְכַּתַּבָה	יִתְכַּתְּבָן	
2mp	הִתְכְּתֵבְתּוּן	תִּתְכַּתְבוּן	הִתְכְּתִבוּ	הִתְכַּתַּבְתּוּן	תִּתְכַּתְּבוּן	הִתְכַּתַּבוּ

2fp	הִתְכְּתִבְתֵּן	תִּתְכַּתְבָן	הִתְכְּתִ֫בָה	הִתְכַּתַּבְתֵּן	תִּתְכַּתְּבָן	הִתְכַּתַּ֫בָה
1cp	הִתְכְּתֵ֫בְנָא	נִתְכְּתֵב		הִתְכַּתַּ֫בְנָא	נִתְכַּתַּב	
inf	הִתְכְּתָבָה			הִתְכַּתָּבָה		
part	מִתְכְּתֵב			מִתְכַּתַּב		

I-nun roots in pə ʿal

	נפל *to fall*		נפק *to go or come out*		נתן *to give*
	pə ʿal		**pə ʿal**		**pə ʿal**
	prefix	**imperative**	**prefix**	**imperative**	**prefix**
3ms	יִפֵּל		יִפֵּק		יִנְתֵּן
3fs	תִּפֵּל		תִּפֵּק		תִּנְתֵּן
2ms	תִּפֵּל	פֵּל	תִּפֵּק	פֵּק	תִּנְתֵּן
2fs	תִּפְּלִין	פֵּ֫לִי	תִּפְּקִין	פֵּ֫קִי	תִּנְתְּנִין
1cs	אֶפֵּל		אֶפֵּק		אֶנְתֵּן
3mp	יִפְּלוּן		יִפְּקוּן		יִנְתְּנוּן
3fp	יִפְּלָן		יִפְּקָן		יִנְתְּנָן
2mp	תִּפְּלוּן	פֵּ֫לוּ	תִּפְּקוּן	פֵּ֫קוּ	תִּנְתְּנוּן
2fp	תִּפְּלָן	פֵּ֫לָה	תִּפְּקָן	פֵּ֫קָה	תִּנְתְּנָן
1cp	נִפֵּל		נִפֵּק		נִנְתֵּן
inf	מִפַּל		מִפַּק		מִנְתַּן
part	נָפֵל		נָפֵק		נָתֵן

I-nun roots in aphʿel and haphʿel

	נפק					
	aphʿel			**haphʿel**		
	suffix	**prefix**	**imperative**	**suffix**	**prefix**	**imperative**
3ms	אַפֵּק	יַפֵּק		הַנְפֵּק	יְהַנְפֵּק	
3fs	אַפְּקַת	תַּפֵּק		הַנְפְּקַת	תְּהַנְפֵּק	
2ms	אַפֵּ֫קְתְּ	תַּפֵּק	אַפֵּק	הַנְפֵּ֫קְתְּ	תְּהַנְפֵּק	הַנְפֵּק

2fs	אַפֵּ֫קְתִּי	תַּפְּקִין	אַפִּ֫קִי	הַנְפֵּ֫קְתִּי	תְּהַנְפְּקִין	הַנְפִּ֫קִי
1cs	אַפְּקֵת	אַפֵּק		הַנְפְּקֵת	אֲהַנְפֵּק	
3mp	אַפִּ֫קוּ	יַפְּקוּן		הַנְפִּ֫קוּ	יְהַנְפְּקוּן	
3fp	אַפִּ֫קָה	יַפְּקָן		הַנְפִּ֫קָה	יְהַנְפְּקָן	
2mp	אַפֵּקְתּוּן	תַּפְּקוּן	אַפִּ֫קוּ	הַנְפֵּקְתּוּן	תְּהַנְפְּקוּן	הַנְפִּ֫קוּ
2fp	אַפֵּקְתֵּן	תַּפְּקָן	אַפִּ֫קָה	הַנְפֵּקְתֵּן	תְּהַנְפְּקָן	הַנְפִּ֫קָה
1cp	אַפֵּ֫קְנָא	נַפֵּק		הַנְפֵּ֫קְנָא	נְהַנְפֵּק	
inf	אַפָּקָה			הַנְפָּקָה		
part	מַפֵּק			מְהַנְפֵּק		

I-aleph roots

	אמר			אבד		
	pəʿal			**haphʿel**		
	suff	**pref**	**impv**	**suff**	**pref**	**impv**
3ms	אֲמַר	יֵאמַר		הוֹבֵד	יְהוֹבֵד	
3fs	אֲמֶ֫רֶת	תֵּאמַר		הוֹבְדַת	תְּהוֹבֵד	
2ms	אֲמַ֫רְתָּ or -תְּ	תֵּאמַר	אֱמַר	הוֹבֵדְתְּ	תְּהוֹבֵד	הוֹבֵד
2fs	אֲמַ֫רְתִּי	תֵּאמְרִין	אֱמַ֫רִי	הוֹבֵ֫דְתִּי	תְּהוֹבְדִין	הוֹבִ֫דִי
1cs	אַמְרֵת	אֵמַר		הוֹבְדֵת	אֲהוֹבֵד	
3mp	אֲמַ֫רוּ	יֵאמְרוּן		הוֹבִ֫דוּ	יְהוֹבְדוּן	
3fp	אֲמַ֫רָה	יֵאמְרָן		הוֹבִ֫דָה	יְהוֹבְדָן	
2mp	אֲמַרְתּוּן	תֵּאמְרוּן	אֱמַ֫רוּ	הוֹבֵדְתּוּן	תְּהוֹבְדוּן	הוֹבִ֫דוּ
2fp	אֲמַרְתֵּן	תֵּאמְרָן	אֱמַ֫רָה	הוֹבֵדְתֵּן	תְּהוֹבְדָן	הוֹבִ֫דָה
1cp	אֲמַ֫רְנָא	נֵאמַר		הוֹבֵ֫דְנָא	נְהוֹבֵד	
inf	מֵאמַר			הוֹבָדָה		
part	אָמֵר			מְהוֹבֵד		
pass	אֲמִיר			מְהוֹבַד		

I-yod roots

	יכל	ידע				
	pəʿal	pəʿal		haphʿel		
	prefix	prefix	impv	suffix	prefix	impv
3ms	יִכֻּל	יִנְדַּע		הוֹדַע	יְהוֹדַע	
3fs	תִּכֻּל	תִּנְדַּע		הוֹדְעַת	תְּהוֹדַע	
2ms	תִּכֻּל	תִּנְדַּע	דַּע	הוֹדַעְתְּ	תְּהוֹדַע	הוֹדַע
2fs	תִּכְלִין	תִּנְדְּעִין	דַּ֫עִי	הוֹדַ֫עְתִּי	תְּהוֹדְעִין	הוֹדַ֫עִי
1cs	אִכֻּל	אֶנְדַּע		הוֹדְעֵת	אֲהוֹדַע	
3mp	יִכְלוּן	יִנְדְּעוּן		הוֹדַ֫עוּ	יְהוֹדְעוּן	
3fp	יִכְלָן	יִנְדְּעָן		הוֹדַ֫עָה	יְהוֹדְעָן	
2mp	תִּכְלוּן	תִּנְדְּעוּן	דַּ֫עוּ	הוֹדַעְתּוּן	תְּהוֹדְעוּן	הוֹדַ֫עוּ
2fp	תִּכְלָן	תִּנְדְּעָן	דַּ֫עָה	הוֹדַעְתֵּן	תְּהוֹדְעָן	הוֹדַ֫עָה
1cp	נִכֻּל	נִנְדַּע		הוֹדַ֫עְנוּ	נְהוֹדַע	
inf	-	מִנְדַּע		הוֹדָעָה		
part	יָכֵל	יָדַע		מְהוֹדַע		
pass	-	יְדִיעַ		מְהוֹדַע		

II-waw/yod roots

	קום					
	pəʿal			haphʿel		
	suffix	prefix	impv	suffix	prefix	impv
3ms	קָם	יְקוּם		הֲקִים or הֲקֵים	יְקִים (most common) or יְהָקֵים or יָקֵים or יָקִים	
3fs	קָ֫מַת	תְּקוּם		הֲקִ֫ימַת or הֲקֵ֫ימַת	תְּקִים / etc.	
2ms	קָ֫מְתָּ	תְּקוּם	קוּם	הֲקֵ֫ימְתָּ	תְּקִים / etc.	הֲקִים / הֲקֵים
2fs	קָ֫מְתִּי	תְּקוּמִין	ק֫וּמִי	הֲקֵ֫ימְתִּי	תְּקִימִין / etc.	הֲקִ֫ימִי
1cs	קָ֫מֶת	אֲקוּם		הֲקֵ֫ימֶת	אֲקִים / etc.	

3mp	קָ֫מוּ	יְקוּמוּן		הֲקֵ֫ימוּ or הֲקִ֫ימוּ	יְקִימוּן / etc.	
3fp	קָ֫מָה	יְקוּמָן		הֲקֵ֫ימָה or הֲקִ֫ימָה	יְקִימָן / etc.	
2mp	קָמְתּוּן	תְּקוּמוּן		הֲקֵימְתּוּן	תְּקִימוּן / etc.	הֲקִ֫ימוּ
2fp	קָמְתֵּן	תְּקוּמָן		הֲקֵימְתֵּן	תְּקִימָן / etc.	הֲקִ֫ימָה
1cp	קָ֫מְנָא	נְקוּם		הֲקֵ֫ימְנָא	נְקִים / etc.	
inf	מְקָם			הֲקָמָה		
part	קָאֵם			מְהָקֵים		
pass	קִים			?		

III-aleph/waw/yod verbs, pə ʻal and pə ʻīl

	בני				הוי		
	pə ʻal			pə ʻīl	pə ʻal		
	suffix	prefix	impv	suff	suff	pref	impv
3ms	בְּנָה	יִבְנֵא		בְּנִי	הֲוָה	לֶהֱוֵא	
3fs	בְּנָת	תִּבְנֵא		-	הֲוָת	תֶּהֱוֵא	
2ms	בְּנַ֫יְתָ or בְּנַית	תִּבְנֵא	בְּנִי	-	הֲוַ֫יְתָ	-	-
2fs	בְּנַ֫יְתִי	-	בְּנַי*	-	-	-	הֲוַי*
1cs	בְּנֵית	אֶבְנֵא		-	הֲוֵית	-	
3mp	בְּנוֹ	יִבְנוֹן		בְּנִיו	הֲווֹ	לֶהֱוֹן	
3fp	בְּנָה*	יִבְנְיָן		-	-	לֶהֶוְיָן	
2mp	בְּנֵיתוּן	תִּבְנוֹן	בְּנוֹ	-	-	-	הֱווֹ
2fp	בְּנֵיתֵן	תִּבְנְיָן	-	-	-	-	-
1cp	בְּנֵ֫ינָא	נִבְנֵא		-	-	-	
inf	מִבְנֵא				מֶהֱוֵא*		
part	בָּנֵה				הָוֵה		
pass	בְּנֵה				-		

III-aleph/waw/yod verbs, pa‘‘el and haph‘el

	בני						אתי	
	pa‘‘el			haph‘el			haph‘el	huph‘al
	suff	pref	impv	suff	pref (ha./aph.)	impv	suff	suff
3ms	בַּנִּי	יְבַנֵּא		הַבְנִי	יְהַבְנֵא or יַבְנֵא		הַיְתִי	-
3fs	בַּנִּיַת*	תְּבַנֵּא		הַבְנִיַת*	תְּהַבְנֵא or תַּבְנֵא		-	הֵיתָיִת
2ms	בַּנִּיתָ	תְּבַנֵּא	בַּנִּי	הַבְנִיתָ	תְּהַבְנֵא or תַּבְנֵא	הַבְנִי	-	-
2fs	בַּנִּיתִי	-	בַּנִּי*	הַבְנִיתִי	תְּהַבְנֵין* or תַּבְנֵין*	הַבְנִי*	-	-
1cs	בַּנִּית	אֲבַנֵּא		הַבְנִית	אֲהַבְנֵא or אַבְנֵין		-	-
3mp	בַּנִּיו	יְבַנּוֹן		הַבְנִיו	יְהַבְנוֹן or יַבְנוֹן		הַיְתִיו	הֵיתָיו
3fp	בַּנִּיָה*	יְבַנְּיָן		הַבְנִיָה*	יְהַבְנְיָן or יַבְנְיָן		-	-
2mp	בַּנִּיתוּן	תְּבַנּוֹן	בַּנּוֹ	הַבְנִיתוּן	תְּהַבְנוֹן or תַּבְנוֹן	הַבְנוֹ	-	-
2fp	בַּנִּיתֵן	תְּבַנְּיָן	-	הַבְנִיתֵן	תְּהַבְנְיָן or תַּבְנְיָן	-	-	-
1cp	בַּנִּינָא	נְבַנֵּא		הַבְנִינָא	נְהַבְנֵא or נַבְנֵא		-	-
inf	בַּנָּיָה			הַבְנָיָה			הַיְתָיָה	-
part	מְבַנֵּה			מְהַבְנֵה			-	-
pass	מְבַנֵּי			מְהַבְנֵי			-	-

Geminate verbs

	עלל					
	pəʿal			haphʿel		
	suff	pref	impv	suff	pref	impv
3ms	עַל	יֵעֹל (ye‘‘ol)		הַעֵל or הַנְעֵל	יְהַעֵל or יַעֵל	
3fs	עַלַּלת	תֵּעֹל		הַעֶלֶת or הַנְעֶלֶת	תְּהַעֵל or תַּעֵל	
2ms	עֲלַלְתָּ	תֵּעֹל	עֹל	הַעֵלְתָּ / etc.	תְּהַעֵל / etc.	הַעֵל
2fs	עֲלַלְתִּי	תֵּעֲלִין	עֹלִי	הַעֵלְתִּי	תְּהַעֲלִין	הַעִלִי
1cs	עַלֵּת	אֵעֹל		הַעֶלֶת	אֲהַעֵל	
3mp	עַלּוּ	יֵעֲלוּן		הַעִלּוּ	יְהַעֲלוּן	
3fp	עַלָּה	יֵעֲלָן		הַעִלָּה	יְהַעֲלָן	
2mp	עֲלַלְתּוּן	תֵּעֲלוּן	עֹלּוּ	הַעֵלְתּוּן	תְּהַעֲלוּן	הַעִלּוּ
2fp	עֲלַלְתֵּן	תֵּעֲלָן	עֹלָּה	הַעֵלְתֵּן	תְּהַעֲלָן	הַעִלָּה
1cp	עֲלַלְנָא	נֵעֹל		הַעֵלְנָא	נְהַעֵל	
inf	מֵעַל			הֶעָלָה or הַנְעָלָה		
part	עָלֵל			מְהַעֵל		
pass	עֲלִיל			מְהַעַל		

Glossary of grammatical terms

absolute one of three states in which nouns and adjectives occur. The absolute state is the most basic state, the form of the noun/adjective found in a dictionary entry. It is usually translated into English by a noun with an indefinite article (*a*, *an*).

assimilation The absorption of one consonant into another, as when the nun of נפל is absorbed into the peh: יִפֵּל *he will fall* from an earlier *yinpel. The shift in the pronunciation of a consonant towards that of another, neighbouring consonant is also called assimilation, as when the taw of the hitpa‘‘al assimilates towards the emphatic articulation of sadeh, such that the taw becomes a tet: יִצְטַבַּע *he will be drenched* (hitpa‘‘al of צבע) from an earlier *yiṣtabba‘.

begadkephat letters This is the set of letters (ב *b*, ג *g*, ד *d*, כ *k*, פ *p*, ת *t*) that were pronounced either *hard* (i.e. non-spirantized = b, g, d, k, p, t) or *soft* (i.e. spirantized = v, gh, dh, ch, ph, th). Today, only the ב *b/v*, כ *k/ch*, and פ *p/ph* are pronounced in a *soft* manner. The rest are always pronounced *hard*. Graphically, the two pronunciations are distinguished through a dagesh (or dot) in the centre of a consonant when it is pronounced *hard*. A *hard* or *soft* pronunciation never presupposes a different meaning. A begadkephat consonant will generally be *soft* when preceded directly by a vowel and *hard* when not preceded by a vowel or when the consonant is doubled.

closed syllable a syllable that is composed of the sequence consonant + vowel + consonant.

compensatory lengthening The lengthening of a short vowel into a long vowel to compensate for the lack of the doubling of a following guttural consonant or resh (e.g. מִתְעָרַב mit‘ārab hitpa‘‘al m.s. part of ערב – from an earlier *mit‘arrab) or to compensate for the loss of an aleph in pronunciation (e.g. מֵאמַר mēmar *to say* from an earlier *mi’mar).

construct one of three states in which nouns and adjectives occur. A noun or adjective in the construct state forms a single expression with the following word or words. Usually, this expression consists of two nouns (the first in the construct and the second in the absolute or determined state). The expression is usually translated with a preposition (most commonly *of*) between the two nouns (*X of Y*), though other prepositions can be used depending on context. In terms of their forms, masculine singular nouns often have the same form as in the absolute state; masculine plural nouns are marked by a final ◌ֵי- ending. Feminine singular nouns in the construct state are marked by final ת- or ◌ַת- ending and feminine plural nouns by a final ◌ָת- ending.

dagesh a dot in the centre of a non-guttural letter. A dagesh in a begadkephat consonant indicates either that it is doubled and/or that it is pronounced *hard*. A dagesh in any non-begadkephat consonant always indicates doubling.

demonstrative pronouns words that function like the English pronouns *this*, *that*, *these*, *those*.

determined one of three states in which nouns and adjectives occur. The determined state marks a noun or adjective as specific, in the same way that the English *the* marks nouns as specific. The determined state is characterized by a final -ā ending and this vowel is typically marked by an aleph mater, though alternatively sometimes by a he mater.

geminate a root whose second and third root consonants are the same (e.g. עלל *to enter*).

guttural a consonant pronounced in the back of the mouth, close to the throat, including aleph (א), he (ה), het (ח), 'ayin (ע). In addition, resh (ר) often behaves like a guttural.

imperative a verbal form that indicates a speaker's wish or demand for something to happen, exclusively in the second person (e.g. *do it*); the imperative has nearly the same form as the jussive but lacks the jussive's prefixal component.

jussive a verbal form that indicates a speaker's wish for something to happen (*let her do it, may she do it*), formally distinct from the prefix conjugation only in the 2fs and plural forms which lack the final nun ending (e.g. jussive יִכְתְּבוּ *let them write* vs. prefix conjugation יִכְתְּבוּן *they will write*).

mappiq a dot in a final he that indicates that the he is not a mater, but instead a true consonant. The mappiq appears primarily in only two places, in the 3m/fs pronominal suffix (ֵהּ- *his* and ַהּ- *her*) and in roots whose third root consonant is he (e.g. אֱלָהּ *God*).

maqqeph a line (like a dash) that connects independent words and often implies a single stress for the entire group of words that are connected.

mater (lectionis) *a mother (of reading)*, an aleph, he, waw, or yod that represents the presence of a preceding long vowel. In later dialects of Aramaic, like those of the Dead Sea Scrolls and targums, a mater may also represent a short vowel.

metathesis The shift in the sequence of consonants, typically found in the hitpəʻel and hitpaʻʻal stems with roots whose first consonant is a sibilant (zayin ז, samekh ס, sadeh צ, śin שׂ, or shin שׁ), resulting in the sibilant coming before the taw: הִשְׁתְּכַח *he was found*. When the first root consonant is a zayin, the taw also assimilates in pronunciation to the sibilant: הִזְדְּמֵן *he conspired* (hitpəʻel of זמן). When the first root consonant is a sadeh, the taw also assimilates in pronunciation to the sibilant: יִצְטַבַּע *he will be drenched* (hitpaʻʻal of צבע).

morpheme a component of a noun, adjective, or verb that marks the word as feminine, plural, or (with verbs) of the first, second, or third person. For example, the final -$\bar{a}^{h}$ of מַלְכָּה *queen* is a feminine singular morpheme. The ending -$t\bar{\imath}^{y}$ is a 2fs ending of the suffix conjugation: כְּתַבְתִּי *you wrote*.

nasalization The introduction of a nun (n) to break up a doubled consonant. For example, through nasalization יִדַּע yiddaʻ *he will know* becomes יִנְדַּע yindaʻ *he will know*.

open syllable a syllable that is composed of the sequence consonant + vowel.

prefix conjugation a verbal form that usually indicates future tense or nuances of possibility (*we might do it, we could do it*), obligation (*we should do it*), necessity (*we must do it*), formally distinct due to prefixes (and some suffixes) to a verbal stem that indicate person, number, gender.

relative pronoun words that function like English *who, whose, whom, which, that, where*.

shewa a symbol that represents in Biblical Aramaic either the absence of a vowel or a muttered vowel. In the vowel system found in Targum Onqelos, the shewa represents only a muttered vowel (the absence of a vowel being marked by the absence of any symbol).

stem one of the categories of verbal inflection. The three main stems are the pəʿal, paʿʿel, and haphʿel, each of which has a corresponding internal passive stem (pəʿīl, puʿʿal, and huphʿal/hophʿal) and t-stem (hitpəʿel, hitpaʿʿal, hittaphʿal). Those stems that begin with a he (like the haphʿel) have alternative forms that begin with aleph and are called, respectively the aphʿel, itpəʿel, itpaʿʿal, ittaphʿal.

suffix conjugation a verbal form that usually indicates past tense or action seen as complete, formally distinct due to suffixes to a verbal root that indicate person, number, gender.

Syriac a variety of Aramaic which is attested in several separate dialects. It is preserved in a great many texts dating from around the turn of the era to the present day. It has several distinctive alphabets, but a largely standardized grammar. Students familiar with Biblical Aramaic usually can learn Syriac fairly quickly.

Targum an Aramaic translation of Hebrew scripture. Targum Onqelos is the earliest (first centuries CE) and most authoritative translation of the Pentateuch and, although presumably first written in a Western Aramaic dialect, reflects also some aspects of Eastern Aramaic. Targum Jonathan is like Targum Onqelos linguistically and preserves the translations of most other books of the Hebrew Bible through Kings. Targum Neofiti is another translation of the Pentateuch, and is later than Onqelos, reflecting only a Western variety of Aramaic. Targum Pseudo-Jonathan is a third translation of the Pentateuch and represents Aramaic from the last part of the first millennium CE. There are many other Aramaic translations of Hebrew scripture, including those in Samaritan Aramaic, Christian Palestinian Aramaic, and Syriac.

theme vowel A vowel that occurs between root consonants especially in a suffix or prefix conjugation verb form. For example, the theme vowel of כתב in the suffix conjugation is a (כְּתַב *he wrote*) and in the prefix conjugation is u (יִכְתֻּב *he will write*).

virtual doubling The apparent doubling of a guttural (especially he, het, and ʿayin) though the doubling is not indicated with a dagesh (e.g. נַהִירוּ nahīʸrūʷ but reflecting an earlier *nahhīʸrūʷ *illumination*).

vowel reduction the partial or complete elimination of a short vowel, often associated with the inflection of words (סָפַר *scribe* exhibits reduction of the short a to a muttered vowel ə in the determined form, סָפְרָא *the scribe*). From a historical perspective, vowel reduction can be described as taking place only with short vowels in open, non-stressed syllables, primarily in the syllable before the stress (e.g. an earlier *sāparâ *the scribe* became sāpərâ = סָפְרָא). A vowel will entirely disappear as long as this does not result in an irregular type of syllable (like a long vowel in a closed non-stressed syllable or a cluster of consonants). The second a in *malakān *queens* disappears entirely and the word becomes malkān = מַלְכָן *queens*; in *sāparâ, on the other hand, the short a must reduce to a muttered vowel (ə) since this would otherwise result in **sāprâ where the first non-stressed syllable would have a long vowel. The initial short vowel of *malakān is preserved (malkān = מַלְכָן) since vowel reduction of the second a leaves the first a in a closed syllable. If there are short vowels in open syllables further away from the stress, these are reduced to a muttered vowel. In the singular determined form of צִדְקָה *charity* note the development (simplified for pedagogical purposes) *ṣidaqatâ → *ṣidaqtâ (a before stress disappears) → ṣədaqtâ = צְדַקְתָּא (reduction of i to a muttered vowel in the first syllable).

Aramaic–English glossary

Note that nouns are listed with their construct and/or determined forms only when the forms are attested and unpredictable or irregular. In cases where the form of the noun in the construct or determined state is not attested or is entirely predictable, then just the absolute is given. Similarly with plural forms. If a noun ends with -āʰ or -ūʷ it should be inferred that it is feminine; if not, it should be assumed that the noun is masculine. Only exceptions are noted. Verbs that are etymologically III-aleph/waw/yodh are all listed as though they were III-yod (e.g. etymological **מלא** is listed as **מלי**). Verbs of strong roots that appear in the pəʿal are listed with the theme vowels with which they appear in the suffix and prefix conjugations. For example, the parenthetical note "pə. (a/u)" indicates that the verb **כתב** *to write* occurs with an a theme vowel in the suffix conjugation and a u theme vowel in the prefix. Irregular or unusual verb forms are listed in brackets. No theme vowel is listed if a verb is not attested in the suffix or prefix conjugations (e.g. only appearing as a participle). For the sake of consistency, all words with vowels are listed with the vowel symbols of Biblical Aramaic.

אַב	(sing. det. **אַבָא**; w/suff. **אַ֫בִי** and **אֲב֫וּהִי**; pl. **אֲבָהָן**; w/suff. **אֲבָהָתִי**) *father*
אֵב	(det. **אִנְבֵּא**) *fruit*
אבד	pə. (3ms pref. **יֵאבַד** ; targ. 3ms pref. **יֵיבַד**) *to perish, disappear*; ha. (3ms suff. **הוֹבֵד** 3mp pref. **יְהוֹבְדוּן**) *to destroy, abolish*; hu. /ho. (3ms suff. **הוּבַד**) *to be destroyed*
אֲבָהָה	see **אַב**
אֶ֫בֶן	(det. **אַבְנָא**) *stone* (fem.)
אַבְרָם	*Abram*
אִגְּרָה	(det. **אִגַּרְתָּא**) *letter*
אדושיא	Iranian word, *troubles*
אֱדַ֫יִן	conj. *then* (cf. **בֵּאדַ֫יִן**)
אֲדְמָה	*ground*
אוּמָּה	see **אֻמָּה**
אַזְדָּא	*certain*
אזי	pə. (1cp pref. **נֵזֵא** or **נֵזֵי**; inf. **מֵזֵא**) *to heat*; pəʿīl (m.s. pass. part. **אֲזֵה**) to be heated; itpə. (3ms pref. **יִתְזֵה**) *to become hot*
אזל	pə. (a/e) (3ms pref. **יֵיזֵל**; m.s. imv. **אֱ֫זֶל**) *to go*
אַח	(sing. w/suff. **אַ֫חִי** and **אֲח֫וּהִי**; pl. w/suff. **אֶחָיךְ**) *brother*
אַחִטָב	*Aḥitab*
אֲחִידָה	*riddle*
אֲחִיקָר	*Aḥiqar*

אַחְמְתָא	*Ecbatana*
אָחֳרִי	*another*
אָחֳרֵין	*last, in expression* עַד אָחֳרֵין *at last*
אָחֳרָן	(m.p. abs. אָחֳרָנִין) *another*
אֲחַשְׁדַּרְפְּנִין	(only pl.) *satraps*
אֲחָת	*sister*
אַחָתָה	see נחת
אִילָּא	*if not* (= אִין לָא)
אִילָן	*tree*
אִין	*if* (cf. אִם and הֵן)
אִיקָר	*glory, honour*
אִישׁ	*man, person*
אִיתַי	(abbreviated אִת) *there is, it is, there are; with suff. (e.g., 2mp* אִיתֵיכוֹן*) used to mark subject of following verb*
אִיתְּתָא	see אִנְתָּה
אכל	pə. (a/u or o) (3ms pref. יֵאכֻל; targ. יֵיכוֹל) *to eat*
אַל	adv. *no, not*
אֶל	prep. *to*; this occurs in Egyptian texts primarily; it takes suffixes like עַל.
אֵל	*God*
אֵל	*these* (c.p.)
אֵלה	*these* (c.p.)
אֵ֫לֶּה	*these* (c.p.)
אֱלָהּ	*god, God*
אֲלוּ	*lo, behold*
אִלֵּין	*these, those* (c.p.)
אִלֵּךְ	*these, those* (c.p.)
אלף	pə. (a/a) (3ms pref. יֵילַף; targ. m.s. part. אָלֵיף) *to learn*; pa. (3ms pref. יַלֵּיף from earlier יְאַלֵּף*; targ. m.s. imv. אַלֵּיף) *to teach*
אֲלַף	(det. אַלְפָּא; cstr. sing. is אֶ֫לֶף) *thousand*
אֶ֫לֶף	see אֲלַף
אַלְפּוֹן	*teaching*
אִם	*if* (cf. אִין and הֵן)
אֵם	(det. אִמָּא) *mother*
אַמָּה	(pl. אַמִּין) *cubit*
אֻמָּה	*people, nation*

אמן	ha. (3ms suff. הֵימַן) *to trust*
אמר	pə. (a/a) (3fs suff. אֲמֶ֫רֶת and 3ms pref. יֵאמַר; inf. מֵאמַר and מֵמַר; targ. 3ms pref. יֵימַר) *to say, speak, command, order*
אִמַּר	*lamb*
אִמַּת and אִמַּתִי	conj. *when*; עַד אִמַּתִי *how long?*
אִנְבֵּהּ	see אֵב
אֲנָה	*I*
אִנּוּן	*they, these* (c.p.)
אֱנוֹשׁ	*Enosh, person* (= אֱנָשׁ and אֲנָשׁ)
אֲנַחְנָא	*we*
אִנִּין	*they*
אנס	pə. *to trouble, oppress*
אנפי	see אַף
אֱנָשׁ and אֲנָשׁ	(det. אֲנָשָׁא) *person, man, humans, people, humanity*; כָּל־אֱנָשׁ *anyone*
אַנְתְּ	(targ. אַתְּ ='att) *you* (m.s.)
אַנְתְּה	*you* (m.s.)
אִנְתְּה	(targ. cstr. אִתַּת; targ. det. אִתְּתָא and אִיתְּתָא; DSS w/suff. אִנְתְּתִי; pl. abs. נְשִׁין; targ. pl. det. נְשֵׁי) *woman, wife*
אַנְתּוּן	*you* (m.p.)
אַנְתִּי	*you* (f.s.)
אֱסוּר	*fetter, bond*; pl. אֱסוּרִין *imprisonment*
אָסְפַּ֫רְנָא	adv. *properly*
אֱסָר	*prohibition*
אֵסַרְחַאדֹּן	*Esarhaddon*
אסרשת	’sršt (personal name, unknown pronunciation)
אָע	*wood*
אַף	conj. *also, indeed*
אַף	(det. אַפָּא; DSS w/suff. אַנְפַּהּ; pl. abs. אַפִּין; DSS w/suff. אַנְפַּיְהָא) sing. *nose*; pl. *face, surface*
אֱפוֹ	conj. *also*
אַפִּילוּ	conj. *even if*
אֲפִיךְ	*perverted*
אֲפַרְסְכָי	*official*
אַפְּתֹם	*revenue*; in the phrase אַפְּתֹם מַלְכִין *royal revenue* (lit. *revenue of kings*)
אֶצְבַּע	(pl. אֶצְבְּעָן) *finger* (fem.)

אַרְבַּע	*four* (masc. in form but used with fem. nouns)
אַרְבְּעָה	*four* (fem. in form but used with masc. nouns)
ארג	’rg (personal name, unknown pronunciation)
אַרְגְּוָן	*purple*
אֲרֵה	*lo*
אֲרוּ	*lo*
אֲרוּם	conj. *because, since*
אֲרוֹן	*ark*
אֲרַז	(det. אַרְזָא) *cedar*
אֹ֫רַח	(det. אָרְחָא) *way, path*
אַרְיוֹךְ	*Arioch*
אֲרֵי	conj. *that, because*
אַרְיֵה	(m.p. det. אַרְיָוָתָא) *lion*
אַרְיָוָתָא	see אַרְיֵה
אֲרִיךְ	*long*
אֲרִיךְ	*fitting, proper*
ארך	ha. to lengthen
אַרְכָה	*length*
אַרְכֻבָּה	*knee*
אֲרַמָּי	*Aramean*
אֲרַע	(det. אַרְעָא) *earth* (fem.)
אַרְעִי	*bottom*
אֲרַק	(sing. det. אַרְקָא) *earth* (fem.) This is an old spelling of אֲרַע.
אַרְתַּחְשַׁשְׂתְּא	*Artaxerxes*
אֹשׁ	(sing. det. אֻשָּׁא pl. det. אֻשַּׁיָּא) *foundation*
אֲשָׁם	*guilt-offering*
אֻשַּׁרְנָא	*furnishings*
אשׁף	pə. *to conjure*
אֶשְׁתַּדּוּר	*revolt, insurrection*
אֶשְׁתּוֹמַם	see שׁמם
את	see אִיתַי
אָת	sign
אַתְּ	(’att) targ. for אַנְתְּ
אַתּוּן	*you* (2mp) (alternative form to אַנְתּוּן)
אַתּוּן	*furnace*

אֲתוּר	*Assyria*
אתי	pə. (3fs suff. אֲתָת; inf. מֵתֵא) *to come*; ha. (3ms suff. הַיְתִי and 3mp suff. הַיְתִיו; inf. הַיְתָיָה) and aph. (targ. 3mp pref. יַיְתוֹן Egypt. f.s. imv. w/ suff. אֲתַיֵהּ) *to bring*; hu./ho. (3fs suff. הֵיתָיִת and 3mp suff. הֵיתָיו) *to be brought*
אֲתַר	(det. אַתְרָא) *place*, אֲתַר דִּי / אֲתַר זִי *where*
אַתַּרוּ	see נתר
בְּ	prep. *in, with, by, through, due to, by means of, because of*
בֵּאדַיִן	conj. *then* (cf. אֱדַיִן)
בְּאִישׁ	*evil, bad*
בְּאִישָׁה	*evil thing, harm*
בָּב	*gate*
בָּבֶל and בָּבַל	*Babylon*
בָּבְלָי	*Babylonian*
בְּגוֹא	see בְּ and גַּו
בְּגֵין	conj. *because*
בְּגֵין כֵּן	adv. *therefore*
בדי	pə. *to invent, fabricate*
בְּדְיָה	(pl. abs. in DSS בְּדְיָאן) *falsehood*
בְּדִיל	prep. (with 2fs suff. בְּדִילֵיכִי) and conj. *because*
בדר	pa. *to scatter*; itpa. *to be scattered*
בהל	pa. *to disturb, terrify*; hitpa. *to be alarmed, terrified, afraid*
בְּהִילוּ	*haste*
בזע	pə. (a/-) *to tear*
בטל	pə. (3fs suff. בְּטֵלַת) *to cease*; pa. *to make cease*
-בְּטַל	this is a variation of בְּטְלַל that occurs with suffixes of the m.s. noun (e.g. בְּטַלֵהּ *because of him* and בְּטַלֵיכִי *because of you*)
בְּטְלַל	prep. *due to the help of, with the help of, because of*
בֵּין	prep. (w/suff. בֵּינֵיהוֹן) *between, among*, used alone or in the construction בֵּין . . . וּבֵין or בֵּין . . . לְ
בִּירָה	(det. בִּירְתָא) *fortress*
בַּיִת	(cstr. בֵּית; det. בַּיְתָא; pl. בָּתִּין) *house, place, palace, temple*
בית	pə. *to spend the night*
בֵּית אֵל	*Bethel*
בֵּית שְׁקְיָא	*irrigated land*
בכי	pə. (3fs suff. בְּכָת) *to weep*

בְּכֵין	adv. *then, therefore*
בלבל	see בלל
בָּל	*mind*
בְּלוֹ	*tax*
בִּלְחוֹדֵי	prep. (with suffixes for m.p. nouns) *alone* (בִּלְחוֹדַיְהָה *by herself*)
בלל	palpel (1cp pref. נְבַלְבֵּיל) *to mix, confuse*
בֵּלְשַׁאצַּר	*Belshazzar*
בְּנֵה	see בני
בני	pə. (3mp pref. יִבְנוֹן ; 3ms suff. + 3ms obj. בְּנָהִי; inf. מִבְנֵא) *to build*; pass. part. (m.s. בְּנֵה) to be built; hitpə. *to be built, under construction*
בְּנֵי	pl. cstr. of בַּר
בְּנִין	pl. abs. of בַּר
בִּנְיָן	*building*
בנס	pə. to grow angry
בָּנִת	*Banit* (goddess)
בנתסרל	Bntsrl (personal name, unknown pronunciation)
בעי	pə. (3ms suff. בְּעָה) *to seek, seek out, pray, request* (with inf.) *to be about to, on the verge of*
בָּעוּ	*petition*
בְּעֵל	(det. בַּעֲלָא) *master, lord*; בְּעֵל טְעֵם *commander*; בְּעֵל דְּבָב *enemy*
בְּקַדְמֵיתָא	adv. *at first*
בְּקָל	see בְּ and קָל
בִּקְעָה	(det. בִּקְעֲתָא) *valley*
בקר	pa. *to seek, enquire,* search; hitpa. *to be sought*
בַּר	(det. בְּרָא; pl. abs. בְּנִין) *son, child*; in construct with a following noun, it can be used to describe something (not necessarily human) that bears the characteristics of the following noun, as with בַּר־אֱלָהִין *a divinity*. Note also בְּנֵי אֱנָשׁ *humans*
בַּר	(det. בָּרָא) *field, outside*; with lamed preposition and adverbial he ending לְבָרָה* = adv. *outside, outward*
ברי	pə. (targ. 3ms suff. בְּרָא) *to create*; itpə. *to be created*
בְּרִיךְ	*blessed*
ברך	pə. (m.s. pass. part. בְּרִיךְ) *to kneel, bless*; pa. (3ms suff. בָּרִךְ; m.s. pass. part. מְבָרַךְ) *to bless*
בְּרַךְ	(det. בִּרְכָּא) *knee*
בְּרַם	conj. *nevertheless*

בְּשַׂר	(det. בִּשְׂרָא) *flesh*
בְּשְׂרוֹן	*disgrace*
בַּת-	see בַּיִת
בִּתְדִירָא	adv. *continuously*
בְּתוּלָה	*young woman*
גַּב	(det. גַּבָּא) *back*
גֹּב	(det. גֻּבָּא) *pit, den*
גְּבוּרָה	*wonder, might*
גְּבַר	(det. גֻּבְרָא and/or גַּבְרָא) *person, man*
גִּבָּר	*hero, warrior*
גדד	pə. *to chop down*
גַּו	(cstr. גו and גוֹא; det. גַּוָּא) *midst*
גוֹא	see גַּו
גוֹב	see גֹּב
גֵּוָה	*pride*
גזר	pə. *to cut, determine by astrology*, part. *astrologers; hitpə. to be cut*
גְּזֵרָה	(cstr. גְּזֵרַת) *decree*
גֵּיהִנָּם	*Gehenna*
גֵּין	see בְּגֵין
גִּיר	*plaster*
גָּלוּ	*exile*
גלי	pə. *to reveal*; pəʿīl (targ. m.p. part. גְּלַן) *to be revealed*; ha. *to take into exile*; itpə. *to appear, reveal oneself*
גְּלָל	*hewn stone*
גְּנָאי	*disgraceful*
גִּנּוּי	(pl. abs. in DSS גנואין) *disgrace, disgraceful thing*
גִּנּוּן	*bridal chamber*
גְּנַז	(det. גִּנְזָא) *treasure, official documents*, בֵּית גִּנְזַיָּא *archives*
גַּף	(det. גַּפָּא) *wing*
גְּרַם	(det. גַּרְמָא) *bone*
גרס	pa. *to grind*
גְּשֵׁם	(det. גִּשְׁמָא; w/suff. גֶּשְׁמְהוֹן) *body*
דְּ-	see דִּי
דָּא	*this, that* (f.s.); דָּא לְדָא *this against that*
דאת	aph. (3fs pref. תַּדְאֵית) *to sprout, produce vegetation*

דֹּב	(det. דֻּבָּא) *bear*
דְּבוֹרָה	*Deborah*
דבח	pə. *to sacrifice*
דְּבַח	(det. דִּבְחָא) *sacrifice*
דבר	pə. *to lead*; pəʿīl *to be led, taken*
דִּבְרַת	see עַד
דְּהַב	(det. דַּהֲבָא) *gold*
דוק	ha. and aph. *to look at*
דור	pə. (m.p. part. דָּאְרִין) *to dwell*
דוּשׁ	pə. *to crush, trample*
דְּחִיל	*terrifying*
דחל	pə. *to fear*; pa. *to frighten, make afraid*
דִּי and -דְּ	pron./conj. (in Egypt. Aram. זִי) *of, that, which, who (whose, whom), where, so that, because*; it also marks direct speech; conj. כְּדִי *when, as soon as*; conj. מִן־דִּי and מִן־דְּ *because, after*; conj. עַד דִּי *until*; דִּיל with poss. suffixes = *belonging to* (e.g. דִּילַהּ *belonging to her*)
דייר	read דַּיָּר
דִּיל	see דִּי
דין	pə. (m.p. part. דָּאְנִין; targ. f.s. part. דָּיְנָא) *to judge*
דִּין	*judgment, justice*
דֵּין	*this*
דַּיָּן	*judge*
דַּיָּר	(pl. cstr. דיירי) *dweller*
דָּךְ	*this, that* (f.s.)
דֵּךְ	(in Egypt. Aram. זֵךְ) *this, that* (m.s.)
דִּכֵּן	*this, that* (m.s. or f.s.)
דִּכְרוֹן	memorandum
דָּכְרָן	*record, memorandum*
דִּלְמָא	conj. *lest*
דמי	pə. (m.s. part. דָּמֵה, f.s. part. דָּמְיָה) *to be like, resemble*
דְּמַע	(det. דִּמְעָא) *tear* (fem.)
דֵּן	*this, that* (m.s. and f.s.)
דְּנָה	(in Egypt. Aram. זְנָה) *this, that* (m.s.)
דָּנִיֵּאל	*Daniel*
דְּקַל	(det. דִּקְלָא) *date-palm*

דקק	pə. *to shatter, fall apart, crush*; ha. (3mp suff. הַדִּקוּ) *to shatter something*
דָּר	*generation*
דרי	pa. (3ms suff. דָּרִי) *to scatter*; itpa. (targ. 1cp pref. נִדָּרֵי) *to be scattered*
דָּרְיָוֶשׁ	Darius
דְּרָע	*arm* (fem.)
דָּת	*decree, law, verdict* (fem.)
דֶּתֶא	(det. דִּתְאָא) *grass, plants*
הֲ	interrogative particle, marking a question; הֲלָא is it not (marking rhetorical question)
הָא	*lo*
הַב and הַבוּ	pə. imv. of יהב, often used as interjection: *come!*
הַדָּבַר	*counsellor*
הַדָּם	*limb*
הדר	pa. *to glorify, honour*
הֲדַר	*honour*
הַהוּא	*that* (always following m.s. det. noun, as in עִדָּנָא הַהוּא *that time*)
הַהִיא	*that* (always following m.s. det. noun, as in אַרְעָא הַהִיא *that land*)
הוּא	(in Egypt. Aram. הוּ) *he*
הוֹבֵד	see אבד
הוי	pə. (1cs suff. הֲוֵית and 3ms pref. לֶהֱוֵא; targ. 3mp suff. הֲווֹן; 3fs pref. תִּהְוֵי; Egypt. f.s. imv. הֲוַי) *to be, become*
הוך	pə. (3ms pref. יְהָךְ; inf. מְהָךְ) *to go*; for suff. see הלך
הוֹקַר	see יקר
הֲזָדָה	ha. inf. of זיד
הִזְמִנְתּוּן	see זמן
הִי	see הִיא
הִיא	*she*
הֵיבֵל	see יבל
הֵיכַל	*temple, palace*
הֵימָן	*Heman*
הַיְתָיָה	ha. inf. of אתי
הַיְתִיו	ha. 3mp suff. conj. of אתי
הֲלָא	see הֲ
הלך	pə. (for pref. and inf. see הוך) *to go*; pa. *to walk*; for מַהְלְכִין (ha.) read מְהַלְּכִין

הֲלָךְ	*toll*
הִמּוֹ	*them* (m.p.)
הִמּוֹן	*them* (m.p.)
הַמְונִךְ	*necklace* (= הַמְנִיךְ / perhaps הֲמוֹנָךְ (K))
הֵן	conj. *if, whether*; הֵן לוּ *even though, lest* (cf. אִין and אִם)
הַצְדָא	adv. *is it true?*
הַרְהֹר	*thought*
וְ and וּ	conj. *and, but, then, or* (the conj. has the form וִ if the following word begins with יְ (yə), in this situation the shewa following yod is not written (e.g., וְיְקָר* *and glory* becomes וִיקָר))
זבן	pə. (a/u) *to buy*
זְהִיר	*cautious*
זוּגִי	(det. זוּגִיתָא) *glass, crystal*
זון	pə. *to feed*; hitpə. (3ms pref. יִתְּזִין) *to be fed*
זוע	pə. (3mp suff. זָעוּ) *to tremble*
זִי	see דִּי
זיד	ha. (inf. הֲזָדָה) *to act arrogantly*
זִיו	*brightness, appearance*
זִיל	pron. (זִי) + prep. (לְ) *belonging to*; see דִּי
זַיִת	(targ. det. זֵיתָא) *olive, olive tree*
זֵךְ	see דֵּךְ
זָכוּ	*innocence*
זַכָּי	*innocent*
זְכַרְיָה	*Zekaryah*
זמן	hitpə. (2mp suff. הִזְדְּמִנְתּוּן = הִזְמְנְתּוּן) *to conspire*
זְמַן	(det. זִמְנָא) *time*; מַשְׁכַּן זִמְנָא *the tent of meeting*
זְמָר	*music*
זַמָּר	*musician*
זַן	(det. זְנָא) *kind, type*
זְנָה	*this* (Egyptian and Samarian spelling of דְּנָה)
זְעֵיר	*small, little*
זעק	pə. (i/-) *to cry*
זַעְרָרָה	*medlar fruit*
זקף	pə. *to raise*; pəʿīl *to be raised*
זְרֻבָּבֶל	Zerubbabel

זרע	pə. *to sow*; itpə. (m.s. part. מִזְדְּרַע) *to be sown*
זְרַע	(det. זַרְעָא) *seed*; בַּר זְרַע *seed*
חֲבוּלָה	*damage, harm*
חבל	pa. *to destroy, harm*; hitpa. *to be destroyed*
חֲבָל	*injury*
חֲבַר	(det. חַבְרָא) *companion*
חַגַּי	*Haggai*
חַד	(f.s. חֲדָה) *one, a*; חַד־שִׁבְעָה *seven times*
חֲדָה	see חַד
חֲדֵי or חֲדֵה	(w/suff. חַדְיֵהּ) *breast*
חֶדְוָה	*joy*
חדי	pə. (3ms pref. יֶחֱדֵא*) *to rejoice*
חֲדַת	(f.s. abs. חַדְתָּה; f.s. det. חֲדַתָּא = ḥădattâ from *ḥadatatâ) *new*
חוט	see יחט
חָוכְמָה	see חָכְמָה
חוי	pa. (1cs pref. אֲחַוֵּא) and ha. (2mp pref. + 1cs obj. תְּהַחֲוֻנַּנִי; inf. הַחֲוָיָה) *to declare, show, explain, tell*
חוּלָק	*portion*
חִוָּר	*white*
חֱזֵו	(det. חֶזְוָא) *vision* (cf. חזיו Neof. to Gen 39:6 = חֱזֵיו) (masc.)
חֲזוּ	(det. חֲזוּתָא) *appearance, sight*
חזי	pə. (m.s. pass. part. חֲזֵה) *to see*; ha. *to cause to see, show*; hitpə. and ittaphʿal *to be seen*
חֲטָי or חֲטָא	*sin*
חֹטַר	*rod*
חַי	(m.s. cstr. חֵיל, det. חַיָּא; f.s. abs. חַיָּה) *alive, one alive*
חֵיוָה	*beast, beasts* (collective)
חִיוָּר	see חִוָּר
חיי	pə. (3ms pref. יֶחֱיֵא*; DSS 1cs pref. אֱחֵה) *to live*; ha. and aph. *to keep alive*
חַיִל	*power, valour, host, army*; קרא בְּחַיִל *to call loudly*
חֵמַר or חֵימַר	(det. חֶמְרָא or חֵימְרָא) *bitumen*
חַכִּים	*wise, sage, wise person*
חכם	pə. *to be wise*; pa. *to instruct*
חָכְמָה	(det. חָכְמְתָא ḥokmətâ) *wisdom*
חֲלוּז	(w/suff. חֲלוּזֵהּ) *garment*

חלז	pə. (targ. 3fs suff. חֲלֵ֫יזַת) *to gird, pull up* (clothing)
חלם	pə. (1cs suff. חַלְמֵת) *to dream*
חֵ֫לֶם	(det. חֶלְמָא) *dream*
חלף	pə. (-/u) *to replace, exchange*
חֲלָק	*share, portion*
חֱמָא	see חֲמָה
חֲמָה	(also חֱמָא) *rage*
חמי	pə. (targ. and DSS inf. מַחְמֵי) *to see*
חֲמִיד	*desirable*
חֲמס	*violence*
חמר	pə. *to be angry; vinegar-like*
חֲמַר	(det. חַמְרָא) *wine*
חַנָּה	*Hannah*
חֲנֻכָּה	*dedication*
חנן	pə. (inf. מִחַן) *to favour, show mercy*; hitpa. *to implore favour*
חַסִּין	*strong*
חַסִּיר	lacking
חסן	aph. *to give or take a possession*
חֱסֵן	(det. חִסְנָא) *power*
חֲסַף	(det. חַסְפָּא) *clay*
חַסִּר	see חַסִּיר
חצף	ha. (f.s. pass. part. מְהַחְצְפָה), aph. (f.s. pass. part. מַחְצְפָה) *to insist, urge*, *pass. part. one that is urgent*
חרב	ho./hu. (3fs suff. הָחָרְבַת) *to be laid waste*
חֲרַב	(det. חַרְבָּא) *sword (fem.)*
חֲרוּץ	*Ḥorudj*
חַרְטֹם	*magician*
חרך	hitpa. *to be singed*
חֲרַץ	(det. חַרְצָא) *hip*
חַשִּׁיךְ	*one (or something) in need*
חשׂך	ha. *to spare*
חשׁב	pə. *to think, consider*; pə'īl *to be considered*; pa. (f.s. part. מְחַשְּׁבָה) *to ponder, concentrate on, plot*
חֲשׁוֹךְ	*dark, darkness*
חשׁח	pə. *to need*

חַשְׁחָה	*something needed*
חשׁי	pə. *to be silent*
חתם	pə. *to seal*
טאב	pə. (e/-) *to be good*
טָב	*good*
טָבוּ	*goodness, beneficial actions*
טוּר	*mountain*
טוּר מַלְכָּא	*Tur-Malka* (lit. *The Mountain of the King*)
טְוָת	adv. *fasting*
טִין	*clay*
טַל	(det. **טַלָּא**) *dew*
טַלְיָה	(det. **טְלִיתָא**) *young girl*
טלל	aph. *to shade*
טמי	pa. *to defile*
טָעוּ	(pl. det. **טָעֲוָתָא**) *idols*
טעי	pə. *to wander, err*
טעם	pə. (a/a) *to taste, perceive*; pa. *to feed*
טְעֵם	(det. **טַעְמָא**; cstr. is **טְעֵם** or **טַ֫עַם**) *taste, decree, proclamation, judgment, report, command, influence, matter*
טַ֫עַם	see **טְעֵם**
טְפַר	(det. **טִפְרָא**) *nail, claw*
טַר	see **נטר**
טרד	pə. *to chase away*; pəʿīl *to be chased*
יָאֵה / יָאֵא or **יָאֵי**	(f.p. **יָאיָן**) *perfect*
יֵב	*Yeb* or *Elephantine*
יַבִּישָׁה	(det. **יַבִּישְׁתָּא**) *dry ground*
יבל	pə. *to bring*; ha. (3ms suff. **הֵיבֵל**; inf. **הֵיבָלָה**) *to carry, bring*; oph./uph. (3ms juss. **יֻבַל**) *to be brought*
יַבְּשָׁה	(det. **יַבַּשְׁתָּא**) *dry ground*
יַד	(det. **יְדָא**; du. **יְדַ֫יִן**) *hand, arm, power* (fem.)
ידי	ha. and aph. (m.s. part. **מוֹדֵא**) *to praise, give thanks*
ידע	pə. (a/a) (1cs pref. **אִנְדַּע**) *to know*; **יְדִיעַ** pass. part. be known; ha. (3ms suff. **הוֹדַע**) *to inform, make known (to)*
יהב	pə. (a/-) *to give, set*; pəʿīl (3ms suff. **יְהִיב**) *to be given*; hitpə. *to be given, paid, be made*

יְהוּד	*Yehud, Judah*
יְהוּדָי	(m. pl. det. **יְהוּדָיֵא**) *Judean*
יְהָךְ	see **הוך**
יוֹאֵל	*Joel*
יָיָ	(also **ייי**) a spelling of the name of God, which is **יהוה** in the Hebrew text, and is commonly translated as *the Lord* or *Yahweh*
יוּכַל	see **יכל**
יוֹם	(pl. **יוֹמִין**; pl. cstr. **יוֹמָת**) *day* (fem.)
יחט	pa. *to set in place*
יֵיבַד	see **אבד**
יֵימַר	see **אמר**
ייי	see **יָיָ**
יכל	pə. (i/u) (3ms suff. **יְכִל** , 2ms suff. **יְכֵ֫לְתָּ**; pref. **יִכֻּל**, also irregularly **יוּכַל**) *to be able*
יָנֵק	*child*
יַם	(det. **יַמָּא** in BA and **יְמָמָא** in Onq.) *sea*
יְמָמָא	see **יַם**
יסף	hu./ho. (3fs suff. **הוּסְפַת**) *to be added*
יעט	pə. *to advise*; itpa. *to deliberate*
יָעֵט	*counsellor*
יצב	pa. *to make certain*
יַצִּיב	*certain*
יַצִּ֫יבָה	*certainly*
יצף	pə. (-/a) *to worry over*
יקד	pə. to burn
יקיה	Yqyh (a personal name, the pronunciation of which is not known)
יקר	ha. (m.s. impv. **הוֹקַר**) *to make heavy, insensitive, numb*
יְקָר	*glory*
יְרוּשְׁלֵם	*Jerusalem (fem.)*
יְרַח	(det. **יַרְחָא**) *month*
יְרִיחוֹ	*Jericho*
יִרְמְיָה	*Jeremiah*
יִשְׂרָאֵל	*Israel*
יֵשׁוּעַ	Jeshua
ישר	aph. (2fs juss. **תּשְׁרִי**) *to send*

יָת	(w/suff. יָתִי) direct object marker
יתב	pə. (i/e) (3ms suff. יְתִב; targ. יְתִיב; targ. m.s. part. יָתֵיב; targ. f.s. part. יָתְבָא) *to sit, dwell*; ha. *to settle*; (h)itpə. *to be given, to be made*
יַתִּיר	(f.s. abs. יַתִּירָה and יַתִּירָא) *great, more, superior, surpassing*
יַתִּירָא	*surpassingly, exceedingly*
כְּ	prep. *like, as*
כְּבָר	adv. *perhaps*
כַּד	conj. *when*
כְּדַב	(det. כִּדְבָא) as adj.: *deceitful*, as noun: *lie*
כַּדּוּן	adv. *now*
כְּדִי	conj. *when, as soon as, just as*
כְּדֵין and כְּדֵן	adv. *thus, so*
כהל	pə. (-/a) *to be able*
כָּהֵן	*priest*
כַּוָּה	(pl. כַּוִּין) *window*
כּוֹל	see כֹּל
כּוֹרֶשׁ	*Koresh = Cyrus*
כְּוָת	adv. *thus, just so*
כּוּתָא	adv. *thus*
כְּזִי	see כְּדִי
כַּחְדָה	adv. *as one, together*
כין	see כֵּן
כֹּל	(cstr. כֹּל and כָּל; det. כֹּלָּא; targ. w/suff. כּוּלְהוֹן) *all, any, every*
כֹּלָּא	adv. *entirely*
כַּלָּאן	see כַּלָּה
כַּלָּה	(abs. pl. in DSS כַּלָּאן) *bride*
כלי	aph. (3fs suff. אַכְלִיאַת) *to scream*
כְּלִיל	*flawless*
כלל	see שׁכלל
כָּל־קֳבֵל	prep. in expression כָּל־קֳבֵל דְּנָה *as a consequence of this, because of this*; conj. כָּל־קֳבֵל דִּי *because, although*
כְּמָא	see כְּמָה
כְּמָה	*how!*
כֵּן	adv. *thus, so*; עַל כֵּין *therefore*
כְּנָוָן	see כְּנָת

כְּנֵישָׁה	(targ. det. כְּנִשְׁתָּא) *assemblage, gathering*
כְּנֵמָא	adv. thus, *accordingly*
כנע	itpə. (targ. inf. אִתְכְּנָעָא) *to humble oneself*
כִּנָּר	*lyre*
כנשׁ	pə. *to gather*; (h)itpa. *to be assembled, gathered*
כְּנִשְׁתָּא	see כְּנֵישָׁה
כְּנָת	(pl. כְּנָוָן) *associate, colleague*
כַּסְדָּי	see כַּשְׂדָּי
כְּסַף	(det. כַּסְפָּא) *silver*
כְּסֵת	*clothing*
כְּעַן	adv. *now*
כְּעֶנֶת	adv. *now*
כְּעֶת	adv. *now*
כַּף	(det. כַּפָּא) *palm* (fem.)
כפר	pa. *to atone for* (עַל)
כפת	pəʿīl (3mp suff. כְּפִתוּ) *to be bound*; pa. *to bind*
כַּרְבְּלָה	*helmet, hat*
כרז	ha. *to proclaim*
כְּרֵם	(det. כַּרְמָא) *vineyard*
כָּרְסֵא	(also כֻּרְסֵי) *throne* כֻּרְסֵי see כָּרְסֵא
כַּשְׂדָּי	(pl. abs. כַּשְׂדָּאִין) *Chaldean*
כתב	pə. (a/u) *to write*; pəʿīl (3ms suff. כְּתִיב) *to be written*
כְּתָב	*writing, order, limit, decree*
כִּתּוּן	*tunic*
כְּתַל	(det. כֻּתְלָא) *wall*
כתשׁ	pə. *to strike, afflict*
לְ	prep. *to, for, belonging to, according to, at, as*; marker of object of verb
לָא	*no, not, nothing* (in phrase כְּלָה (read כְּלָא) *as nothing*)
לֵב	(det. לִבָּא; targ. w/suff. לִיבַּה) *heart, mind*
לְבַב	(det. לִבְבָא) *heart, mind*
לְבוּשׁ	*garment*
לבן	(-/a) *to make bricks*
לְבַן	(det. לַבְנָא) *white, white thing, whiteness*
לִבְנָה	(det. לְבֵנְתָא; pl. לִבְנִין) *brick*
לִבְנִין	see לִבְנָה

לְבָרָה*	see בַּר
לבשׁ	pə. (-/a) *to wear*; ha. *to clothe*
לְבֻשׁ	see לְבוּשׁ
לִבַּת	*rage*
לָהֵן	*therefore, except, however*
לוּ	see הֵן
לֵוִי	(m.p. det. לֵוָיֵא) *Levite*
לושׁ	*to knead*
לְוָת	(w/suff. לְוָתָהּ; targ. w/suff. לְוָתֵיה) *toward;* מִן־לְוָת *from*
לְחֵם / לְחֶם	(det. לַחְמָא) *feast, food*
לְחֵנָה	*concubine*
לִיבַּה	see לֵב
לֵיוָי	see לֵוָי
לֵילֵא	(cstr. לֵילֵא; det. לֵילְיָא) *night*
לִישָׁן	see לִשָּׁן
לֵית	*there is not*
לְמָה	*why?* (לְ + מָה)
לְעָלְמִין	prep. לְ followed by עָלַם
לַפִּידוֹת	*Lapidot*
לְקֳבֵל or לָקֳבֵל	prep. *before, due to*; לָקֳבֵל דִּי (or לָקֳבֵל זִי) conj. *because*
לקח	pə. (a/-) *to take, tack back*; itpə. *to be taken*
לִשּׁוֹן	irregular form of לִשָּׁן
לִשָּׁן	*tongue, language group*
מָא	see מָה
מְאָה	*hundred*
מאזַנְיָא	(pl. det. מאזְנַיָּא) *scales*
מַאְכָל	(targ. w/suff. מַאכְלֵיה) *food*
מֵאמַר	*word*; also the pə. inf. of אמר
מָאן	(pl. det. מָאנַיָּא) *vessel*
מִבְנֵא	see בני
מִגְדַּל and מַגְדַל	*tower*
מְגִלָּה	*scroll*
מגר	pa. *to overthrow*
מַדְבַּח	*altar*
מִדָּה	see מִנְדָּה

מְדוֹר	*dwelling place*
מָדַי	*Media, Medes*
מְדִינָה	(cstr. מְדִינַת) *province*
מַדְּעַם	*something*
מָה and מַה	*what?*
מָה־דִּי	*what, whatever*
מִהְוֵא	pə. inf. of הוי
מְהָךְ	see הוך
מוּסַר	*instruction*
מות	pə. *to die*
מוֹת	(det. מוֹתָא) *death*
מָזוֹן	*food*
מַחֵא	aph. participle of חיי
מַחֲזֵה	*appearance*
מחי	pə. *to strike*; pa. *to prevent;* hitpə. *to be impaled*
מַחְלְקָה	*division*
מחמי	see חמי
מִחַן	pə. infin. of חנן
מטי	pə. *to reach, attain, happen*
מְטַר	(det. מִטְרָא) *rain*
מִיטַל	see נטל
מֵיכָלָא	*food*
מִין	see מִן
מַיִן	(det. מַיָּא) *water*
מֵיעַל	prep. *above* (min + ʻal), also in the construction מֵיעַל . . . לְ
מֵישַׁךְ	Meshach
מַכִּבְנִת	Makkibanit
מַכְדָּשׁ	*plague, pestilence* (variant of מַכְתָּשׁ *plague, pestilence*)
מַלְאַךְ	*angel, messenger*
מִלָּה	(pl. מִלִּין fem.) *word, statement, verdict, thing, matter*
מלח	pə. (a/-) *to eat salt*, implying an affiliation and loyalty
מְ֫לַח	*salt*
מלי	pə. *to fill*; hitpə. *to be filled*
מֶ֫לֶךְ	(det. מַלְכָּא, pl. abs. מַלְכִין) *king*
מְלֵךְ	(det. מִלְכָּא) *counsel*

מַלְכָּה	*queen*
מַלְכוּ	*kingdom, realm, kingship, reign*
מִלִּין	pl. of **מִלָּה** (fem.)
מלל	pa. (3ms suff. **מַלִּל**) *to speak*
מַלָּלָה	pa. inf. of **מלל**
מִלְּרַע	adv. and prep. *below* (min + lǝraʿ); **מִלְּרַע . . . לְ** *below . . .*
מַמְלַל	*speech*
מֵמַר	see **אמר**
מַן	*who? what?*
מִן	prep. *from, by, due to, on account of, against, more than, some (rarely, the nun assimilates to the following consonant, as in* **מִטַּל** *from dew (***טַל***) and* **מִקַּדְמַת** *before (lit. from before); see also* **קַדְמָה***)*
מְנֵא	*mina* (measurement of weight)
מִנְדָּה	*tribute*
מַן־דִּי	*who, whom, whoever, whomever*
מִן־דִּי	conj. *because, after*
מַנְדַּע	*knowledge, intelligence*
מִנְחָה	*offering*
מַנְטְרָה	*concern, something to watch out for*
מני	pǝ. *to count, assess, determine*; pa. *to assign, appoint*
מִנְיָן	*number*
מִן־לְוָת	*from*
מנע	pǝ. *to withhold*; itpǝ. *to be withheld, prevented*
מִן־קֳדָם	*before*
מִסְכֵּן	(det. **מִסְכֵּנָא**) *poor*
מִסְכֵּין	see **מִסְכֵּן**
מַעֲבַד	*work* and the pǝ. inf. *of* **עבד**
מֶעָל	*entering* (unusual spelling of pǝʿal inf. of **עלל**)
מְצִיעוּ	*middle*
מִצְרַ֫יִן	*Egypt*
מִקַּדְמַת	before, see **מִן**
מַקְדַּשׁ	*temple*; **בֵּית מַקְדַּשׁ** *holy temple*
מְקָם	*position*
מְקִים	aph. m.s. part. of **קום**
מִקְרַב	see **קרב**

מָרֵא and מָרֵה	(w/suff. מָרִי and מָרִאי) *master, lord*
מָרָד	*rebellious*
מְרַד	*rebellion*
מָרֵה	see מָרֵא
מְרוֹמֵם	polel m.s. part. of רום
מָרִי	see מָרֵא
מָרִיר	(f.s. det. מְרִרְתָּא) *bitter*
מְרַע	(det. מַרְעָא) *sickness*
מְשַׁח	*oil*
מִשְׁכַּב	*bed*
מִשְׁכַּן and מַשְׁכַּן	*abode, dwelling place, tent*; מַשְׁכַּן זִמְנָא *the tent of meeting*
מַשְׁרוֹקִי	*pipe*
מִשְׁתֵּא	(det. מִשְׁתְּיָא) *banquet*
מִשְׁתְּיָא	see מִשְׁתֵּא
מִשְׁתַּעַיִן	see שׁעי
מָת	*country*
מִתְּחוֹת	adv. and prep. *under, below* (min + təḥōt)
מתל	aph. (1cs pref. אַמְתֵּל) *to pose a riddle*
מְתַל	(det. מַתְלָא) *riddle*
מַתְּנָה	(det. מַתַּנְתָּא) *gift*
נְבוּ	*Nabu*
נְבוּאָה	*prophecy*
נְבוּכַדְנֶצַּר	*Nebuchadnezzar*
נְבוּנְתַן	*Nabunetan*
נְבוּסֻמִּסְכֵּן	*Nabusummiskun*
נְבִזְבָּה	(pl. det. נְבָזְבְיָתָא) *reward*
נבט	pə. (targ. m.s. part. נָבֵיט*) *to sprout, spew forth, ooze*; aph. (targ. m.s. part. מַבִּיט) *to spew (something) forth*
נבי	hitpa. to prophecy
נְבִיא	(det. נְבִיָּאה = nəbiyyâ; consonants = nəbīʾā^h and נְבִיָּא) *prophet (male)*
נְבִיָּא	see נְבִיא and נְבִיאָה
נְבִיאָה	(also spelled נְבִיָּא = nəbiyyâ from nəbīʾā^h; targ. det. נְבִיאֲתָא) *prophet (female)*
נְבֵל	(det. נִבְלָא) *harp*
נֶבְרַשְׁתָּא	*lamp*

נֶ֫גֶד	prep. *in front of*
נְגַהּ	(det. נָגְהָא noghâ) *daylight*
נדב	hitpa. (m.s. part מִתְנַדַּב) *to volunteer, donate*
נִדְבָּךְ	*layer of wall*
נדד	pə. *to flee*
נָדִן	*Nadin*
נְהוֹר	*light* (i.e. photons and the source of photons)
נַהִירוּ	*illumination*
נְהַר	(det. נַהֲרָא) *river*
נוד	ha. and aph. *to disturb*
נוח	pə. (3ms suff. נָח) *to rest*
נְוָלִי	*rubbish dump*
נור	aph. *to illuminate, shine*
נוּר	*fire*
נזק	pə. *to be injured*; ha. *cause injury*
נְחָשׁ	*copper, bronze*
נחת	pə. *to fall, descend*; ha. and aph. (2ms pref. תַּחֵת; m.s. imv. אֲחֵת; inf. אַחָתָא) *to deposit*; hu./ho. (3ms suff. הָנְחַת) *to be deposed*
נטל	pə. (targ. inf. מִיטַל) *to lift, move, travel*; pə'īl *to be lifted*
נטר	(-/a) to guard
נִיחוֹחַ	*incense-offering*
נְכַס	(pl. abs. נִכְסִין) only pl. *wealth, property*
נְמַר	*leopard*
נֵס	(det. נִסָּא) *miracle*
נסח	hitpə. *to be pulled away, torn*
נסך	pa. to pour out
נסע	aph. (3mp suff. אַסְּעוּ) *to remove*
נסק	see סלק
נִפְטָא	*naphtha*
נפל	pə. (a/e) *to fall*
נפק	pə. (a/u) *to go or come out, emerge*; ha. and aph. *to bring out, remove*
נִפְקָה	*expenses*
נְפַשׁ	(det. נַפְשָׁא) *throat, breath, life, soul*
נֵץ	*blossom*
נצח	hitpa. *to distinguish oneself*

נַצִּיחַ	*splendid*
נצל	ha. (inf. + 3ms suff. הַצָּלוּתֵהּ) and aph. (m.s. part. מַצִּל) *to rescue, deliver, save*
נקשׁ	pə. *to knock*
נשׂי	pə. (m.s. imp. שֵׂא) *to lift, take; hitpa. to rise up*
נשׁב	pa. *to blow*
נְשִׁין	see אִנְתָּה
נִשְׁמָה	*breath*
נִשְׁפֵּךְ*	see שׁפך
נְשַׁר	(det. נִשְׁרָא) *eagle*
נִשְׁתְּוָן	*letter*
נתן	pə. (a/e) (3ms pref. יִנְתֵּן; with 3fs obj. suff. יִתְּנִנַּהּ) *to give*
נתר	aph. *to strip off*
סָב	see שָׂב
סבל	pa. *to support*; po‘‘el *to lay foundation*
סגד	pə. (i/u) *to bow down, worship*
סִגְדָּה	*worship, object of worship, idol*
סְגַן	(det. סִגְנָא) *prefect*
סגר	pə. (a/-) *to shut*
סְדַר	(det. סִדְרָא) *order, battle line*
סהד	pə. and pa. *to testify, bear witness*
סוּמְפֹּנְיָה	*wind instrument, trumpet*
סְוֵן	*Syene*
סוף	pə. *to be fulfilled; aph. (3fs pref.* תְּסִיף*) to bring to an end, destroy*
סוֹף	*end*
סוּפֹּנְיָה	see סוּמְפֹּנְיָה
סלק	pə. (e/a) (3ms pref. יִסַּק) *to ascend, come up*; ha. (3mp suff. הַסִּקוּ) *to lift up*; hu./ho. (3ms suff. הֻסַּק) *to be lifted up*
סַנְחֵארִיב	*Sennacherib*
סעד	pa. *to support*
סְפַר	(det. סִפְרָא) *book, letter, writing, document*; בֵּית סִפְרַיָּא *archives*
סָפַר	*scribe*
סרב	pə. (a/) *to refuse*; pa. *to refuse*
סַרְבָּל	*garment*
סָרַךְ	*official, minister*
סתר	pə. (3ms suff. w/suff. סַתְרֵהּ) *to destroy*

עבד	pə. (a/e) *to make, do, bear, work, prepare, get ready*, with **דָּת** *to observe the law*; **. . . עבד דין מן** *to make judgment against . . .*; (h)itpə. *to be made, done*
עֲבֵד	(det. **עַבְדָּא**; pl. abs. **עַבְדִין**) *slave, servant*
עֲבֵד נְגוֹ	*Abed-Nego*
עֲבִידָה	(cstr. **עֲבִידַת**) *work, labour*
עבר	pə. (targ. 3fs pref. **תִיעבַר**) to cross, go over
עֲבַר	*area across, beyond*
עֲבַר נַהֲרָה	*Abar-Nahara* (lit. *Across-the-River*, i.e., upper Mesopotamia)
עַגְלָה	(det. **עֲגַלְתָּא**) *cart, wagon*
עַד	conj. / prep. *until, up to, while, before*; **עַד אָחֳרֵין** adv. *at last*; **עַד דִּבְרַת דִּי** conj. *so that*; **עַד דִּי** (or **עַד זִי**) conj. *until*; **עַד צֵית** prep. *towards*; for **קֳדָם** **עַד לָא** see **קֳדָם**
עדי	pə. *to pass on, over, away*, to touch; ha. (1cs suff. **הֶעְדִּית**) and aph. *to take away, remove*
עִדָּן	*time, time period, year*
עוֹבָד	*deed, work*
עוֹד	*yet, still, again*
עור	itpə. (1cs suff. **אִתְעִירֶת**) *to awake*
עִזְקָה	(det. **עִזְקְתָא**) *signet ring*
עֶזְרָא	*Ezra*
עֵטָה	(det. **עֵטְתָא**) *counsel*
עַטְרוֹת	*Atarot*
עַיִן	(sing. cstr. **עֵין**; det. **עַיְנָא**; pl. abs. **עַיְנִין**; cstr. **עַיְנֵי** or **עֵינֵי**) *eye* (fem.)
עִיר	*watcher, wakeful one*
עַל	prep. *on, over, on account of, against, about, concerning*; **עַל דִּי** (or **עַל זִי**) conj. *because* (or, *concerning what*); **עַל כֵּין** adv. *therefore*
עֵלָּא	*over, above*
עֲלָה	(pl. **עֲלָוָן**) *burnt-offering*
עִלָּה	*pretext, matter*
עִלָּי	*highest, unsurpassed*
עִלִּי	*roof chamber*
עֶלְיוֹן	*the Most High*
עלל	pə. (3ms suff. **עַל**; inf. **מֵעַל**) *to go in, come in*; ha. (3ms suff. **הַנְעֵל**; inf. **הַנְעָלָה**) *to bring in*; hu./ho. *to be brought*
עָלַם	(det. **עָלְמָא**) *eternity, ever, world*; **יוֹמָת עָלְמָא** *days of old*

עֲלַע	(det. עִלְעָא) *rib, side*
עַם	(det. עַמָּא; pl. det. עַמְמַיָּא) *people, nation*
עִם	prep. *with, for*
עֲנֵה	(pl. עֲנַיִן; in pause עֲנָ֫יִן) *poor*
עַנְוָה	*poverty* or *humiliation*
עני	pə. *to answer, respond, speak up*; this is often used in conjunction with אמר to introduce direct speech
עֲנָ֫יִן	see עֲנֵה
עֲנָשׁ	*fine, punishment*
עֲסַב	(det. עִסְבָּא) see עֲשַׂב
עֲסַר	see עֲשַׂר
עֳפִי	*foliage*
עֲפַר	(det. עַפְרָא) *dust, mud, soil*
עֲצִיב	*pained, despairing*
עצב	itpə. *to be sad*
עָקָה	*trouble*
עקר	pə. *to uproot*; itpə. (3f.p. suff. אֶתְעֲקַ֫רָה) *to be uprooted*
עִקַּר	*stump, root*
עָר	*enemy*
ערב	pa. to mix; pa‘lel (1cs and 1cp pref. נְעַרְבֵּב) *to mix, confuse*; hitpa. *to be mixed*
עָרֵב	*guarantor, surety*
עַרְבֵּב	see ערב
עֲרָד	*wild donkey*
עַרְוָה	*dishonour*
עַרְפִּלָּא	*cloud, shadow*
עֲשַׂב	(det. עִשְׂבָּא) *grass, plants*
עֲשַׂר	in combination with other numerals to indicate 11–19 (e.g. אַרְבְּעַת עֲשַׂר *14*)
עֶשְׂרִין	*20*
עשת	pə. (3ms suff עֲשִׁית = ‘ăšit) *to think*
עֲתִיד	*ready*; together with a following verbal form (part. or inf.), it expresses the future (e.g. עֲתִיד לְמֶהֱוֵי *he will be*)
עַתִּיק	*old*
פּוּם	see פֻּם

פּוּרְעָנוּת	*punishment*; פּוּרְעָנוּת נִסָּא *miraculous punishment* (lit. *the punishment of the miracle*)
פֶּחָה	(sing. cstr. פַּחַת; pl. det. פַּחֲוָתָא) *governor*
פַּחַת	see פֶּחָה
פַּטֵּשׁ	*garment, legging*
פֵּירִין	see פְּרִי
פלג	pə. *to divide*
פְּלֻגָּה	*division*
פלח	pə. (a/-) *to serve, worship*
פלט	pə. (a/u) *to be spared*, pa. *to rescue*
פְּלִשְׁתָּי	*Philistine*
פֻּם	(w/suff. פֻּמֵּהּ) *mouth*
פַּס	(det. פַּסָּא) *hand, end of the arm*
פְּסַח	(det. פִּסְחָא) *Passover*
פסמי	Psmy (personal name, the pronunciation of which is unknown)
פְּסַנְתֵּר	harp
פַּרְדֵּס	(det. פַּרְדֵּסָא) *garden*
פַּרְדֵּיס	see פַּרְדֵּס
פַּרְזֶל	*iron*
פְּרִי	(pl. פֵּירִין) *fruit*
פרנס	palpel (targ. f.s. part. מִתְפַּרְנְסָא) *to support oneself*
פרס	pə. (a/-) *to spread, divide*; pəʿīl *to be split, divided*
פָּרַס	*Persia, Persians*
פְּרֵס	(pl. abs. פַּרְסִין) *half-mina (a measurement of weight)*
פְּרָס	*salary*
פָּרָס	Persia
פרע	itpə. *to be avenged*
פַּרְעֹה and פַּרְעוֹ	*Pharaoh*
פרק	pə. (-/u) *to redeem*; itpə. *to be redeemed, rescued*
פֻּרְקָן	*redemption, deliverance*
פרשׁ	pa. (m.s. pass. part. מְפָרַשׁ) *to explain*; aph. *to separate, divide*
פַּרְשֶׁגֶן	(also spelled in targ. פַּרְשְׁגַן) *copy*
פשׁר	pə. (-/a) and pa. *to explain, interpret*
פְּשַׁר	(det. פִּשְׁרָא) *interpretation*
פִּתְגָם	*command, answer, affair, verdict*

פתח	pə. *to open*; pə‘īl *to be opened*; itpə. *to be opened*
פְּתַח	*Ptaḥ* (god)
פְּתָי	*breadth*
צְבוּ	*thing, matter*
צבי	pə. *to desire, wish, be pleased*
צָבִית	*keeper*
צבע	pa. *to drench*; hitpa. (3ms pref. יִצְטַבַּע) *to be drenched*
צַד	*side*
צְדָא	see הַצְדָא
צדי	pə. *to be desolate*
צַדִּיק	*righteous*
צִדְקָה	(det. צִדְקְתָא) *righteousness, charity*
צַוַּאר	*neck*
צֵית	see עַד
צלח	ha. and aph. *to prosper promote*
צלי	pa. *to pray*
צְלֵם	(det. צַלְמָא, cstr. is צְלֵם or צֶלֶם) *image*
צמח	pə. *to sprout*; pa. (inf. צַמָּחָא) *to make grow*
צְנְפַּר	see צִפַּר
צֹעַן	*Zoan*
צפן	ha. *to hide*
צְפַר	(det. צַפְרָא) *morning*
צִפַּר	*bird*
צְרוֹךְ	*need, use*
קַב	a measure for dry goods
קבל	pə. *to complain against*; pa. *to receive, accept*
קֳבֵל and קֳבֵל	see לָקֳבֵל and כָּל־קֳבֵל
קַדִּישׁ	*holy, holy one*
קְדָם and קֳדָם	(with suff. קֳדָמוֹהִי) prep. *before*; קְדָם עַד לָא conj. *before*
קַדְמָה	*period previous*; in expression מִן־קַדְמַת דְּנָה *before this*; קַדְמַת *before*
קַדְמָי	(f.s. det. קַדְמָיְתָא; m.p. det. קַדְמָיֵא; f.p. det. קַדְמָיָתָא) *first*
קַדמִין	*previously*; בְּקַדמִין *at first*
קַדְמֵית	see בְּקַדְמֵיתָא
קֳדָמַן	*previously*
קַדְמַת	see קַדְמָה

קְדֹשׁ (det. קֻדְשָׁא) *holiness*

קום pə. *to arise*; pa. and ha. *to erect, establish, re-establish, appoint*; hu./ho. (3fs suff. הֳקִמַת) *to be lifted, established, erected*

קְטִין *small, thin*

קטל pə. (a/u) *to kill*; pəʿīl *to be killed*; pa. *to slay, kill many*; hitpə. *to be slain*

קְטֵל *killing*

קְטַר (det. קִטְרָא) *knot, joint, difficult task, problem*

קְיָם *statute*

קַיָּם *long-lasting*

קַיתְרֹס *lute* (pronounced קַתְרֹס)

קָל voice, sound

קִלְקְלָה (det. קִלְקִלְתָּא) *disgrace*

קני pə. *to acquire, buy*

קְצֵה (pl. cstr. קִצְוֵי) *end, outer extreme*

קצץ pə. (3mp suff. קַצּוּ; 2mp juss. תִּקֹּוצוּ; inf. מִקַּץ) *to chop off*

קְצָת *end*

קרא see קרי

קרב pə. (i and e/-) (inf. מִקְרַב) *to approach*; pa. and ha. *to bring near, to offer sacrifice*

קְרָב *war*

קֻרְבָּן *offering*

קְרֵבְתָּא *immediately after, right then*

קרי pə. *to call, name, read*; pəʿīl *to be read*; hitpə. *to be summoned*

קִרְיָה (det. קִרְיְתָא) *city* (cf. קְרַת)

קֶרֶן (sing. det. קַרְנָא; du. det. קַרְנַיָּא) *horn (fem.)*

קְרַץ (det. קַרְצָא) *piece, morsel*; in the idiom אֲכַל קַרְצֹוהִי *he slandered him* (lit. *he ate his morsels*)

קְרַת (det. קַרְתָּא) *city* (fem.) (cf. קִרְיָה)

קשׁט ha. *to make true, justify*

קְשֹׁט (det. קֻשְׁטָא) *truth*

קַשִּׁיט *true*; as substantive: *truth*

ראמ (Iranian loanword) *joy*

רֵאשׁ (det. רֵאשָׁא; DSS w/suff. רֵאישַׁהּ) *head, top*

רַב (m.s. det. רַבָּא; f.s. det. רַבְּתָא; m.p. abs. רַבְרְבִין; f.p. abs. רַבְרְבָן; in Aḥiqar the m.p. const. is רַבֵּי) *great, great one, noble, ruler*

רְבוּ	*greatness*
רִבּוֹ	(pl. רִבְוָן, in oral trad. רִבְבָן / written trad. רִבְּוָן) *ten thousand*
רבי	pə. (m.s. part. רָבֵא, det. רָבְיָא) *to grow great, grow up*; as part. official
רְבִיעָי	(f.s. abs. רְבִיעָיָה) *fourth*
רַ֫בַע	fourth generation
רַבְרְבִין	m.p. abs. of רַב
רַבְרְבָן	f.p. abs. of רַב
רַבְרְבָן	*noble*
רַבְּתָא	see רַב
רְגִג and רְגִיג	*precious*
רגז	ha. *to enrage, anger*
רְגַז and רְגֹז	(det. רֻגְזָא, targ. det. רוּגְזָא, w/suff. רוּגְזִי) *rage*
רְגַל	(det. רַגְלָא; du. רַגְלַ֫יִן) *foot*
רגשׁ	ha. *to come together quickly*
רֵו	*face, facial expression*
רוּגְזִי	see רְגַז
רוּחַ	*spirit, wind*
רום	pə. (3ms suff. רִם; targ. 3fs suff. רֵימַת) *to be lifted up*; aph. (m.s. part. מְרִים) *to lift*; polel (m.s. part. מְרוֹמֵם) *to exalt*; hitpolal (2ms suff. הִתְרוֹמַ֫מְתָּ) *to exalt oneself*
רוּם	*height*
רוֹקָנִי	(f.s. רוֹקָנְיָא) *barren*
רָז	(det. רָזָא) *secret*
רְחוּם	*Rehum*
רְחִיק	*far*
רחם	pə. *to love*
רְחֵם	(det. רַחְמָא) *womb*; pl. רַחֲמִין *compassion*
רחץ	hitpə. to trust
רֵיחַ	*smell*
רֵימַת	see רום
רֵישׁ	see רֵאשׁ
רַכִּיךְ	*soft*
רמי	pə. *to throw, make (bricks)*; pə'īl *to be thrown*; hitpə. idem
רְמַשׁ	*evening*
רָמְתָא	*Rama*

רְעוּ	*will, pleasure*
רֶעְיָה	*Reiah*
רַעְיוֹן	*thought*
רַעְנַן	*serene*
רפס	pə. *to crush, tread*
רְקִיעַ	*sky, firmament*
רַקִּיק	*fine*
רַשִּׁיעַ	*evil, wicked*
רשׁם	pə. *to inscribe, write, sign*; pəʻīl *to be inscribed*
שָׂב	*old, elder*
שַׂבְּכָא	*lyre*
שְׂגֵא and שְׂגֵה	*multitude*
שׂגי	pə. *to increase, be abundant*
שַׂגִּיא	*many, great, abundant, as adv. greatly*
שְׂטַר	*side*
שׂים	pə. (3ms suff. **שָׂם**; w/suff. **שָׂמֵהּ**) *to set, make*; pəʻīl (3ms suff. **שִׂים**) *to be set, made*; hitpə. (3ms pref. **יִתְּשָׂם**) idem
שָׂכְלְתָנוּ	*insight*
שָׂם	see **שׂים**
שׂני	pə. *to hate*; part. **שָׂנְאָיךְ** *those who hate you*
שְׂעַר	(det. **שַׂעְרָא**) *hair*
שָׂרַי	Sarai
שׂרף	pə. (-/o) *to burn, bake (bricks)*
שׁאט	see **שׁוט**
שׁאל	pə. (e/-) *to ask, look after*
שְׁאֵלָה	(det. **שְׁאֵלְתָא**) *request, response*
שְׁאָר	*remainder, rest*
שְׁבָא	*Sheba*
שְׁבִיב	*flame*
שׁבח	pa. (m.s. part. **מְשַׁבַּח**) *to praise*
שְׁבַע	*seven* (masc. in form but used with fem. nouns)
שִׁבְעָה	(cstr. **שִׁבְעַת**) *seven* (fem. in form but used with masc. nouns)
שׁבק	pə. (a/u) *to leave alone, permit;* pəʻīl (3ms suff. **שְׁבִיק**) *to be left alone*
שׁבשׁ	hitpa. and itpa. (3mp pref. **יִשְׁתַּבְּשׁוּן**) *to be confused*
שֵׁגְלָה	*consort*

שׁדר	hitpa. (m.s. part. מִשְׁתַּדַּר) *to struggle*
שַׁדְרַךְ	*Shadrach*
שׁוט	pə. (targ. m.s. part. שָׁאֵיט) *to despise*
שׁוי	pa. *to transform something into* (w/ עִם), *be made like*
שׁוֹם	see שֵׁם
שׂוֹפַר	see שֹׂפַר
שׁוּר	*wall*
שׁזב	see שׁיזב
שְׁחִיתָה	as adj.: *corrupt*; as noun: *corrupted thing, fault*
שׁיזב	(orig. shaph'el) (3ms suff. שֵׁיזִב) *to deliver, save*
שְׁיָע	*mortar, plaster*
שׁיצי	itpə. (3mp pref. יִשְׁתֵּיצוֹן) *to be destroyed*
שׁיציא	(orig. shaph'el) (3ms suff. שֵׁיצִיא) *to bring out*
שִׁירָה	*song* (also spelled שִׁירָא)
שׁכח	ha. and aph. to find; hitpə. *to be found*
שְׁכִינָה	*dwelling, Shekinah = the divine presence*
שׁכלל	(orig. shaph'el) (3ms suff. שַׁכְלֵל) *to complete*
שׁכן	pa. *to cause to dwell, establish*
שְׁלֵה	*at ease*
שָׁלוּ	*fault, error, fail*
שְׁלֵוָה	*prosperity*
שׁלח	pə. (a/a) *to send*; pə'īl *to be sent*; pa. *to release*; itpə. *to be sent*
שׁלט	pə. (e/a) (3mp suff. שְׁלִטוּ) *to rule, to have power*; ha. *to make rule*
שִׁלְטוֹן	*ruler*
שָׁלְטָן	*dominion*
שַׁלִּיט	*having authority, ruler, sovereign*
שׁלם	pə. (e/a) *to complete*; pass. part. (m.s. שְׁלִם) *to be completed*; ha. *to finish, deliver, bring to completion, destroy*
שְׁלָם	*peace, welfare; in the introduction of a letter: greetings, (may the gods seek) well-being*
שְׁלֹמֹה	*Solomon*
שֻׁם	(det. שְׁמָא; pl. cstr. שְׁמָהָת) *name, fame, reputation*
שׁמד	ha. *to destroy*
שְׁמָהָת	see שֻׁם
שְׁמוּאֵל	*Samuel*

שְׁמַ֫יִן	(det. שְׁמַיָּא) *heavens*
שׁמם	itpoʿal (3ms suff. אֶשְׁתּוֹמַם) *to be dumbfounded*
שׁמע	pə. (a/a) *to hear, understand*; pa. *to sing*
שָׁמְרָ֫יִן	Samaria
שְׁמַשׁ	(det. שִׁמְשָׁא) *sun* (fem.)
שִׁמְשַׁי	*Shimshai*
שֵׁן	(du. שִׁנַּ֫יִן) *tooth, set of teeth*
שְׁנָה	(cstr. שְׁנַת; det. שִׁנְתָּא; pl. שְׁנִין) *year*
שְׁנָה	(w/suff. שִׁנְתֵּהּ) *sleep*
שׁני	pə. *to change, be different*; pa. *to change (something)*; pass. part. (f.s. מְשַׁנְּיָה) *to be different*; (h)itpa. *to be changed*; ha. *to change (something), alter*
שְׁנִין	see שְׁנָה
שִׁנַּ֫יִן	see שֵׁן
שָׁעָה	(det. שַׁעֲתָא) *moment*; בַּהּ־שַׁעֲתָא in that moment, immediately; כְּשָׁעָה חֲדָה *for one moment*
שׁעי	itpa. (m.s. imv. אִשְׁתַּעִי; m.p. part. מִשְׁתַּעִין) *to tell, narrate, talk, converse*
שָׁפֵט	*judge, magistrate*
שַׁפִּיר	*beautiful*
שׁפך	(a/u) (targ. pə ʿīl 3ms suff. שְׁפִיךְ*) *to spill, pour forth*
שׁפל	pə. *to be low*; ha. *to humble, make low* or *bring down, vanquish*
שְׁפַל	*low, one who is low*
שׁפר	pə. (a/a) *to be attractive, pleasing*
שְׁפַר	(det. שָׁפְרָא; targ. det. שׁוּפְרָא; targ. w/suff. שׁוּפְרִיךְ) *beauty* (fem.)
שָׁק	(du. שָׁקַ֫יִן) *thigh* (fem.)
שָׁקֵה	(det. שָׁקְיָא) *server*
שִׁקְיָא	see בֵּית שִׁקְיָא
שְׁקַר	*conspiracy*
שרדר	Šrdr (personal name, unknown pronunciation)
שֵׁרוּי	(det. שֵׁרוּיָא) *beginning*
שׁרי	pə. (targ. 3ms suff. שְׁרָא) *to loosen, dwell*; pass. part. *be loosened*; pa. (BA and Onq. 3mp suff. שָׁרִיו; Neof. 3mp suff. שָׁרוֹן) *to begin, solve*; hitpa. (m.p. part. מִשְׁתָּרַיִן) *to be loosened*
שְׁרֹשׁ	(det. שָׁרְשָׁא) *root*
שְׁרֹשִׁי	*corporal punishment*
שֵׁשְׁבַּצַּר	*Sheshbazzar*
שֵׁת	*six* (masc. in form but used with fem. nouns)

שׁתי	pə. *to drink*
שׁתי	(Iranian loanword) *happiness*
שִׁתִּין	*sixty*
שׁתיצי	see שׁיצי for יִשְׁתֵּיצוֹן
שְׁתַר בּוֹזְנַי	*Shethar Boznai*
תְּדִירָא	*constantly*; בִּתְדִירָא *constantly*
תֵּבֵל	*world, specifically the world's dry lands*
תבר	pa. *to shatter*
תְּהוֹם	*abyss*
תוב	pə. *to return* (intransitive); ha. and aph. (2mp pref. תְּתִיבוּן; f.s. part. מְתִיבָה; targ. inf. + 3mp suff. אָתָבוּתְהוֹן) *to return (something), to respond, answer*
תוה	pə. (a/-) *to be startled*
תֹּוקַף	see תְּקַף
תּוֹר	*bull*
תְּחוֹת	(w/ suff. תְּחֹתוֹהִי) *beneath, under*
תִּיעַבַר	see עבר
תְּלַת	(det. תַּלְתָּא) *third*
תְּלָת	*three* (masc. in form but used with fem. nouns)
תְּלָתָה	*three* (fem. in form but used with masc. nouns); תְּלָתֵהוֹן the three of them
תַּלְתָּי	*third*
תְּלָתִין	*thirty*
תַּמָּה	*there*
תְּמַהּ	(det. תִּמְהָא) *wonder*
תַּמָּן	*there*
תַּמְרָה	(det. תְּמַרְתָּא) *palm tree*
תְּנָה	*here*
תַּנִּין	*sea serpent, monster*
תִּנְיָן	(f.s. abs. תִּנְיָנָה) *second*
תַּקִּיף	*mighty, powerful, mighty act*
תקל	pə. *to weigh*; pəʿīl *to be weighed*
תְּקֵל	*shekel (a measurement of weight)*
תקן	ha. and aph. (targ. 3ms suff. אַתְקֵין) *to establish*; hu./ho. (suff. 1cs הָתְקְנֵת) *to be established*
תקף	pə. (i and e/-) *to grow strong, bold*; pa. *to strengthen, make strong*

תְּקַף and תְּקֹף	(det. תָּקְפָּא) *strength, force*
תְּרֵין	(cstr. תְּרֵי) *two* (masc.)
תְּרַע	*gate, door*
תַּרְתֵּין	*two* (fem.)
תשי	Tšy (personal name, the pronunciation of which is unknown)
תַּתְּנַי	*Tattenay*

Bibliography and further reading

BIBLIOGRAPHY

Brock, Sebastian. *The Hidden Pearl: The Syrian Orthodox Church and its Ancient Aramaic Heritage*. 3 vols. Rome: Trans World Film Italia, 2001.

Cook, John A. *Aramaic Ezra and Daniel: A Handbook on the Aramaic Text* (Waco: Baylor, 2019).

Dupont-Sommer, André. 'L'Inscriptione araméene.' *Journal Asiatique* 246 (1958): 19–32.

Elgvin, Torleif. 'Trials and Universal Renewal – The Priestly Figure of the Levi Testament, 4Q541.' Brill Open Access. Leiden: Brill, 2020.

Fassberg, Steven E. *A Grammar of the Palestinian Targum Fragments from the Cairo Genizah* (Atlanta: Scholars Press, 1988).

Fitzmyer, Joseph A. *A Wandering Aramean*. 2 vols. Grand Rapids: Eerdmans, 1997 (first published 1979).

-----. *The Genesis Apocryphon of Qumran Cave 1* (1Q20). Biblica et Orientalia 18/B. Rome: Pontifical Biblical Institute, 2004.

Fraade, Steven D. 'Rabbinic Views on the Practice of Targum and Multilingualism in the Jewish Galilee of the Third–Sixth Centuries.' Pp. 253–86 in *The Galilee in Late Antiquity*. Ed. Lee I. Levine. New York and Jerusalem: Jewish Theological Seminary of America, 1992.

Geller, M. J. 'Philology versus Linguistics and Aramaic Phonology.' *Bulletin of the School of Oriental and African Studies* 69 (2006): 79–89.

-----. 'The Aramaic Incantation in Cuneiform Script (AO 6489 = TCL 6, 58).' *Jaarbericht ex Oriente Lux* 35–6 (1997–2000): 127–46.

Golomb, David M. *A Grammar of Targum Neofiti. Harvard Semitic Monographs* 34. Chico: Scholars Press, 1985.

Kaufman, Stephen A. 'On Vowel Reduction in Aramaic.' *Journal of the American Oriental Society* 104 (1984): 87–95.

Khan, Geoffrey. 'Shewa, Pre-Modern Hebrew.' In *Encyclopedia of Hebrew Language and Linguistics*. Leiden: Brill, 2013.

Li, Tarsee. *The Verbal System of the Aramaic of Daniel: An Explanation in the Context of Grammaticalization*. Leiden: Brill, 2009.

Lindenberger, James M. *The Aramaic Proverbs of Ahiqar*. Baltimore: The Johns Hopkins University, 1983.

Machiela, Daniel A. *The Dead Sea Genesis Apocryphon: A New Text and Translation with Introduction and Special Treatment of Columns* 13–17. STDJ 79. Leiden: Brill, 2009.

Mazar, B. et al. 'Ein Gev Excavations in 1961.' *Israel Exploration Journal* 14 (1964): 27–9.

Mukherjee, B. N. *Studies in the Aramaic Edicts of Aśoka*. Calcutta: Indian Museum, 2000.

Nyberg, Henrik Samuel, Bo Utas, and Christopher Toll. *Frahang I Pahlavīk*. Wiesbaden: Harrassowitz, 1988.

Porten, Bezalel. 'Loan of Grain (3.81).' Vol. 3, pp. 197–8 in *COS*.

Porten, Bezalel, and Ada Yardeni. *Textbook of Aramaic Documents from Ancient Egypt: Newly copied, edited, and translated into Hebrew and English*, vol. 1: Letters (1986), vol. 2: Contracts (1989), vol. 3: Literature, accounts, lists (1993), vol. 4: Ostraca and assorted Inscriptions (1999). Winona Lake, Ind.: Eisenbrauns, 1986–99.

Skjærvø, Prods Oktor. 'Aramaic in Iran.' *Aram* 7 (1995): 283–318.

-----. 'Aramaic Scripts for Iranian Languages.' Pp. 515–35 in *The World's Writing Systems*. Ed. Peter T. Daniels and William Bright. Oxford: Oxford University Press, 1996.

Steiner, Richard. *The Aramaic Text in Demotic Script*. Vol. 1, pp. 309–27 in *COS*.

Steiner, Richard and Charles F. Nims. 'The Aramaic Text in Demotic Script: Text, Translation, and Notes, 2017.' At https://www.academia.edu/31662776/The_Aramaic_Text_in_Demotic_Script_Text_Translation_and_Notes. Published 2017. Accessed Feb. 13, 2020.

Toorn, Karel van der. *Papyrus Amherst 63*. Münster: Ugarit-Verlag, 2018.

-----. 'Eshem-Bethel and Herem-Bethel: New Evidence from Amherst Papyrus 63.' *Zeitschrift für die Alttestamentliche Wissenschaft* 128 (2016): 668–80.

LEXICONS

Among the free-to-use websites that concern Aramaic, there is none more thorough than the aptly named *Comprehensive Aramaic Lexicon* (i.e. *CAL*), found at cal.huc.edu. At this single website you will find many texts that you can read. Each word of each text is linked to its entry in the lexicon itself. So, by clicking on a word you can immediately see its definitions. The *CAL* covers all the ancient dialects of Aramaic, including Syriac, so you could spend years exploring everything it has to offer. Another resource is *Dukhrana Biblical Research* (dukhrana.com). The website contains the major lexicons for the study of Syriac. And, in addition to these, you can find Jastrow's Hebrew/Aramaic dictionary (described below).

Although the *CAL* should always be consulted, there are other lexicons that are sometimes cited and may be of interest to those who do not wish to be tied to their computer. The old, standard lexicon of Biblical Aramaic is BDB, though the Aramaic section of this dictionary is not terribly accurate. More helpful is *HALOT*, though this is still quite expensive. More thorough and affordable is E. Vogt, *A Lexicon of Biblical Aramaic: Clarified by Ancient Documents* (trans. J. A. Fitzmyer; 2nd revised ed.; Rome: Pontifical Biblical Institute, 2008).

For the Aramaic of the targums, always refer to *CAL*, but you can also use Marcus Jastrow, *Dictionary of the Targumim, Talmud Babli Yerushalmi, and Midrashic Literature*. New York: Judaic Press, 1992 (first ed. 1903) and available online for free at dukhrana.com. The dictionary of Michael Sokoloff, *A Dictionary of Jewish Palestinian Aramaic of the Byzantine Period* (2nd ed.; Ramat Gan: Bar Ilan / Baltimore: John Hopkins, 2002 (first ed. 1992)) covers early midrashic works and the targums like Neofiti. If one knows German, a useful early resource is G. Dalman, *Aramäisch-Neuhebräisches Handwörterbuch zu Targum, Talmud, Midrasch* (3rd ed.; Göttingen: n.p., 1938).

For the Dead Sea Scrolls, consult the *CAL* as well as Edward M. Cook, *Dictionary of Qumran Aramaic* (Winona Lake, Ind.: Eisenbrauns, 2015).

TEXT EDITIONS AND TRANSLATIONS

The basic scholarly edition of the Bible is that of BHS, though this is slowly being supplanted by its successor *Biblia Hebraica Quinta*, the fascicle on *Ezra and Nehemiah* having been published relatively recently (eds. D. Marcus, et al.; Stuttgart: Deutsche Bibelgesellschaft, 2007). A handy resource is Donald R. Vance, et al., *Biblical Aramaic: A Reader and Handbook* (Peabody, Mass.: Hendrickson, 2017). A very influential commentary on the book of Daniel is that of John J. Collins (*Daniel: A Commentary on the Book of Daniel* (Hermeneia; Minneapolis: Fortress, 1993)).

Most texts (including those from the Bible) are found at *CAL*, though the website does not provide translations. The standard edition of Targum Onqelos is that of Alexander Sperber, *The Bible in Aramaic Based Upon Old Manuscripts and Printed Texts* (5 vols.; Leiden: Brill, 1959). Individual translations of the targums are offered in various places, including online at the website Sefaria (sefaria.org) as well as in the multi-volume work *The Aramaic Bible* (ed. Martin McNamara et al.; Wilmington, Del.: Glazier, 1986–2008).

In addition to the editions of the Genesis Apocryphon cited in the bibliography by Fitzmyer and Machiela, the texts and translations of the Dead Sea Scrolls are presented in Florentino García Martínez and Eibert J. Tigchelaar, *The Dead Sea Scrolls Study Edition* (2 vols.; Grand Rapids: Eerdmans, 2019). Vocalized versions of most Aramaic Dead Sea Scrolls (together with French translations) can be found in Ursula Schattner-Rieser, *Textes araméens de la Mer Morte, Édition bilingue, vocalisée et commentée* (Brussels: Safran, 2005).

For translations of many Old and Official Aramaic texts, you can consult *COS*. For specifically the Aramaic letters from Egypt, consult James M. Lindenberger, *Ancient Aramaic and Hebrew Letters* (Atlanta: Society of Biblical Literature, 2003) and for the letters and legal material from Egypt, Bezalel Porten, et al., *The Elephantine Papyri in English* (2nd ed.; Atlanta: Society of Biblical Literature, 2011). Neither of these contains a translation of Aḥiqar for which one may consult two older resources: A. E. Cowley, *Aramaic Papyri of the Fifth Century B.C.* (Oxford: Clarendon, 1923 (available now online at various sites)) and James M. Lindenberger, 'Ahiqar', in *The Old Testament Pseudepigrapha* (ed. James H. Charlesworth; 2 vols.; Peabody, Mass.: Hendrickson, 2010 (originally published 1983)) 2:479–508. Unfortunately, these are a bit outdated and do not take into account the new organization of the text as presented in *TAD C*, which also contains a translation.

GRAMMARS

There are many other grammars of Aramaic. For Biblical Aramaic, the standard for English speakers is Franz Rosenthal, *A Grammar of Biblical Aramaic* (7th ed.; Wiesbaden: Harrassowitz, 2006). Another work, which includes all the biblical texts plus several non-biblical texts not in the present grammar, is Frederick E. Greenspahn, *An Introduction to Aramaic* (2nd Edition; Atlanta: Society of Biblical Literature, 2003). One disadvantage of both of these is that they assume a knowledge of Hebrew at the beginning; however, a person having read the present grammar will easily be able to understand and make use of these grammars.

Contemporary grammars of the targums are still being written. You may consult for the time being several older works, one in English (William B. Stevenson, *Grammar of Palestinian Jewish Aramaic* (Oxford: Oxford University, 1924)) and one in German (G. Dalman, *Grammatik des jüdisch-palästinischen Aramäisch* (Darmstadt: Wissenschaftliche Buchgesellschaft, 1960; first ed. 1927)). For the Aramaic of the scrolls consult T. Muraoka, *A Grammar of Qumran Aramaic* (Leuven: Peeters, 2011). For Official Aramaic from Egypt, look at T. Muraoka and Bezalel Porten, *A Grammar of Egyptian Aramaic* (2nd ed.; Atlanta: Society of Biblical Literature, 2014).

CULTURAL STUDIES

The history of the Aramaic language has recently been surveyed by Holger Gzella (*A Cultural History of Aramaic: From the Beginnings to the Advent of Islam* (Leiden: Brill 2015)). A history of the early Aramean kingdoms has also recently been written by K. Lawson Younger (*A Political History of the Arameans: From Their Origins to the End of Their Polities* (Atlanta: Society of Biblical Literature, 2016)). A more specific study is Wayne T. Pitard's *Ancient Damascus* (Winona Lake, Ind.: Eisenbrauns, 1987). Paul V. M. Flesher and Bruce D. Chilton offer an introduction to the targums (*The Targums: a Critical Introduction* (Waco: Baylor University, 2011)). Karel van der Toorn presents a fresh perspective on the Judean residents of Elephantine in his book *Becoming Diaspora Jews: Behind the Story of Elephantine* (New Haven: Yale University Press, 2019).

OTHER CORPORA AND GRAMMARS

The number of ancient Aramaic texts is quite diverse. The dialect of Aramaic called Syriac contains entire libraries. A useful and easy to use grammar of this dialect is J. F. Coakley, *Robinson's Paradigms and Exercises in Syriac Grammar* (5th ed.; Oxford: Oxford University, 2003). From there, you can explore numerous other works available at the *CAL* and at the electronic *Syriac Studies Reference Library* maintained by Bringham Young University and Catholic

University of America (https://lib.byu.edu/collections/syriac-studies-reference-library/). Sebastian Brock offers an introduction to Syriac literature in his *An Introduction to Syriac Studies* (Piscataway, New Jersey: Gorgias, 2006).

Most of the texts in the following printed books are available online through the *CAL*, but again are cited here in case readers wish to explore the texts in more depth. Old Aramaic inscriptions (from the era preceding Official Aramaic) can be found in *KAI*. Among texts in Official Aramaic, one can consult J. B. Segal, *Aramaic Texts from North Saqqâra* (London: Egypt Exploration Society, 1983); I. Ephal and J. Naveh, *Aramaic Ostraca of the Fourth Century BC from Idumaea* (Jerusalem: Magnes, 1996); Douglas M. Gropp, 'Wadi Daliyeh II: the Samaria Papyri from Wadi Daliyeh' in *Wadi Daliyeh II: the Samaria Papyri from Wadi Daliyeh and Qumran Cave 4 XXVIII: Miscellanea, Part 2* (Discoveries in the Judean Desert 28; Oxford: Clarendon, 2001).

For texts from the first centuries of the Common Era, you can consult John F. Healey, *Aramaic Inscriptions and Documents of the Roman Period* (Oxford: Oxford University, 2009); Ada Yardeni, *Textbook of Aramaic, Hebrew, and Nabataean Documentary Texts from the Judaean Desert and Related Material* (2 vols.; Jerusalem: Hebrew University, 2000); Y. Yadin, et al., *The Documents from the Bar Kokhba Period in the Cave of the Letters: Hebrew, Aramaic, and Nabatean-Aramaic Papyri* (2 vols.; Jerusalem: Israel Exploration Society, 2002).

For reading the Babylonian Talmud, you can consult Elitzur A. Bar-Asher Siegel, *Introduction to the Grammar of Babylonian Aramaic* (2nd ed.; Münster: Ugarit Verlag, 2016). For magical texts of the same era, consider Hannu Juusola, *Linguistic Peculiarities in the Aramaic Magic Bowl Texts* (Helsinki: Finnish Oriental Society, 1999) and consult the texts in Charles D. Isbell, *Corpus of Armaic Incantation Bowls* (Missoula, Mont.: Society of Biblical Literature and Scholars Press, 1975); and Dan Levene, *A Corpus of Magic Bowls: Incantation Texts in Jewish Aramaic from Late Antiquity* (London: Kegan Paul, 2003).